Documentality

Trends in Classics – Supplementary Volumes

Edited by
Franco Montanari and Antonios Rengakos

Associate Editors
Stavros Frangoulidis · Fausto Montana · Lara Pagani
Serena Perrone · Evina Sistakou · Christos Tsagalis

Scientific Committee
Alberto Bernabé · Margarethe Billerbeck
Claude Calame · Kathleen Coleman · Jonas Grethlein
Philip R. Hardie · Stephen J. Harrison · Stephen Hinds
Richard Hunter · Giuseppe Mastromarco
Gregory Nagy · Theodore D. Papanghelis
Giusto Picone · Alessandro Schiesaro
Tim Whitmarsh · Bernhard Zimmermann

Volume 132

Documentality

New Approaches to Written Documents
in Imperial Life and Literature

Edited by
Jacqueline Arthur-Montagne, Scott J. DiGiulio
and Inger N.I. Kuin

DE GRUYTER

ISBN 978-3-11-153666-8
e-ISBN (PDF) 978-3-11-079191-4
e-ISBN (EPUB) 978-3-11-079192-1
ISSN 1868-4785

Library of Congress Control Number: 2022942765

Bibliographic information published by the Deutsche Nationalbibliothek
The Deutsche Nationalbibliothek lists this publication in the Deutsche Nationalbibliografie; detailed bibliographic data are available on the Internet at http://dnb.dnb.de.

© 2024 Walter de Gruyter GmbH, Berlin/Boston
This volume is text- and page-identical with the hardback published in 2022.
Editorial Office: Alessia Ferreccio and Katerina Zianna
Logo: Christopher Schneider, Laufen

www.degruyter.com

Acknowledgements

It has taken several years for this volume to come to fruition, and the editors want to thank first and foremost the contributors. We are grateful for their patience, their unwavering commitment to this project, and, most importantly, their willingness to engage in an interdisciplinary dialogue with each other about documents in the ancient world, guided by the modern theoretical concept of documentality. This project stems from a conference held in 2016 at the France-Stanford Center for Interdisciplinary Studies, and we are grateful to the Center for the generous Collaborative Research Grant that they awarded us to organize the conference. We also thank Grant Parker at the Classics Department at Stanford University, who has supported this project from the start. We owe a great debt to Hester Higton, who did a wonderful job copy-editing the manuscript. The anonymous reader for De Gruyter provided many fruitful insights, which improved this manuscript in important ways. We thank the editors of the *Trends in Classics Supplementary Volumes* series, Franco Montanari and Antonios Rengakos, for their help in seeing the publication of this volume through to the end, as well as the team at De Gruyter Classical Studies. The three of us first met at the Advanced Seminar in the Humanities at Venice International University, where the idea for a project on documents and documentality was born. We want to thank, in particular, its conveners Ettore Cingano and Lucio Milano, without whom this project would not exist.

Contents

Acknowledgements —— V
Abbreviations —— IX
List of Figures —— XI

Jacqueline Arthur-Montagne, Scott J. DiGiulio, Inger N.I. Kuin
Introduction —— 1

Part I: Approaches to Ancient Documentality

John Bodel
Documenting Identity in the Early Roman Empire —— 35

Jacqueline Arthur-Montagne
Copying the Canon: Imperial School Texts as Documentary Traces —— 57

Karen ní Mheallaigh
Documenting Wonderland: Lucian's *True Stories* and the Documentary *imaginaire* —— 79

Part II: Documentary Communities and Landscapes

Inger N.I. Kuin
Cities Full of Words: Illiteracy and Epigraphy in Lucian of Samosata —— 107

Pierre Schneider
Documenting the *oikoumenê*: What "Documents" Supported the Description of the Inhabited World in the Hellenistic and Imperial Periods? —— 133

Sjoukje M. Kamphorst
A Community Set in Stone? Monumental Decrees as Instruments of Greek Interactions —— 153

Part III: Between Documents and Literature

Scott J. DiGiulio
Dead Letters, Documentality, and the *Noctes Atticae* of Aulus Gellius —— 181

Jean-Luc Fournet
The Relationship between Documents and Literature in Late Antiquity: The Case of the Petition, between Document, Adaptation and Literary Creation —— 209

Yasmine Amory
When the Letter Speaks Up: Living and Lifeless Letters —— 233

Epilogue

Mireille Corbier
The Ancient Historian and His Documents: Reader, Interpreter and/or Author? —— 253

List of Contributors —— 279
Index Locorum —— 281
Index Rerum —— 285

Abbreviations

Abbreviations in the citations of ancient sources follow the Oxford Classical Dictionary, supplemented with H.G. Liddell, R. Scott and H.S. Jones, *A Greek-English Lexicon* (Oxford 1996) and G.W.H. Lampe, *A Patristic Greek Lexicon* (Oxford 1969). Citations of modern scholarship primarily follow the abbreviations given in *L'Année Philologique*.

Other abbreviations used throughout this volume:

ACO   E. Schwartz and J. Straub (eds.), *Acta Conciliorum Oecumenicorum*, (Berlin 1914–1984)
BKT   *Berliner Klassikertexte, herausgegeben von der Generalverwaltung der Kgl. Museen zu Berlin* (Berlin 1904–)
CIL   *Corpus Inscriptionum Latinarum* (Berlin 1863–)
EDR   *Epigraphic Database Roma* (www.edr-edr.it/default/index.php)
FIRA² S. Riccobono (ed.), *Fontes Iuris Romani Antejustiniani* (2nd edn., Florence 1941–1943)
IG   *Inscriptiones Graecae* (Berlin 1873–)
IK   *Inschriften griechischer Städte aus Kleinasien* (Bonn 1972–)
SB   F. Preisigke et al. (eds.), *Sammelbuch griechischen Urkunden aus Ägypten* (1915–)
TH   *Tabulae Herculanenses*, as published in G. Camodeca, *Tabulae Herculanenses. Edizione e commento* (Rome 2017)

List of Figures

Fig. 1: *P.Lond.Lit.* 253, British Library, MS 34186, tablet 1 recto. © The British Library Board Add 34186. —— **62**
Fig. 2: This graph shows the chronological distribution of all decrees listed in the inventory in Rhodes with Lewis 1997, and in the appendices of Rhodes 1972. —— **155**
Fig. 3: This map shows the locations of the cities mentioned in IGR IV.39 (=*IG* XII 2.58). —— **167**
Fig. 4: *Tabulae dealbatae*, the Forum of Pompei, House of Julia Felix. Museo Archeologico Nazionale, Napoli, inv. 9068. —— **257**
Fig. 5a and b: Military diplomas outside (5a) and inside (5b). In: Corbier 2006, 133–134, fig. 98 a-b. —— **265 and 266**
Fig. 6: Bronze tablet dedicated by the *Vigiles*. Museo Capitolino, Roma. —— **269**
Fig. 7: Cartaceum Museum. British Museum, inv. 2005,0927.52. —— **270**
Fig. 8: *CIL*, VI, 220. —— **271**
Fig. 9: Graffiti in the barracks of the *Vigiles*. Roma, Trastevere. —— **272**
Fig. 10: Graffiti on a tegula. Pietrabbondante. —— **275**

Jacqueline Arthur-Montagne, Scott J. DiGiulio, and
Inger N.I. Kuin

Introduction

In the Roman Empire, documents held a strong sway over everyday life, so much so that the form and implications of the document seeped into the realm of literature as well. Epigraphic monuments populated provinces from Britannia to Mesopotamia and dotted the imaginary landscapes of the ancient novels. Papyri preserve an abundance of "real" letters written during the same centuries that the epistolary form found new expression in the poetry of Ovid, and in the sophistic collections of Alciphron and Aelian. Although Roman record-keeping and archival traditions had originated from Greek epigraphic practices and the administrations of the Near East,[1] a new documentary consciousness began to take hold under the Empire. Authors in this period displayed a heightened awareness of the authority of documents, and how they could be used and abused by the opportunistic forger. In contrast to surviving works of classical literature, which catered primarily to elite readers, ancient documents — including inscriptions, letters, monuments, contracts, laws, and testaments — intervened in the public and private lives of nearly everyone.

From the outset of modern philological study, classicists and historians have collected and categorized ancient documentary texts. Their efforts have culminated in the widespread digitization of epigraphic and papyrological corpora and the steady publication of documentary anthologies.[2] The past two decades have also witnessed new research on the role of documents within classical literature. From epistolary fictions to pseudo-documentarism, scholars have become increasingly interested in how classical authors incorporated and manipulated documentary genres within their works.[3] To a large extent, howev-

---

[1] Brosius 2003, 1–16.
[2] Among other more specific digital projects, see the Epigraphische Datenbank Clauss-Slaby (http://www.manfredclauss.de/, accessed March 21, 2022); the Duke Databank of Documentary Papyri (https://papyri.info/docs/ddbdp, accessed March 21, 2022); the Epigraphic Database Roma (http://www.edr-edr.it/default/index.php, accessed March 21, 2022); the Epigraphic Database Heidelberg (https://edh-www.adw.uni-heidelberg.de/home, accessed March 21, 2022); the U.S. Epigraphy Project (http://usepigraphy.brown.edu, accessed March 21, 2022); and the broader EAGLE project, accessed March 21, 2022).
[3] Rosenmeyer 2001 remains the seminal publication on fictitious letters within classical literature. See also Rimell 2000; Rosenmeyer 2006; and Whitmarsh 2013, 86–100. On writing in Latin literature broadly, from books to letters to inscriptions, see now Frampton 2019. Morello and Morrison 2007 unite studies of both literary and documentary letters (although with a prefer-

er, these fields of study have operated in isolation from one another: those investigating fictitious documents often do so in strictly literary terms, while those who work on "real" documents rarely engage with imaginary versions.[4] Accordingly, scholarly expertise is concentrated at opposite ends of what was, in the Roman world, an interconnected system of documentary communication and production.

This volume unites scholars of ancient history, epigraphy, papyrology, and classical literature in order to reexamine fundamental questions about the document in the Roman Empire. Drawing on recent philosophical theories of the document, the chapters here analyze the form and function of an array of documentary genres, from letters and monumental decrees to school compositions and forgeries. Although the documentary media within this volume are diverse, our contributors focus their analyses on three interconnected topics: the use of documents within Imperial societies, the heightened consciousness of documents among Imperial readers and writers, and the extent to which the latter distinguished documents from literature. Each chapter advances individual claims about documentation within specific genres and contexts, and yet the contributors to this volume achieve broad consensus on two central points. First, the boundary between ancient literary genres and documentary genres of writing appears more fluid than prior scholarship has allowed. Second, documents provoked a greater degree of scrutiny and active engagement in the Imperial period than do the ubiquitous and often unnoticed documents of the modern world.

---

ence for the former) and situate these texts within a broader frame of epistolary literature. The term "pseudo-documentarism" was coined by Hansen 2003, 302 and further developed in ní Mheallaigh 2008.

4 For inscriptions in literature, see the latter half of Liddel/Low 2013. This collection resolves some of the division between strictly literary and epigraphical studies; numerous contributions in the second half of the volume survey the use of epigraphy within the literary realm. There is still a need, however, to consider the intersection of these documents and literary material within the context of the Roman Empire, and especially to explore the areas of overlap between literary and non-literary versions of these documents.

1 Documentality: The Sphere of Social Objects

The contributions of this volume represent a collective effort to place current analyses of Roman documentary texts into conversation with twenty-first-century philosophies of documentation. These most recent theoretical interventions themselves engage earlier debates on historiography, the ontology of objects, and the nature of different types of texts. The term "document," in spite of its Latin derivation,[5] came "to denote the materials reserved for the use of professional historians" only in the mid-nineteenth century, and it has been argued that describing ancient texts as "documents" is anachronistic.[6] Nonetheless, ancient historians freely and frequently use the term "document." One case in point is *Brill's New Pauly*, which defines "document" simply as "a written declaration regarding a legal transaction" and adds that "documents include all non-literary and partially literary texts," such as poetry on amulets, as well as "business documents, trial and administrative documents, letters and accounts."[7] Our chapters are situated between these divergent perspectives: we employ the term "document" and its cognates in reference to ancient texts, but in doing so problematize the mismatch between the commonplace meaning of "document" and the ancient circumstances and attitudes under consideration.[8]

The nineteenth-century way of doing history, including its positivistic use of "documents," came under intense pressure in the late twentieth century.[9] The American historian Hayden White, in his 1980 article "The Value of Narrativity in the Representation of Reality," argued influentially that historiography cannot but narrativize and thereby moralize recorded events into a chosen plot structure. He traced the evolution from medieval annals, to chronicles, and all

---

[5] On the derivation and Latin meaning of the word, see section 2 below, "Defining Documents in the Roman Empire."
[6] Hedrick 2015, section 1.
[7] Hengstl/Schiemann/Gröschler 2006. It should be noted that this *BNP* article for "Documents" is a translation of the German entry for *Urkunden*.
[8] The modern usage of "document," due in part to the revolution of information technology, is now very broad, as is evident from, for instance, Merriam-Webster's dictionary definition: "1 (*law*) a (*archaic*): proof, evidence; b: an original or official paper relied on as the basis, proof, or support of something; c: something (such as a photograph or a recording) that serves as evidence or proof; 2a: a writing conveying information; b: a material substance (such as a coin or stone) having on it a representation of thoughts by means of some conventional mark or symbol; 3: a computer file containing information input by a computer user and usually created with an application (such as a spreadsheet or word processor)."
[9] On nineteenth-century attitudes to documents, see Schneider in this volume.

the way up to nineteenth-century historiography, as a development of ever-increasing emplotment, which imposes on real events "the coherence, integrity, fullness, and closure of an image of life that is and can only be imaginary."[10] The first seeds of this development are already present in the medieval annals, even if they appear as simple lists of dates and events. Some years listed in the left-hand column have no events associated with them in the right-hand column; this betrays both a particular understanding of time and an implicit criterion for judging which events merit inclusion. White writes: "All of the events are extreme, and the implicit criterion for their selection is their liminal nature."[11] The consequence is that even this type of text is no longer "just" a document, and that we must read it as we would a literary text, paying attention to who the narrator is and in what ways reality has been shaped to fit this particular "plot."

Contemporaneously with White's challenge to historiography, critical literary theorists and philosophers of language were testing the connections between texts, meaning, authors, and readers in broader and more radical ways. The two most important voices in this arena, while emphatically disagreeing with one another, both featured in later theoretical approaches to documents. Jacques Derrida's proposed deconstruction of the text removed the intentionality of the writer as the primary determining factor for meaning, instead tasking the reader (or, rather, the critic) with revealing or even inventing a text's alternative meanings.[12] John Searle, responding directly to Derrida, wrote that "to the extent that the author says what he means the text is the expression of his intentions... the situation as regards intentionality is exactly the same for the written word as it is for the spoken."[13] For Searle, the creation and authority of documents hinged on "collective intentionality": the primitive biological phenomenon of shared "intentional states such as beliefs, desires, and intentions."[14] To use his example, collective intentionality is what celebrates two men sparring in a prizefight as collective cooperative behavior but criminalizes one man beating another in a back alley. Within Searle's framework, documents acquire their documentary status through collective intentionality: physical object x counts as social object y in context c.[15] A printed piece of paper or a

---

10 White 1980, 27.
11 White 1980, 11.
12 See esp. Derrida 1988 [1977], 1–24 and 1998 [1996].
13 Searle 1977, 202.
14 Searle 1995, 23.
15 Searle 1995, 28.

laminated card constitutes a birth certificate or a driver's license respectively because societies collectively determine that they do.

The work of White, Derrida, and others precipitated in the philosophy of history the so-called "linguistic turn," a focus on language as "constitutive of intellectual and social life,"[16] in response to which current historians have formulated several challenges. White's work has been criticized for taking us ever further away from "history itself," while instead historians should pursue "a real, authentic, and 'experiential' relationship with the past… not contaminated by historiographical tradition, disciplinary presuppositions, and linguistic structures."[17] For proponents of what is now known as the "mnemonic turn," the concept of memory takes the place of history, because by memory "an experience or re-experience of the remembered past" can be achieved.[18] In this context, places, landscapes, and objects have come to be understood as important sites and carriers of historical memory that can embody and activate the past.[19]

The current volume emerges from what some have already identified as a (second) material turn: an increased awareness of and focus on embodiment, objects, landscapes, and sensory experience in history, and in the humanities and social sciences more broadly.[20] In this context the ways in which ancient texts functioned *as* objects have recently received increased attention as well.[21] It appears that it would be timely for fundamental questions about the status of (physical) documentary objects, their influence on reality, and the role of subjectivity and intentionality in their creation and reception to be raised once again. The Italian philosopher Maurizio Ferraris has done exactly this. Since the early 2000s, Ferraris has reevaluated the function of documents as social objects: physical, digital, or even mental records of our social actions. Across several articles and his 2009 book, *Documentalità. Perché è necessario lasciar trac-*

---

16 Surkis 2012, 704.
17 Ankersmit 2005, 4.
18 Ankersmit 2005, 5.
19 Especially Pierre Nora's work (1984–1992; 1989) on *lieux de mémoire* has been enormously influential. On memory and history, with reference to Nora, see Assmann 2011, 1–59. For a critical appraisal of the mnemonic turn, especially in the field of ancient history, see Berliner 2005; also Grigoropoulos *et al.* 2017. On Ankersmit's notion of experiential history, see also Carr 2014. On objects as carriers of historical memory, see Runia 2006, 2010.
20 If, that is, we take the materialism of Engels and Marx as the first "material turn"; for an introduction to these issues, see Bennett/Joyce 2010.
21 See e.g., Howley 2017; Petrovic/Petrovic/Thomas 2018.

ce, he introduces the concept of "documentality" as the "sphere in which social objects are generated."[22]

Ferraris's explanation of documents, and especially the way in which social acts are transformed into documents, makes an important departure from the document theory of Searle. Ferraris disputes the mysterious and immeasurable forces of collective intentionality and instead calls attention to the role of recording in the construction of the social world. It is not, he argues, any specific context or cooperative will that generates documents, but rather the act of inscription. "The very fact of recording makes us responsible," he writes. "This is why the world is filled with paper, files, archives and registries."[23] For Ferraris the document results from recording a social act (involving two or more people) within any medium — even the memory. Crucial to this definition is the idea that documents, while dependent on human minds for creation, can exist independently of human knowledge or even consciousness. State constitutions and financial recessions have existence and power in reality, even if the majority of people are unaware of them. Divorcing documents from collective intentionality also illuminates why recorded social acts do not lose their status *as* documents with the passing of time or the revolution of political regimes. Inscribed decrees from Roman Asia no longer extend any political authority, but that does not prevent them from preserving the initial social act that led to their generation. Ferraris's revision to Searle's theory therefore acknowledges the individual and collective intention required to *create* documents, but understands that such intention need not persist in order for objects to *remain* documents. Indeed, Mireille Corbier's epilogue to this volume demonstrates how artifacts can be "made into documents by historians" for purposes quite different from the ones their creators intended.[24]

Ferraris's writings present a concept of "document" that is at once more restrictive and more liberating for the ancient historian than Searle's constructionism. On the one hand, it is more restrictive, in that it requires us to identify the social act at the heart of any record which we hope to define as a "document." At the core of any true document, in Ferraris's estimation, there must be a social act. Even when a new context in time or space negates the authority of that social act, the document still records it. This function-driven definition may narrow the field of what many scholars have long categorized as documentary

---

[22] We cite here the English edition of *Documentalità*, Ferraris 2012, 208, as do all other chapters of the volume.
[23] Ferraris 2015, 431–432.
[24] Corbier in this volume.

texts of one kind or another. Diary entries, notes to self, and even letters may not constitute true "documentary" texts if they fail to register some social act beyond the inner monologue of the author.[25] On the other hand, Ferraris's emphasis on the function of documents also liberates us from the need to classify them according to the precise criteria of form. Scholars of the ancient world have often been preoccupied with the formal prerequisites of documentary genres: how does the shape, size, style, or length of a text adhere to or depart from the established features of a document? Can a text really be counted as a document if it is pseudepigraphic? Ferraris's documentality encourages scholars to assess what documents *do* rather than what they *look like*; pseudepigraphic texts may look like documents, and may have been intended as documents, but do not in fact qualify as documents because they do not preserve a social act.

The collaborative initiative from which this volume has emerged had already adopted the name 'Documentality' as its working title before encountering the scholarship of Ferraris. But his ideas have subsequently shaped our own work in important ways. The authors in this volume find their research invigorated by Ferraris's insights into the materiality, traceability, and social agency of documents. By the same token, their chapters should not be regarded as direct applications of Ferraris's documentary formula that "social object = inscribed act."[26] They instead explore and appraise the merits of his formulation for the study of documents in the Roman Empire, and in many instances challenge the "virtuous cycle" of practices and documents that Ferraris postulates for the evolution of human society. In their efforts to identify both the potential and the limitations of documentality for the ancient world, our contributors have also drawn upon the 2014 "Documentality" issue of *The Monist*, in which eight philosophers elaborate and critique Ferraris's theory (including Ferraris himself). Ferraris's critics in *The Monist*, while agreeing upon the inadequacy of Searle's collective intentionality and the need for a new ontology of social reality, identified some gaps in the theory of documentality as well — many of which our contributors, too, have probed. For Enrico Terrone, more research needs to be done in order to understand "how documents work" — a subject that Bodel and Arthur-Montagne evaluate in the

---

25 Then again, a semiotic view of documentation recognizes that human societies can interpret all sorts of artifacts as documents and apply them for new social purposes, as discussed in Buckland 2014, 180.
26 Ferraris 2014, *passim*.

opening section of the volume.²⁷ In contrast, Buckland's contribution to *The Monist* expresses dissatisfaction with the social element of Ferraris's documentality, noting that it overlooks private documents written to one's future self and the category of objects "considered as documents."²⁸ Buckland's three categories of information and his corresponding definitions of documentation have provided helpful analytic models in the chapters of Schneider and Corbier. Finally, Koepsell and Smith's efforts in their *Monist* article to more precisely describe the relationship between oral, mental, and material documents have been reinforced by the findings of Kuin and Amory, who reveal in their chapters how (il)literacy and orality shaped the social experience of documents in antiquity.²⁹ Our volume thus explores the implications of Ferraris's documentality for the study of life and literature in the Roman world on its own merits *and* with this first wave of critiques in mind.

One irony of using Ferraris and his critics as a springboard for the study of Imperial documents is that their theories arose with the advent of the internet revolution. Throughout the writings of Ferraris and the other *Monist* authors runs a deep interest in the web as a producer of infinite records. The concept of defining documentary status in terms of inscription rather than physical material is deeply indebted to the internet, which Ferraris describes as a "document-producing *device*" that functions as a "performative rather than a descriptive system."³⁰ As scannable boarding passes and e-payment apps gradually obviate the need for paper tickets and plastic credit cards, it is clear that the "hard copy" is only one of many possible forms that the document of today can adopt. This appreciation for the fluidity of the documentary form in the digital age is paradoxically useful for the study of documents in the Roman Empire — a period that also witnessed the proliferation of written texts but did not necessarily prioritize them above other methods of recording. Imperial authors, both Greek and Latin, give voice to new anxieties about the emergence of written forms of documentation in a way analogous to modern concerns about the mass transfer of information (personal and otherwise) to the internet. In several chapters of this volume, we find instances where memorized or recited methods of documentation were even deemed preferable to the written word.

In sum, the contributions in this volume adopt the theory of documentality not as a programmatic, let alone definitive, model, but rather as a heuristic

---

27 Terrone 2014, 163.
28 Buckland 2014, 180–181.
29 Koepsell/Smith 2014, 230–234.
30 Ferraris 2015, 424, emphasis in the original.

starting point. Collectively, the contributors reflect on what these philosophical forays into documentality may bring to bear on the definition of the document in the Roman Empire.

2 Defining Documents in the Roman Empire

This volume initiates a fundamental conversation about the meaning of "document" in the Roman Empire. When we consider the comparatively low rates of literacy in the Imperial period, it follows that readers could not have relied upon written documentation to the same degree that we do today. Written texts were not always formatted to facilitate ease of reading, and documents were often placed in locations inaccessible to the public.[31] On a more basic level still, our volume investigates whether Imperial readers and writers recognized the document as a coherent genre. Ancient Greek and Latin possess robust vocabularies for letters, inscriptions, and contracts, but were these forms of writing classified together in the ancient imagination?

The English word "document" derives from *documentum*, which Varro defined in the *De lingua latina* as *quae exempla docendi causa dicuntur*, "those which are called examples in order to teach."[32] Documents can indeed teach us about historical details or stand as proofs of the facts we set out to illustrate; but Varro tells us nothing about what forms these *documenta* take, instead emphasizing that they are *exempla* first and foremost. His definition deviates significantly from our derived term, yet seems to have been shared by other ancient authors. Livy in his preface, for instance, frames his entire historical enterprise in terms of the *exempla* that he provides, explicitly labeling such *exempla* as *documenta* (Livy, *Praef.* 10):

> hoc illud est praecipue in cognitione rerum salubre ac frugiferum, omnis te exempli documenta in inlustri posita monumento intueri; inde tibi tuaeque rei publicae quod imitere capias, inde foedum inceptu, foedum exitu quod vites.
>
> That which is especially beneficial and profitable in the study of history is this, namely beholding the lessons (*documenta*) of every example set on an illustrious monument; from

---

31 Small 1997, 59, who points to Roman taxation documents as a notable exception. See also Cribiore 1996, 2–5.
32 Varro *Ling.* 6.62. See also *TLL*, s.v. *documentum*, 5.1.1804.19–1805.44. Unless noted, all translations are our own.

there, you may take what you or your own state may imitate, and what you might avoid that is shameful in the conception and shameful in the outcome.

As Livy's programmatic statement about his work indicates, the historical examples in the *Ab urbe condita* are selected for their educative value, and contribute to the didactic fabric of the work.[33] He reinforces this understanding in framing the disaster that befell Gnaeus Scipio's forces in Spain during the Second Punic War, describing the fickleness of the *auxilia* as a *documentum* for future Roman commanders.[34] *Documenta* contain lessons, and within Livy's historical narrative they link the historical events that they describe with the present and future generations for whom these lessons are intended.

Livy's history also abounds with documents in the modern, quotidian sense of the word. Perhaps the most notable inclusion of a written document is Augustus' personal investigation into the *spolia opima* in the Temple of Jupiter Feretrius, which comprised, among other things, an inscribed linen corselet (4.20.5–11). Livy's inclusion of this document is predicated upon his recognition of Augustus as the ultimate source (4.20.7). In articulating his reasons for including the corselet in his narrative, the historian suggests to his audience the purpose of documentary texts writ large: to serve as witnesses to historical events, much like Augustus' comments serve as a witness to the veracity of the inscribed corselet.[35] Livy's terminology for the corselet is notable too in that he deploys the conventional language of epigraphical texts in Latin: *titulus ipse* (4.20.6).[36] His discussion of the *spolia opima* expands the horizon of what might constitute a document for the Roman historian, serving as a testament to both the scholarly enterprise of Augustus and the valor of Cornelius Cossus.

Later examples from historiography demonstrate that documents in the modern sense continued to be common and powerful sources of information.

---

33 On Livy's use of *exempla*, see Crosby 1980, which discusses the connection between *exemplum* and *documentum*; Chaplin 2000, 1–31; and Lushkov 2015, which builds on Chaplin's work on exemplarity.
34 Livy 25.33.5: *id quidem cavendum semper Romanis ducibus erit exemplaque haec uere pro documentis habenda, ne ita externis credant auxiliis ut non plus sui roboris suarumque proprie uirium in castris habeant* ("Indeed, Roman commanders must always be on guard, and must always truly consider these examples as lessons, to not trust foreign auxiliaries to such an extent that the auxiliaries not have more of their own strength and fighting resources in the camps").
35 On the episode, see Sailor 2006.
36 OLD^2 s.v. *titulus*, which suggests that, while the word initially meant a flat piece of wood or other surface on which words were written, by the time of the Principate it metonymically referred to the documentary texts themselves, rather than just the material support.

Suetonius in his *Lives of the Caesars*, for instance, availed himself of a whole range of available texts in order to provide a comprehensive biography of each emperor.³⁷ In the *Life of Gaius Caligula*, when Caligula ascends to the throne in 37 CE, he makes a theatrical display of publicly burning all of the texts containing incriminating evidence about family enemies (*Calig.* 15.4). The destruction of the evidence, which Suetonius suggests comprises the trial records controlled by the *princeps* himself, has a powerful effect on the populace.³⁸ Burning the texts is symbolic: they represent the threat of prosecution itself, and the palpable relief that Suetonius observes at their destruction reveals the weighty status of such records in the Roman imagination. However, the anxieties which result from the ultimate revelation that Caligula only feigned destroying the evidence (*Calig.* 30.2) underscore that, in this case, the existence of the physical documents was thought to vouchsafe the testimony included within them. On this occasion, the physical medium and the information it carried were understood as intrinsically connected, thereby according privileged status to these documents.

Finally, Tacitus suggests that, while written documents of all stripes can be authoritative in the minds of his audience, we must approach them with caution.³⁹ In his description of the Pisonian conspiracy, his narrative reveals the evidentiary force that the written document can possess: Nero publishes the evidence that he has in his possession, for fear that it would not be taken seriously if the conspirators were condemned by the words of the edict alone.⁴⁰ Without publishing the evidence, Nero risks being disbelieved. It is only by producing the collated, written material to support the execution of the Pisonians that his claims hold any veracity. In this case, the production of *conlata in*

---

37 On Suetonius' use of documentary material, and his respect for such sources, see generally Wallace-Hadrill 1983, 88–96.
38 Wardle 1994, 166–167.
39 For Tacitus, the inscription is perhaps the most prevalent, and potent, documentary source in his works, but his history includes a broad range of documents, including the *acta senatus*. On Tacitus' sources generally, see Potter 2011; on inscriptions in Tacitus, including a catalog of all citations, see Bérard 1991, 3010–3015 (catalog); on the *acta senatus* generally, the best study remains Talbert 1984.
40 Tac. *Ann.* 15.73.1–2: *Sed Nero oratione inter patres habita, edictum apud populum et conlata in libros indicia confessionesque damnatorum adiunxit. Etenim crebro vulgi rumore lacerabatur, tamquam viros claros et insontis ob invidiam aut metum extinxisset* ("but Nero, after his speech was given in among the senators, gave an edict among the people and added evidence collected into books and the confessions of the condemned. For in fact he was frequently attacked by a rumor among the people that he had killed famous and innocent men because of envy or fear").

libros indicia — physical, material documents supporting his claims — lends authority to his words. As a counter-example, however, Tacitus cautions against uncritical adoption in recording the statements of the Senate. Discussing the reign of Tiberius, he notes that he elected not to include any motions advanced in the Senate during this period because of the sycophancy of the time.⁴¹ He feels the need to explain to his readers why he omitted this documentary evidence, reaffirming its importance. Simultaneously, his exclusion of the motions underscores the complexity and risks inherent to authoritative texts: if these texts were included, readers might have taken these motions at face value because of their official status. Tacitus intervened precisely to prevent this.

Because this volume inquires into Greek texts as well as Latin, it is worthwhile to briefly address document-terminology in ancient Greek. In contrast to Latin, Greek does not generate the problem of a false friend like *documentum*. The relevant Greek terms can be divided into, on one hand, words that emphasize the act that created the document (typically the act of writing) and, on the other hand, words that emphasize the function of the document. γράφω, "to write," and all its derivations, in particular γράμμα, "letter," and its plural γράμματα, had a wide range of meanings. Inscriptions on stone are often referred to simply as τὰ γεγραμμένα, terminology which requires one to infer from context that the text has been written on a stone or another object, since the phrase can also describe texts written on papyrus. γράμματα can refer to a treatise, to legal documents, or even, in a general sense, to education and to learning. In our second category, important terms are μνήματα, "records" or "remembrances"; σημεῖα, "marks," "signals," "tokens," but also (in the singular) "tomb"; and, γνωρίσματα, a less common word that means "tokens" or "marks." All three words emphasize what documents *do*. Unlike documents that are explicitly referred to as "writings," a document in this sense stands in and communicates for something or someone who is otherwise absent, temporarily or permanently. To be clear, μνήματα, σημεῖα, and even γνωρίσματα can be written or drawn symbols (as in Xen. *Cyr.* 2.1.27), but by not referring to them as γεγραμμένα or γράμματα their function is emphasized over their form.⁴²

---

41 *Ann.* 3.65.1: *Exequi sententias haud institui nisi insignis per honestum aut notabili dedecore, quod praecipuum munus annalium reor ne virtutes sileantur utque pravis dictis factisque ex posteritate et infamia metus sit* ("I have decided not to record proposals in the senate except those that were remarkable for their honesty or their noteworthy shamelessness, since I consider it to be the special duty of historians that virtue is not left in silence and that fear of future disgrace accompany crooked words and actions"). See Potter 2011, 127.
42 For a fuller treatment of vocabulary and concept of documents in Greek and Greece see Sickinger 2002; Davies 2003; and Kirk 2018.

An indication that in early Greek thought there was already a strong awareness of what might constitute a proper record or token is provided by the various iterations of the recognition scene of Electra and Orestes. In Aeschylus' *Libation Bearers*, Electra infamously infers Orestes' return from locks of hair and footprints left at her father's grave. The shortcomings of both pieces of evidence as reliable tokens — does she really recognize the hair? How could a footprint point to an individual (before shoes had profiles, of course)? — prompted Euripides to parody Aeschylus' recognition scene in his *Electra*. The recognition scenes in the *Odyssey* show that tokens can be necessary to identify someone who is present, when the passage of time has made facial and bodily features unreliable as evidence. Finally, in Lucian's *True Stories*, we encounter a collaboration of documents referred to as written and unwritten γνωρίσματα in the sense of "traces": the traveler named Lucian infers that Dionysus and Heracles preceded him on his journey from an inscription *and* their footprints; here γράμματα and ἴχνη (traces) together constitute a record of the past presence of the gods (*VH* 1.7).[43]

In sharp contrast to the complex and flexible ancient vocabulary for different types of texts and records, modern scholars have traditionally adopted an essentializing distinction between "literary" and "documentary" texts, in which, as Charles Hedrick has recently pointed out, "literature is the normative 'unmarked term'. The category of the document serves as an accommodating receptacle for everything else."[44] Furthermore, this dichotomy has traditionally privileged the literary, as Hedrick explains:

> Literature is thought to make its bed in the intellect: like scholarship its excellence is correlated with its separation from the social: the banal, the workaday contingencies of life; it is defined precisely by its isolation from other kinds of writing. Literature is philosophical; documents are historical; literature is transcendent and speaks to modern readers across the expanse of time, as if they were coevals; the significance of documents is pragmatic, contextually limited.[45]

By drawing attention to the importance of documentary practices within literature, as well as the literary tendencies in documentary texts, the chapters in this volume seek to challenge and move beyond this binary.

The contributors to the volume broadly adopt the following definition of documents: records of social acts, or "social objects," with their own agency to

---

43 On this, see both ní Mheallaigh and Kuin in this volume.
44 Hedrick 2015, section 1.
45 Hedrick 2015, section 1.

(intentionally or unintentionally) shape realities.[46] The act of recording was essential to the creation of documents, though not necessarily through writing, as the chapters of Bodel, Amory, and Schneider in particular show. As both Bodel and Corbier explain, documentality in the Roman Empire resists the historical teleology implicit to Ferraris's work, which renders the document as an inevitable product of modernity. The world-creating and world-recording capacities of texts were already deeply felt in antiquity, as the chapters of ní Mheallaigh and Kuin underscore. Another important difference is the degree of engagement and scrutiny among the users of documents. In his article "Total Mobilization," Ferraris describes a modern world awash in documentation, through which most users move passively. This is a new reality, where the internet is "identical in scale with the whole of the human social world," and where "we are surrounded by systems recording events and making them permanent" in nearly every public location.[47] Ferraris observes that, within such a society, people today use and react to the recordings around them unthinkingly: the social reality that documents help construct is "passively undergone" and we rarely question the intrinsic value of money or an official's right to inspect a passport or driver's license.[48]

The chapters of this volume reveal a very different set of norms surrounding the creation and consumption of documentation in the Roman Empire. Ancient readers and writers did not accept written documents unquestioned, but instead probed the media and the voices behind documents. This could entail testing the reliability and authority of a canonical author or, in different circumstances, requiring witnesses or oral testimony in the authentication of documentary texts. Written documents to or from famous figures, such as petition letters in the later Roman Empire, became models for new literary genres of their own in Late Antiquity and beyond (see Fournet's contribution in this volume). This heightened attention to the creators and contexts of written documentation in the Imperial period meant that documents demanded scrutiny, as Kuin's analysis of Lucianic descriptions makes clear: "whoever lives with documents can be seduced and therefore snared, sooner or later, by the semblance of authoritative text."[49] In the Roman Empire, legal and civic documents represented not the last word, but the first step in "tracing" the validity of a social act.

---

46 This formulation borrows Kamphorst's phrasing in this volume, which in turn draws on Ferraris 2012, 120–174.
47 Ferraris 2014, 208, 201.
48 Ferraris 2014, 218.
49 Kuin in this volume.

3 Documents and Empire

The review of Greek and Latin terminology for documents in the section above underscores that both the literary and material artifacts of the Roman world provide a robust lexicon by which Imperial societies imagined and described their written records. It may be less clear to readers, however, why "life and literature in the Roman Empire" constitute natural and necessary spheres in which to analyze ancient documentality. The Imperial period does not, after all, mark the first time that the inhabitants of the classical world used written documents. Some of the most innovative scholarship on ancient inscriptions and the materiality of written records has taken Classical Athens as its focal point.[50] The record-keeping of the Hellenistic empires, especially Ptolemaic Egypt, has also received substantial attention in recent years, showing these eras as formative periods in the standardization and proliferation of documentary texts.[51] The value of anchoring this volume in the Roman Empire — and in defining "empire" broadly — lies in the contributors' ability to illuminate two waves of innovation in how Imperial societies engaged with documents.

The first of these "waves" is the spread of documentary writing across the Mediterranean as a consequence of imperial conquests by Romans from the late Republic to the high Empire. The "high intensity of written interchange" in this period can be observed not only in the dissemination of military documents and the growing demand for papyrus after the Roman conquest of Ptolemaic Egypt.[52] It is also visible in the "notable pattern of rise and fall" in the production of monumental inscriptions between the first and third centuries CE.[53] This resulted from the spread of urban culture and provincial governance, especially in the western half of the Mediterranean, which had less exposure to the scribes and local bureaucracies prevalent in the Near East and Egypt. But even in the eastern provinces, whose contact with royal decrees and inscribed letters grew substantially in the age of Alexander, Roman rule expanded systems of record-keeping and state archives. The administration of the Roman army can also be credited with creating a vast body of records. New recruits were obligated in the course of enlisting to provide some written evidence of free status and, for some offices, Roman citizenship. The composition of the *pridianum*, an annual report of military personnel, entailed substantial record-keeping across the Empire.

---

50 See, e.g., Sickinger 1999; Gagarin 2008; Meyer 2017; Day 2018; and Kirk 2018.
51 McLean 2002; Bagnall 2011; and Shear 2017.
52 Jördens 2011, 243.
53 Meyer 2011, 192.

The Roman army's "almost modern ... love of documentation" in the Principate, in the words of William Harris, occurred against the backdrop of rising literacy levels in the Roman Empire.[54] "[U]nder Roman rule many regions reached higher levels of literacy than before, while some regions which had scarcely known writing at all came to have partly literate populations," he writes.[55] Military men and their families increasingly found themselves surrounded by documents, as illustrated by the wooden tablets from Vindolanda.[56] So too the profusion of papyrological remains from Roman Egypt, ranging from receipts to book rolls to personal letters to official correspondence, suggests the degree to which Romans were constantly surrounded by documentation of various forms, including building out their own collections of literary texts.[57] Even for those who could not read the text of the documents surrounding them, the visual form of different types had begun to ossify by the first century CE to the extent that one might intuit the contents of a given document or textual form based solely on their visual engagement with the shape of its form or its *mise en pierre*.[58] Setting aside the question of precisely how many people could read and write *per se*, what becomes clear is that in the Roman world, writing and responding to letters (albeit it through intermediaries), owning books, and establishing one's identity through written evidence were no longer the sole purview

---

[54] Harris 1989, 217.
[55] Harris 1989, 175. Harris's discussion in the main focuses on attempting to calculate the percentage of people that could read and write in the ancient world, and he concludes that full literacy never exceeded 20%; responses to his arguments and methods are collected in Humphrey 1991. More recent reappraisals of literacy focus instead on the variety in kinds of literacy that manifested in the ancient world, including functional literacies and their applicability in different contexts: see, for instance, the essays collected in Johnson and Parker 2009, Woolf 2015, and Kuin in this volume. Habinek 2009 calls attention to the interconnected nature of oral and literate cultures and stresses that while writing took time to become an established practice at Rome, its spread nevertheless correlates with broader social shifts (in property, in status, in identity) from the Republic into the Empire.
[56] The *Tabulae Vindolandenses* have been published in four volumes, Bowman/Thomas 1983–2011.
[57] On everyday writing in the papyri such as contracts, letters, and receipts see Bagnall 2011, 27–53. On papyrological evidence for personal library collections, see Houston 2009 and Johnson 2010, 179–199. On the interdependence between such literary texts and contemporary documentary forms, particularly in the later Roman Empire, see Fournet and Amory in this volume.
[58] Kruschwitz 2008 and Kruschwitz/Campbell 2010 (arguing the point from the visual representations of different document types in the graffiti from Pompeii); cf. Bodel 2015.

of the *literati*. The written word was becoming a constant presence in the daily lives of a larger cross-section of Roman society.[59]

Documents possessed a broad reach, shaping many levels of Roman societies, and certain classes of text are, by virtue of their public nature, more overtly official than others.[60] The debt records housed in the *aerarium*, for instance, are documents of the Roman state and would have impacted the lives of everyday Romans, as they contained the records of their outstanding obligations to the same.[61] The physical texts and the debts they represented were so connected that emperors who offered remission of these debts publicly burned the associated documents.[62] The incineration of some 900 million sesterces of debt under Hadrian ca. 118 CE alleviated a significant burden by eliminating the sole authoritative records of these debts, and the act was also memorialized on coinage and in the Anaglypha Traiani.[63] These events and the various media in which they are commemorated suggest the importance of the physical document itself in the Roman mind — destruction of the record erases the debts themselves — as these texts had an intrinsic authority. Likewise, Octavian's strategic publication

---

[59] Even beyond documentary texts, Romans across social classes were increasingly presented with a multitude of text in their daily lives that reflected the increasing accessibility of the literate world. The proliferation of graffiti at Pompeii, which included quotations of literature scribbled on the walls alongside more official announcements and political campaign materials, suggests both increasing literacy levels as well as the existence of multiple intersecting forms of literacy within these graffiti and dipinti; see, e.g., Franklin 1991 and Milnor 2014. "Literary" games like the *tabulae Iliacae* and *tabulae lusoriae* also became more prevalent, demonstrating the penetration of literary culture and the written word into all facets of Roman social life; see Purcell 1995 and Habinek 2009, 124–136 (who includes acrostics as part of the same phenomenon).

[60] The distinction between public and private documents existed in the Roman consciousness at least as early as the time of Cicero, as several of his letters and forensic speeches suggest; see DiGiulio in this volume.

[61] On the physical form of the *tabulae* that would constitute these records, see Meyer 2004, 148–163.

[62] A practice that began with Augustus, as in Suet. *Aug.* 32.2; cf. Cass. Dio 49.15.3, 53.2.3. Similar remissions of texts, accompanied by public destruction of the documentary records themselves, occurred under Nero (Tac. *Ann.* 13.23), Vespasian (Cass. Dio 66.10.2), and Hadrian (SHA *Hadr.* 7.6; Cass. Dio 69.8.1); see Zadorojnyi 2006, 372–373. On the public destruction of these records and the Augustan precedent, which is seen as distinct from the destruction of literary material, see Howley 2017, 219–220.

[63] On the Anaglypha Traiani, see Hammond 1953; Torelli 1983, 89–118 (including discussion of the comparable Chatsworth relief); and Plattner 1998. On coinage, see Howley 2017, 220 n. 48. For possible connections between Trajanic issues and the Anaglypha imagery, see Thill 2014, 128–129.

of Antony's will, seized from the Temple of Vesta where it had been stored and vouchsafed, thrust into the public eye a text whose authority was guaranteed by the Roman state and the priestesses charged with safeguarding it. The signed and sealed document, deposited with the Vestals, thus possessed several guarantees of its authority: signatures and seals, but also the imprimatur of the cult and ultimately Roman law itself. By even claiming to read from Antony's will, Octavian imbued his accusations against his rival with each of these guarantees of authority, thus ensuring his audience's trust in the authenticity of the document that he read.[64]

The second "wave" of innovation in document and empire is the robust tradition of writing about or with documentation in the Imperial period: the literary reaction to a Roman landscape now teeming with inscriptions, letters, tablets, wills, recorded debts, and so on.[65] While the proliferation of the written word across the physical, lived world of antiquity is not new (one may think of the massive tribute lists displayed on the Athenian acropolis, or the numerous epigrams adorning monuments throughout the Attic countryside), their integration into the literature of the Roman Empire represents a marked shift from earlier Greek literature or even Republican-era Latin. Whereas Peter Bing could suggest that many Greeks of the fifth and fourth centuries BCE reacted to the texts around them with indifference, in this later period documents become such omnipresent and essential features of daily life that they permeate the social and literary psyche of Rome in fundamentally new ways.[66] This response marks an equally important path to

---

64 The authenticity of the will was further guaranteed by the seals of Octavian's informants, Titius and Plancius, on the document itself (Cass. Dio 50.3.3; cf. Plut. *Ant.* 58.2–3, Suet. *Aug.* 17.1–2). Nevertheless, whether the will was entirely a propagandistic forgery has remained an open question, as noted by Wardle 2014, 147–148; see, for instance, Johnson 1978, 494–503, and, arguing the other side, Sirianni 1984, 236–241.

65 On the epigraphic habit in the Roman world, which was first discovered and so described by MacMullen 1982, see Corbier 2006; Beltrán Lloris 2015; and Bolle/Machado/Witschel 2017.

66 Bing 2002, 44, responding in part to the arguments of Sickinger 1999, 160–187 and others that Attic inscriptions were widely read and consulted. Using epigram as his test case, he suggests that the physical location of most inscriptions impeded access while also noting that their content, with their imprecations to stop and read the text, suggests an ultimately futile attempt to impose upon the attentions of passers-by. While Greeks of the Classical period may have ultimately ignored the texts around them as we might ignore many roadside billboards today, Bing concedes that a change in approach becomes evident in Hellenistic world as ancient scholars began to assemble collections of inscribed epigrams. In fact, Cic. *Tusc.* 5.23 (discussed at Bing 2002, 59–60, who sees it as evidence of "the utter inattention of the Greeks to their monuments"), in which Cicero enthusiastically relates his visit to Archimedes' tomb,

understanding ancient documentality and requires the chronological scope of our chapters to extend beyond the Principate.

In this volume, Kamphorst's chapter analyzes the earliest source material in the form of late Hellenistic inscriptions, while the concluding chapters by Fournet and Amory take us into the fourth and fifth centuries, revealing a remarkable degree of overlap between the realms of documentation, written literature, and oral performance in Late Antiquity. We trace a new documentary consciousness emerging as early as the Augustan Age, while the extent and sophistication of interplay between documentation and literature amplifies after the second century CE and well into the fifth. The sustained interest in documentary texts in this later period, together with new and experimental genres including or imitating documents, marks an important continuity with the early Empire, and thereby advances the broader scholarly effort to consider Late Antiquity *as* antiquity. While the case can be made that either the third century or the years 410 or 476 mark distinctive turning points in the tastes and political organization of the Roman world,[67] the analyses of documentality in the latter chapters of this volume reinforce the notion that "Late Antiquity's distinctiveness did not arise from a clear break with the past ... but from the transformations that took place in it."[68] In the polymathic tendencies of Gellius, the versified petitions of Dioscorus, and the "living" letters of the Eastern Empire, the realms of the documentary, literary, and metaliterary merged.

Documentary consciousness is manifest in descriptions of the variety and visibility of written records within the Roman world. The *Periegesis* of Pausanias, for instance, presents a panoramic view of the Mediterranean landscape, dotted with the documentary evidence of a Greek world long past. Through his gaze, we read or at least envision the dedicatory inscriptions attached to Enodeus' Athena (1.26.4) or the statue of Asclepius at Epidaurus (2.27.2). Even the absence of documents in this travelogue can speak to Pausanias' persistent reliance on inscribed information, as when he notes the Sicyonian tendency *not* to add inscriptions to the tombs of their dead (2.7.2). One of the few inscriptions that Pausanias quotes in full is not inscribed on stone but on Celtic armor, recording the victory of King Pyrrhus over the Gauls (1.13.3). Although these

---

suggests that already by the late Republic attitudes had begun to shift among the Romans, prefiguring the new mentality towards documents of all forms under the Empire.

67 Recent proponents of the notion of a distinct chronological break, especially in the Western Roman Empire, include Heather 2005 and Ward-Perkins 2005.

68 Marcone 2008, 10 reflecting on the approach of Bowersock/Brown/Grabar 1999 and Liebeschuetz 2006.

shields and greaves would constitute only the weakest types of records in Ferraris's ambit, in that they merely preserve information, such inscribed records of victories were of paramount importance for Imperial authors.

A useful test case of the scope of this newfound documentary consciousness can be seen in the impulse to document one's presence at cultic sites or other locations of religious or social significance. Such texts abound in Roman Egypt, and the palimpsestic set of inscriptions that accreted on the Memnon Colossus, for instance, demonstrates the degree to which individuals felt the need to record their visits to the site.[69] These *proskynêmata*, which stand in for an individual before the god of a particular shrine, record their presence in generally formulaic language; in this regard, they may be interpreted as documentation of visitors' acts of worship, and declarations of their belonging within the social community of devotees to a god or cult.[70] These formulaic inscriptions were positioned in dialogue with inscriptions by others who came to the site before, and served as evidence of the visitor's presence for future pilgrims or tourists. They are physical instantiations of a social act and as such operate as documents, while they also afford opportunities for visitors to commemorate themselves by fashioning their own self-portraits.[71] By recording their acts of pilgrimage and reifying their presence, average Romans produced documents of their own that inscribed their social acts of worship and asserted their membership within the broader community of visitors to these sacred sites.

Other genres of Imperial literature show that documentary consciousness was not confined to writing. In prose fiction, a variety of objects and signs could exert the "strong" documentary power of evidence or proof. In Apuleius' *Metamorphoses*, a revived corpse points to the waxen nose and ears of Thelyphron as proof of the supernatural circumstances of his death (*dabo vobis intemeratae veritatis documenta perlucida*, 2.30).[72] In a similar vein, the recognition scenes in

---

[69] On the Memnon Colossus and its inscriptions, see Rosenmeyer 2018.
[70] On *proskynêmata* generally see Geraci 1971; on those affixed to the Memnon Colossus see Rosenmeyer 2018, 21–27.
[71] Compare Rosenmeyer 2018, 34, understanding the inscriptions on the Memnon Colossus within the frame of social memory: "One can argue that, in addition to commemorating something that happened at a specific place and time, these inscriptions also fulfill what has been called the "*mnema* function," or the function of social memory aimed at a human audience, in which the inscription extends the memory of the dedicator's name in connection with the monument beyond the time it would be remembered without the act of writing. Many of the inscribers supplement their public, socially sanctioned narrative act of commemoration (*mnema* function) with a personal, particularized narrative act of self-fashioning."
[72] On the body as a source of corroboration, see Gleason 2002, 294–299.

the Greek romances create special opportunities for Imperial readers to explore the dimensions of identity and proof. The eponymous protagonists of *Daphnis and Chloe* discover the true circumstances of their births through "tokens" (γνωρίσματα, 3.19), luxury goods that mark their noble origins. In the *Alexander Romance*, by contrast, it is a painting that allows Queen Kandake to identify Alexander the Great in disguise: "You just so happen to be King Alexander, and now I will show you your document" (τὸ συμβόλαιόν σου, 3.22). In all three episodes, characters rely upon non-textual objects to confirm or refute verbal testimony.

The literature of the later Roman Empire gives the impression that the profusion of documents in everyday life also fueled an industry of counterfeit and pseudepigraphy. In the adjudication of Romans' wills, for instance, forgery was so common an accusation that charges of *falsum* and *captatio* ("legacy hunting") became a literary trope.[73] The very formulaic nature of final testaments, as Edward Champlin has observed, made counterfeiting remarkably easy to do and notoriously difficult to prosecute. The later Empire also gave rise to the production of false documentation about figures from the first and second centuries CE, both pagan and Christian. A fifth-century CE letter known as the *Anaphora Pilati* falsifies correspondence between Pontius Pilate and Tiberius. The author's deliberate effort to adopt the frame of an authentic first-century epistle and to imitate the style of a Roman governor has led Anne-Catherine Baudoin to categorize this letter as an instance of forgery rather than pseudepigraphy: "It is unlikely that those texts would be considered pseudepigraphical ... wrongly attributed to an author — since the texts themselves claim their authorship."[74] The prevalence of these forgeries has prompted William Hansen to identify a related phenomenon in the Imperial period as pseudo-documentarism: a false claim that the author has discovered and now transmits an authentic document.[75] Such "revelations" about the document that readers now hold in their hands appear, for instance, in the fourth-century *Journal of the Trojan War of Dictys of Crete* — diary entries purportedly written by an Iliadic veteran, on wooden tablets no less.

At the same time, asserting a hard line between "forged" and "authentic" elides some of the nuance inherent to the imitative practice that underlies

---

[73] Champlin 1991, 87.
[74] Baudoin 2016, 220.
[75] Hansen 2003, 302: "An author's untrue allegation that he (or she) has come upon an authentic document of some sort that he (or she) is drawing upon or passing on to his (or her) readers."

pseudepigraphy, which in turn illuminates the very nature of the documentary consciousness that emerged in the early Empire. Though the Alexandrian critics imposed strong barriers between these categories (as attested by Quintilian *Inst.* 1.4.3), the iterative and mimetic nature of Greco-Roman literature, and the centrality of creative imitation in the ancient educational system in many instances suggest a complementary interpretation of this "pseudepigraphic habit" as a process of coming to terms with the nature of these documents, and of reinterpreting their vital roles within Roman society.[76] Even as the forgery of certain legal documents like wills was becoming a legitimate cause for concern, the contemporary pseudepigraphic and pseudodocumentarian tendencies in literature are attempts to reconceptualize the textual forms that documented, and dominated, the social life of the Roman Empire. Authors examine the role of documents through these creative imitations, and their mimetic efforts provide a window into their own interpretations of documentary forms and the centrality of such forms to the lived experiences of their audiences. These efforts, which vacillate between the parodic and the deliberately fraudulent, allow us to see authors in the Roman Empire thinking through the very nature of these documents in real time. By manipulating their forms and presenting them in new, potentially fraught contexts, Imperial pseudepigraphists and pseudodocumentarians reflect an effort to understand the limits of what documents could do, and to reassess their function amidst the shifting social landscape of the Roman Empire.

The "long Roman Empire" — encompassing the imperial expansions of the second century BCE to the postclassical expressions of the early fifth century CE — provides a valuable setting for the study of ancient documentality. This is not because Imperial societies used records in a radically different way than in the Classical or Hellenistic periods. Nor do the expressions of documentary consciousness in the Imperial period mark the first instances when Greeks or Romans concerned themselves with the authority, veracity, or materiality of written records. But the Imperial period does bear witness to tandem transformations in the Mediterranean world: a new political order that required increased production and standardization of written records, and a host of diverse voices from across that Empire reading, responding to, and reworking the documentary landscape around them.

---

76 Cf. Najman/Peirano Garrison 2019, 351: "In reframing pseudepigraphy as an act of interpretation or as a generative mechanism than enables the growth of a tradition, we can study these texts not as intruders or interlopers into the canon but as creative responses to their respective traditions."

4 Structure of the Volume

The chapters of this volume reexamine familiar categories of written records in the Roman world by analyzing documents as social objects, using Ferraris's theory of documentality as a starting point. Each contribution places ancient source materials into dialogue with the fundamental conversation about the nature of documents outlined above, exploring the interstices between modern and ancient concepts to recover the documentary consciousness of the Roman Empire. In so doing, the volume eschews the simple dichotomy between literary and documentary texts. For that reason, and in an effort to bridge traditional disciplinary boundaries, we have organized the chapters on the basis of shared methodologies and lines of inquiry, rather than chronology or types of sources studied.

The chapters of the first section, "Approaches to Ancient Documentality," engage directly with the social ontology of Ferraris and his critics in order to question the applicability of this paradigm to documentary practice in the ancient world. The opening contribution by John Bodel, "Documenting Identity in the Early Roman Empire," examines the role that written records played in legal discussions of identity and citizenship in ancient Rome. For Bodel, the evolutionary narrative of documentality as posited by Ferraris and Enrico Terrone must be reevaluated. Some modern assumptions about the nature of documents are shared with ancient jurists like Ulpian, including the irrelevance of material and the requirement of an initial social act in constituting a document. Indeed, the manner in which Romans attested to the identities of individuals in two case studies suggest that Roman evidentiary practice appears to transcend the written document in cases of identity, given their dependence on witness testimony and oral utterance. Even Roman texts that aimed to establish identity were largely ineffective at imposing social reality until the Edict of Caracalla. This relative slowness to move beyond the oral document appears to violate the teleology inherent in Ferraris's model, and Bodel ultimately suggests that Roman Imperial documentary practice never truly set off the virtuous cycle of practices and documents postulated in *Documentality*.

Jacqueline Arthur-Montagne's chapter, "Copying the Canon: Imperial School Texts as Documentary Traces," turns to Terrone's model of the documentary trace: the concept of the document as that which connects us to past social action. Although, like Bodel, she challenges the teleological conception of documents, she also applies Terrone's notion of documentary traces to the study of copying exercises in Imperial school papyri, which provided testimony of the students' efforts to achieve *paideia* and assemble a library of the mind. By examining copying exercises from the Roman schoolroom, and by raising the question of whether such exercises could be considered documents, Arthur-Montagne recognizes memory as a key tool in demonstrating one's knowledge of the canon. Her focus on the cognitive facets of ancient pedagogical practice aligns with the model of the documentary trace, since these school exercises inscribed their lessons simultaneously onto wax tablets and into the minds of Roman learners.

The first section concludes with a chapter by Karen ní Mheallaigh, titled "Documenting Wonderland: Lucian's *True Stories* and the Documentary *Imaginaire*," on what fiction can tell us about ancient documentality. Starting from the position that fiction and documents are both founded on agreement between author and reader about their veracity, she examines in detail three inscriptions from Lucian's *True Stories*, showing how they evoke specific documentary texts and practices from antiquity such as boundary-marking, seal-making, inscribed treaties, funerary epigraphy, and the literary peritext. In each of her case studies, ní Mheallaigh shows that interest in the materiality of the purported documents increases in direct proportion to the degree of anxiety about the authoritativeness of the document. Ultimately, she argues that Lucian is interested precisely in the boundary between documents and literature, and that his fiction offers insight into the complex semiotics of documents in antiquity.

From documentality's terms and definitions in the first section of the volume, the second section — "Documentary Communities and Landscapes" — transitions to applied approaches to documentality in the Roman world. The chapters of this section interrogate Roman interactions with publicly visible objects and texts that contributed to the construction of ancient social reality, and they also situate the study of those inscribed records in the everyday, embodied experiences of the Empire's inhabitants. Contributors investigate how epigraphy shaped social communities in urban centers and, conversely, in what ways the natural world itself could function or be interpreted as a document in the ancient imagination. Inger Kuin's chapter, "Cities Full of Words: Illiteracy and Epigraphy in Lucian of Samosata," seeks to reconstruct the lived experiences of (il)literate individuals through an analysis of the imagined epigraphic objects in the Lucianic corpus. Even as the ancient cityscape surrounded Greeks and Romans with texts, interactions with these texts and their authority varied based on the degree of literacy of the observer. Lucian's use of inscriptions, and the challenges that they present in his fictions, offer one avenue for reconstructing broader attitudes towards these abundant texts and their documentary status. By exposing the differing receptions that realistic and fantastical inscriptions receive in the Lucianic corpus, Kuin reveals a paradox in Lucian's documentary messaging: though illiteracy hardly marginalized Greek-speakers economically or politically, even those who *could* read had to learn to fear the snares and seductions of written records.

Where Kuin's chapter focused on individual (would-be) readers, the next chapter in this section considers the collective attitude towards documentary evidence among ancient geographers. In "Documenting the *oikoumenê*: What 'Documents' Supported the Description of the Inhabited World in the Hellenistic and Imperial Periods?" Pierre Schneider studies geographical writing and descriptions of the *oikoumenê gê* from the Hellenistic period onward in order to discern attitudes towards documentary source materials. He demonstrates that ancient authors, in an effort to compile a robust body of geographical knowledge, employed even plants, animals, and objects as documentary material. Schneider finds Ferraris's theory of the document as social object to be inadequate for understanding how the ancient geographers envisioned their sources. He instead argues that a fundamentally different way of knowing the world emerges from these authors, dependent on an expansive, almost universal interpretation of what constitutes a document.

The final chapter in this section considers documentality in a civic context. Sjoukje Kamphorst's contribution, "A Community Set in Stone? Monumental Decrees as Instruments of Greek Interactions," looks at civic inscriptions in Greek cities during the late Hellenistic and early Imperial periods as media for coordinating cooperation. She utilizes Michael Chwe's concept of "rational rituals" and Josiah Ober's notion of "common knowledge" as foils to Ferraris's understanding of documents as the material representations of events and decisions. Kamphorst then argues that the prevalence of inscribed civic documents to record interstate relations suggests their role in documenting and performing community-building in Hellenistic and Roman Greece. In the transition to Empire, civil decrees may have lost their agency to foster diplomacy between *poleis*, but nonetheless remained "informational beacons" within communities.

The third section of the volume, "Between Documents and Literature," moves from documents and documentality in the lived experience of Imperial communities to the dynamic fluidity between documentary and literary writing in the later Roman Empire. The chapters challenge conventional approaches to letters, allusions, and literary quotation by observing the overlap between genres; in so doing, they aim to demonstrate the permeability of these textual forms in the ancient world and the artificial disciplinary divides between literature and document. These chapters illustrate the reach of the period's documentary consciousness, which enveloped the production and interpretation of literature as well. Scott DiGiulio, in "Dead Letters, Documentality, and the *Noctes Atticae* of Aulus Gellius," explores Aulus Gellius' miscellany and its use of documents (especially letters and inscriptions). In contrast to other antiquarian projects, Gellius' treatment of these texts as analogous to the literary works that he quotes suggests that, for him, the divide between the documentary and the literary was more permeable than we might otherwise imagine. As authoritative pieces of evidence for Latin language and style, literary works and documents stand side by side, together constituting the broader text-world that Gellius depicts with his miscellany.

Jean-Luc Fournet's chapter, titled "The Relationship between Documents and Literature in Late Antiquity: The Case of the Petition, between Document, Adaptation and Literary Creation," makes the first foray into Late Antiquity with a study of third- and fourth-century CE petition letters. By looking at extant petitions both on papyrus and in literary sources, including those that survive in multiple forms, he demonstrates the complementarity of documentary and literary texts. If earlier instances of the petition appear in the expected form when included in historiographical or other comparable works as a form of rhetorical ornamentation, by the sixth century CE the cross-pollination of the "literary" and "documentary" petition is complete, with poetic versions of the petition staking a claim to status as both literature and functional text. Yet, despite their more literary nature, these texts may still deservedly claim the status of document, reinforcing the difficulty of drawing a dividing line between "literature" and "document."

In the third and final chapter of this section, "When the Letter Speaks Up: Living and Lifeless Letters," Yasmine Amory uncovers the oral elements of the ancient epistolary experience. She considers the role of late antique letter-carriers, who would animate written letters by reading them aloud and conveying other personal messages from sender to recipient. Amory's emphasis on epistolary performances and the personification of the letter-writer by the messenger shows once again that written text was not necessarily perceived as the most authoritative medium in ancient Roman record-keeping. Simultaneously, the evidence she presents demonstrates the utility of Ferraris's notion that social acts can be inscribed as immaterial documents in memory, to be passed on subsequently via the messenger's oral utterances. Amory's interpretation of "living letters" reflects our still-evolving understanding of the Graeco-Roman epistolary habit, and also challenges the primacy of physical textual records in ancient documentary practice.

The final chapter of the volume is titled "The Ancient Historian and His Documents: Reader, Interpreter and/or Author?" and serves as an epilogue. Mireille Corbier explores how modern historians' attitudes towards inscribed documents shape these texts and condition their interpretation; in so doing, her reflections about the historical enterprise touch on many of the central themes addressed in the preceding chapters. Over time, scholars' understanding of what constitutes a document — not only text, but also shape and context — has changed, and this has in many cases influenced the preservation of ancient materials. Noting that epigraphists and historians invert the terms of Ferraris's formulation, making every written act an object (rather than making every social object a written act), Corbier reiterates that what students of the ancient Mediterranean have traditionally considered "documents" are in effect traces that only gain their particular status and authoritative nature when examined through the scholarly lens. She argues that Buckland's response to Ferraris, and especially his tripartite division of documents, is most readily applicable to the study of the Roman world. Surveying an array of epigraphical texts, including the second-century CE identity documents of Babatha and military diplomas, her essay demonstrates the very instability of some of these documents as scholarly approaches have advanced, and as new readings and interpretations have reshaped the documents themselves. Ultimately, in bringing modern theory into dialogue with ancient evidence, Corbier raises a series of provocative questions about what it means for classicists and Greco-Roman historians to utilize documents. Her chapter problematizes the nature of the documents that constitute such a vital dossier of ancient Roman historical evidence.

Collectively, the chapters in this volume address the materiality, authority, use, and literary interactions of Roman documents, examining different modes of documentation from the early Empire into Late Antiquity. The Roman Empire saw a proliferation of texts and documents that was of a piece with, if not on the scale of, our own times. Just as our shifting landscape of information technologies has sparked reconsideration of what constitutes a document, so too did the Romans reflect on their experience of more information being recorded on stone, on papyrus, and (increasingly) in codices than in any previous period. Contributors to this volume reconsider several orthodoxies about ancient document study from a range of methodological perspectives. Rather than maintaining the traditional siloes in which these texts and objects are studied, the volume unites the contributors' diverse, multidisciplinary expertise in order to assess the cognitive and social space occupied by documents. As such, our goal is not to provide a singular methodology through which one should study the ancient document. Rather, the variety of materials, and the juxtaposition of the different approaches required for such study, suggests that a single, narrow definition of "document" in antiquity may be beyond reach and ultimately undesirable. Such a conclusion may seem frustratingly aporetic. Nonetheless, we, as the editors of this volume, see value in demonstrating the instability of the document as a category. Our contributors' search for ancient mentalities towards documents, both real and imagined, as traces, records, memories, and objects, brings their function and power within Imperial societies into focus. In this way we hope to encourage others to reflect further upon the role of documents — "ours" and "theirs" — in translating lived experiences from the Roman Empire to the present day.

References

Ankersmit, F. (2005), *Sublime Historical Experience*, Stanford.
Assmann, J. (2011 [1992]), *Cultural Memory and Early Civilization: Writing, Remembrance, and Political Imagination*, Cambridge.
Bagnall, R. (2011), *Everyday Writing in the Graeco-Roman East*, Berkeley.
Baudoin, A.-C. (2016), "Truth in the Details: The Report of Pilate to Tiberius as an Authentic Forgery", in: E.P. Cueva/J. Martínez (eds.), *Splendide mendax: Rethinking Fakes and Forgeries in Classical, Late Antique, and Early Christian Literature*, Groningen, 219–238.
Beltrán Lloris, F. (2015), "The 'Epigraphic Habit' in the Roman World", in: C. Bruun/J. Edmonson (eds.), *The Oxford Handbook of Epigraphy*, Oxford, 131–148.
Bennett, T./ Joyce, P. (eds.) (2010), *Cultural Studies, History and the Material Turn*, London.
Bérard, F. (1991), "Tacite et les inscriptions", in: *ANRW* II.33.4, 3007–3050.
Berliner, D. (2005) "The Abuses of Memory: Reflections on the 'Memory Boom'", in: *Anthropological Quarterly* 78, 197–211.
Bing, P. (2002), "The Un-Read Muse? Inscribed Epigram and its Readers in Antiquity", in: M.A. Harder/R.F. Regtuit/G.C. Wakker (eds.), *Hellenistic Epigrams*, Leuven, 39–66.
Bodel, J. (2015), "Inscriptions and Literacy", in: C. Bruun/J. Edmonson (eds.), *The Oxford Handbook of Epigraphy*, Oxford, 745–763.
Bolle, K./Machado, C./Witschel, C. (eds.) (2017), *The Epigraphic Cultures of Late Antiquity*, Stuttgart.
Bowersock, G.W./Brown, P./Grabar, O. (eds.) (1999), *Late Antiquity: A Guide to the Postclassical World*, Cambridge, MA.
Bowman, A.K./Thomas, J.D. (eds.) (1983–2011), *Tabulae Vindolandenses*, 4 vols., Cambridge/London.
Brosius, M. (2003), "Ancient Archives and Concepts of Record Keeping", in: M. Brosius (ed.), *Ancient Archives and Archival Traditions: Concepts of Record-Keeping in the Ancient World*, Oxford, 1–16.
Buckland, M. (2014), "Documentality beyond Documents", in: *The Monist* 97, 179–186.
Carr, D. (2014), *Experience and History: Phenomenological Perspectives on the Historical World*, New York.
Champlin, E. (1991), *Final Judgments: Duty and Emotion in Roman Wills, 200 B.C.–A.D. 250*, Berkeley.
Chaplin, J. (2000), *Livy's Exemplary History*, Oxford.

Corbier, M. (2006), *Donner à voir, donner à lire. Mémoire et communication dans la Rome ancienne*, Paris.
Cribiore, R. (1996), *Writing, Teachers, and Students in Graeco-Roman Egypt*, Atlanta.
Crosby, T.P. (1980), "*Exemplum* and *Documentum* in Livy", unpublished PhD thesis, King's College London.
Davies, J.K. (2003), "Greek Archives: From Record to Monument", in: M. Brosius (ed.), *Ancient Archives and Archival Traditions: Concepts of Record-Keeping in the Ancient World*, Oxford, 323–343.
Day, J. (2018), "The 'Spatial Dynamics' of Archaic and Classical Greek Epigram: Conversations among Locations, Monuments, Texts, and Viewer-Readers", in: A. Petrovic/I. Petrovic/E. Thomas (eds.), *The Materiality of the Text: Placement, Perception, and the Presence of Inscribed Texts in Classical Antiquity*, Leiden, 73–104.
Derrida, J. (1988 [1977]), *Limited Inc*, transl. S. Webber, Evanston, IL.
Derrida, J. (1998 [1996]), *Monolingualism of the Other or the Prosthesis of Origin*, transl. P. Mensah, Stanford.
Ferraris, M. (2009), *Documentalità. Perché è necessario lasciar tracce*, Rome.
Ferraris, M. (2012), *Documentality: Why It Is Necessary to Leave Traces*, transl. R. Davies, New York.
Ferraris, M. (2014), "Total Mobilization", in: *The Monist* 97, 200–221.
Ferraris, M. (2015), "Collective Intentionality or Documentality?", in: *Philosophy & Social Criticism* 41, 423–433.
Frampton, S.A. (2019), *Empire of Letters: Writing in Roman Literature and Thought from Lucretius to Ovid*, New York.
Franklin, J.L., Jr. (1991), "Literacy and the Parietal Inscriptions of Pompeii", in: J.H. Humphrey (ed.), *Literacy and the Roman World*, Ann Arbor, 77–98.
Gagarin, M. (2008), *Writing Greek Law*, Cambridge.
Geraci, G. (1971), "Ricerche sul proskynema", in: *Aegyptus* 51, 3–211.
Gleason, M. (2002), "Truth Contests and Talking Corpses", in: J. Porter (ed.), *Constructions of the Classical Body*, Ann Arbor, 287–313.
Grigoropoulos, D./Di Napoli, V./Evangelidis, V./Camia, F./Rogers, D./Vlizos, S. (2017), "Roman Greece and the 'Mnemonic Turn': Some Critical Remarks", in: T.M. Dijkstra/I.N.I. Kuin/M. Moser/D. Weidgenannt (eds.), *Strategies of Remembering in Greece under Rome (100 BC–100 AD)*, Leiden, 21–35.
Habinek, T. (2009), "Situating Literacy at Rome", in: W.A. Johnson/H. Parker (eds.), *Ancient Literacies: The Culture of Reading in Greece and Rome*, Oxford, 114–140.
Hammond, M. (1953), "A Statue of Trajan Represented on the 'Anaglypha Traiani'", in: *MAAR* 21, 125–183.
Hansen, W. (2003), "Strategies of Authentication in Ancient Popular Literature", in: S. Panayotakis/M. Zimmerman/W. Keulen (eds.), *The Ancient Novel and Beyond*, Leiden, 301–314.
Harris, W. (1989), *Ancient Literacy*, Cambridge, MA.
Heather, P. (2005), *The Fall of the Roman Empire: A New History of Rome and the Barbarians*, New York.
Hedrick, C. (2015), "Written Media in Antiquity", in: D. Selden/P. Vasunia (eds.), *The Oxford Handbook of the Literatures of the Roman Empire*, Oxford, doi.org/10.1093/oxfordhb/9780199699445.001.0001.
Hengstl, J./Schiemann, G./Gröschler, P. (2006), "Documents", in: *Brill's New Pauly*, Leiden.

Houston, G.W. (2009), "Papyrological Evidence for Book Collections and Libraries in the Roman Empire", in: W.A. Johnson/H.N. Parker (eds.), *Ancient Literacies: The Culture of Reading in Greece and Rome*, Oxford, 233–267.

Howley, J. (2017), "Book-Burning and the Uses of Writing in Ancient Rome: Destructive Practice between Literature and Document", in: *JRS* 107, 213–236.

Humphrey, J.H. (ed.) (1991), *Literacy in the Roman World*, Journal of Roman Archaeology, Supplementary Series 3, Ann Arbor.

Johnson, W.A./Parker, H.N. (eds.) (2009), *Ancient Literacies: The Culture of Reading in Greece and Rome*, Oxford.

Johnson, J.R. (1978), "The Authenticity and Validity of Antony's Will", in: *AC* 47, 494–503.

Johnson, W.A. (2010), *Readers and Reading Culture in the High Roman Empire: A Study of Elite Communities*, Oxford.

Jördens, A. (2011), "Communicating with Tablets and Papyri", in: M. Peachin (ed.), *The Oxford Handbook of Social Relations in the Roman World*, Oxford, 227–247.

Kirk, A. (2018), "What is an ἐπιγραφή in Classical Greece?", in: A. Petrovic/I. Petrovic/E. Thomas (eds.), *The Materiality of the Text: Placement, Perception, and the Presence of Inscribed Texts in Classical Antiquity*, Leiden, 29–47.

Koepsell, D./Smith, B. (2014), "Beyond Paper", in: *The Monist* 97, 222–235.

Kruschwitz, P. (2008), "Patterns of Text Layout in Pompeian Verse Inscriptions" in: *Studia Philologica Valentina* 11, 225–264.

Kruschwitz, P./Campbell, V.L. (2010), "What the Pompeians saw: representations of document types in Pompeian drawings and paintings (and their value for linguistic research)", in: *Arctos* 43, 57–84.

Liddel, P./Low, P. (eds.) (2013), *Inscriptions and Their Uses in Greek and Latin Literature*, Oxford.

Liebeschuetz, J.H.W.G. (2006), *Decline and Change in Late Antiquity: Religion, Barbarians, and Their Historiography*, Aldershot.

Lushkov, A.H. (2015), *Magistracy and the Historiography of the Roman Republic: Politics in Prose*, Cambridge.

MacMullen, R. (1982), "The Epigraphic Habit in the Roman Empire", in: *AJPh* 103, 233–246.

Marcone, A. (2008), "A Long Late Antiquity? Considerations on a Controversial Periodization", in: *JLA* 1, 4–19.

McLean, B. (2002), *An Introduction to Greek Epigraphy of the Hellenistic and Roman Periods from Alexander the Great down to the Reign of Constantine (323 B.C.–A.D. 337)*, Ann Arbor.

Meyer, E.A. (2004), *Legitimacy and Law in the Roman World:* Tabulae *in Roman Belief and Practice*, Cambridge.

Meyer, E.A. (2011), "Epigraphy and Communication", in: M. Peachin (ed.), *The Oxford Handbook of Social Relations in the Roman World*, Oxford, 191–226.

Meyer, E.A. (2017), "Inscribing Columns in Fifth-Century Athens", in: I. Berti/K. Bolle/F. Opdenhoff/F. Stroth (eds.), *Writing Matters: Presenting and Perceiving Monumental Inscriptions in Antiquity and the Middle Ages*, Berlin, 205–261.

Milnor, K. (2014), *Graffiti and the Literary Landscape in Roman Pompeii*, Oxford.

Morello, R./Morrison, A.D. (eds.) (2007), *Ancient Letters: Classical and Late Antique Epistolography*, Oxford.

Najman, H./Peirano Garrison, I. (2019), "Pseudepigraphy as an Interpretative Construct", in: M. Henze/L. Ingeborg Lied (eds.), *The Old Testament Pseudepigrapha: Fifty Years of the Pseudepigraph Section at the SBL*, Atlanta, 331–355.

ní Mheallaigh, K. (2008), "Pseudo-Documentarism and the Limits of Ancient Fiction", in: *AJPh* 129, 403–431.
Nora, P. (1984–1992), *Les lieux de mémoire*, 3 vols., Paris.
Nora, P. (1989), "Between Memory and History: Les lieux de mémoire", in: *Representations* 26, 7–24.
Plattner, G.A. (1998), "Die ‚Anaglypha Hadriani' in Rom", in: *Forum Archaeologiae* 7, https://homepage.univie.ac.at/elisabeth.trinkl/forum/forum0698/07traian.htm, accessed March 31, 2022.
Potter, D.S. (2011), "Tacitus' Sources", in: V. Pagán (ed.), *A Companion to Tacitus*, Malden, MA, 125–140.
Purcell, N. (1995), "Literate Games: Roman Urban Society and the Game of *Alea*", in: *P&P* 147, 3–37.
Rimell, V. (2000), "Epistolary Fictions: Authorial Identity in *Heroides* 15", in: *CCJl* 45, 109–135.
Rosenmeyer, P. (2001), *Ancient Epistolary Fictions: The Letter in Greek Literature*, Cambridge.
Rosenmeyer, P. (2006), *Ancient Greek Literary Letters: Selections in Translation*, London.
Rosenmeyer, P. (2018), *The Language of Ruins: Greek and Latin Inscriptions on the Memnon Colossus*, Oxford.
Runia, E. (2006), "Presence", in: *History and Theory* 45, 1–29.
Runia, E. (2010), "Inventing the New from the Old: From White's 'Tropics' to Vico's 'Topics'", in: *Rethinking History* 14, 229–241.
Sailor, D. (2006), "Dirty Linen, Fabrication, and the Authorities of Livy and Augustus", in: *TAPhA* 136, 329–388.
Searle, J.R. (1977), "Reiterating the Differences: A Reply to Derrida", in: *Glyph* 2, 198–208.
Searle, J.R. (1995), *The Construction of Social Reality*, New York.
Shear, J. (2017), "Writing Past and Present in Hellenistic Athens: The Honours for Demosthenes", in: I. Berti/ K. Bolle/F. Opdenhoff/ F. Stroth (eds.), *Writing Matters: Presenting and Perceiving Monumental Inscriptions in Antiquity and the Middle Ages*, Berlin, 161–190.
Sickinger, J.P. (1999), *Public Records and Archives in Classical Athens*, Chapel Hill, NC.
Sickinger, J.P. (2002), "Literacy, Orality, Legislative Procedure", in: I. Worthington/J.M. Foley (eds.), *Epea and Grammata: Oral and Written Communication in Ancient Greece*, Leiden, 147–169.
Sirianni, F.A. (1984), "Was Antony's Will Partially Forged?", in: *AC* 53, 236–241.
Small, J. (1997), *Wax Tablets of the Mind: Cognitive Studies of Memory and Literacy in Classical Antiquity*, London.
Surkis, J. (2012), "When Was the Linguistic Turn? A Genealogy", in: *AHR* 117, 700–722.
Talbert, R.J.A. (1984), *The Senate of Imperial Rome*, Princeton.
Terrone, E. (2014), "Traces, Documents, and the 'Puzzle of Permanent Acts'", in: *The Monist* 97, 161–178.
Thill, E.W. (2014), "The Emperor in Action: Group Scenes in Trajanic Coins and Monumental Reliefs", in: *AJN* 26, 89–142.
Torelli, M. (1983), *Typology and Structure of Roman Historical Reliefs*, Ann Arbor.
Wallace-Hadrill, A. (1983), *Suetonius: The Scholar and His Caesars*, London.
Wardle, D. (ed.) (2014), *Suetonius: Life of Augustus*, Oxford.
Ward-Perkins, B. (2005), *The Fall of Rome and the End of Civilization*, Oxford.
White, H. (1980), "The Value of Narrativity in the Representation of Reality", in: *Critical Inquiry* 7, 5–27.

Whitmarsh, T. (2013), *Beyond the Second Sophistic: Adventures in Greek Postclassicism*, Berkeley.
Woolf, G. (2015), "Ancient Illiteracy?", in: *BICS* 58(2), 31–42.
Zadorojnyi, A. (2006), "Lords of the Flies: Literacy and Tyranny in Imperial Biography", in: B. McGing/J. Mossman (eds.), *The Limits of Ancient Biography*, Swansea, 351–394.

Part I: **Approaches to Ancient Documentality**

John Bodel
Documenting Identity in the Early Roman Empire

Abstract: This chapter examines the role that written records played in legal discussions of identity and citizenship in ancient Rome, and demonstrates that the evolutionary narrative of documentality, as posited by Maurizio Ferraris and Enrico Terrone, must be reevaluated. The manner in which Romans attested to the identities of individuals suggests that Roman evidentiary practices transcend the written document in cases of identity, given their dependence on witness testimony and oral utterance. Even Roman texts that aimed to establish identity were largely ineffective at imposing social reality until the Edict of Caracalla. This relative slowness to move beyond the oral document appears to violate the teleology inherent in Ferraris's model, and ultimately suggests that Roman Imperial documentary practice never truly set off the "virtuous cycle" of practices and documents postulated in Ferraris's *Documentality*.

Maurizio Ferraris's theory of "documentality" rests on his fundamental rule of social reality: that social objects are the recordings, in any medium (even when only in the minds of two participants), of social acts. The essence of a document for Ferraris is thus neither material nor formal but intentional, in the sense that it is willed and collaborative, and recorded, in the sense that the intention is noted in a way that can be recognized and acknowledged by a third party.[1]

Recording is essential to the creation of a document, since it instantiates the idea embodied in a collaborative intent and renders the intent verifiable. Ferraris distinguishes three fundamental stages of marking, which, in the chapter of his book entitled "Ichnology," he arranges in an ascending order of development, from "traces" (any sort of modification of a surface that recalls something not present) to "registrations" (traces laid down in the mind) to what he calls "inscriptions in the technical sense," that is, registrations endowed with social

---

[1] Ferraris 2012 [2009]. Ferraris helpfully summarizes his argument in a brief Introduction (1–6), and enumerates its eleven theses in an Epilogue (316–320). (Page references are to the 2012 English edition.)

value by being shared by two or more persons.² Without this final stage of inscription, at the summit of the hierarchy, there can be no social objects: "In line with the law Object = Inscribed Act, if the inscription does not follow the expression, then the object does not come into being." What is more, "whatever fixes a social act and brings social objects into being should be called an inscription to signal that it is not a private registration" (Ferraris 2012, 237). In this process, the medium of delivery is irrelevant: "thus, it is not strictly necessary that there be writing on paper or some other medium for there to be an inscription. It is easy to think of times when there were only acts, inscribed with easily remembered formulas in the minds of persons" — formulas such as "I promise" or "I swear," which created mutual understandings.³ It is only through the mechanism of inscription that such speech acts become enduring social objects. Indeed, the importance of recording and inscription in the construction of social reality is manifested and sustained precisely through the production of documents.⁴

In certain respects Ferraris's ideas about documents and inscriptions are fully in line with the thinking of classical theorists of Roman law (jurists) and modern students of writing on durable surfaces (epigraphists). All agree, for example, that material and medium are irrelevant. For the jurist Ulpian, writing in the early third century, the phrase "tablets of a will" was to be understood to mean any form of written expression of testamentary intent. Although popular usage referred to a last will and testament as "tablets," Ulpian is at pains to emphasize, through the circumlocution *omnis materiae figura* ("every form of material"), that any medium of written testamentary expression should be regarded as valid. The document consisted in the publicly recognized expression of intent, however transcribed.⁵ The issue of central interest to legal histori-

---

2 The cumbersome gloss is necessary because Ferraris uses "inscriptions" in a non-technical sense in expounding Derrida's idea of "archiwriting" as a primordial stage of human evolution from prehistory to history: see Ferraris 2012, 206 and 235–241, respectively; further below, n. 3.
3 Ferraris 2012, 239. More recently Ferraris has rethought his use of the term "inscription," precisely because of its spurious specificity, and, in reformulating the fundamental law "object = inscribed act," has replaced "inscribed" with "recorded," in the same sense: see Ferraris 2015, 425 and 432 n. 5.
4 Ferraris 2015.
5 Ulp. 37.11.1.pr: *Tabulas testamenti accipere debemus, omnem materiae figuram: sive igitur tabulae sint ligneae sive cuiuscumque alterius materiae, sive chartae sive membranae sint vel si corio alicuius animalis, tabulae recte dicentur.* ("As 'tablets of a will' we ought to understand the entire form of the material [on which the will is written], whether the 'tablets' are of wood or any other material, whether papyrus or parchment or the skin of some animal, they are

ans — whether the written record was merely declaratory, affirming the oral statement (which was the effective binding instrument), or was itself constitutive of the obligation — is of no consequence for Ulpian's point that intention and recording are at the heart of the idea of a document and that medium and form make no difference for its legal validity.

So, too, for one modern epigraphist, the late Silvio Panciera, the medium and material of a written communication are not what make an inscription; rather, it is the intent of the author as signaled by choice of audience and mode of address that defines the form. With Ulpian (and in contrast to Ferraris), Panciera considered writing to be essential, but with Ferraris (in contrast to Ulpian), he regarded the nature of the communicative relationship between author and audience to be constitutive of the form. To illustrate the idea, Panciera imagined different contexts for a declaration of affection:

> If I say to a girl, in person or on the telephone, "Francesca, I love you," I am making an oral, interpersonal, communication; ... if I write it to her in a letter or ... email or text message, I produce a document; but if I spray-paint it in block capitals on the Aurelian Wall and broadcast it, through its location and through the chosen method of writing, not only to her but to the entire community ... I am producing an inscription.[6]

Panciera was obviously using the terms "inscription" and "document" in senses different from those intended by Ferraris: for Ferraris, there can be no document without inscription; for Panciera, inscriptions are not themselves documents but merely records of them. But for our purposes it is enough to observe that all three theoreticians — the Roman jurist, the modern scholar of inscriptions, and the new realist philosopher — agree in their understanding of the essence of a document as consisting in a recognized expression of intent rather than in any particular material form.[7]

---

correctly called 'tablets (of a will).'" Cf. Paulus, *Sent.* 4.7.6. For the materiality of Roman tablets, their uses, and the related associations, see Meyer 2004, 21–43, esp. 22–36.
6 Panciera 2012, 8.
7 Panciera 2012, 7: "Inscriptions, even if they provide records of many documents (thus confirming the importance of epigraphic communication) are not themselves documents." Another epigraphist, Mireille Corbier, working from a tripartite classification proposed by Buckland 2014, 179–181 — "made as a document," "made into a document," and "considered as a document" — argues that the categories often overlap and that, for a historian, the intent of the author is not essential; rather, "it is the researcher who 'makes the document'." The issue for Corbier is less the essence of the form than the practices of modern historians: see Corbier in this volume.

The authors of a useful collection of responses and reactions to Ferraris's book published in a special issue of *The Monist* in 2014 for the most part acknowledge the timelessness of this essential feature but nonetheless focus mainly on physical documents and their contemporary use to constitute and authenticate personal identity. In this discussion the modern passport figures prominently. Enrico Terrone, for example, asks to what extent documents as social objects constrain or determine social reality; he compares the passport and the boarding pass as markers of identity. Both allow "a suitable beholder to trace back to the relevant acts and persons involved in the production of the document," but they are constituted differently: whereas a boarding pass can be infinitely replicated but is used (i.e. authenticated) only once, a passport is produced only once — that is, "it is the sole particular allowed to represent the act that constituted it as a document" — but can be authenticated numerous times.[8] The latter form of document — unique but repeatedly verifiable — creates a stable social entity of the sort that "arises where social practices and documents historically reinforce each other." This process, and the environment that supports it, according to Terrone, create a "virtuous cycle" of practices and documents, whereby history proceeds according to fluctuations in a culture's documentary behavior:

> On the one hand, documents can exist only within a framework of practices that supports processes of tracing back from documents to the acts constituting them. On the other hand, documents allow practices to create more stable social entities by making acts permanent in effective and reliable ways. We can thus outline the construction of social reality by telling a story like this: through a gradual process social practices began to make room for documents, which then made room for further social entities, including entities of a more stable sort, which in turn made room for further types of documents and for more efficient document practices, which in turn made room for significantly more stable social entities, and so on without end. In this way, the social world historically unfolds along a virtuous cycle of practices and documents.[9]

Terrone presents this theory not as a hypothesis but as a historical narrative of evolutionary progress ("telling a story ... through a gradual process"). Ferraris speaks in the same way, framing his theory of "documentality" not as a timeless

---

8 Terrone 2014, 171–173, quotes from 173 and 171 respectively. On passports, see also Buckland 2014, 181–183; Koepsell/Smith 2014, 224, 226, 228; and Hennig 2014, 246–247. In comparing passports with boarding passes, Terrone does not note the inverse relation of replicability and possibility of authentication, but this aspect enhances his argument about the difference between the two otherwise ontologically similar forms.

9 Terrone 2014, 176.

idea or a discrete set of social practices, such as literacy or philanthropy, but as a particular stage of human history.[10] If we accept this premise, it is fair to ask where the documentary practices of the early Roman Empire fit into this virtuous cycle. In order to investigate that question, we may turn to an issue that has preoccupied modern researchers — how personal identity is constituted and ascertained — since the issues raised by the prominence of the passport in contemporary discussions of the concept of documentality were fundamentally no different in antiquity than they are today. What were the modes, documentary or other, of establishing and verifying personal identity during the first centuries CE, and to what extent did they support and advance social practices?

1 Unstable Social Entities

Two more or less contemporary stories about establishing identity during the later decades of the first century CE — one from the highest end of the social spectrum, the other from a lower register — together illustrate both the inevitability and the inadequacy of a recourse to documents in one of the social practices in which they were most closely implicated. In the early 70s CE, a woman from Herculaneum "who claimed to be Petronia Iusta" found herself embroiled in a legal dispute concerning the status of her birth, whether she had been born a slave or free. We know of the case from a cache of documents preserved on wax tablets, some eighteen in all, collected by Iusta's opponent, Calatoria Themis, and found together in the 1930s stored in a small chest in a modest room above the peristyle of a well-appointed private house (the so-called House of the Bicentenary, V,13–18) at Herculaneum.[11]

---

10 E.g., Ferraris 2012, 176–178, 286–291; see also Ferraris 2015, 423. And yet Ferraris 2015, 431 frames the origins of the phenomenon in resolutely ahistorical terms: "Imagine some Crusoe figure...".

11 The documents, collectively known as *Tabulae Herculanenses* and (for now) numbered consecutively according to a detailed system designed to distinguish a pair of sequences established by a first set of editors (*TH* 1–115 and *TH* D1–18) from a pair of notations (*TH²* and *TH²* A, B, etc.) designating documents newly revised or read, are currently being re-edited by Giuseppe Camodeca, who has identified some 160 legible texts, many still unpublished, mostly dating from the period 40–75 CE: see, for now, Camodeca 2017, especially 9–23, with 21–22 for the numbering. For Calatoria's archive, see Camodeca 2017, 46–47, 169–176 (*TH²* 60); for the legal issues raised by Iusta's case, see Weaver 1991, 166–169; Metzger 2000; and Lintott 2002, 560–565, with further bibliography at 555 n. 3.

The legal situation was complicated, and many important aspects of the case remain obscure. We do not know the precise nature of the lawsuit, or if — or how — the matter was resolved. The procedure attested in the *testimonia* was evidently an *actio per sponsionem* (an action arising from a sworn promise) involving a preliminary determination whether or not Iusta was freeborn (*praeiudicium an ingenua sit*), but it is unclear whether the tablets preserved by Calatoria Themis comprised all the relevant written evidence or only those parts of it pertinent to her case. Most of the documents are undated, and to a large extent our reconstruction of their chronology depends upon our overall understanding of the case, and vice versa.[12]

That said, the parties to the litigation and the nature of the dispute are clear: Iusta was the natural daughter of a woman, Petronia Vitalis, who had been a slave in the household of Petronius Stephanus and his wife, Calatoria Themis. This much was agreed. At some point Stephanus and Themis had manumitted Vitalis — whether formally or informally is unknown (probably the latter) — and for some time after that Vitalis' daughter Iusta had lived with Stephanus and Themis, before Vitalis sought to reunite with her and offered to make payment to Stephanus and Themis for the expenses they had incurred for Iusta's upkeep. At least twenty years had passed since the birth of Iusta, and it seems that, at the time of the lawsuit, both Vitalis (her mother) and Stephanus (her patron and, in all likelihood, father) had died. Although the cache of documents was found at Herculaneum and some of the agreements to appear in court (*vadimonia*) were evidently executed locally, most of the proceedings took place before the urban praetor in Rome. Iusta maintained that she had been born after her mother, Vitalis, had been manumitted and was therefore freeborn, whereas Calatoria Themis claimed that Iusta was her freedwoman and had been manumitted by her husband, Stephanus, only after she had been born a slave.[13]

The case of "the woman who claims to be Petronia Iusta" has become celebrated among Roman social and legal historians for the light it sheds on Roman documentary practices and the questions it raises about the status of Junian Latins, the peculiar category of citizenship to which, following the manumis-

---

[12] Camodeca's ongoing re-edition of the documents relevant to Iusta's case is clarifying the chronology and elucidating other obscurities, but uncertainties remain: see Metzger 2000, 151–152; Lintott 2002, 560, 563–565; Camodeca 2015, 272–282; and Camodeca 2017, 47.

[13] Iusta styles herself "*Sp(uri) f(ilia)*" in her nomenclature, from which it is clear that she claimed to be freeborn but not from a legitimate union (*s(ine) p(atre)*: cf. Gai. *Inst.* 1.64). That both Vitalis and Stephanus were deceased at the time of the proceedings can be inferred from the circumstances of the suit: see Metzger 2000, 153 and Lintott 2002, 563.

sion reforms of Augustus, informally manumitted slaves during the early Empire were relegated, which granted them limited property and procedural rights during their lifetimes but denied them testamentary privileges upon death.[14] With the dossier of private documents collected by a Jewish woman, Babatha, fleeing the emperor Hadrian's Jewish campaign in the early 130s and discussed by Mireille Corbier in the final chapter of this volume, the archive of Calatoria Themis provides vivid evidence of the densely documented private lives of two early Imperial women of sub-elite status and diverse geographical, social, and cultural circumstances (the documents of Babatha are written in Greek, Aramaic, and Nabataean-Aramaic) but similarly diverse legal entanglements. The issue at the center of Iusta's case — a determination of civil status based upon specific criteria of eligibility — lies at the heart also of a similar and roughly contemporary case pursued at Herculaneum by a certain L. Venidius Ennychus (also discussed by Corbier in this volume). Both exemplify documentary practices in central Italy of the first century CE and raise similar questions about the status of written evidence in proving identity in the early Roman Empire.[15]

The most striking aspect of Calatoria's dossier, despite the evident centrality of the hoarded documents to the conduct of the proceedings, is the complete absence from it of anything that we might regard as documentary proof, or even evidence, of the principal claims advanced by the two opposing parties. Iusta had no birth certificate or other document attesting to her status at the time of birth to substantiate her claim, nor did Calatoria Themis have any record to show how and when Iusta had been manumitted or redeemed. Instead the archive consists of various forms of indirect verbal testimony, mostly from witnesses or between the litigating parties. Specifically, the tablets comprise three *vadimonia*, agreements to appear in court at a fixed date, two executed at Her-

---

[14] For the extensive literature on Junian Latins, see Balestri Fumagalli 1985; Mouritsen 2011, 84–88; and Rawson 2010, 195–221, all with further references. For their suspected prominence in the civic life of Pompeii and Herculaneum, see Camodeca 2006; Emmerson 2011 (esp. 161–164); Silver 2013; and Camodeca 2017, 57–84, esp. 70–76, with Corbier in this volume.

[15] Corbier rightly notes that Ferraris's theory of documentality, which focuses on intentionally produced written records capable of authentication, ignores or distorts many types of evidence that historians use as documents, often with purposes very different from those for which the "documents" were originally created. For her, dossiers of tablets such as those collected by Calatoria Themis and Venidius Ennychus show how artifacts made as documents for one purpose can be put to use by modern scholars for other purposes and thus illustrate only a small part of what historians regard as the documentary record. Our concern here is rather with the inadequacy of the documents, as documents, in meeting the purposes for which they were created and saved.

culaneum on the order of a local magistrate, the third executed in Rome for an appearance there a year later; seven *testimonia*, sworn statements of witnesses — essentially written records of oral declarations — all concerning Iusta's status, with five giving testimony in favor of her free birth and two against; and eight tablets that now preserve only the names of witnesses. Only two of the *vadimonia* are precisely dated: one was executed on September 7, 74 CE, the other six months later, on March 12, 75 CE. Most of the other documents, including all the *testimonia*, seem to concern earlier stages of the suit and are only generally datable on the basis of the persons mentioned in them, some from as much as a dozen or more years earlier.[16]

The dossier of Venidius does contain documentary proofs of the sort missing from Calatoria's archive — a birth certificate and a copy of an official decision (*edictum*) by a Roman magistrate awarding full citizenship — but, far from creating stable social entities, these documents reveal a complexity and cumbersomeness in the procedures required for obtaining and authenticating the proofs, including the production of supporting documents, that exposes the fundamental instability of the system they are designed to support.[17] Thus, despite these collections presenting a social reality thick in documentary practices and rich in the production of documents, the picture we receive of the Roman world of the early Imperial period from the dossiers of Babatha, Calatoria, and Venidius is one in which documents, by themselves, appear singularly ineffective in constructing social entities capable of sustaining themselves. The reasons why are worth considering.

The most conspicuous feature common to the documents collected by Babatha, Calatoria, and Venidius is the prominence in all of them, regardless of their form or textual content, of witnesses — seven Roman citizens for each transaction in the Calatoria archive, eight and twelve respectively for the birth certificate and the copy of the decree of citizenship preserved by Venidius — whose names and seals authenticated the written records as accurate statements. The reason for such witness ubiquity is that the documents were not themselves considered to be proofs but rather mnemonic devices, preserving in

---

16 In this reconstruction I follow Metzger 2000, with details updated from Camodeca 2017. The relevant documents are: *TH* 13, 14 (September 7, 74 CE), 15 (March 12, 75 CE) (*vadimonia*); *TH* 16, 17, 18, 19, 20 (*testimonia* on Iusta's behalf); *TH* 23, 24 (*testimonia* against Iusta, of 74–75 CE); *TH* 21, 22, 25–29, 30 [= *EDR* 128323, ca. 60–65 CE] (names only); Metzger 2000, 152–153 nn. 3–7, with further references; Camodeca 2017, 176 n. 23, 215 n. 32 (*TH* 29), 229 n. 76 (*TH* 16, of 74 CE).
17 For Venidius' dossier, see Camodeca 2006 and 2017; and Corbier in this volume.

more permanent form oral testimony that could later be verified.[18] This basic concept is well illustrated in the normative document known as the Praetor's Edict, a tralatician code of legal principles, annually renewed, that over time grew in scope from the cumulative accretions that kept it up to date with an evolving legal system.[19] Although developed mainly during the last two centuries BCE, the law remained in force throughout the early Imperial period, when it mandated that a majority of the Roman citizen signatory witnesses to a will be present at the unsealing of it in order to authenticate its contents; if four or more of the witnesses had predeceased the testator or were otherwise indisposed, a new will would have to be drawn up and ratified.[20] The written record — the document — provided only a bridge between the event witnessed and confirmation of it by renewed oral testimony.

Recently, however, the provocative thesis of a comprehensive study of writing tablets (*tabulae*) in Roman life has bid to turn this orthodoxy on its head. According to Elizabeth Meyer, writing tablets held intrinsic authority for the Romans and were from the beginning regarded as constitutive of the ritual acts they formalized. It was only during the first century CE that the authority of tablets qua tablets began to be subverted by the introduction of new forms of composing (in first-person chirographs rather than third-person *testationes*) and recording (on triptychs instead of diptychs) legal documents of various forms for use in daily life, which placed increased value on the reliability (*fides*) of witnesses — a development we see mainly through the private documents buried by Vesuvius. For Meyer, in other words, documentary practices developed in exactly the opposite direction from that envisioned by Ferraris and Terrone, who see oral witnessing as historically preceding the advent of a social world created by documents. Although ultimately unpersuasive, Meyer's closely argued analysis of the relationships among textual style, physical form, and the issue of verification or authenticity usefully highlights the essential role played by witnessing as a means of validating both oral and written testimony.[21]

One of the two *testimonia* against Iusta's claim to free birth illustrates explicitly this distinction between the written record and the sworn oath it recorded:

---

18 Legal historians debate only the extent to which this principle was enacted in practice: see, e.g., Kaser 1971, 231 (normally constitutive when written evidence was required); Gardner 1986, 12–13 (declaratory only and always); Metzger 2000, 159.
19 See Lenel 1927; Watson 1970, 105–119.
20 *Edict.* 25.167; cf. Gai. *Inst.* 2.104; Paulus, *Sent.* 4.6.1; Martini 1968.
21 Meyer 2004 (esp. 125–168).

> I, [– M]ammius, have written at the request of Marcus Calatorius Marullus and in his presence, because he said that he was illiterate, that he has sworn by the *genius* of the emperor Vespasian Augustus and his sons that: "I know that Calatoria Themis manumitted the girl along with me, from which I know that the girl is a freedwoman of Calatoria Themis" — which is the matter at issue.[22]

Here it is clearly the oral declaration that is binding and not the written record of it, which merely reports the event. A second declaration offers a good example of the sort of hearsay evidence — not only testimony reported at second hand but also inferences drawn indirectly from it — that would not normally be admissible in court today:

> I, Quintus Tamudius Optatus, have written and sworn by the *genius* of the emperor Vespasian Caesar Augustus and his sons that I was present with Petronia Vitalis when she discussed the girl, her daughter, with Calatoria Themis, and I heard Stephanus, the husband of Themis, there and then say to Petronia Vitalis, "Why do you begrudge us a daughter, since we are treating her as our own daughter?" — from which I know that the woman about whom the case is brought is the daughter of Petronia Vitalis and is freeborn — which is the matter at issue.[23]

Nothing in the reported conversation or its circumstances establishes that the girl was freeborn, but the document is duly witnessed at the time that Optatus was deposed, so that if he were unable to verify his testimony in person at a later date, one or more of the signatories could authenticate the statement.

Ferraris saw the necessity of witnessing as an early development in the construction of a social universe, since it led to the creation of "inscriptions in a technical sense" and thus marked a major advance in human evolution:

> very early in the construction of the social world there emerges the figure of the witness as someone who, by being present at an act, has the role of third-party guarantor of the fact that has taken place. When inscription in this technical sense emerges, humankind makes

---

[22] TH 24: [--- M]*ammius* [---] *scripsi rogatu M. Calatori Marulli coram* [ip]*so, quod is se negaret lit(t)eras scire, eum iurasse per genium Imperatoris Vespasiani Aug(usti) liberorumque eius: me scire puellam mecum Calatoriam Themidem manumisisse: ex e*[o] *me s*[c]*ire puellam liberta(m) Calatoriae Themidis esse — q(uae) r(es) a(gitur)*.
[23] TH 20 = AE 1951, 217 = EDR 073856: *Q(uintus) Tamudius Optatus scripsi iura/vique per Genium Imp(eratoris) Ves/pasiani Caes(aris) Aug(usti) liberorumque / me adfuisse Petroniae Vitali / cum haberet cum Calatoria / Themide de pu*[e]*lla filia / sua ibi me audisse dicen/tem Stephanu(m)* [*mari*]*t*[*um*] */ Themidis Petroniae / Vitali quid invides f*[i]/*liae cum eam nos / filiae loc*[o *fa*]*ciamus / ex eo me* [*scire*] *mulie/rem q(ua) d(e) a(gitur) Petroniae / Vitalis fi*[*l*]*iam et ingenuam esse q(uae) r(es) a(gitur)*. See also Gardner 1986, 13.

a decisive step forward, because it gives rise to the world of social objects, of shared intentions, and of the transmission of technology.[24]

Indeed, some of our earliest written records, dating from the end of the third millennium (2100–2000 BCE), during the so-called Neo-Sumerian renaissance in southern Mesopotamia, show witnesses helping to establish the status of slaves in ways similar to those offered by Marullus and Optatus in the case of Petronia Iusta. In one instance, a slave representing himself in a suit for his own freedom argued that his father had been manumitted more than fifteen years previously and that he had been born free, but his current master produced witnesses who affirmed that they had seen the father receive food rations from the household — clearly a sign that he was still living as a slave — and the slave plaintiff evidently lost his case.[25] In Roman society, no slave had legal standing to bring a suit for liberty (or for anything else) — in this respect Roman and Neo-Sumerian law differed fundamentally — but the role of eye-witness testimony in both legal systems was the same. We are left with the impression that the status of documentary proof in establishing free birth had advanced very little in the two millennia that separate the two worlds. The only substantive innovation evident in Iusta's case is the device of a written record of the names of witnesses whose presence was required by parties involved in the suit to authenticate not facts but the reporting of facts. The names served to verify that the signatories had been present at the time the document was transcribed but did nothing to authenticate or substantiate the claims of the witnessed declaration.

2 Authoritative Documents of Identity?

Establishing personal identity was no more certain for those at the opposite end of the social scale from Iusta. In the twenty years following the death of the emperor Nero in 68 CE, no fewer than three "false Neros" presented themselves to supporters as the emperor himself, with sufficient plausibility to rouse consternation at the capital. The details of their various impersonations and the motivations and historical implications of the disturbances they caused have been well discussed and need not concern us here.[26] For our purposes it is

---

24 Ferraris 2012, 178.
25 Falkenstein 1956–1957, no. 34, cited by Snell 2011, 8–9.
26 The ancient sources — Tac. *Hist.* 2.8–9; Cass. Dio 63.9.3; Zonar. 11.15 (p. 45 D), 11.18 (p. 55 D); Suet. *Nero* 57 — are thoroughly reviewed by Tuplin 1989. A similar impersonation (by a slave,

enough to notice how easy it seems to have been in the later first century CE to impersonate even a figure as prominent as Nero. Wishful thinking in some no doubt discouraged close scrutiny of the false claims, but others who had doubts were unable either to confirm or to refute them by recourse to documentary proof or probative evidence about the supposed emperor's identity. For the false Neros seeking to establish authenticity, there was no need to forge any documents because there was no expectation that such documents would exist, or, if they existed, that they would be regarded as valid and decisive.

When, if ever, did the Romans develop the concept of an autonomously authoritative document of identity, one not dependent upon witnesses for probative force but, like a coin, accepted as authentic because of widespread familiarity with the conventions of its use and confidence in the issuing authority? One famous legal case of the late Republican period centering on a question of identity paints a dim picture of the value of documents when eye-witness oral testimony was available. In 62 BCE the Greek poet Archias found himself charged with illegal residency in Rome on the grounds that, in contravention of a law passed three years previously, he was an alien (*peregrinus*) with no recognized home in Italy. Born in Syrian Antioch, Archias had been awarded Roman citizenship twenty-seven years earlier, in 89 BCE, by the *lex Plautia Papiria* passed at the end of the Social War, which granted Roman citizenship to nonresident aliens of allied cities, as Archias was by virtue of having previously been granted citizenship by the allied town of Heraclea in Lucania. A further requirement that such nonresident aliens should register themselves with the praetor at Rome within sixty days of the law's passage Archias had duly met. At issue was the question of his citizenship at Heraclea.[27]

In the brilliant defense that Cicero mounted for his client, the relative reliability and authority of oral testimony and written documents became a point of importance: envoys sent from Heraclea had entered public testimony and had personally declared that Archias was enrolled as a citizen there; a Roman citizen, Marcus Lucullus, present at the time of Archias' registration had furthermore corroborated their testimony. Despite these proofs, the prosecution was demanding documents. In recalling the role of the witnesses, Cicero emphasizes above all their presence in court (*Adest vir … Adsunt Heraclienses legati*), but also their general probity and trustworthiness (*vir summa auctoritate et religione et fide … Heraclienses legati, nobilissimi homines*), and finally, in the case of

---

Clemens) followed the assassination of Agrippa Postumus in 14 CE: see Suet. *Tib.* 25.1, 3; Cass. Dio 57.16.3–4; and Tac. *Ann.* 2.29.2–2.40.3; with Mogenet 1954.

27 For the historical background and circumstances, see Cic. *Arch.* 4–7 with Coşkun 2010 *ad loc.*

Lucullus, the quality and extent of his knowledge of the facts (*se non opinari sed scire, non audisse sed vidisse, non interfuisse sed egisse dicit*). With these merits he contrasts the uncertainty and unreliability of public documents, which in this case had been irretrievably lost:

> Are you now asking for the public records of Heraclea (*tabulas Heracliensium publicas*), which we all know were destroyed in the Social War when the record hall burned? It is absurd to say nothing about what evidence we do have and to seek evidence we cannot have; to be silent about what men remember and to demand the memory preserved in written records (*litterarum memoriam*); and, when you have the oath of a man of great honor and the sworn and trustworthy statement of a town of the highest integrity, to reject evidence that cannot possibly be corrupted and to seek documents (*tabulas*) that you yourself acknowledge are often corrupted.[28]

Cicero goes on to impugn the integrity of the citizenship lists (*tabulae*) of two of the praetors of 89 BCE — those of Appius Claudius Pulcher (the father of Cicero's enemy) were said to have been carelessly kept (*neglegentius adservatae*), while those of P. Gabinius were vitiated by his inconstancy in office and subsequent conviction of extortion — and to extol the scrupulous rectitude of Metellus, whose records alone held "the authority of public records" (*publicarum tabularum auctoritatem*).[29] For Cicero, the integrity even of public documents rested entirely on the reputation and reliability (*fides*) of those who kept them, since the documents themselves were subject to tampering and falsification.[30]

---

[28] Cic. *Arch.* 8: *Hic tu tabulas desideras Heracliensium publicas, quas Italico bello incenso tabulario interisse scimus omnis? Est ridiculum ad ea quae habemus nihil dicere, quaerere quae habere non possumus et de hominum memoria tacere, litterarum memoriam flagitare et, cum habeas amplissimi viri religionem, integerrimi municipi ius iurandum fidemque, ea quae depravari nullo modo possunt repudiare, tabulas, quas idem dicis solere corrumpi, desiderare.* Translation adapted from Zetzel 2009, 177. For M. Licinius (later M. Terentius Varro) Lucullus, consul in 73 BCE, see *RE*, s.v. "Licinius," 109. What type of records Cicero means by the phrase *tabulae publicae Heracliensium* is unclear: see Coşkun 2010, 58–59.

[29] Cic. *Arch.* 9: *Immo vero eis tabulis professus, quae solae ex illa professione conlegioque praetorum obtinent publicarum tabularum auctoritatem. Nam, cum Appi tabulae neglegentius adservatae dicerentur, Gabini, quam diu incolumis fuit, levitas, post damnationem calamitas, omnem tabularum fidem resignasset, Metellus, homo sanctissimus modestissimusque omnium, tanta diligentia fuit ut ad L. Lentulum praetorem et ad iudices venerit et unius nominis litura se commotum esse dixerit. In his igitur tabulis nullam lituram in nomine A. Licini videtis.*

[30] Naturally, Cicero's rhetorical stance was to some extent adapted to suit his case. When confident that documents would not be produced, he could grant them greater probative value: cf. *Q. Rosc.* 2–3, *2 Verr.* 1.61. Meyer 2004, 218–227 recognizes that personal reputation (*fides* and *auctoritas*) underlay the rise in late Republican courts of the use of *tabulae* for written declarations of testimony (*testationes*) but regards the medium as more significant than the credibility

In raising the specter of forgery, Cicero invokes a criticism often leveled against the validity of written records, one first addressed formally by a senatorial decree of 61 CE, which mandated that tablets bearing any kind of public or private document be sealed by witnesses only after being pierced (*pertusae*) and wrapped three times around with wire, and which further required that the sealed contents be duplicated for reference on the outside of the tablets.[31] These measures against forgery taken during the time of Nero mark an important stage in the evolution of oral *testationes* preserved in written form into autonomously authoritative documents, to the extent that they represent an effort to impose order on the social and administrative turmoil introduced into the comparatively undocumented world of Archias and Cicero by a series of early Imperial laws, beginning with the first emperor, Augustus, aimed at regulating the orders of society. None of these well-known laws specifically required the use of documents, but they laid down rules and introduced incentives that encouraged the production of documents by individuals like Petronia Iusta and Venidius Ennychus, now motivated to establish biographical information about aspects of private life that previously had been the preserve of custom and convention — circumstances of birth, age, origin, periods of military service, and the like. The specific reforms can be rehearsed briefly, since it is their cumulative effect rather than the impact of any single one of them that first, toward the end of the Julio-Claudian period, prompted the Senate to enact comprehensive regulations to ensure the verifiable authentication of both public and private documents.[32]

Before the time of Augustus there was no formal way to register the birth of a child, probably because there was no perceived need to do so, but with the passage of the *lex Aelia Sentia* in 4 CE, which laid down rules concerning manumission based on age, an ex-slave's Roman citizen status would depend upon

---

(however established) of the persons whose words are reported (227). The question of the relative value of oral and written communication persisted throughout antiquity and shaped documentary behavior in various ways: compare Amory's acute analysis of the double role of the messenger/letter-bearer in epistolary exchanges, both literary and actual, of the early Byzantine period of the eastern Mediterranean (Amory in this volume).

31 See Suet. *Nero* 17 (with wills, only the names of the testators were to be displayed on the exterior) and Paulus, *Sent.* 5.25.6 with Camodeca 1993, 353–364. Forgery and falsification of documents were an ongoing concern for early Imperial authors: see the Introduction by Arthur-Montagne, DiGiulio, and Kuin in this volume.

32 Meyer 2004, 163–168 connects the measures taken against forgery with a particular concern with wills and sees their extension to other forms of document as "probably a fortuitous association or afterthought" (166). More probably, in my view, the Neronian regulations were meant from the start to be all-encompassing.

proving not only his or her own age but the age of a manumitting master. For slaves freed before the age of thirty and therefore not entitled to full Roman citizenship, the latter could be earned by marrying a Roman woman (freed or freeborn) and producing a child who reached the age of one year — a situation requiring both a birth certificate and a second proof of having reached a first birthday, as is well illustrated by the case of L. Venidius Ennychus discussed by Corbier in this volume (pp. 259–264). The *lex Papia Poppaea* of 9 CE encouraged marriage, in part by granting privileges to married Romans who could prove their parenthood of three legitimate children. Such privileges were awarded only after legitimate children had been officially registered within thirty days of birth by a Roman magistrate.[33] Registration was never compulsory, however, and, according to the Augustan laws, registering the births of illegitimate children was explicitly forbidden.[34] Many inhabitants of the Roman Empire probably went through life without ever having to prove, or even to know, their own ages. The widely noticed propensity toward age-rounding in Latin inscriptions from the provinces recording ages at death and in tax returns and census declarations from Egypt suggests that ignorance of one's exact age was not uncommon.[35]

As a consequence of the new legislation, however, certain categories of persons — notably those with resources and aspirations to join the political classes, or newly enfranchised resident foreigners like Archias, or ex-slaves with limited peregrine or Latin rights — would have had incentive to avail themselves of the opportunities for formal registration, where such possibilities existed. A *lex Junia* of (probably) the early Tiberian period regularized the status of informally freed slaves and provided further incentives for them to upgrade to full citizen status by marrying and producing legitimate children. A *lex Visellia* of (probably) 24 CE made it a crime for freedpersons to claim to be freeborn. Each of these regulations added categories to the list of persons who could benefit from being able to prove their age or civil status or periods of service in order to gain personal advantages or to establish the freeborn status of their offspring. Several of these categories — unmarried freedwomen mothers, Junian Latins of either sex, and above all auxiliary soldiers — were unable to register legitimate Roman births, but they could "pre-enroll" their children in the citizen lists by obtaining

---

[33] For the Augustan laws on manumission and marriage, see, e.g., Mouritsen 2011, 80–92 and McGinn 1998, 70–104, respectively; for registrations of birth, see Lévy 1952, 454–463 and Dolganov 2021, 199–207.
[34] See *PMich.* 3.169 with Lévy 1952, 458.
[35] See, e.g., Scheidel 1996, 53–91, esp. 87–91.

informal proofs of their circumstances of free birth through *testationes*, declarations authenticated by seven citizen witnesses, which could be "activated" when other secondary conditions were met (such as survival of the child through the first year). Such copies of birth certificates as we have are not the official records, which were recorded by a magistrate in an *album*, a whitened board for public display, and then transferred into codices or papyrus rolls and stored in a building known as a *Kalendarium*, but are instead these informal copies, made by professional scribes and certified by the signing witnesses.[36]

By far the most common type of document of identity we have from the Roman period, however, are the so-called military *diplomata* issued upon honorable discharge from the military to peregrine soldiers who had dutifully fulfilled twenty-five or twenty-six years of service in the auxiliary troops (mainly *auxilia* and navy) and who were thereby entitled upon discharge to have their informal marriages legitimized and to earn citizenship for themselves and their spouses and, with various qualifications, their children.[37] It used to be thought that the issuing of *diplomata* was universal and regular from the time of Claudius, but it now seems that, for the first twenty years of their use (ca. 50–70 CE), military *diplomata* were issued with increasing frequency but only irregularly to those who had participated in some significant military campaign or other notable "qualifying" event, and it remains uncertain whether they were ever issued routinely, as a matter of course, other than during their heyday of the first sixty years of the second century CE.[38] During these early years the texts engraved on the inner faces of the diptych tablets — those that bore the official discharge formulae and names of authenticating witnesses, in contrast to the texts etched on the exterior faces, which were merely reference copies — were carefully composed and written, but over time they became more and more abbreviated and perfunctory, until the trend abruptly reversed itself in 153 CE (no doubt in response to an imperial intervention), when an official notation indicating that

---

36 See Lévy 1952, 459–461 and, generally on the offspring of mixed marriages, Lavan 2021.
37 *Diplomata* were informal copies, usually in bronze, of the imperial *constitutiones* (discharge certificates) granting discharge (normally) to entire auxiliary units; the original documents were displayed on the Capitoline Hill in Rome, until a fire of 69 CE destroyed most of them: see Corbier 2006, 131–146 and in this volume. For an overview of our evolving understanding of practices involving military *diplomata*, see Eck/Wolff 1986; Wilkes 2003; Lavan 2019, 28–37; and Dolganov 2021, 211–214. New finds continue to enrich and complicate the picture. For the status of military marriages generally, see Phang 2001 and Lavan 2021.
38 After the death of Antoninus Pius, the numbers drop precipitously: see Lavan 2019, 34 fig. 2. For the early years, see Dušanić 1982.

the text had been "copied and checked" (*descriptum et recognitum*) reappeared systematically, and the texts themselves were once again written out in full.³⁹

Over this same period, the nature of the witnesses underwent a complementary evolution: originally most were veterans from the same units as the soldiers discharged, but in 73 or 74 CE Vespasian transferred the witnessing function to public clerks, and under Hadrian a more hierarchical ranking of witnesses of higher social position becomes pronounced — at precisely the time when the formal "authentication" formula (*descriptum et recognitum*) disappears from the interior texts.⁴⁰ Taken together, these developments in the form of military *diplomata* over the first hundred years of their use suggest a gradual erosion of the perceived importance of the documentary text, despite administrative efforts to shore up the basis of its authority, in favor of a return to the traditional underwriting of credibility by witnesses whose probity (*fides*) is commensurate with their social status. As in Cicero's defense of Archias, so still in the time of Hadrian, personal reputation and social stature are the guarantors of authority.

Both aspects of the use of military *diplomata* during the early Imperial period — the pattern of restricted use for a particular group spreading to other groups wishing to avail themselves of specific personal advantages, and the ultimate failure of the associated documentary practices to unseat the traditional alignment of authority — recur repeatedly during the first two centuries of the Roman Empire. A basic sequence of events can be outlined as follows. First, a new regulation introduced by a Julio-Claudian emperor with the aim of granting privileges to, or imposing liabilities on, a designated segment of the population prompts but does not mandate the creation of documents to establish evidence of qualification for or exemption from the newly defined rights or liabilities. This privilege or exemption, along with its attendant documentary apparatus, is then sought by and extended to similar groups, which in turn helps to normalize the documenting practices. With time, the original social aim of the measures is fulfilled or abandoned, but the residual documentary habit seems not so much to give rise to new social formations (*pace* Terrone) as to reshape itself to accommodate the deeply embedded social structures that are themselves continuously undergoing subtle transformation. Documents in this world are not so much drivers and shapers of behavior as symptoms (and, for us, telltale markers) of more fundamental underlying social forces.

---

39 For these developments see Eck 2003 and Eck/Pangerl 2015. Shortly thereafter, in 158 CE, a change in wording of the discharge formula may have been introduced in order to deter fraudulent declarations: Lavan 2019, 32 n. 35.
40 Morris/Roxan 1977.

The aim of these early Imperial regulations, collectively, was to demarcate and, to a certain extent, to hierarchize particular segments of the population, but in this they seem singularly to have failed. Not only do we find that the irregular, voluntary issuing of identity documents and the haphazard way they seem to have been used led to their rapid extension to persons at the margins of the originally designated groups, who wished to stabilize their position in the world, but the documents themselves, being purely voluntary, never acquired the authority they might have gained had their use been mandatory and enforced. As a result, despite the efforts of Augustus and his successors to reform Roman society and to renew the citizen population, over time the extension of the Roman franchise to ever larger numbers of persons and the division of the citizenry into two broad groups, conventionally identified from the middle of the second century as the "more honorable" (*honestiores*) and "more humble" (*humiliores*), led to a flattening of the social universe, even as the use of documents in daily life proliferated.[41] Finally, the distinction in privileges between the two broad groups came to be defined more sharply, but qualification for membership in the *honestiores* no longer depended upon proof of a certain status at birth but rather upon membership in one of the higher orders, which might be inherited in the case of senatorial families but which could also be earned by service to the civil government as an equestrian official or town councilor in a *municipium* or colony.[42] The extension by Caracalla in 212 CE of full Roman citizenship to all free inhabitants of the Roman Empire removed at one stroke many of the contexts in which demonstrating a particular qualification for citizenship might be useful.

It is therefore the more noteworthy that only around then do we begin to see the idea of documents as self-authenticating proofs being raised. As with many social developments during the third century, evidence is spotty and difficult at times to piece together chronologically, but it seems to be during the first decades of the century that we find the first indications of documents being recognized as valid on the basis of a governmental issuing authority rather than citizen witnesses, and with those indications come also the first signs of a deprecation of the latter. Beginning early in the century, it seems, the officials in charge of registering legitimately born children on the citizen rolls began issu-

---

[41] So, for example, a change in the form of military *diplomata* around 140 CE corresponds with an abrupt decline in their use as *testationes*, apparently because auxiliary soldiers no longer had reason to prove the birth of any children born before their discharge: see Roxan 1986, Sánchez-Moreno Ellart 2008 and Lavan 2019, 31.
[42] See, in general, Garnsey 1970 and Rilinger 1988.

ing authenticated duplicate copies to individuals at the time of registration.⁴³ At around the same time, a rescript of the emperor Alexander from 223 CE declared that the evidence of witnesses on informal *testationes* was insufficient to establish free birth incontrovertibly.⁴⁴ The two developments seem to be related: the effect of the *Constitutio Antoniniana* was to reduce to a single criterion — free status, as established by free birth or legitimate manumission — the sorts of qualifying circumstances that previously had aimed to create distinctions of rank within the Roman social order. As a result, the importance of proving free birth increased, even as all other criteria for membership in the citizenry faded.

Alexander was evidently responding to a perception that the system was being compromised by false testimony and so attempted to minimize and reduce the reliance on witnesses, but his effort to subvert the authority of the older form of orally witnessed proofs did not last. Little more than half a century later, a rescript of the emperor Probus reassured a petitioner that, in the event that a document (*tabulae*) certifying the birth of a daughter had not been made, the common knowledge of neighbors and others sufficed to prove the child legitimate.⁴⁵ And at the end of the century, a response of Diocletian issued under the name of the tetrarchs declared that the loss of a birth certificate did not affect the civil condition of the holder.⁴⁶ After Constantine, the documentary habit for ordinary Romans seems to have declined, along with the significance of proofs of status. It is only when the phenomena reappear in the time of Justinian that we find a ruling allowing kinship relations to be authenticated by presentation of a publicly issued document alone, without the need for witnesses.⁴⁷

If we restrict our gaze to the first three centuries of the Roman Empire, however, we can see that classical antiquity never fully emerged from the oral stage of documentary development, in which written declarations depended upon witness verification for validity. Documents of identity and even a classical form of documentality were introduced in the Augustan era, developed, and spread, without ever acquiring unquestioned or even primary authority in policing the traffic of status verification that they were meant to regulate.⁴⁸ The "virtuous

---

43 See Lévy 1952, 461–462.
44 *Cod. Iust.* 2.42 [43] 1; Lévy 1952, 463 n. 3 proposes to resolve the apparent inconsistency by declaring the passage to be interpolated — unconvincingly.
45 *Cod. Iust.* 5.4.9.
46 *Cod. Iust.* 4.21.6.
47 *Cod. Iust.* 4.20.15.6 (of 527? CE); cf. Lévy 1952, 463 nn. 2–3.
48 Ando 2020, 166–172 shows both the ubiquity of documentary recording practices in official proceedings of late antiquity and the cooption by rival Christian sects of similar practices in order to legitimize their claims with the state. The probative authority manifested in documents

cycle" of practices and documents envisioned by Terrone and adumbrated by Ferraris in his teleological narrative of social progress is nowhere apparent in the era of ancient Roman history most often credited with establishing an efficient administrative bureaucracy. For the first three centuries of the Roman Imperial era, documentality, that rough beast of an as yet unimagined modernity, lurched and stumbled, hesitated and stalled, as it slouched toward Byzantium to be born.

References

Ando, C. (2020), "The Certainty of Documents. Records of Proceedings as Guarantors of Memory in Political and Legal Argument", in: C. Ando/W.P. Sullivan (eds.), *The Discovery of the Fact*, Ann Arbor, 155–174.
Balestri Fumagalli, M. (1985), *Lex Iunia de Manumissionibus*, Milan.
Buckland, M. (2014), "Documentality beyond Documents", in: *The Monist* 97, 179–186.
Camodeca, G. (1993), "Nuovi dati dagli archivi campani sulla datazione e applicazione del 'S.C. Neronianum'", in: *Index* 21, 353–364.
Camodeca, G. (2006), "Per una riedizione dell'archivio ercolanese di L. Venidius Ennychus. II", in: *CErc* 36, 187–209.
Camodeca, G. (2015), "I consoli degli anni di Nerone nelle Tabulae Herculanenses", in: *ZPE* 193, 272–282.
Camodeca, G. (2017), *Tabulae Herculanenses. Edizione e commento I*, Rome.
Corbier, M. (2006), *Donner à voir, donner à lire. Mémoire et communication dans la Rome ancienne*, Paris.
Coşkun, A. (ed.) (2010), *Cicero und das römische Bürgerrecht. Die Verteidigung des Dichters Archias. Einleitung, Text, Übersetzung und historisch-philologische Kommentierungen*, Göttingen.
Dolganov, A. (2021), "Documenting Roman Citizenship", in: M. Lavan/C. Ando (2021), 196–228.
Dušanić, S. (1982), "The Issue of Military Diplomata under Claudius and Nero", in: *ZPE* 47, 149–171.
Eck, W. (2003), "Der Kaiser als Herr des Heeres: Militärdiplome und die kaiserliche Reichsregierung", in: Wilkes (2003), 55–87.
Eck, W./Pangerl, A. (2015), "Fragment eines Militärdiploms aus der Zeit Neros vielleicht aus dem Jahr 59 (?)", in: *Acta Musei Napocensis* 52, 69–72.
Eck, W./Wolff, H. (eds.) (1986), *Heer und Integrationspolitik. Die römischen Militärdiplome als historische Quelle*, Cologne.

---

recording public meetings spread more slowly to written proofs of personal identity. For a more optimistic assessment, based on the uncertain assumption that recording practices attested for males residing in *metropoleis* in Egypt were widespread and universal for all inhabitants throughout the provinces, see Dolganov 2021, esp. 225–228.

Emmerson, A.L.C. (2011), "Evidence for Junian Latins in the Tombs of Pompeii?", in: *JRA* 24, 161–190.
Falkenstein, A. (1956–1957), *Die neusumerischen Gerichtsurkunden*, Munich.
Ferraris, M. (2012), *Documentality: Why It Is Necessary to Leave Traces*, transl. R. Davies. New York. First published as (2009), *Documentalità. Perché è necessario lasciare tracce*, Rome.
Ferraris, M. (2015), "Collective Intentionality or Documentality?", in: *Philosophy and Social Criticism* 41, 423–433.
Gardner, J.F. (1986), "Proofs of Status in the Roman World", in: *BICS* 33, 1–14.
Garnsey, P.D.A. (1970), *Social Status and Legal Privilege in the Roman Empire*, Oxford.
Hennig, B. (2014), "Documents: Fillers of Informational Gaps", in: *The Monist* 97, 246–255.
Kaser, M. (1971), *Das römische Privatrecht*, vol. 1, 2nd edn., Munich.
Koepsell, D./Smith, B. (2014), "Beyond Paper", in: *The Monist* 97, 222–235.
Lavan, M. (2019), "The Army and the Spread of Roman Citizenship", in: *JRS* 109, 27–69.
Lavan, M. (2021), "Roman Citizenship, Marriage with Non-citizens and Family Networks", in: M. Lavan/C. Ando (2021), 155–174.
Lavan, M./Ando, C. (eds.) (2021), *Imperial and Local Citizenship in the Long Second Century CE*, Oxford.
Lenel O. (1927), *Das Edictum perpetuum. Ein Versuch zu seiner Wiederherstellung*, 3rd edn., Leipzig.
Lévy, J.-P. (1952), "Les actes d'état civil Romains", in: *RHD* 29, 449–486.
Lintott, A. (2002), "Freedmen and Slaves in the Light of Legal Documents from First-Century A.D. Campania", in: *CQ* 52, 555–565.
Martini, R. (1968), "Sulla presenza dei 'signatores' all'apertura del testamento", in: *Studi in onore di Giuseppe Grosso*, vol. 1, Turin, 483–495.
McGinn, T.A.J. (1998), *Prostitution, Sexuality, and the Law in Ancient Rome*, Oxford.
Metzger, E. (2000), "The Case of Petronia Iusta", in: *RIDA* 47, 151–165.
Meyer, E.A. (2004), *Legitimacy and Law in the Roman World:* Tabulae *in Roman Belief and Practice*, Cambridge.
Mogenet, J. (1954), "La conjuration de Clemens", in: *AC* 23, 321–330.
Morris, J./Roxan, M. (1977), "The Witnesses to Roman Military *Diplomata*", in: *AArchSlov* 28, 299–333.
Mouritsen, H. (2011), *The Freedman in the Roman World*, Cambridge.
Panciera, S. (2012), "What Is an Inscription? Problems of Definition and Identity of an Historical Source", in: *ZPE* 183, 1–10.
Phang, S.E. (2001), *The Marriage of Roman Soldiers (13 B.C.–A.D. 235): Law and Family in the Imperial Army*, Leiden.
Rawson B. (2010), "Degrees of Freedom: *Vernae* and Junian Latins in the Roman *Familia*", in: V. Dasen/T. Spaeth (eds.), *Children, Memory, and Family Identity in Roman Culture*, Oxford, 195–221.
Rilinger, R. (1988), *Humiliores — Honestiores. Zu einer sozialen Dichotomie im Strafrecht der römischen Kaiserzeit*, Munich.
Roxan, M. (1986), "Observations on the Reasons for Changes in the Formula of Diplomas circa AD 140", in: Eck/Wolff (1986), 265–292.
Sánchez-Moreno Ellart, C. (2008), "'Ipsis liberis posterisque eorum': Die Bedeutung der Geburtsurkunden von Soldaten der Auxiliareinheiten und der Wandel im Formular von diplomata militaria im Jahre 140 n. Chr. ausweislich RMD I 39 und RMD IV 266", in: *ZRG* 125, 348–374.

Scheidel, W. (1996), *Measuring Sex, Age, and Death in the Roman Empire*, Ann Arbor.
Silver, M. (2013), "The Status of the 'Incerti' in the Herculaneum 'Album': Freed Self-Sellers or Promoted Junian Latins", in: *Hephaistos* 30, 105–115.
Snell, D. (2011), "Slavery in the Ancient Near East", in: K. Bradley/P. Cartledge (eds.), *Cambridge World History of Slavery, Volume I: The Ancient Mediterranean World*, Cambridge, 4–21.
Terrone, E. (2014), "Traces, Documents and the Puzzle of 'Permanent Acts'", in: *The Monist* 97, 161–178.
Tuplin, C.J. (1989), "The False Neros of the First Century", in: C. Deroux (ed.), *Studies in Latin Literature and Roman History* 5, Brussels, 364–404.
Watson, A. (1970), "The Development of the Praetor's Edict", in: *JRS* 60, 105–119.
Weaver, P.R.C. (1991), "Children of Freedmen (and Freedwomen)", in: B. Rawson (ed.), *Marriage, Divorce, and Children in Ancient Rome*, Oxford, 166–190.
Wilkes, J.J. (ed.) (2003), *Documenting the Roman Army: Essays in Honour of Margaret Roxan*, BICS suppl. 81, London.
Zetzel, J.E.G. (2009), *Marcus Tullius Cicero: Ten Speeches*, Indianapolis.

Jacqueline Arthur-Montagne
Copying the Canon: Imperial School Texts as Documentary Traces

Abstract: This chapter analyzes ancient school compositions through the lens of Terrone's model of the documentary trace: the understanding of the document as that which connects us to past social action. Although Ferraris's teleological conception of documents merits challenges, Terrone's notion of documentary traces can be fruitfully applied to the study of copying exercises in Imperial school papyri, which provided testimony of the students' efforts to achieve *paideia* and assemble a library of the mind. Memory's function as a key tool in demonstrating individual knowledge of the canon becomes visible when we examine copying exercises from the Roman schoolroom and explore whether such exercises could be considered documents. The cognitive facets of ancient pedagogical practice align with the model of the documentary trace, since these school exercises inscribed their lessons simultaneously into wax tablets and into the minds of Roman learners.

One assumption that undergirds much of the document theory preceding and proceeding from Maurizio Ferraris's concept of "documentality" is that the process of recording social acts has evolved across human history from immaterial to material methods.[1] The oaths, rules, and contracts that could once be conveyed through memory or recitation would eventually find more concrete expression in physical objects. These objects would in turn advance from 'garden-variety' media like "stone tablets, parchment scrolls, dollar bills" to more complex institutions for issuing and preserving documentation, such as "civil registries, safety-deposit boxes, licenses."[2] Classicists too have a tendency to highlight textualization as a turning point in the reception and preservation of ancient literature, laws, and rituals. What begins as a social act in the mind or the mouth eventually takes shape as a text, which can be duplicated and authenticated long after its immediate context. When at last written documenta-

---
[1] See Smith/Searle 2003, 287–291; Salaün 2014, 188–195; and Terrone 2014, 176. But Ferraris 2012, 207–216 warns of the dangers of logocentrism when analyzing the emergence of documentality and proposes that inscription (as thought, memory, and gesture) may even precede spoken language.
[2] Koepsell/Smith 2014, 222–223.

tion has become so prevalent in a society as to pervade the urban landscape and to shape social interactions, then writers within that society may begin to regard documentation as a subject worthy of inclusion — or a genre worthy of imitation — within their own texts. Indeed, in the next chapter, Karen ní Mheallaigh investigates the fiction-writer Lucian's preoccupation with documents and his "mingling [of] documentary fact with fiction" in his literary works to expose the double-edged power of inscriptions in the Roman Principate. The narrowing margin between documents and literature will also return as a focus of the later chapters in this volume, which examine the third and fourth centuries as a distinctive span in the development of the documentary consciousness of authors in the later Roman Empire.[3] These chapters indicate that written documentation in this period had achieved a sort of critical mass such that readers could recognize the form and function of documents deployed in a variety of literary works.

In the preceding chapter of this volume, however, John Bodel challenges the "teleological narrative of social progress" that Ferraris and Enrico Terrone envision in their accounts of the historical emergence of documentary practices. As he sees it, the first three centuries of the Roman Empire neither do away with the need for oral testimony nor invalidate the legitimacy of "the common knowledge of neighbors and others" in authenticating identity.[4] Documentality, he argues, must wait many more centuries to fully materialize. In this chapter, I would like to offer another challenge to the teleologies of modern document theorists by examining copying exercises in Greek school papyri, tablets, and ostraca as a documentary practice in the Roman world. In contrast to the dominant narrative of documentation advancing from immaterial to material media, I argue that written copying exercises were intended to be disposable stepping stones in the creation of a permanent library of memorized documents. In the intellectual communities of the Second Sophistic, which were preoccupied with achieving the status of "learned men" (*pepaideumenoi*), the written evidence of one's literary learning represented only an early step in the pursuit of genuine training in the canon (*paideia*). In this context, the trajectory of documentary development operates in the reverse direction: the reliance on "weak" and erroneous written sources subsides when the student etches on the tablets of his mind a final mental copy of the text he has mastered.

---

3 See Fournet and Amory in this volume.
4 Bodel in this volume.

This chapter proceeds in three parts. The first surveys school copying exercises from the first to fourth centuries CE.⁵ I demonstrate that students copied canonical authors by three ascending methods: first from the teacher's handwritten model, then from dictation, and finally from memory.⁶ This progression, I argue, indicates that copying exercises were intended to liberate students from a textual model and develop literary documents of the mind: a mental library they could consult for the rest of their lives. The second section examines the extent to which such copying exercises can be considered "documents" and precisely what social acts they record. It draws upon Terrone's discussion of the documentary "trace" and his proposed paradigm of documentary status as a spectrum from weak traces to strong documents.⁷ The final section of the paper turns to Imperial reflections on the practices of copying and memorization in literary education. When divorced from teleological accounts of the evolution from primitive to advanced documentation methods, the documentary trace provides a useful model with which to analyze ancient sources that do not conform to the definition of documentation in the modern sense of the word.

1 School Copying Exercises: Form and Function

In the first book of the *Institutio oratoria*, the pedagogue Quintilian recommends a method for teaching the alphabet through tracing. He encourages teachers to etch a wooden tablet with letters, so that students may practice the motion of making letters by copying over them:

> cum vero iam ductus sequi coeperit, non inutile erit eos tabellae quam optime insculpi, ut per illos velut sulcos ducatur stilus. nam neque errabit quemadmodum in ceris (continebitur enim utrimque marginibus neque extra praescriptum egredi poterit) et celerius ac saepius sequendo certa vestigia firmabit articulos neque egebit adiutorio manum suam manu super imposita regentis.

---

[5] The authoritative catalogue of ancient school papyri upon which this paper draws is Cribiore 1996. Cribiore builds upon Debut 1985. Morgan 1998, 275–323 also offers helpful data on the numbers of surviving school papyri, arranged by classical author quoted.

[6] By "ascending," I indicate difficulty and not a unidirectional progress through the levels of education. Students performed copying, dictation, and memorization at every stage of the educational process and might return to any of these exercises even in advanced stages of grammatical and rhetorical training.

[7] Terrone 2014.

> It will be helpful to have [letters] carved as perfectly as possible on a tablet, so that they guide the stylus like furrows. For [the student] will not make mistakes as he would in wax, for he will be held in position on both sides of the margins and incapable of writing beyond what was pre-inscribed. By following the set traces more quickly and frequently, he will strengthen his fingers and have no need of a helping hand placed on his own to guide him.[8]

In the same way that modern schoolchildren copy letters on tracing paper, the ancient pupil learned Greek and Latin scripts by copying the motions of writing on a pre-inscribed wooden tablet. On the one hand, Quintilian's teaching tablet served a clear practical purpose: it enabled the student to repeat correct lettering without supervision and prevented bad compositional habits. As so many lessons in the *Institutio oratoria* do, however, Quintilian's counsel also connotes an ethical dimension: it is far better to follow a perfect *exemplum* at the beginning of one's education than to correct missteps after the fact. Copying therefore represents the first step towards mastery by allowing the copier to connect to the original by tracing its exact words.

Quintilian's instructions in the passage above pertain to the actual practice of tracing letters in order to improve handwriting. But the terms "tracing" and "copying" also describe more profound concepts in the realm of Imperial pedagogy and literary criticism. This is because Greek and Latin authors of the Roman Principate depict their own works as being both shaped and overshadowed by the canon. The writers of the Second Sophistic in particular engage in a paradoxical contest to exhibit novelty and spontaneity through their facility with classical authors of the past. In this setting, "copying" begins with the replication of ancient verses on a wax tablet in school, but also extends to epideictic rhetorical performances in which sophists recite and reinvent the voices of the canon. In a similar fashion, the activity of "tracing" first marks the elementary exercise of composing alphas and betas on a tablet, but eventually represents the propensity of Imperial writers and critics to trace their own artistic heritage back through the centuries to the originators of their genres. The preoccupation with imitation and erudition that so permeates the Imperial literary aesthetic emerges from formative years of schooling in the classical curriculum.

School compositions can also teach us a great deal about the methods of literary learning. Scholars who are mindful of the oral contexts of classical literature tend to assume that learned people acquired that learning through a sort of osmosis — by hearing and reciting classical authors at dinner parties, in the

---

[8] Quint. *Inst.* 1.1.27, ed. Russell 2002. All translations are my own, unless otherwise indicated.

baths, and in public readings.⁹ While there is no doubt that students did learn literature through aural and oral methods, there is documentary proof that students did a great deal of writing as well — copying, more specifically. From simple lists of mythological names to longer passages from the poets, students made copies at all levels of literary education. Furthermore, surviving school exercises suggest that copying took place in three ways: from a textual model, from dictation, and from memory. Although these categories were neither mutually exclusive nor introduced in strict order (advanced students might copy from a textual model as well), the degree of difficulty did increase with each phase and thereby implied a scaffolded path from the material text to the memorized one.

The most obvious indication that a school exercise has been copied from a teacher's model is the repetition of a textual passage: once in the teacher's hand, and once or more in the student's hand. In such documents, the teacher's lines tend to be composed in a strong, confident script and then duplicated by a shakier hand. One well-known example of this exercise is *P.Lond.Lit.* 253, a wax diptych from the second century CE. Its first leaf contains six lines in iambic verse, the first two of which are written on a ruled line in a strong, uncial hand:

σοφοῦ παρ' ἀνδρός προσδέχου συμβουλίαν
μὴ πᾶσιν εἰκῇ τοῖς φίλοις πιστεύεται

Accept advice from a wise man.
Do not trust all friends indiscriminately.¹⁰

These are lines from Menander's *Sententiae*, one of the most popular sources of maxims for students at beginning and intermediate levels of education.¹¹ In the bottom four lines of the tablet are the student's copies (Figure 1). The spacing between letters is less even, leaving some words more tightly compressed than others. Furthermore, the student's letters stand less upright than in the teacher's model: φ, for example, often tilts. While the student did not replicate the elegance of his teacher's hand, he did replicate the content of the model. In fact, the only error in the student's composition derives from the teacher's model: -ται on

---

9 For an overview of the controversy on text, oral recitation, and reading in the Roman world, see Johnson 2010, 4–14. On the intersection of the oral and the textual in Imperial intellectual communities, see Goldhill 2009.
10 Ed. Hesseling 1892–1893; the first maxim is no. 705 and the second resembles no. 460 in Pernigotti 2008, 398 and 323 respectively.
11 See Bonner 2012, 173–175; Karavas/Vix 2014.

the verb πιστεύεται, where we expect a simple epsilon for the imperative (πιστεύετε): "do not trust."[12]

Fig. 1: *P.Lond.Lit.* 253, British Library, MS 34186, tablet 1 recto. © The British Library Board Add 34186.

The faithful reproduction of the text — but not the elegance — of the teacher's hand is a hallmark of this tier of school exercises. On another wax tablet from the third century CE is a similar exercise in which the teacher has copied off lines from Hesiod's *Works and Days*, but once more with an error:

ἔμμορέ τοι **τειμη** ὅς τ' ἔμμορε γείτονος αἰσθλοῦ ...

He who has a good neighbor has a share of value.[13]

---

12 The phonetic nature of this error indicates that the teacher himself was composing from memory or dictation. On the substitution of vowels as phonetic mistakes, see below.
13 *Tabula ceratae graecae Assendelftianae* 1v, ed. Hesseling 1892–1893. Compare Hes. *Op.* 347: ἔμμορέ τοι τιμῆς, ὅς τ' ἔμμορε γείτονος ἐσθλοῦ.

D.C. Hesseling, who published these plates, said he found it "difficult to believe that the schoolmaster would have written τειμη instead of τειμῆς" and attributed the mistake to a possible misreading of a cursive model.[14] More important than the fallibility of Greek teachers, however, are the implications of such mistakes. The fact that student copies often preserve errors within the instructor's model suggests that beginning pupils had not first memorized the lines they were reproducing through oral repetition. In these instances, at least, students gained their first exposure to Menander and Hesiod through writing — perhaps even writing words they did not understand. Copied mistakes are the signs of a writer who does not necessarily know better.[15]

When a student was capable of writing letters and forming syllables with some fluency, a new challenge was to copy passages from external dictation: hearing the teacher recite a passage of poetry or prose aloud. It is challenging to determine on the basis of orthography alone which surviving school exercises were made from dictation; student exercises are naturally erroneous. But compositions that exhibit a large number of phonetic mistakes — as opposed to morphological or syntactic ones — are suspected to be the products of dictation. This is because novice writers often replicate the sounds of orally delivered content, but not necessarily the correct spelling of that content. Rafaella Cribiore notes that the vast majority of these errors are vowel-based: confusing η, ι, and ει; ε and αι; ο and ω; υ and οι. Among the consonants, the most common conflations are between τ and δ, χ and κ, λ and ρ, and the elimination of the final ν.[16]

We find many such errors in *P.Oxy.* II 213, a composition from the early second century. This fragment contains a tragic speech, likely by Tantalus about the fate of his child Niobe, who has become a stone "welling with tears." Scholars have identified this fragment alternately as the *Niobe* of Aeschylus or of Sophocles.[17] For our purposes, it is not important which tragedian wrote this text, but rather how mistakenly the student copies it. Compare, for example, lines 1–6 of the student composition edited by Carden and Barrett with lines 1–6 of the reconstruction of Kalamara:

---

[14] Hesseling 1892–1893, 302.
[15] Cribiore 2009, 327: "In order for students to practice handwriting, teachers made them write their names and copy verses of texts of a very limited extent as soon as they learned their letters ... These students could not read what they had copied but proceeded blindly, committing every sort of mistake and omission."
[16] Cribiore 1996, 92. See also Skeat 1957; Fernández Delgado/Pordomingo 2010.
[17] See Carden/Barrett 1974, 236–243.

]..ω..αυ [
]πετωνδεπιμωγοσφοβων
]θǫυργεσηκονισμαειδητερα
]αικωφαισιγϊκελονπετροις
]εινησǫιδακαιμαγουσπαγας
].γρωικαλαβικοιμηθησεται[18]

].. ω... αυ [
τῶνδ' ἐπεὶ μόνος φόβων
λι]θουργὲς εἰκόνισμ' ἰδεῖν πάρα
]αι κωφαῖσιν εἴκελον πέτραις
]εινης οἶδα καὶ μάγους πάγας
λ]υγρῷ κάλυβι κοιμηθήσεται[19]

... then alone of these fears.
Behold the image worked in stone,
Like silent rocks in color,
But in its shape I see springs welling
With tears. She will be laid to rest in a dank place.

In the first six lines of this fragment there appear a number of the most frequent phonetic swaps outlined by Cribiore. In line 2, for example, the writer has misspelled μόνος and compressed ἐπεί to επι.[20] In line 4, a mispronunciation or mishearing may have caused the erroneous πετροις for πέτραις. Then in line 5 the mysterious και μαγουσπαγας may indicate that the student lost track entirely of the verse he was copying. Word jumbles of this size may reveal that a student did not recognize the words being dictated, especially when the teacher recited an obscure word from tragic poetry.

The final and most difficult group of school exercises are those that required students to transition their copying from written and oral models to memorized models. A number of school compositions from the Roman Empire indicate that students were instructed to memorize long passages of poetry and then copy the exact text by hand. Unsurprisingly, the most commonly memorized Greek author was Homer. In a papyrus from the first century, *P.Köln* II 70, a student has copied out a long passage from the first book of the *Iliad*: lines 108–154, the beginning of the quarrel between Achilles and Agamemnon. The passage below offers an excerpt of the composition:

---

18 *P.Oxy.* II 213 fr. A, col. 1 1–6, ed. Carden/Barrett 1974; Cribiore 1996, no. 265.
19 Kalamara 2019, 13.
20 Carden/Barrett 1974, 236–237: "There are misspellings and some unintelligible series of letters: the writer was presumably a schoolboy with little knowledge of Greek."

[εσθλον δ ουτε τι πω] ειπε̣ [ς ε]πος ουτ ετ[ελ]εσσας
[και νυν εν Δαναοι]σι θεοπροπιας [.] γορεοι [[μενος]] εις
[ως δη τουδ' ενεκα σ]φιν εκηβολος α[λγ]εα τευχιν   110
[ουνεκ εγω κουρης Χ]ρυσε̣ιδος αγ[λα] αποινα
[ουκ εθελον δεξασ]θαι επι πολυ βο̣υλομε αυτην
[οικοι εχειν και γαρ] ρα Κλοιτεμήσστ[ρ]ης προβεβ[υλα]
[κουριδιης αλοχ]ο̣υ, επι ουν εθεν εσι χ[ερειων]
[ου δεμας ουδε φ]οιην ουτ αρ φρενα[ς ουτε τι εργα   115
[αλλα και ως εθελ]ο δομενε παλιν ει [το γ αμεινον]
[βουλομ εγω λα]ω̣ν σον εμμενε η α[πολεσθαι]
...
[Αργειων αγερα]στος ἔω, ἐπεὶ οὐδὲ [εοικε]
[λευσσετε] γὰρ το γε παντες ο̣ [μοι γερας ε]ρχεται ἀλλη   120

> ... but a word of good you have never yet spoken, nor brought to pass. And now among the Danaans you claim in prophecy that for this reason the god who strikes from afar brings woes upon them, that I would not accept the glorious ransom for the girl, the daughter of Chryses, since I much prefer to keep her in my home. For certainly I prefer her to Clytemnestra, my wedded wife, since she is not inferior to her, either in form or in stature, or in mind, or in any handiwork. Yet even so will I give her back, if that is better; I would rather the people be safe than perish. But provide me with a prize of honour forthwith, lest I alone of the Argives be without one, since that would not be proper. For you all see this, that my prize goes elsewhere.[21]

The copy as we have it is far from perfect. There are numerous spelling errors: θεοπροπιας for θεοπροπέων (109), βουλομε for βούλομαι (112), and ουν εθεν for οὔ ἑθέν (114).[22] Line 118 is missing entirely. In line 109, the student has forgotten the second half of the verse (θεοπροπέων ἀγορεύεις) and substituted a different formula. Furthermore, in line 120, we observe the another hand adding a few forgotten words to the end of the line. This is the work of a student who likely toiled to copy forty-five Homeric verses from memory, perhaps even recalling them by self-dictation. As many of us do singing the verses of a familiar song, he occasionally substitutes the wrong phrase or forgets the final words of a line. His mistakes are not wild Homeric variants but slips of memory which his teacher perhaps corrects. In this way, by recollection and correction, the student begins to internalize Homer, to develop a perfect model of the *Iliad* in his memory.

What was the objective of all this copying in Imperial schools? Certainly these exercises improved the speed and fluidity of handwriting, and trained

---

21 *P.Köln* II 70, ed. Kramer/Hagedorn 1978; Cribiore 1996, no. 254. Translation from Murray 1924.
22 Hom. *Il.* 1.109–120, ed. Allen 1920.

students to spell difficult forms correctly. For those whose likely employment included scribal or accounting work, these skill sets would have been paramount. But men of distinction, as Quintilian describes, had little interest in good penmanship (Quint. *Inst.* 1.1.28). For these writers, the true payoff of copying exercises was conditioning the memory. In Book 11, Quintilian counters Plato's anxiety over the detrimental effects of writing by arguing that text facilitates the process of memorization. Modern idioms for memorization — "off the top of one's head" or "to know by heart" — divorce the notions of memorized knowledge and textuality. But Quintilian indicates that, for ancient readers, learning by heart was the equivalent of a mental Xeroxing, in which the document was "imprinted" in the memory (*Inst.* 11.2.32):

> *illud neminem non iuvabit, isdem quibus scripserit ceris ediscere. sequitur enim vestigiis quibusdam memoriam, et velut oculis intuetur non paginas modo sed versus prope ipsos, estque cum dicit similis legenti. iam vero si litura aut adiectio aliqua atque mutatio interveniat, signa sunt quaedam quae intuentes deerrare non possumus.*

> This will assist everyone: to learn by heart from the same wax tablets on which one has written. For [the student] pursues memory by certain traces and will focus not only on the pages but the individual verses as if with his eyes, and when he recites, it is similar to someone reading. Furthermore, if some erasure, addition, or alteration should interrupt, there are certain symbols which, when we focus on them, will prevent us from wandering off.

According to this lesson, the process of memorization begins with making a copy from a model, and then transferring that copy directly from the written text to the memory. This passage resembles Quintilian's earlier description of the teaching tablet.[23] Just as the beginning student wrote out the letters on a wooden board with his stylus, the advanced student traces the words of the canon with his eyes. That Quintilian envisions a memorized text as a mental document is also clear from the final sentence in this passage: memories, too, produce fallible copies. When minds erase, add, or alter the text entered into them, students must rely on the written model to keep along the straight and narrow path.

Extant school exercises from antiquity confirm that the methods of memorization Quintilian recommends here were in fact used to teach students long passages of poetry and prose. *P.Ryl.* III 545, from the third century CE, contains

---

23 Bloomer 2011 argues that Quintilian rejects Platonic metaphors of pruning or molding. Rather, in the highly textualized society of the first century CE, he sees education as the writing of linguistic disposition upon the boy.

a puzzling fragment of the *Odyssey*: while this school hand preserves twenty-eight lines of Homer, they are only half-lines. Cribiore has described these half-lines as a memory challenge. The student likely copied down the first half of the line, and then had to recite the rest by memory.[24] Another challenging memory test survives on a school ostracon from the second century, *O.Bodl.* II 2170. This text preserves only the first words of whole paragraphs from Book 2 of the *Iliad*: line 527 (Λοκρῶν δ' ἡγεμόνευεν), then line 536 (οἳ δ' Εὔβοιαν), then line 546 (οἳ δ' ἄρ' Ἀθήνας). Just as Quintilian described, these portions of text worked as "prompts" (*signa*) that kept the student on track in the process of memorization, until a perfect model of the poem could be sealed in the mind. The young copyist slowly weaned himself from the written word and developed a mental duplicate in the process.

2 Copying Exercises and the Documentary "Trace"

School texts from the Imperial period demonstrate the variety of methods by which students acquired compositional skills and a foundational knowledge of the canonical authors at the core of classical *paideia*. But they also reveal a central paradox about the function of school documents, which challenges the very definition of documentation in the modern sense of the word. On the one hand, the physical and material aspects of copying exercises were crucial to the learning process. Students practiced positioning the hand and the stylus, perfecting the shape of letters on wax or ostracon, and correcting mistakes directly atop or adjacent to the ink of the first attempt. With every new bid to put pen to papyrus, the young writer gained more mastery over the form and content of the written language. On the other hand, in the most elite circles of literary study, the purpose of this training was to liberate the reader and writer from their dependence upon the material text. From modeling off the teacher's hand to filling in the blanks of Homeric half-lines, the student gradually came to "read" long passages of poetry and prose from tablets of the mind. In this sense, the educational system of the early Roman Empire aspired to use copies of literary texts for the express purpose of making text redundant.

This institutionalized practice of copying in antiquity confounds the two dominant schools of thought on the modern document: that documentary status hinges *either* on material form *or* on collective intentionality. The former and

---

24 Cribiore 1994, 3.

more traditional view perceives documents as objects transformed into graphic records: the act of writing defines the document. The latter focuses on the role of collective intent to invest certain signifiers — whether material or immaterial — with documentary authority.[25] But Imperial school texts and the pedagogues who discuss them exemplify a different, perhaps hybrid, attitude towards the value of the written word. This attitude does not privilege the physical text as the ultimate source of authority, for it is the canonical author who serves as the wellspring of poetic genius, along with those who can recite and transcribe his words perfectly. But it does recognize the value of the inscribed object as a tool in the production of mental documents; copying, composing, and correcting are stepping stones to amassing intellectual authority of one's own. In this sense, Imperial school texts suggest that the process of writing was more important than the product. The documentary practice remained crucial, while the material document was disposable. For this reason, it is more helpful to regard ancient documents as "traces" of activity.

The notion of the document as trace has emerged in recent years as philosophers have sought to expand the definition of documents beyond notions of proof and verification. For Ferraris, traces mark the genesis of documentary inscription. Traces are always material, smaller than the support medium in which they appear, and are meaningful "only for minds … which are capable of recognizing them."[26] Terrone calls particular attention to how communities use documenting artifacts to "trace" back to the original acts that produced them:

> Documents, too, are not magic devices that create permanent acts in virtue of some magic power. Documents are used by human beings in a framework of human practices … A document can make an act resistant to fading and disagreement only if the members of the community share a reliable way to trace back from the document to the act that constituted it.[27]

Documents, then, are not random indices to which we assign meaning and value. In Terrone's view, the practice and products of documenting allows readers to connect back to the activities and the agents who preserved that act in a material medium. By producing textual records, and copies thereof, "authors"

---

25 For a sweeping review of approaches to defining the document, see Buckland 1997. Examples of more textualist approaches include Loosjes 1962, 1–8 and Ranganathan 1963. Examples of a more instrumental or semiotic approach include Briet 2006 and Ferraris 2012.
26 Ferraris 2012, 225.
27 Terrone 2014, 163.

construct permanent and traceable links to ephemeral acts, speech, and intentions.

To demonstrate how documents function as traces, Terrone rejects a binary view of documentary status in favor of a spectrum. He outlines the evolution of documents in five phases, from the "causal trace" to the "social document."[28] Causal traces lie at the primitive end of the documentary spectrum: these are natural signs that show the occurrence of an act. Ash proves the existence of fire; a scar proves a past injury. Causal traces are neither intentional nor necessarily the product of human agency. Agency and intention come into play in the second stage of Terrone's spectrum, "documenting traces." These preserve a record of any intentional human activity, but the act of producing them "was not specifically aimed at constituting the trace as a trace."[29] For this reason, we exhibit the crafts and tools of past civilizations in museums, but do not believe that such objects were manufactured with documentation in mind.

The third stage of Terrone's spectrum introduces the first true "document": the fact-driven document. Portraits, photographs, and video and audio recordings are fact-driven documents because they are made to be traces of what they represent. These provide proof of the person, object, or event depicted. At last, in the final two stages of Terrone's spectrum, we find the intentional and self-conscious acts of inscription that constitute strong documents. Stage four is the "act-driven document," which represents traces of the acts that produced it: signatures in wet cement make permanent the act of signing. Perhaps another way to note the difference between fact- and act-driven documents is the function of the trace: the former traces the object, while the latter traces the agent. Terrone's fifth and final stage of the documentary spectrum are "social documents," essential act-driven documents of obligation: documents that can be used to enforce, verify, or validate. In this way, the conventional view of documentary status as proof appears only as the last and most sophisticated stage of documentary development.

Terrone's hierarchy of documentary traces equips historians with a new toolkit for classifying and analyzing the many textual and non-textual sources that survive from the Roman Empire. It allows us to advance beyond questions of authenticity and authority of ancient documents, and to instead examine the diversity of relationships between traces and the acts, speeches, and artifacts they preserve. As such, this spectrum allows us to see how the very same objects can transform from a simple trace to a document. A dog's footprints in the sand

---

28 Terrone 2014, 167–168.
29 Terrone 2014, 167.

are causal traces; photos of footprints at a crime scene, however, are fact-driven documents. This is especially true when we consider that inhabitants of the Roman Empire did not define or use written documents the way that we do, as illustrated by John Bodel in the previous chapter. In these circumstances, positioning ancient texts as traces along a spectrum of human intentions also shifts focus away from the qualifying characteristics that make or break documentary status and onto the historical contexts and communities in which such texts made meaning.

The theory of documentary traces in Ferraris and Terrone is hampered, however, by the unidirectional framework in which they propose that traces develop into documents. The language Terrone adopts as he presents this spectrum is one of progress: "a hierarchy that leads from traces to documents" or "a further step in the hierarchy leads us to traces that are intentionally produced."[30] He differentiates a community without writing that designates its permanent leader with a crown or scepter from a community with writing, in which "the act that assigns leadership to a person can be more efficiently made permanent."[31] Within his hierarchy of documentary status, Terrone assumes that human society must eventually and eagerly gravitate towards the production of more and more verifiable documentation — that "document acts" represent a pinnacle and purpose for documenting practices in the first place. This paradigm does little to illuminate the priorities of a community for whom the goal was to eliminate the necessity of the trace entirely. For the students, teachers, and intellectuals of the Roman Empire, the only skill more distinguished than the ability to summon vast scrolls of literature before the eyes was to make the labor appear effortless. In this setting, documentation was designed to be discarded in every medium but the mind.

3 Ancient Pedagogy and the School "Document"

If ancient documents may profitably be conceptualized as documentary traces, then precisely what are school documents traces of? What act do these school texts "make resistant to fading and disagreement"? School copying exercises represent rare traces of literary learning in the Roman Empire. From the most rudimentary replications of teachers' scripts to advanced half-line exercises,

---

30 Terrone 2014, 167–168.
31 Terrone 2014, 174.

these texts provide the student, the teacher, and the historian with a "trace" back to the crucial processes by which Imperial readers acquired *paideia*. Across the literature of the Second Sophistic, we observe that elite authors — both Greek and Roman — preoccupy themselves with displaying the breadth of their knowledge, and especially the ability to summon a Homeric or Vergilian verse at a moment's notice. But what these performances of high culture often conceal is the hard-won nature of that learning, or the processes of memorization that began with boyhood and continued well into the adolescent years in rhetorical schools. The daily practice, the institutionalized exercises, and the teacher's corrections by which one transformed from an *idiotēs* to a *pepaideumenos* are all preserved on these incomplete and error-prone compositions. As if carved on a tree: "I have learned my Homer. I have been here."

The value of memory within Imperial schools and intellectual communities cannot be overstated. While audiences marveled at archaizing dialects and extemporaneous speeches, an ingrained knowledge of the canonical passages marked the minimum requirement for participation in elite circles of learning. Pedagogical treatises from the Principate emphasize the advantages of a pupil with a good memory, which Plutarch describes as the "treasury of high learning."[32] Even children with poor memories, he asserts, can be aided by rigorous lessons, and parents must therefore "train and habituate" pupils' memories from a young age. One of the principal objectives of literate education therefore was to stock this storehouse with a lifetime's worth of learning, and pedagogical sources from as early as Classical Greece attest memorization as the central component of schooling. In Xenophon's *Symposium*, Niceratus explains that his father "forced me to learn the entirety of Homer," with the result that he could still in his adulthood rattle off the epics "from memory."[33] While his fellow symposiasts are quick to point out that any rhapsode can parrot poetry, Niceratus' account of his tutelage reveals the conventional understanding among elite households of what constituted a well-educated and ethical man. This perception of memory as a moral necessity of the noble and good continued well into the Middle Ages, as Carruthers has observed.[34]

---

32 Plut. *Mor.* 9e: τῆς παιδείας ἐστὶ ταμιεῖον ... ἀσκεῖν καὶ συνεθίζειν.
33 Xen. *Symp.* 3.5: ἠνάγκασέ με πάντα τὰ Ὁμήρου ἔπη μαθεῖν ... ἀπὸ στόματος.
34 Carruthers 2008, 13: "The choice to train one's memory or not for the ancients and medievals, was not a choice dictated by convenience: it was a matter of ethics." See, for example, Augustine's tale of Dioscurus the physician, who fails to memorize the creed before baptism and is punished by God with paralytic seizures until he commits it to memory (August. *Ep.* 52).

What is striking about Imperial discussions of memory, however, is the persistent link between the process of rote memorization and writing. Although the ostensible value of memorization is to free oneself from the text, descriptions of memory are often couched in the vocabulary of the written word. In Diogenes Laertius, for instance, the philosopher Antisthenes reproaches a careless friend who had misplaced his written notes: "You should have recorded them on your soul and not on paper."[35] Quintilian's recommendations for improving memory and internalizing passages of poetry or prose often include the use of textual prompts. The act of tracing, as I have discussed earlier in this chapter, is one way of affixing text in the wax tablets of the mind. But Quintilian also reflects on the way that marking and visualizing an actual page of text can help the student commit more difficult passages to memory (*Inst.* 11.2.29):

> *non est inutile iis quae difficilius haereant aliquas adponere notas, quarum recordatio commoneat et quasi excitet memoriam: nemo enim erit tam infelix ut quod cuique loco signum destinaverit nesciat.*

> It is helpful, for those parts that stick [to the mind] with greater difficulty, to add markings, the remembrance of which may impress upon and, as it were, rouse the memory. For no one will be so unfortunate as not to recognize the mark he affixed in each place.

This advice provides insight into how school drafts and texts contributed to the process of memorization. The annotation of the text allows the pupil to seal the visual image of that papyrus roll within his mind. As the student plans to recite from memory, markings made on the page then reactivate in the mind, allowing him to summon up difficult passages before the eyes. Quintilian even emphasizes the efficacy of pictorial markings like anchors and javelins in prompting the memory (*Inst.* 11.2.19–29). In this way, the pedagogue makes literal Plutarch's notion of the memory as a storehouse that contains personal copies of one's written texts. For both the student and the historian, the annotated text represents a documentary trace of the cognitive act of mental recording. And while longer annotated texts may have been preserved for the future, unlike school composition scraps, Quintilian clearly intends here that the annotation serves the memory of a declaiming student rather than the consultation of future readers.

The notion that copying and annotating school texts equips the student with a library of mental documents is further attested by numerous anecdotes

---

35 Diog. Laert. 6.5, ed. Long 1966 [1964]: ἔδει γάρ, ἔφη, ἐν τῇ ψυχῇ αὐτὰ καὶ μὴ ἐν τοῖς χαρτίοις καταγράφειν.

from ancient readers who did not have immediate access to their texts. Aulus Gellius, for example, explains that the organization of his *Attic Nights* resembles his schoolboy notes, "which I stowed away as an aid to my memory, like some storeroom of literature" (*quoddam litterarum penus*).[36] Now, as an adult, Gellius has amassed a considerable library of real books and has produced written *commentarii* so that he and fellow readers may consult them. When he does not have his books on hand but requires some "subject or word," the notes trigger his memory of the original and allow him to trace back to his original readings.[37]

Seneca the Elder recalls his own exercises in memorization, when his fellow classmates would recite over two hundred lines of poetry and he would then repeat them all in reverse order (*Controv. praef.* 2–3). Of course, it is the Younger Seneca who criticizes such memory feats as a mere façade of wisdom. In a letter to Lucilius, he insists that real men make maxims, rather than memorize them like children (*Ep.* 33.8):

> For it is shameful for an old man — or a man staring down old age — to have his wisdom from a notebook (*ex commentario sapere*) ... Instead, real wisdom is to make something of your own, and not to depend on the model (*ad exemplar pendere*) and to look back at the teacher time and again.

What is illuminating in this passage is the way in which Seneca blends cognitive and pedagogical imagery to describe the performance of wisdom. With his language of notebooks and models, he refers to both the literal copying exercises of the classroom and also the mental processes by which we store and retrieve knowledge. Even in educated conversations, according to Seneca, adult men behave like schoolchildren: they keep an open text of maxims in their minds, and they copy their models to earn the approval of their teachers.[38] In an

---

36 Gell. NA *praef.* 2: *nam proinde ut librum quemque in manus ceperam seu Graecum seu Latinum vel quid memoratu dignum audieram, ita quae libitum erat, cuius generis cumque erant, indistincte atque promisce annotabam eaque mihi ad subsidium memoriae quasi quoddam litterarum penus recondebam, ut quando usus venisset aut rei aut verbi, cuius me repens forte oblivio tenuisset, et libri ex quibus ea sumpseram non adessent, facile inde nobis inventu atque depromptu foret*, ed. Rolfe 1927.

37 Gunderson 2009, 21 observes that Gellius' notes are only "like" a storehouse but are "actually" aids to memory. See also pp. 147–159 on Gellius' unique recommendations of textual annotation.

38 Palmieri 1989, 179 n. 17: "Tale atteggiamento è la conseguenza della radicalizzazione del concetto augusteo di memoria dotta: in un'epoca in cui la cultura rischiava di diventare erudizione, il filosofo condanna l'aspetto deteriore della memoria, e mentre propone il suo più alto concetto del sapere, ribadisce, tuttavia, la ne ribadisce, tuttavia, la necessità del ricordo."

educational system that privileges the memorization of past authorities over the invention of new ones, Seneca worries that maintaining a mental library produces more archivists than true philosophers.

School copying exercises of the sort surveyed in the first part of this chapter therefore represent both traces and templates of the literary learning process that undergirded intellectual status in the Roman Empire. That both Greek- and Latin-speaking authors from the Principate describe learning and cognition in such textual terms emphasizes a clear link in their thinking between the tools of childhood education and the desired outcome of literate instruction. But if Terrone is correct to reformulate documentary status along a spectrum, then the placement of surviving school documents bears further consideration: what sort of traces are these? It is here that the flexibility of a spectrum of documentary status proves especially useful in weighing the significance of such texts: these copying exercises represent different sorts of traces in different contexts. At the bare minimum, school copying exercises could be said to constitute the second tier of Terrone's spectrum: documenting traces, which allow us "trace back to some acts of creating or fabricating."[39] Certainly, for the modern scholar, the school text might be analogous to the ancient bowl or knife on display in the museum. Papyri are often exhibited among other artifacts for precisely this reason: they document the daily lives of ancient people. These texts are imbued with the agency and intentions of student writers but remain disposable. And this impermanence of school copies, which were tailored to be erased with the heating of wax or the scraping of a papyrus layer, challenges the very notion of documentary authority. How could something designed for disposability plausibly constitute a trace?

If, on the other hand, we take into account the function of school documents as propaedeutics for the creation of permanent mental documents, it might be possible to elevate school texts to the tier of fact- or act-driven documents. To qualify as "full-fledged" documents in Terrone's hierarchy, the creator of the artifact must "specifically [aim] at constituting the trace as a trace."[40] That is, the school copying exercise qualifies only as a document if the copyist created it with the intention that an audience might later use it to trace back to a specific act. Fortunately, *testimonia* from antiquity demonstrate that school copies could be used in precisely this way. Students created copies not merely for their own benefit, but in order to earn the approval of the teacher. While it is likely the case that most copying exercises were never checked, the expectation

---

39 Terrone 2014, 167.
40 Terrone 2014, 167.

that any school document might be corrected by the *magister* indicates that students created them with verification in mind. In the *Colloquium Celtis*, the first-person narration of a student's day reports that the young man enters the school, sits at his bench, and begins copying his model on a tablet. After completing the copying, he reports: "I showed my writing to the teacher, and he praised me because I had written well. I read aloud what I had written, with pauses in the right places."[41] In this scene, the written exercise undergoes a two-step verification: the teacher first evaluates the student's written fidelity to the model, and then observes his ability to deliver textual information orally. With the *magister* as audience, the student performs two elementary steps of converting copied documents into internal documents. He has not yet proceeded to memorization, but the foundations of *paideia* have been laid.

School copying exercises, then, are demonstrably created as intentional traces. They may be checked, approved, and rejected. They may be duplicated and faked. They permit the creator and viewer to verify that learning has indeed taken place. Whether these documents constitute fact- or act-driven documents depends in large degree on what aspects we choose to prioritize. To classify these documents as fact-driven would be to emphasize their content: the vitality of the canon in the Imperial educational system. The recreation of Menander, Hesiod, and Homer in school exercises enables the student and the teacher to trace their literary heritage back to the voices of Archaic and Classical Greece. They present snapshots of the classical tradition, preserved and reactivated. If, on the other hand, we describe these texts as act-driven documents, then we underscore the agency and cognitive acts of the student. To return to Terrone, act-driven documents "are produced with the purpose of making the producing act permanent."[42] The examples that Terrone cites emphasize permanency in a material medium. But guest signatures and tree carvings also demonstrate that the significance of the textual document pales in comparison with the act that produced it: the *intention* to leave the mark, rather than the mark itself, imbues the document with relevance. So too in ancient schooling, it was not the tablet, ostracon, or papyrus that held value to the teacher, but the evidence that these documents provided about the student's acquisition of *paideia*. The master copy of the canon would reside in the mental library of each learner and would continue to be tested and enhanced throughout his intellectual life. In this sense, tracing exercises contribute to the construction of intellectual identity and social reality in the Roman Empire.

---

41 *Colloquium Celtis* 27b, transl. by Dickey 2017, 173.
42 Terrone 2014, 168.

4 Conclusion

Mastering the literary traditions of the classical canon is a slow and laborious process. In one of his many letters to Lucilius, the Younger Seneca explains that while "seeming learned" (*eruditus videri*) remained a social requirement of the Roman elite in his generation, not every man of standing had the dedication to become truly educated. A certain Calvisius Sabinus, confronting the limitations of his memory, discovered a short-cut on the path to *paideia* and simply purchased learned slaves instead: "He bought slaves at the highest price: one who mastered Homer, another Hesiod (*unum, qui Homerum teneret, alterum, qui Hesiodum*). Additionally, he assigned individual slaves to the nine lyric poets" (*Ep.* 27.6). Sabinus did not disguise the mnemonic value of these servants but paraded them at dinner parties. Seating them at the foot of his couch, he called upon any of the eleven when he wished to hear a pertinent line of the canon recited before his guests. When one dinner guest commented that Sabinus could have purchased proper book-boxes (*scrinia*) for the price of one specialized slave, the host defended the value of his investment: "He was of the opinion that he had the knowledge of what anyone in his household knew."[43] While Seneca intends this anecdote as a critique on the nouveau riche and the erosion of patrician values, it also reveals a great deal about how Romans understood the mind, the learning process, and the social value of erudition. Sabinus sees little reason to purchase the concrete contents of the library, because he understands that the Imperial intellectual circles did not measure learning by the number of books bought. Rich men with too many books and too little wisdom were, by Lucian's own accounts, a dime a dozen (*Ind.* 4–5). Rather, insiders of the sophistic communities understood the written text as a draft for the library of the mind. For Sabinus and men like him, the easiest solution was not to commit literature to their own memories, but to purchase minds that held copies of the canon within.

This chapter has argued that, from the most elementary tracing exercises to the complex memory challenges of grammar and rhetorical schools, Greek and Roman students of the Principate incentivized readers and writers to liberate themselves from their texts and assemble in their memories a library of mental documents. The necessity and disposability of school texts in this educational process thereby defies traditional paradigms of documentary status and invites

---

[43] Sen. *Ep.* 27.7: *ille tamen in ea opinione erat, ut putaret se scire, quod quisquam in domo sua sciret*, ed. Gummere 1917.

historians to reexamine ancient documentality in the context of a society that did not privilege writing over spoken testimony or memory. Terrone's hierarchy of documentary status tells a story about the unidirectional development of documentation that did not apply to the Imperial world: a history of increasingly sophisticated and "stable" documentation to support the complex social activities that human society sought to undertake. His spectrum of fact- and act-driven documents, however, provides a more inclusive approach to the documentary nature of copied texts in Imperial schools, and how the lived experience of school exercises shaped the habits and thought patterns of educated Greeks and Romans.

References

Allen, T. (ed.) (1920), *Homeri: Opera*, vol. 1, Oxford.
Bloomer, M. (2011), "Quintilian on the Child as a Learning Subject", in: *CW* 105, 109–137.
Bonner, S. (1977), *Education in Ancient Rome: From the Elder Cato to the Younger Pliny*, Berkeley.
Briet, S. (2006), *What Is Documentation? English Translation of the Classic French Text*, Lanham, MD.
Buckland, M. (1997), "What Is a 'Document'?", in: *Journal for the American Society for Information* 48, 804–809.
Carden, R./Barrett, W.S. (1974), *The Papyrus Fragments of Sophocles*, Berlin.
Carruthers, M. (2008), *The Book of Memory: A Study of Memory in Medieval Culture*, Cambridge.
Cribiore, R. (1994), "A Homeric Writing Exercise and Reading Homer in School", in: *Tyche* 9, 1–8.
Cribiore, R. (1996), *Writing, Teachers, and Students in Graeco-Roman Egypt*, Atlanta.
Cribiore, R. (2009), "Education in the Papyri," in: R. Bagnall (ed.), *The Oxford Handbook of Papyri*, Oxford, 320–337.
Debut, J. (1985), "Les documents scolaires", in: *ZPE* 63, 251–278.
Dickey, E. (transl.) (2017), *Stories of Daily Life from the Roman World: Extracts from the Ancient Colloquia*, Cambridge.
Fernández Delgado, J./Pordomingo, F. (2010), "Topics and Models of School Exercises on Papyri and Ostraca from the Hellenistic Period: P.Berol. inv. 12318", in: T. Gagos (ed.), *Proceedings of the Twenty-Fifth International Congress of Papyrology*, Ann Arbor, 227–238.
Ferraris, M. (2012), *Documentality: Why It Is Necessary to Leave Traces*, New York.
Goldhill, S. (2009), "The Anecdote: Exploring the Boundaries between Oral and Literate Performance in the Second Sophistic", in: W. Johnson/H. Parker (eds.), *Ancient Literacies: The Culture of Reading in Greece and Rome*, Oxford, 96–113.
Gummere, R.M. (1917), *Seneca: Epistles*, vol. 1, Cambridge, MA.
Gunderson, E. (2009), *Nox Philologiae: Aulus Gellius and the Fantasy of the Roman Library*, Madison.
Hesseling, D.C. (1892–1893), "On Waxen Tablets with Fables of Babrius (Tabulae Ceratae Assendelftianae)", in: *JHS* 13, 293–314.

Johnson, W. (2010), *Readers and Reading Culture in the High Roman Empire: A Study of Elite Communities*, Oxford.
Kalamara, Z. (2019), "Human and Divine Guilt in Aeschylus' *Niobe*", in: *Frammenti Sulla Scena* (online), 4–16, doi.org/10.13135/2612-3908/3251.
Karavas, O./Vix, J. (2014), "On the Reception of Menander in the Imperial Period", in: A.H. Sommerstein (ed.), *Menander in Contexts*, London, 183–198.
Koepsell, D./Smith, B. (2014), "Beyond Paper", in: *The Monist* 94, 222–235.
Kramer, B./Hagedorn, D. (eds.) (1978), *Kölner Papyri (P. Köln)*, vol. 2, Opladen.
Long, H.S. (ed.) (1966 [1964]), *Diogenis Laertii vitae philosophorum*, Oxford.
Loosjes, T.P. (1962), *Dokumentation wissenschaftlicher Literatur*, Munich.
Morgan, T. (1998), *Literate Education in the Hellenistic and Roman Worlds*, Cambridge.
Murray, A.T. (ed.) (1924), *Homer: The Iliad, Books 1–12*, Cambridge, MA.
Palmieri, N. (1989), "'Alia temptanda est via': allusività e innovazione drammatica nell'Edipo di Seneca", in: *MD* 23, 175–189.
Pernigotti, C. (ed.) (2008), *Menandri Sententiae*, Florence.
Ranganathan, S.R. (ed.) (1963), *Documentation and Its Facets*, London.
Rolfe, J.C. (ed.) (1927), *Gellius: Attic Nights*, vol. 1, Cambridge, MA.
Russell, D.A. (ed.) (2002), *Quintilian: The Orator's Education, Books 11–12*, Cambridge, MA.
Salaün, J.-M. (2014), "Why the Document Is Important ... and How It Is Becoming Transformed", in: *The Monist* 94, 187–199.
Skeat, T. (1957), *The Use of Dictation in Ancient Book-Production*, London.
Smith, B./Searle, J. (2003), "The Construction of Social Reality: An Exchange", in: *American Journal of Economics and Sociology* 62, 285–309.
Terrone, E. (2014), "Traces, Documents, and the Puzzle of 'Permanent Acts'", in: *The Monist* 94, 161–178.

Karen ní Mheallaigh
Documenting Wonderland: Lucian's *True Stories* and the Documentary *imaginaire*

Abstract: This chapter investigates what the fiction of Lucian of Samosata can tell us about ancient documentality. Starting from the position that fiction and documents are both founded on agreement between author and reader about their veracity, it examines in detail three inscriptions from Lucian's *True Stories*, showing how they evoke specific documentary texts and practices from antiquity such as boundary-marking, seal-making, inscribed treaties, funerary epigraphy, and the literary peritext. Each of these case studies reveals that interest in the materiality of the purported documents increases in direct proportion to the degree of anxiety about the authoritativeness of the document. Ultimately, Lucian is interested precisely in the boundary between documents and literature, and his fiction offers insight into the complex semiotics of documents in the Roman world.

This essay tackles aspects of a bigger question: what can fiction tell us about ancient documentality? In her essay in this volume, Inger Kuin addresses this question through examining Lucian's use of inscriptions in *True Stories* and other works, showing how this sheds light on the everyday experience of living with inscriptions from the perspective of both the educated elite and the partly literate. Kuin brilliantly demonstrates how readers at both ends of the literacy spectrum would have distrusted inscriptions for different reasons: the one group because they were well versed in these documents' power to substantiate false realities (not least, Lucian's own imaginary worlds), and the other because they were at the mercy of letters they could not understand. The fact that Lucian himself was writing (and performing) during the height of the popularity of the

---

This article would have been impossible without Lynette Mitchell's sage guidance on Greek inscriptions; any errors are, of course, mine. My warmest thanks are due also to Peter von Möllendorff and Daniel King for helpful comments and discussions, and, finally, to the editors for their patient support and guidance, and for inviting me to participate in a wonderful conference in the first place.

epigraphic habit in the second century CE makes his work a particularly fruitful study for Kuin's attempt to reconstruct the experience of illiteracy.[1]

My own approach to this question follows a different, Chartier-esque path: I will examine in detail three inscriptions from Lucian's *True Stories*, showing how they evoke specific documentary texts and practices from antiquity such as boundary-marking, seal-making, treaty-inscriptions, funerary epigraphy, and the literary peritext. I will argue that Lucian is interested in minute questions, such as: How do documents communicate? Are there different sorts of documents, different ways of recording presence? How does the material nature of a document or its location influence its interpretation? I will also explore the equivocality of Lucian's imaginary documents through analysis of the slippage he creates between epigraphic and literary texts. Lucian is interested in that critical boundary between documents and literature that several contributors to this volume address.[2] I hope to make a convincing case here that Lucian's fiction opens up for us some aspects of the semiotics of documents in antiquity.

1 Fiction vs. Document?

Prima facie, the question "What can fiction tell us about documentality?" appears to be a paradox, for documents represent the real world, as everyone knows (or at least, that is the default assumption), but this is something fiction can only pretend to do. That is to say, readers generally know they are not meant to believe fiction literally, but documents are imbued with a truth status so literal that they are often legally binding. On that basis, fictions and documents are as different, it would seem, as oil and water. In fact, however, they are more closely integrated than we might think. Both work on the basis of implied, contractual agreements between author and reader regarding the truth status of the claims they make,[3] and both have world-building powers. But whereas documents build and hold force in the "real" world we inhabit — Ferra-

---

[1] See Kuin in this volume: "Together the inscriptions of *Verae historiae* bear testimony to how the epigraphic habit can seep into even the most outlandish corners of the literary imagination."
[2] Fournet in this volume; DiGiulio in this volume. Schneider (in this volume) treats separately the question of what *we* think a document is, and whether ancient writers (specifically geographers) shared that concept. Though I do not share his pessimism about the second question, his discussion is illuminating.
[3] See Ferraris 2015, 425 and DiGiulio in this volume: "Documents require a degree of complicity between reader and writer in order to have authoritative force."

ris argues that our very society is built on documents, whilst at the same time documents build the real world —⁴ fictions build worlds of make-believe with no binding force on the world in which we live.⁵

Yet, that assertion is not wholly true, for at least two reasons. First of all, because *some* fictions do indeed *lay claim to* documentary status in order to breach the boundaries of the fictional world and intervene in the affairs of the real. The Trojan war 'diaries' ascribed to Dictys of Crete and Dares of Phrygia are good examples of this because they feign the status of historical, autographic documents in order to challenge the canonical account of the war received from the Homeric poems.⁶ William Hansen coined the term "pseudo-documentary fiction" for this special, transgressive sub-category. ⁷ Secondly, although the status of the material text itself is not usually a prominent concern in fictions generally — in vivid contrast with documents, where it is central to the document's authenticity and therefore its authority (think: the watermarks and other authenticating features of banknotes, passports, and similar documents) — pseudo-documentary fictions often work very hard indeed to convince the reader of their documentary materiality, as I shall explain further in a moment. These exceptions substantially narrow the gap between the documentary realm and the fictional. Of course, fictional worlds are themselves often filled with fictional documents: letters, inscriptions, and the like which lend the storyworld a *frisson* of textuality and a *trompe l'oeil* depth (the so-called "reality-effect"), helping to authenticate it by importing into fictional societies the documentary habits of the real.⁸ However, troubling (and thrilling) frictions are generated by the metaleptic traffic of documentality between the real and fictional worlds — a kind of literary contraband — since this weakens the boundary separating the two. Phlegon of Tralles offers us a good example of the disrup-

---

4 On documents as social objects, see Ferraris 2015; and cf. Ferraris 2012, 247 on documents as "inscriptions of acts." On the "virtuous cycle" of mutual reinforcement between the social world, practices, and documents, see Terrone 2014, 176.
5 See Kuin in this volume: "Literary texts represent a special type of document, because they have the capability to create discrete, imagined worlds, which can be reflective of the real world, but cannot be contained by it."
6 On Dictys, see Merkle 1989; on Dares, see Berschorner 1992.
7 Hansen 2003; ní Mheallaigh 2008. On the motif of "book discovery" in antiquity, see Speyer 1970.
8 On the role of inscriptions in ancient prose fictions, especially novels, see Stoneman 1995 (on the *Alexander Romance*); Sironen 2003; Slater 2009. Zadorojnyi 2013, with which I intersect at several points here, offers an excellent analysis of the use of inscriptions to explore questions relating to power, identity, and authority in imperial literary texts generally. The term "reality-effect" is from Barthes 1989, 141–148.

tive interpolation of documentary practices into fiction: at the end of an apparently fictional love-story, in a surprise that is an accidental result of the text's incomplete transmission, we suddenly discover that we were reading a bureaucratic letter all along (*Mir.* 1).[9] The fact that we hesitate in deciding if this letter is *actually* documentary or (more likely) *pseudo*-documentary illustrates the kind of interpretative trouble — and pleasures — that such transgressive documentary strategies generate for the reader.

As I pointed out above, in order to substantiate their documentary status in the real world, pseudo-documentary fictions often work very hard to convince the reader of the authenticity and autonomous existence of the putative ur-documents on which they are (allegedly) based. At the very least, this requires fabricating for these documents a carefully calibrated 'thingness' or materiality, along with a history and narrative of discovery or transmission. As part of this, the ur-document usually undergoes putative translation — sometimes several stages of translation — which exonerates the author from the need to fabricate a distinctive voice or style for it as well. Ironically, it is this very work that tends to betray these texts as make-believe. Out of this a simple rule of thumb emerges: the more vividly an author strives to evoke a putative document — and the more exotic its nature — the greater the probability that it is make-believe. To put it another way: preoccupation with the details of a document's material nature increases in direct proportion to anxiety about its authenticity.

At one end of the spectrum, therefore, we find the regular citation of documents in law-court speeches, where no special attention is paid to the material nature of the document, be it a decree, law, contract, or other documentary evidence. This is because its material existence is simply a given, a mundane fact; the document has been preselected and stored safely in the sealed evidence jar (the *ekhinos*), it is presumably visible to all present at the trial, and no one harbors anxiety about its existence or authenticity.[10] At the opposite end of the spectrum, the archives of the literary imagination are filled with exotic texts that are evoked in crisp detail: golden inscribed columns, ivory books, cryptoglyphic writing, and buried memoirs inscribed on slabs of antique wood, each one endowed with its own elaborate tale of discovery and transmission.[11] These

---

9 See Morgan 2013.
10 The procedures for handling documentary evidence in court are set forth in Arist. *Ath. Pol.* 53.2–3 (claim courts); see also Theophr. *Char.* 6.8 with Diggle 2005, 258–262.
11 In Euhemerus' *Sacred Inscription*, Hermes has inscribed an account of the gods' exploits on a golden column (Diod. Sic. 5.46.7). Menelaus' eye-witness account of the Trojan war was allegedly recorded in a hieroglyphic inscription in Egypt (see Dio Chrys. *Or.* 11.37–38, with incisive comments by Zadorojnyi 2013, 372 n. 30). For Dictys' Trojan War diary engraved in

authors work very hard to convince the reader that their documents exist, quite simply because they do not exist. But lest we grow too complacent about this, we should also bear in mind that — just occasionally — vivid and unusual artifacts were indeed to be found on the shelves of ancient libraries. The famous "linen books" (*lintei libri*) of Rome are a case in point and a salubrious reminder of the dangers of being too readily dismissive of pseudo-documentary claims.[12] Of course, it is precisely this moment of hesitation — the mere whiff of a possibility that the document *might actually exist* — that makes these fictions all the more exciting.

This essay examines the documentary–fictional frontier in order to gain a clearer understanding of the theoretical implications that we can extract from deliberate and transgressive crossings thereof. My case study will be Lucian's *True Stories* (*Verae historiae*, or *VH* for short). Of all authors to survive from the imperial period, Lucian is arguably the most obsessively preoccupied with fraud as a cultural phenomenon, with the interplay of truth and lies, and with texts' ability to create authority and to deceive. His fascination with these themes surfaces again and again in his satires on pretentious or gullible intellectuals, in essays about charismatic confidence tricksters, and in his treatise on how to write history.[13] He is no stranger to the world of documentary and literary fraud, either, as attested by his detailed account of the holy man Alexander's clandestine team of seal-breakers and forgers, and by his own composition of a Heraclitean hoax to dupe a philosophical expert.[14] Even Lucian's own fictions are directed, metafictionally, toward self-surgery and investigation of their own

---

Phoenician letters on tablets of linden wood, see *Eph. Epist.* 2–4 and *Prol.* 7–8. Deinias, the wondrous traveler of Antonius Diogenes' novel, recorded his adventures on tablets of cypress wood (Phot. *Bibl.* 111a). On the "ivory books" of the *Historia Augusta*, see the following note.

12 On the *libri lintei*, see Livy 4.7.12; 4.20.8; 4.23.2–3. The question of their authenticity is discussed in detail by Walt 1997, who concludes that they are not likely to have been a fabrication, however unreliable their contents may have been; for a succinct summary of the debate, see Oakley 2013. The "ivory books" (*libri elephantini*) — one of which could be found in Chest 6 in the Ulpian Library, according to SHA, *Tac.* 8.1 — look like a spoof of the *libri lintei*, exploiting ivory's well-known association with deception in the ancient literary imagination (on which, see Elsner 1991, 162–164).

13 On Lucian's social satire, see Hall 1981; Jones 1986; Whitmarsh 2001, 247–294. He is also well aware of his own powers to deceive, which align him subversively with the very tricksters he seeks to expose: see Fields 2013 (on *Peregrinus*) and ní Mheallaigh 2018 (on *Alexander the false prophet*).

14 See esp. *Alex.* 21, with Speyer 1971, 56–59 and ní Mheallaigh 2018. On Lucian's Heraclitean hoax, see Strohmaier 1976 and Macleod 1979.

mechanics.¹⁵ The acme of this tendency is the paradoxically titled *True Stories* itself, which Lucian presents as an entertaining exercise in the telling of plausible lies and an exposé of less scrupulous writers before him who exploited their readers' good faith by telling lies in the guise of truth. These authors include philosophers, travel-writers, and historiographers. In contrast with them, Lucian promises that his approach will be more honest, for he warns his readers *not* to believe a word he has written, but to savor instead the artfulness of his lies (*VH* 1.3–4).

In the gathering wave of scholarship on this text, much work has been done to explore Lucian's parodic literary allusions, especially showing how he exploits the techniques of historiography to imbue his fantasy with an air of verisimilitude.¹⁶ But comparatively little attention has been paid to the documentality of his fiction specifically, namely, how he evokes documentary sources and practices as well.¹⁷ This oversight is surprising, especially in light of Lucian's evident interest in documents — and more specifically inscriptions — as unstable sites of authority, as illustrated in his famous anecdote about the inscription in the Pharos lighthouse, with its (literally) hidden layer of meaning.¹⁸ As Alexei Zadorojnyi points out, this "quirky epigraphic manoeuvre in Lucian is a trope for narrative that authorizes itself as an unbiased and true monument to the political past."¹⁹ Lucian's deceptive epigraphic habit in the *VH* intensifies that text's central paradox as an honest record of things that never happened. The *VH* therefore offers us an exposé not only of authors' slippery wiles, but also of the potential for documentary fraud. As Kuin shows, this gives Lucian's fantasy traction beyond the confines of the library, in the real world of an empire that was built on an elaborate infrastructure of information technology.

---

15 See ní Mheallaigh 2014 on this tendency in *Toxaris*, *Philopseudes*, and *True Stories*.
16 Von Möllendorff's magisterial commentary (2000) is invaluable. On (parodic) historiographical allusions in Lucian's work and the *VH* more specifically, see Georgiadou and Larmour 1994; Saïd 1994; Avery 1997; Georgiadou and Larmour 1998, 28–40; Fusillo 1999; Bartley 2003.
17 Kuin's essay in this volume is a welcome expansion of this question. Previous work includes: Householder 1940, who compares the mock decrees in Lucian's work with epigraphical evidence, but does not discuss the *VH*; Saïd 1994, 160–162, who presents Lucian's use of inscriptions as parodic of Herodotean and Thucydidean practice; and ní Mheallaigh 2008, 419–422, on pseudo-documentarism in the *VH* more generally.
18 Luc. *Hist. conscr.* 62. For discussion, see Kuin in this volume; Zadorojnyi 2013, 372; and ní Mheallaigh 2014, 178–179.
19 Zadorojnyi 2013, 372.

My analysis will focus on three inscriptions in the text. First, I will examine the documentary landscape of the Island of the Vine-Women (*VH* 1.7). Significantly, this is the very first adventure in Lucian's fantasy; it therefore plays an important role in highlighting the documentality of his fantasy and foregrounding the interpretation of documents itself as a theme in the work as a whole. Thereafter I examine the alliance between the Sun and the Moon (*VH* 1.20) and the inscription recording Lucian's presence on the Isle of the Blessed (*VH* 2.28). All of these documents are imagined in their material detail, and all three challenge the boundary between the documentary and the fictional, offering us insight into the ancient documentary *imaginaire*.

2 Reading Signs: The Documentary Detective Work of *VH* 1.7

The first adventure in Lucian's fantastic *True Stories* presents the reader with a miniature drama of documentality, with semiosis in action. After crossing a mysterious river of wine, Lucian and his men stumble across an inscription that records the former presence of the gods Heracles and Dionysus and the limit of their worldly travels:

> προελθόντες δὲ ὅσον σταδίους τρεῖς ἀπὸ τῆς θαλάττης δι' ὕλης ὁρῶμέν τινα στήλην χαλκοῦ πεποιημένην, Ἑλληνικοῖς γράμμασιν καταγεγραμμένην, ἀμυδροῖς δὲ καὶ ἐκτετριμμένοις, λέγουσαν Ἄχρι τούτων Ἡρακλῆς καὶ Διόνυσος ἀφίκοντο. ἦν δὲ καὶ ἴχνη δύο πλησίον ἐπὶ πέτρας, τὸ μὲν πλεθριαῖον, τὸ δὲ ἔλαττον – ἐμοὶ δοκεῖν, τὸ μὲν τοῦ Διονύσου, τὸ μικρότερον, θάτερον δὲ Ἡρακλέους. προσκυνήσαντες δ' οὖν προῆμεν· οὔπω δὲ πολὺ παρῆμεν καὶ ἐφιστάμεθα ποταμῷ οἶνον ῥέοντι ὁμοιότατον μάλιστα οἶόσπερ ὁ Χῖός ἐστιν. ἄφθονον δὲ ἦν τὸ ῥεῦμα καὶ πολύ, ὥστε ἐνιαχοῦ καὶ ναυσίπορον εἶναι δύνασθαι. ἐπῄει οὖν ἡμῖν πολὺ μᾶλλον πιστεύειν τῷ ἐπὶ τῆς στήλης ἐπιγράμματι, ὁρῶσι τὰ σημεῖα τῆς Διονύσου ἐπιδημίας.

> Having advanced as much as three *stades* from the sea, we saw through a wood a column made of bronze and inscribed in Greek letters, faint and worn off, saying: "Thus far Heracles and Dionysus came." And there were two footprints in rock nearby – one 100 feet long, the other smaller – the latter, smaller one belonging to Dionysus, I reckoned, and the other one to Heracles. We made obeisance and moved on. We had not yet gone on very far when we happened upon a river flowing with wine very like Chian. The current was so abundant and full that in some places it was possible to sail in it. And so it occurred to us to put far greater trust in the inscription of the column, since we saw the signs of Dionysus' presence.[20]

---

[20] Citations of the *VH* are from Macleod's *OCT*. Unless otherwise declared, all translations are my own.

The abundance of records in this passage is striking: not just the inscription, but footprints and other environmental traces of the gods' former presence (e.g., the wine river).

In this scene Lucian heavily evokes the documentary practices that clustered around boundaries in antiquity. The combination of natural and artificial boundary markers, the one corroborating the other, is absolutely typical of ancient practice, since manmade markers like *horoi* (inscribed boundary stones) and inscribed pillars (*stêlai*) often served to formalize divisions that were already suggested by natural features such as rivers or mountain passes. Plutarch records Theseus' famous pillar, which bore inscriptions marking the boundary between Attica/Megara and the Peloponnese in two trimeter verses: one facing east that read "This is not the Peloponnese, but Ionia"; and the other facing west that said "This is the Peloponnese, not Ionia." The pillar was located on the Isthmus, a natural boundary between the two.[21] Lucian's contemporary Pausanias, on his tour around mainland Greece, records several types of boundary document, including stone herms, inscribed pillars and statues, which reinforce natural boundaries, usually rivers or mountains. Often, these borders are further marked by shrines and temples or similar religious structures.[22]

In addition to such reports, we have many surviving examples of inscriptions that deal with *polis* borders, as well as documents, such as boundary stones (*horoi*), that demarcated more local boundaries of agricultural land, sacred space, or civic spaces like the Athenian *agora*.[23] *Horoi* could take the form of movable stones bearing a simple inscription such as the word ὍΡΟΣ. Alternatively, in so-called rupestral *horoi*, the word ὍΡΟΣ was simply carved into an exposed shelf of bedrock, converting a natural feature of the landscape

---

21 Plut. *Thes.* 25.4.
22 Examples include Paus. 2.38.7: the border region known as Hermai, after the stone herms that marked the triple boundary between Argos, Arkadia, and Lakonia, with the River Tanaos and Mount Parnon nearby; Paus. 8.25.1: the ancient inscribed pillar that marked the boundary between Psophis and Thelpousa in Arcadia, with the River Ladon nearby; Paus. 8.34.6: a boundary between Messenia and Megalopolis, which was marked by a temple of Hermes plus a pillar carved with a figure of Hermes; Paus. 8.35.2: another point on the boundary between Messenia and Megalopolis, which was marked by a shrine to Hermes, statuettes of Persephone, Demeter, Hermes, and Heracles, and an ancient wooden statue (*xoanon*) made (Pausanias thinks) by Daedalus for Heracles; and Paus. 8.38.7: the peak shrine of Zeus Lycaeus, from where much of the Peloponnesus was visible, where one could find two columns facing east. References are from Ober 1995, 108 n. 33.
23 Ober 1995, 108 n. 33 cites the following as illustrative of *polis* border inscriptions: *SIG*³ 933–935; *SEG* 23.297; *SEG* 35.406; *IG* V 1 1371–1372; *IG* VI 1 2792.

into an unmovable document.²⁴ As is well known, these documents served not only to organize space formally (e.g., by designating the different functions of different spaces, territorial borders, or the limits of legal ownership); they also had a social function, influencing human behavior by reminding their readers of the need to adjust their behavior appropriately to the space they were about to enter. A good example of this was the *horos* of the Athenian *agora*, whose presence implicitly reminded visitors of the law that prohibited certain types of criminals (e.g., murderers) from entering that space.²⁵

To return to Lucian, it is notable that, in terms of its physical geography, this part of the mountainous island is a landscape not far (three *stades*) from the sea and adjacent to a river, both of which form natural boundaries. For his ancient readers, this was clearly a frontier landscape, or ἐσχατιά (the formal designation for such border regions that were abutted by mountains or sea).²⁶ Reinforcing (and reinforced in turn by) these natural features, the pillar of bronze with its inscription, and the impression of footprints in the adjacent rock evoke *horos* stone and rupestral *horos* respectively.

These are no ordinary *horos* documents, however; they are *horoi* in a psychogeographical and metaliterary sense as well, marking the boundaries of the known world and the threshold to the realms of fantasy. The reader who crosses these boundaries must therefore adjust his or her expectations about what is believable. Lucian has sailed through the Pillars of Heracles — the Straits of Gibraltar — which were widely believed to mark the western edge of the inhabited world. Now he discovers a new frontier beyond, marked by a new "Pillar of Heracles," this time a more literal instantiation of the toponym.²⁷ He specifically

---

24 On rupestral *horoi* of Attica, see Ober 1995, 114–123, esp. 115: "the rupestral inscription is, by definition, *in situ*."

25 Ober 1995 explores the problems that arise from the contingency of meanings proclaimed by *horoi*; see 91–96 on the *horos* of the Athenian *agora* specifically.

26 Harpocration s.v. Ἐσχατιά· (146) Ἐσχατιά· ... τὰ πρὸς τοῖς τέρμασι τῶν χωρίων ἐσχατιὰς ἔλεγον, οἷς γειτνιᾷ εἴτε ὄρος εἴτε θάλασσα ("Frontier: ... They used to call the regions at the limits of territories, abutted by either mountains or sea, 'frontiers'"). Schol. Aeschin. 1.97: ἐσχατιαί εἰσι τόποι ἔσχατοι τῆς χώρας περατούμενοι ἢ εἰς ὄρη ἢ εἰς θάλασσαν ("The frontiers are places at the outer edges of the land, finishing either in mountains or in the sea"). At *VH* 1.6, Lucian describes the island, as seen from the sea, as "lofty and thickly wooded" (ὑψηλὴ καὶ δασεῖα).

27 Lucian seems to evoke an ancient controversy over what, precisely, the "Pillars of Heracles" were. According to Strabo (3.5.5), many people identified them with the Straits of Gibraltar, a natural feature on the coast of Gades (Cadiz), but there was also a more literal interpretation: οἱ δὲ τὰς ἐν τῷ Ἡρακλείῳ τῷ ἐν Γαδείροις χαλκᾶς ὀκταπήχεις, ἐν αἷς ἀναγέγραπται τὸ ἀνάλωμα τῆς κατασκευῆς τοῦ ἱεροῦ, ταύτας λέγεσθαί φασιν· ἐφ' ἃς ἐρχόμενοι οἱ τελέσαντες

evokes the network of texts and monuments that were thought to mark the margins of the known world, especially monuments to the peregrinations of Dionysus and Heracles in farthest India, and those left by Alexander the Great, who strived to exceed these gods' achievements and push the world's boundaries back even farther.[28]

All three adventurers are evoked in Lucian's text: Dionysus and Heracles explicitly, and Alexander implicitly, through Lucian's Alexander-like surpassing of the limits of the gods' exploration, and through the piety he shows while doing so.[29] Albeit a great breaker of boundaries, Alexander habitually showed reverence at the monuments of his predecessors. According to Arrian, he offered sacrifice after he gained control of a rocky outcrop in India that Heracles had failed to capture (Arr. *Anab.* 4.28–30). In the *Alexander Romance*, Alexander reports that, when he encountered two *stêlai* (one of gold, the other of silver), which Heracles was said to have set up as boundary markers in the territory of Babylon, he decided to bore a hole in one of the pillars in order to see if it was solid gold — but not before offering sacrifice to Heracles.[30] Lucian's gesture of reverence (*proskynêsis*) on passing the bronze pillar mirrors this behavior, more specifically evoking the religious worship (*proskynêmata*) of Greek pilgrims or perhaps the obeisance that Alexander famously (and controversially) demanded when he was in the East.[31] Lucian's travels beyond this point in the text cast

---

τὸν πλοῦν καὶ θύοντες τῷ Ἡρακλεῖ διαβοηθῆναι παρεσκεύασαν, ὡς τοῦτ' εἶναι καὶ γῆς καὶ θαλάττης τὸ πέρας. τοῦτον δ' εἶναι πιθανώτατον καὶ Ποσειδώνιος ἡγεῖται τὸν λόγον … ("Others say that what is meant are the bronze pillars, eight cubits tall, in the Temple of Heracles in Gades, on which the cost of the construction of the sanctuary is inscribed. Those who reach them at the end of their voyage and offer sacrifice to Heracles ensure it is bruited abroad that this is the end of land and sea. Posidonius also believes this is the most plausible account …").

28 On local Indian tales of Dionysus' and (separately) Heracles' conquests in India, see Diod. Sic. 2.38–39. For accounts of how Alexander surpassed the achievements of Heracles and/or Dionysus, see Arr. *Anab.* 4.28–30 and the Letter to Aristotle (Latin version) of the *Alexander Romance* 78. On representations of Alexander as a breaker of boundaries, see Stoneman 1992, 97–98; Zadorojnyi 2013, 378.

29 Note that in Plutarch's essay *On the fortune of Alexander* 332a, the Macedonian king declares that he imitates Heracles, emulates Perseus, and *follows the footsteps of Dionysus*, who was a founder of his family and ancestor: Ἡρακλέα μιμοῦμαι καὶ Περσέα ζηλῶ, καὶ τὰ Διονύσου μετιὼν ἴχνη, θεοῦ γενάρχου καὶ προπάτορος.

30 *Alexander Romance rec.* α 3.27.3–4, dated to the third–fourth century CE. Elsewhere in the novel, we are told that Alexander's gesture of covering Sesonchosis' epitaph with his cloak (*rec.* γ 2.31) is ostensibly a gesture of respect, but in fact an attempt to conceal the inscription from his soldiers.

31 On pilgrimage and *proskynêma*-inscriptions at Philae in Egypt, see Rutherford 1998. On the cultural contentiousness of Alexander's behavior in the East, especially with regard to

him, therefore, into the role of a Munchausen-esque hyper-Alexander, whose desire for whatever glory he can garner through fantasy adventures (*kenodoxia*, 1.4) is the antithesis of — or perhaps more subversively an extension of — the Macedonian king's near-fabulous accomplishments.

The pillar is made of bronze, which (in contrast with the more extraordinary inscriptions we find in fantasy-land subsequently) was indeed a material used for inscriptions in antiquity, and, in Roman thought especially, was felt to advertise authority, permanence, and inviolability.[32] Bronze was also proverbial for its longevity, which means that the inscription's weathered letters denote a document of great antiquity indeed.[33] This detail serves as an authenticating strategy, enhancing both its credibility and (presumably) its authority. There is, however, a tension between the verisimilitude of the artifact and the extraordinary nature of the text's claim (*gods* were here!), as well as the marvelous surrounding landscape, whose features come straight from the world of paradoxography. The river of wine evokes springs and rivers of miraculous substances from Ctesias and paradoxographers,[34] while Heracles' gigantic footprint has been lifted (with fantastical amplification) from Herodotus 4.82, where it is described as the only wonder-worthy feature of Scythia apart from that country's enormous rivers. These boundary markers conjure a frontier where fact meets fantasy, and one is not sure what to believe.

But, in fact, we have not just two documentary records of the gods' visit to the island (inscription and footprints), but three, for the river of *wine* attests to the presence of Dionysus specifically. As we have seen from Pausanias, it was not unusual for boundaries to be marked by clusters of documents in this way. However, the three markers on Lucian's border are carefully interleaved so as to complement each other, not duplicate. With this artfully selected trifecta of proofs, Lucian seems to be exploring, quite deliberately, the nature and reliability of different records of past events, as well as how they interlock and reinforce each other.

---

proskynêsis, see Plut. *Alex.* 45, with Schmidt 1999, 287–299; Whitmarsh 2002, 186–191; Mossman 2006, 289–291.
32 Williamson 1987.
33 Noted also by Kuin in this volume. Von Möllendorff 2000, 79–80 suggests that this evokes the inscription on the tomb of Osiris (a god identified with Dionysus) in Arabian Nysa. This document recorded Osiris' round-the-world travels, but the text was badly eroded with time (Diod. Sic. 1.27.5–6).
34 E.g., Ctesias *ap.* Photius *cod.* 72, 46a33 (a spring of wine). Further references are cited in Georgiadou and Larmour 1998, 73; von Möllendorff 2000, 84 with n. 4.

In his discussion of documentality, Enrico Terrone distinguishes between what he calls the *trace* and the *document* on the basis of purpose and intentionality: "[T]he trace is the product of a causal process that makes its cause recognizable… In this sense a trace can represent its subject independently of whether it was intentionally produced by some creator." As an example of a trace, Terrone cites ash, which is a trace of fire, whether or not it had been intentionally produced by the person who lit the fire. Moreover, as he notes: "Traces are signs that even nonlinguistic animals can properly understand."[35] In contrast, a document is an "intentionally produced trace": "In order to be a document…a trace has to be *intentionally produced through an act that was aimed at creating a trace*. A footprint is a trace; but to the extent that it was caused by an act that was not aimed at creating a footprint it is not a document. A fingerprint taken in a public office, in contrast, does constitute a document *since it is caused by acts aimed at producing this very trace*."[36]

One might argue, therefore, that from the modern perspective, the footprint and wine-river in Lucian's landscape are collateral *traces* of the gods' visit to the island, in contrast with the deliberately engraved and therefore *documentary* inscription recording that event. However, I would argue that all three features have the full status of documents — for two reasons. First, because, within the grammar of ancient epiphanies, which are evoked in this scene through Lucian's reference to the famous Heraclean footprint and to Dionysus' transformation of his captors' ship into vines and wine in his *Homeric Hymn*, such signs are interpreted or given by the gods *in order to* attest to their presence and divinity. They are not, therefore, casual "traces" in Terrone's definition, but intentional, epiphanic documents. Secondly, *all* traces within a fictional world are, in a more general metafictional sense, documents, inasmuch as they have been planted deliberately in that world by the author. To put it differently, since the world of the *VH* is a fictional one, none of the "traces" or "documents" within it can *ever* correspond to any real social act; they can *only* lead back, solipsistically, to the author's design, which is an intentional disposition of the components of his fictional world. In this more general sense, therefore, *traces* may "accidentally" record fictional events in the story-world, but in a metafictional sense they are always *documents* of the author's world-building acts.[37] From this, it would seem that documentality works rather differently within fictional worlds.

---

35 Terrone 2014, 163–164.
36 Terrone 2014, 165, with my italics.
37 I would like to thank James Healy for this observation.

Whether we regard them formally as traces or documents, all three features described in Lucian's landscape attest (fictionally) to the gods' presence on the island a long time ago, and explain or corroborate each other. But there are further crucial differences between them. The river and footprints are autographic, unique documents. Innate documents like these are, by definition, non-replicable and forged only with the greatest difficulty. In contrast, the inscription is an "auxiliary" document, which bears witness to the past event or presence through its asseverative function. Since auxiliary documents are always potentially allographic (i.e., possibly written by someone else), they are replicable and relatively easy to forge. This explains why Lucian needs the corroboration of the innate documents in order to verify the inscription. Interlaced with these generic differences are the distinctions between different types of *horoi* more specifically: the bronze pillar, like a *horos* stone, could presumably be moved (albeit with difficulty), whereas the topographical features, like rupestral *horoi*, are fixed *in situ*. The mobile text, as always, is attended by a potential crisis of authenticity, but the documentary landscape is imbued with evidentiary authority.

Each of the innate documents in this landscape, however, carries a distinctive semiotic charge. To evoke Peirce's classic taxonomy of signifiers, the wine river is a symbol, and the footprints an index.[38] As such, each presents the reader with a distinct interpretative challenge: the symbol because its connection with its referent is arbitrary, and specific cultural learning is required if a reader is to make the connection (i.e., one must first know that Dionysus is the god of wine in order to understand that the wine river denotes his presence). *Prima facie*, the index should be less troublesome, since it denotes its referent in a literal way: footprints inevitably denote the presence of a foot and therefore a person. Yet footprints have innumerable referents, potentially. While one might reasonably surmise that only gods could produce footprints of the proportions Lucian describes here, without intimate knowledge of every deity's individual foot size and shape, it would be impossible to identify the exact pedestrian from each print.

This particular problem had a long genealogy in ancient recognition scenes stretching back to Aeschylus' *Libation Bearers* (205–210), where Electra correctly divines the presence of her brother Orestes, whom she has not seen for years, from a lock of his hair, a piece of his clothing, and his footprint, which is unmistakably similar to her own. In fact, Aeschylus' scene — like Lucian's — features *two* footprints: in this case, one belonging to Orestes and the other to "some fellow-traveler" (καὶ γὰρ δύ' ἐστὸν τώδε περιγραφὰ ποδοῖν, / αὐτοῦ τ' ἐκείνου

---

38 Peirce 1998 [c. 1894].

καὶ συνεμπόρου τινός·, *Cho.* 207–208). In Euripides' rewriting of the same scene, Electra exposes the ludicrous improbability of this detective work, pointing out, first, the unlikelihood that anyone could make a footprint in the rock-hard soil, and secondly, the implausibility of the idea that a man's footprint would be similar to a woman's, even if they were brother and sister (Eur. *El.* 532–537). In her subtle analysis of this scene, Isabelle Torrance reveals that the tokens as well as Electra's questions are metapoetically charged: Electra's refusal to interpret the recognition tokens "correctly" is a parody of the conventions of recognition scenes generally; but more specifically, her comment on the difficulty of making a footprint "in stony ground" (ἐν κραταιλέωι πέδωι, Eur. *El.* 534–535) can be construed as an authorial reflection on the challenges of producing novel poetry: "The metapoetic question implied … asks 'how can one make one's mark on established poetic tradition?'"[39] Lucian's text, similarly, features two footprints "on rock" (ἐπὶ πέτρας, *VH* 1.7) and an interplay of documents that, as I have argued elsewhere, are metapoetically charged, opening this adventure up to allegorical interpretation as a drama about the "crisis of posterity."[40] It is not surprising, for a work that is so candid about its own "secondariness," that this initial boundary is so heavily marked with the documentary vestiges of Lucian's literary forebears.

These documents reverberate as literary allusions in their own right, inscribing the works of earlier writers — especially Herodotus and Ctesias — into Lucian's work, just as he had promised in the prologue. As Manuel Baumbach and Peter von Möllendorff have argued, these allusions — which are recognizable to the reader of the *VH* — render the otherwise unknown landscape "readable." Consequently, the documentality of the scene operates on two levels: within the story world, where the inscription, footprints, and river attest to the gods' presence; and at the level of the text, where they attest to the intertextual presence of other literature.[41] This converts *True Stories* into a sort of literary-documentary archive: a text that contains multiple vestiges of other texts, somewhat like a prose *cento*, and — since Lucian expects his readers to recog-

---

39 Torrance 2013, 26; as she points out, this key phrase is thought to be an Aeschylean allusion, from the lost beginning of *Libation Bearers*. For the metapoetic reading of the scene more generally, see Torrance 2013, 14–31, with further references.
40 ní Mheallaigh 2014, 208–216. The expression "crisis of posterity" is from Whitmarsh 2001, 41 and *passim*.
41 Baumbach and von Möllendorff 2017, 84.

nize these allusions — also a quasi-documentary about the reading practices of the educated elite.⁴²

3 A Document in Outer Space: The Solar–Lunar Treaty (*VH* 1.20)

The next document we encounter is the alliance treaty between the Sun and the Moon. It marks the culmination of the Thucydidean-style narrative of the Lunar–Solar War,⁴³ and, uniquely in the *VH*, it is a legally binding document from the sphere of interstate relations. Lucian does not quote the inscription *verbatim*, presumably because it is imagined to be a longer text. Instead, he summarizes it in Thucydidean fashion:

Κατὰ τάδε συνθήκας ἐποιήσαντο Ἡλιῶται καὶ οἱ σύμμαχοι πρὸς Σεληνίτας καὶ τοὺς συμμάχους,⁴⁴ ἐπὶ τῷ καταλῦσαι μὲν Ἡλιώτας τὸ διατείχισμα καὶ μηκέτι ἐς τὴν σελήνην ἐσβάλλειν, ἀποδοῦναι δὲ καὶ τοὺς αἰχμαλώτους ῥητοῦ ἕκαστον χρήματος,⁴⁵ τοὺς δὲ Σελη-

---

42 For detailed analysis of different aspects of metapoetic themes in the *VH*, see von Möllendorff 2000, 512–538; Baumbach and von Möllendorff 2017, 80–85. On Lucian and *cento*-composition, see Baumbach and von Möllendorff 2017, 209–216.
43 It is generally agreed that there are similarities between Lucian's account of the war and Thucydidean battle narratives, though scholars differ in the weight that they assign to these similarities. Stengel's list of specific Thucydidean influences in the episode (1911, 29–30) is expanded further by Bartley (2003), who adopts the maximalist view, interpreting allusions as praise for specific aspects of the historian's technique, in contrast with the poor historiographical practice that Lucian parodies elsewhere. In contrast, Bompaire (1958, 640) is skeptical about particular Thucydidean allusions in the terms of the treaty: "En réalité les termes sont des plus généraux ... Il suffice de réminiscences vagues, à la portée de quiconque a un peu pratiqué l'histoire classique ..." See also von Möllendorff 2000, 134. My own position is that Lucian imparts to the episode a general Thucydidean flavor (especially in the sequence of events that lead to the cosmic war), without identifying specific Thucydidean passages as targets: i.e., pastiche rather than parody.
44 Ἡλιῶται καὶ οἱ σύμμαχοι πρὸς Σεληνίτας καὶ τοὺς συμμάχους: Ponderously symmetrical expressions like this are typical of treaty texts, e.g., Thuc. 5.18.4: ὅπλα δὲ μὴ ἐξέστω ἐπιφέρειν ... μήτε Λακεδαιμονίους καὶ τοὺς ξυμμάχους ἐπ' Ἀθηναίους καὶ τοὺς ξυμμάχους μήτε Ἀθηναίους καὶ τοὺς ξυμμάχους ἐπὶ Λακεδαιμονίους καὶ τοὺς ξυμμάχους. Compare, e.g., *IG* II³ 1 912, 70–72 (in square brackets); *IG* I³ 83, 4–6 (in square brackets).
45 ἀποδοῦναι δὲ καὶ τοὺς αἰχμαλώτους: The return of prisoners is also a condition of the Thirty Years' Peace (Thuc. 5.18.7): ἀποδόντων δὲ καὶ Ἀθηναῖοι ... καὶ τοὺς ἄνδρας ὅσοι εἰσὶ Λακεδαιμονίων ἐν τῷ δημοσίῳ τῷ Ἀθηναίων. Compare, e.g., *IG* I³ 118, 8–10 (partly in square brackets).

νίτας ἀφεῖναι μὲν αὐτονόμους τούς γε ἄλλους ἀστέρας,⁴⁶ ὅπλα δὲ μὴ ἐπιφέρειν τοῖς Ἡλιώταις, συμμαχεῖν δὲ τῇ ἀλλήλων, ἤν τις ἐπίῃ·⁴⁷ φόρον δὲ ὑποτελεῖν ἑκάστου ἔτους τὸν βασιλέα τῶν Σεληνιτῶν τῷ βασιλεῖ τῶν Ἡλιωτῶν δρόσου ἀμφορέας μυρίους, καὶ ὁμήρους δὲ σφῶν αὐτῶν δοῦναι μυρίους, τὴν δὲ ἀποικίαν τὴν ἐς τὸν Ἑωσφόρον κοινῇ ποιεῖσθαι, καὶ μετέχειν τῶν ἄλλων τὸν βουλόμενον·⁴⁸ ἐγγράψαι δὲ τὰς συνθήκας στήλῃ ἠλεκτρίνῃ καὶ ἀναστῆσαι ἐν μέσῳ τῷ ἀέρι ἐπὶ τοῖς μεθορίοις.⁴⁹ ὤμοσαν δὲ Ἡλιωτῶν μὲν Πυρωνίδης καὶ Θερείτης καὶ Φλόγιος, Σεληνιτῶν δὲ Νύκτωρ καὶ Μήνιος καὶ Πολυλάμπης.⁵⁰

The Heliots and their allies agreed a treaty on the following terms with the Selenites and their allies: on the condition that the Heliots dismantle the blockade wall, desist from further acts of aggression against the Moon, and return prisoners, each one for a specified sum; that the Selenites, in turn, allow the other stars to govern themselves and do not bear arms against the Heliots; and that they should be mutual allies, if anyone should attack. Furthermore, the King of the Selenites should pay ten thousand amphorae of dew each year as tribute to the King of the Heliots; he should surrender ten thousand of his own people as hostages; both parties should jointly undertake the colonization of the

---

46 ἀφεῖναι μὲν αὐτονόμους τούς γε ἄλλους ἀστέρας: The condition that the Selenites should respect the independence of other stars echoes the condition of the Thirty Years' Peace that both Athenians and Spartans should respect the independence of the panhellenic shrines (Thuc. 5.18.2: τὸ δ' ἱερὸν καὶ τὸν νεὼν τὸν ἐν Δελφοῖς τοῦ Ἀπόλλωνος καὶ Δελφοὺς αὐτονόμους εἶναι) and also that the autonomy of other city-states should be respected (Thuc. 5.18.5: τὰς δὲ πόλεις ... αὐτονόμους εἶναι); see also Thuc. 5.77.5. Compare, e.g., IG I³ 118, 10–12 (partly in square brackets).

47 ἐπὶ τῷ ... μηκέτι ἐς τὴν σελήνην ἐσβάλλειν; ὅπλα δὲ μὴ ἐπιφέρειν ... συμμαχεῖν δὲ τῇ ἀλλήλων, ἤν τις ἐπίῃ: Similar conditions (i.e., desisting from hostilities, plus defensive alliance) are stipulated as part of the Thirty Years' Peace (Thuc. 5.18.4) and the Peace of Nicias (Thuc. 5.23.1): ἢν [δέ] τινες ἴωσιν ἐς τὴν γῆν πολέμιοι τὴν Λακεδαιμονίων ... ὠφελεῖν Ἀθηναίους Λακεδαιμονίους. For a similar condition that the Athenians should desist from siege activity, cf. Thuc. 5.18.7: καὶ τοὺς ἐν Σκιώνῃ πολιορκουμένους Πελοποννησίων ἀφεῖναι. Compare, e.g., IG I³ 83, 8–10 (in square brackets); IG II³ 1 912, 74–81 (partly in square brackets).

48 μετέχειν τῶν ἄλλων τὸν βουλόμενον: The syntax mirrors a clause in the Thirty Years' Peace (Thuc. 5.18.2): θύειν καὶ ἰέναι καὶ μαντεύεσθαι καὶ θεωρεῖν ... τὸν βουλόμενον.

49 ἐγγράψαι τὰς συνθήκας στήλῃ ἠλεκτρίνῃ καὶ ἀναστῆσαι ἐν μέσῳ τῷ ἀέρι ἐπὶ τοῖς μεθορίοις: The stipulation that an inscription should be set up in a particular location is standard in treaties. Multiple copies of the inscription of the Thirty Years' Peace were to be erected at panhellenic sanctuaries (Olympia, Delphi, and the Isthmus), as well as in Sparta and Athens (Thuc. 5.18.10: στήλας δὲ στῆσαι Ὀλυμπίασι καὶ Πυθοῖ καὶ Ἰσθμοῖ καὶ Ἀθήνησιν ἐν πόλει καὶ ἐν Λακεδαίμονι ἐν Ἀμυκλαίῳ). Two copies of the Peace of Nicias were to be set up: one in the Temple of Apollo at Amyclae in Sparta, the other in the Temple of Athene at Athens (Thuc. 5.23.5: στήλην δὲ ἑκατέρους στῆσαι, τὴν μὲν ἐν Λακεδαίμονι παρ' Ἀπόλλωνι ἐν Ἀμυκλαίῳ, τὴν δὲ ἐν Ἀθήναις ἐν πόλει παρ' Ἀθηνᾷ). Compare, e.g., IG I³ 118 c. 26–28; IG II³ 1 912, 95–96 (partly in square brackets); AIUK 3 no. 1, lines 30–32.

50 ὤμοσαν: Another realistic detail; Lucian's names are transparently puns, but the formula itself is standard: cf. Thuc. 5.19.1; 5.24.1. Compare, e.g., IG I³ 118 c. 28–31.

Evening Star, and any of the others who so wished should participate; and they should inscribe the treaty on a column of electrum and set it up in mid-air at the borders. Sworn by: McFyre, Summers, and Burns (for the Heliots); Knightley, Mooney, and Allbright (for the Selenites).

The similarities with the (randomly selected) epigraphic sources that I have highlighted in the notes are due to the fact that Lucian models his treaty on Thucydides, who is himself using documentary sources and — as far as we can tell — tends to adhere closely to the wording of the documentary text.[51] In other words, Lucian's inscriptions are inspired by the historiographer; I do not think we need to envisage any special epigraphic research on his part.[52] But does this make his document a plausible imitation of a treaty text, or an artful Thucydidean pastiche? Actually, its status as document or literary text is less than clear.

One way or another, however, the net result is that Lucian's language smacks of documentary authenticity. Once again, we find a document located at a boundary (ἐπὶ τοῖς μεθορίοις) — this time, a political and territorial boundary between states. This too mirrors real-life practice, for the boundary lines between *poleis* were, in fact, a standard location for the posting of treaties in antiquity. The liminal location was both symbolic and practical, for it reflected the contractual nature of these public documents, and also ensured that they were visible to the peoples of each city as they were about to enter the other. (Additional copies were usually housed separately within temples inside the respective cities.) We therefore enjoy a pleasurable friction between the cunning verisimilitude of the document and the fantastical nature of its context and referent: the terms of the agreement and its very wording are boiler-plate material, yet we are in outer space, the signatories are denizens of the Sun and the Moon, and the pillar itself is to be set up (how?) in mid-air. By providing the precise names of those who swore the oath — something that treaties regularly do — Lucian enhances the reality effect, but this too is instantly undermined by the fantastical nomenclature, which is an obvious comical invention.

---

51 For Thucydides' quoting of treaties see Thuc. 4.118; 5.18–19; 5.23–24; 5.47; 5.77; 5.79. There is only one instance where the surviving epigraphic evidence enables us to check his citation practice (*IG* I³ 83; Thuc. 5.47). In this instance, the historian adheres closely to the wording and forms of the inscription. For a reconstruction of Thucydides' documentary research, see Lane Fox 2010.

52 This echoes Householder 1940, who, through a painstaking comparative analysis with the epigraphic evidence, arrives at a similar conclusion about the origins of the mock decrees in Lucian's works: that they are derived, directly or indirectly, from historiographical sources (e.g., Ephorus), or that they evoke documentary language in an impressionistic way, in a pastiche or "burlesque" of documentary language (Householder 1940, 211).

Zooming in closer on the physical details of the document, we find further conflicting messages. The prescription for inscribing and setting up the treaty is a clear gesture toward verisimilitude, and many ancient treaty inscriptions contain clauses exactly like this. However, the material to be used for this document immediately activates suspicions about its veracity; it is one of Niall Slater's aptly named "unreality effects."[53] Ancient treaties were inscribed typically on *stêlai* of bronze or stone.[54] Lucian's treaty, in contrast, is to be carved into a slab of ἤλεκτρον, which denotes either amber or electrum (an alloy of silver and gold). Throughout his works, Lucian shows himself highly attuned to the semiotics of material substances.[55] Although it is not clear which substance he had in mind here, either one would import an element of fantasy into the document, and both are semiotically charged in distinctive ways. Amber arguably suits Lucian's subversive purposes in the *VH*, since its mysterious provenance, which was bound up with questions about truth and lies, was a theme even in Lucian's own work.[56] But the metal alloy electrum is perhaps the more likely candidate in this case, since gold and silver represent the Sun and the Moon respectively, making the document — through a sort of political alchemy — embody the peaceful symbiosis of the two celestial states in a literal way.[57] This floating inscription might even represent a new star, a point of metallic light glittering in the sky. Albeit imaginary, Lucian's document demonstrates that the artifactual status of an inscription, the material on which it is carved, and its location are all co-conspirators in reinforcing, or complicating, the message of the text itself.[58]

---

[53] Slater 2009, 64.
[54] Bronze: e.g., *IG* II³ 1 912, alliance between Athens and Sparta 269–268 BCE. Stone: e.g., *AIUK* 3 no. 1, treaty between Athens and Halieis, prob. 424–423 BCE; *IG* I³ 118, ratification of Alcibiades' treaty with Selymbria, probably 408–407 BCE.
[55] See Romm 1990.
[56] See Georgiadou and Larmour 1998, 120–121 on amber as "a material which represents … lies and improbabilities." On the origins of amber, see Plin. *HN* 37.31–46; Luc. *Electr.* with Popescu 2013, 69–74.
[57] Philostratus (*VA* 5.5) mentions pillars of gold and silver in the sanctuary of Heracles in Gadeira. On the link between the celestial bodies and metals, which originated with the Babylonians, see Berthelot 1887, 92–104; Partington 1937–1938; Nilsson 1958; Evans 2004, esp. 4 and 15.
[58] On the "paratextual" aspects of epigraphical documents, see Fontanille 2005.

4 "Lucian was Here": A Documentary Gem (*VH* 2.28)

Much has already been written about the final document I wish to examine, the inscription at *VH* 2.28, in particular about Lucian's play with authority and his own name.[59] I shall not reiterate this here, but focus instead on the satisfying juxtaposition of the quotidian, even banal, nature of the inscription itself and the exquisite material on which it is (improbably) carved, and how Lucian once again creates a slide between the documentary and the literary. The making of the document is relayed as follows:

> τῇ δὲ ἐπιούσῃ ἐλθὼν πρὸς Ὅμηρον τὸν ποιητὴν ἐδεήθην αὐτοῦ ποιῆσαί μοι δίστιχον ἐπίγραμμα· καὶ ἐπειδὴ ἐποίησεν, στήλην βηρύλλου λίθου ἀναστήσας ἐπέγραψα πρὸς τῷ λιμένι. τὸ δὲ ἐπίγραμμα ἦν τοιόνδε·
> Λουκιανὸς τάδε πάντα φίλος μακάρεσσι θεοῖσιν
> εἶδέ τε καὶ πάλιν ἦλθε φίλην ἐς πατρίδα γαῖαν.

> But on the following day, I approached the poet Homer and asked him to compose a two-verse inscription for me. And when he had composed it, I set up and inscribed a pillar of beryl stone beside the harbor. The inscription was as follows:
> Lucian, dear to the blessed gods, saw all these things,
> and went back home again to his dear native land.

Lucian's verse inscription, situated here in the land of the dead, smacks of an epitaph. As Peter von Möllendorff argues, its location links it with the mighty inscribed arch which Alexander built after his own attempt to visit the Isles of the Blessed, at the spot that he believed marked the end of the world.[60] Lucian's monument, which is made of unbelievably costly material and is inscribed in verse by Homer himself, roundly trumps Heracles and Dionysus' comparatively "pathetic" pillar of bronze at 1.7, with its prose inscription that is barely legible. This is a literal version of Horace's famous claim *exegi monumentum aere perennius*.[61]

---

[59] See, e.g., Goldhill 2002, 65; ní Mheallaigh 2014, 255–258.
[60] *Hist. Alex.* 2.41 rec. β, with von Möllendorff 2000: 420. However, Alexander's inscription serves a different purpose to Lucian's *stêlê*, offering directions to future travelers, rather than recording the author's achievements: "Those who wish to enter the land of the blessed, go right so that you may avoid death" (οἱ βουλόμενοι εἰσελθεῖν ἐν τῇ μακάρων χώρᾳ, δεξιᾷ πορεύεσθε, μήποτε ἀπόλησθε).
[61] Hor. *Carm.* 3.30.1; von Möllendorff 2000, 420–421.

Lucian's deepening immersion in fantasy-land is mirrored in the increasingly exotic material of his documents: from bronze (on the threshold of the imaginary world), to gold and silver (in outer space), to a magnificent pillar of precious green stone here in the land of the dead. There were fabled parallels for such a marvelous artifact: the elder Pliny mentions an obelisk in the Temple of Zeus Ammon in Egypt and a large pillar (*stêlê*) in the Temple of Heracles at Tyre, both reportedly made of "emerald" (*smaragdus*), and Herodotus mentions the latter object too.[62] Usually, Lucian's pillar of beryl is explained by evoking the paradisiacal opulence of the Isle of the Blessed with its golden edifices, emerald walls, ivory pavements, and fragrant cinnamon timber, all awash with a river of myrrh (*VH* 2.11). There can be no doubt that this context is crucial, for nowhere else would one find rare substances like this put to such everyday use. Notably, the gods' temples are also made of beryl, thus connecting Lucian's inscription to the urban architecture and hinting, perhaps, at the immortality that he will ultimately share with the gods, as Rhadamanthus had predicted.[63]

But what has not, as far as I am aware, been noted before, is how Lucian's inscription also evokes the art of gem engraving, albeit in a grotesquely distorted fashion, for this is no miniaturist artwork carved onto a tiny area of precious stone, but a public declaration on a great slab of jewel, visible to all. More particularly (and more incongruously still), this combination of jewel and verse arguably evokes the Alexandrian poetics of Posidippus' *Lithika*, a collection of epigrams about jewels. In other words, this is not just a documentary moment in the fiction, but a rare metapoetical moment in Lucian's prose as well. This interpretation finds support in the intensely metapoetical environment on Lucian's Isle of the Blessed, where poetry and music pervade the soundscape, and the population consists largely of poets (and their characters).[64] The island itself is a version of the idealized afterlife landscapes imagined by Homer, Pindar, and others,[65] and even the activities are metapoetical in nature: for example, the poetic competition between Homer and Hesiod (a reenactment of the *Certamen Homeri et Hesiodi*) which Hesiod wins (though Lucian assures us that Homer is really robbed of the prize).[66]

---

62 Plin. *HN* 37.75; Hdt. 2.44.2; cf. Theophr. *De lap.* 24–25. As How and Wells 1928 note on the Herodotus passage, the material was more likely to be malachite or green jasper.
63 Von Möllendorff 2000, 421. For Rhadamanthus' prediction, see *VH* 2.27.
64 Kim 2010, 140–174.
65 The landscape and the symposium are described at *VH* 2.11–22. For similar landscapes, see Hom. *Od.* 4.563–568 (the Elysian Plain); Pind. *Ol.* 2.71–80. Further examples and discussion in Georgiadou and Larmour 1998, 182–184 and von Möllendorff 2000, 286–308.
66 *VH* 2.22, with Georgiadou and Larmour 1998, 205–206 and von Möllendorff 2000, 388–389.

The beryl pillar gains special significance in this metapoetical context. With their high value based on a combination of rarity and craftsmanship, their exquisite luster, varied hues, and multifaceted surfaces, gems were metaphors in antiquity for poetical refinement and intertextuality. As a gem that bears a Homeric poem, moreover, this inscription is an obvious intertextual artifact (or an artifactual intertext).[67] Symbolically, the absurdly huge chunk of beryl distends the precious poetics of the Alexandrians, most pointedly the lithopoetics of the Alexandrian gem poet *par excellence*, Posidippus.[68] At the same time, the verse inscription shrinks Homeric grandeur down to the smallest scale. Multiple layers of friction and paradox are generated by carving this tiny poem — composed by an epic poet — onto a gem of gigantic proportions. The result is a new and unlikely poetic hybrid of Homero-Hellenistic verse — a grotesque genre that befits Lucian's often grotesque fantasy with its populations of grossly magnified and cross-bred monsters.[69] In contrast to its Alexandrian models, Homer's flat verse is a flagrant waste of the material on which it is carved; Homer is obviously having a bad day (perhaps, in view of his defeat by Hesiod, a series of them).

But Lucian's gem evokes documentary practices too. Inscribed gems were used as seal or *sphragis* stones, whose imprint in malleable substances like clay or wax imparted to documents a guarantee of authenticity and authority.[70] As I have argued elsewhere, Lucian's inscription fulfills the function of the *sphragis* or the literary "seal," a *topos* in which an author effectively signed his name into his text in the first person and thereby documented his authorship.[71] The literary *sphragis* was often located at the start or end of the text.[72] However, the *VH* famously professes to be an incomplete text, which means that the end of Book 2 is (fictionally) not the end of the work as a whole. Lucian has therefore relocated his *sphragis* to another sort of "end" — the world of the dead. In Lucian's case, moreover, we have evidence of just such a sphragistic document that may have accompanied an ancient edition of his work: the "epigram of the book" that is preserved for us by Photius and ascribed to Lucian himself. From deep within the story world of the *VH*, Lucian's inscription calls to this peritextual document that seals the text as his own.

---

67 On another intertextual jewel, the engraved pantarbe ring in Heliodorus, see Bowie 1995.
68 On Posidippus' "lithopoetics," see Elsner 2014.
69 On the metapoetic significance of the hybrid body in Lucian's works, see ní Mheallaigh 2014, 1–38, with further references; Baumbach and von Möllendorff 2017, 171–216.
70 On seals and seal usage, see Plantzos 1999, 18–32. On the philosophical ramifications of seals, see Platt 2006.
71 ní Mheallaigh 2014, 171–183.
72 Kranz 1961, esp. 44–46.

It is not accidental, I think, that we encounter here yet another instance of a document that is located on a boundary — this time at the island's harbor. Documents are repeatedly associated with liminality in Lucian's imaginary world. As I have hinted above, the liminality that particularly fascinates me in this case pertains to the edges of the physical text, the peritext. This collective term denotes the features that cluster around borderlands of the text, such as its title, prologue, table of contents, author's name, and *sphragis*. If I am right that Lucian's document evokes the peritext specifically, we can draw two important conclusions from it.

First, by casting the *sphragis* into the form of a fictional inscription, Lucian implicitly acknowledges the documentary status of the peritext. In other words, Lucian recognizes that like all documents, the role of the peritext is to attest to the text, e.g., to its structure, theme, genre, and authorship, and to valorize it, to authenticate its credentials.[73] The peritext, moreover, has a contractual role with the reader, and as with all documents it is assumed (not always wisely) to be genuine and truthful. Lucian is not the only author to recognize the documentary quality of the peritext; many other authors do this implicitly by representing it in the form of documents such as letters. This points us to the likelihood that the ancient peritext evolved partly from documents that accompanied the text independently (dedicatory letters and so on), which gradually became physically integrated into the text, and sometimes were even absorbed into the fiction or story (the multiple imaginary letters cited in the peritext to Antonius Diogenes' novel *The Wonders beyond Thule* are an excellent illustration of this). This highlights the fact that the experience of reading literature is always partly documentary; the two types of text are entwined in what we might call the "bookscape," and readers intuitively (more or less) adjust their expectations as they maneuver through the different regions of the text. Documentality, in other words, is an integral part of the experience of literature and fiction.

The corollary of that idea leads me to the second conclusion. By taking a peritextual element that was, by default, assumed to be documentary and truthful, and relocating it into the middle of his fantasy where *nothing* is true, Lucian confronts the reader, once again, with the disturbing possibility that even the documentary parts of a text (like all documents) are not necessarily to be trusted. As I have argued also with the Lunar–Solar treaty, it is not clear precisely what sort of text Lucian's inscription *is*. The question is not just "Are its claims true or not?" (a question one can ask of every statement in *True Stories*), but,

---

[73] See DiGiulio in this volume on the documentary role of the table of contents in Gellius' work.

more specifically, "What type of text is this — a literary verse or an epigraphical document? Can it be both? How do we tell?" The fact that the inscription is composed by Homer intensifies its equivocality, so that we might legitimately read it as a poem: a tiny, trashy literary text. Or we might legitimately read it as an asseverative documentary text, albeit an exotic one. No matter what documentary practice we believe underlies the beryl pillar — and it evokes several (e.g., funerary epigraphy, boundary inscription, sealing practices, peritext) — this is obviously a playful gesture, as Lucian enfolds documentary practice into fiction, confronting us once again with that slender margin between the two.

5 Conclusion

Lucian's pseudo-history powerfully appropriates the world-creating authority of documents in order to enhance the believability of his fantasy world. In this respect, we can align him with the practices of the novelists who similarly buttress their fictions with documentary texts, especially inscriptions.[74] But Lucian also reveals himself in his works as an author who is captivated by fakery in all its manifestations, and the explicit aims of the *VH* as an exposé of specious truth-creating make his use of documents in this work distinctive: they are thickly entangled in the ruses of this most slippery of fictional texts, and are offered up for scrutiny under the most exacting metafictional eye. Lucian shows a nuanced interest in the semiotics of documents, paying attention not just to their texts, but to how they communicate through their artifactual status, materiality, and location as well.

Lucian's treatment of documents suggests an understanding that they are sites of negotiated meaning, where (as Kuin will show in the next chapter) the potential for deception is always lurking. As such, they appear to be microcosms for the tricky reading protocols of the *VH* itself. The margin between what constitutes "literature" and what constitutes a "document" is narrow indeed; at this point, we may remember that the *VH* presents itself as a quasi-documentary record of Lucian's greatest non-achievements, a sort of parodic *res non gestae* (*VH* 1.4). The implication of Lucian's "plausible lies" is a subversive one: if fiction can be documentary, cannot documents, in turn, be fictions?

---

74 See Kuin in this volume on Lucian's use of documents to create imaginary worlds; Sironen 2003 on inscriptions in the novels.

References

Avery, J.R. (1997), "Herodotean Presences in Lucian", unpublished PhD thesis, Yale University.
Barthes, R. (1989), *The Rustle of Language*, trans. Richard Howard, Berkeley/Los Angeles.
Bartley, A. (2003), "The Implications of the Influence of Thucydides on Lucian's 'Vera Historia'", in: *Hermes* 131, 222–234.
Baumbach, M./Möllendorff, P. von (2017), *Ein literarischer Prometheus. Lukian aus Samosata und die Zweite Sophistik*, Heidelberg.
Beschorner, A. (1992), *Untersuchungen zu Dares Phrygius*, Tübingen.
Berthelot, M. (1887), *Collection des anciens alchimistes grecs*, vol. 1, Paris.
Bompaire, J. (1958), *Lucien écrivain. Imitation et création*, Paris.
Bowie, E.L. (1995), "Names and a Gem: Aspects of Allusion in Heliodorus' *Aethiopica*", in: D. Innes/H. Hine/C. Pelling (eds.), *Ethics and Rhetoric: Classical Essays for Donald Russell on His Seventy-Fifth Birthday*, Oxford, 269–280.
Diggle, J. (ed.) (2005), *Theophrastus: Characters*, Cambridge.
Elsner, J. (1991), "Visual Mimesis and the Myth of the Real: Ovid's Pygmalion as Viewer", in: *Ramus* 20, 154–168.
Elsner, J. (2014), "Lithic Poetics: Posidippus and His Stones", in: *Ramus* 43, 152–172.
Evans, J. (2004), "The Astrologer's Apparatus: A Picture of Professional Practice in Greco-Roman Egypt", in: *JHA* 35, 1–44.
Ferraris, M. (2012), *Documentality: Why It Is Necessary to Leave Traces*, New York.
Ferraris, M. (2015), "Collective Intentionality or Documentality?", in: *Philosophy and Social Criticism* 41, 423–433.
Fields, D. (2013), "The Reflections of Satire: Lucian and Peregrinus", in: *TAPhA* 143, 213–245.
Fontanille, J. (2005), "Du support matériel au support formel", in: M. Arabyan/I. Klock-Fontanille (eds.), *L'écriture entre support et surface*, Paris, 183–200.
Fusillo, M. (1999), "The Mirror of the Moon: Lucian's *A True Story* — From Satire to Utopia", in: S. Swain (ed.), *Oxford Readings in the Greek Novel*, Oxford, 351–381.
Georgiadou, A./Larmour, D.H.J. (1994), "Lucian and Historiography: 'De Historia Conscribenda' and 'Verae Historiae'", in: *ANRW* II.34.2, 1448–1509.
Georgiadou, A./Larmour, D.H.J. (1998), *Lucian's Science Fiction Novel, True Histories: Interpretation and Commentary*, Leiden.
Goldhill, S. (2002), "Becoming Greek, with Lucian", in: *Who Needs Greek? Contests in the Cultural History of Hellenism*, Cambridge, 60–107.
Hall, J. (1981), *Lucian's Satire*, New York.
Hansen, W. (2003), "Strategies of Authentication in Ancient Popular Literature", in: S. Panayotakis/M. Zimmerman/W. Keulen (eds.), *The Ancient Novel and Beyond*, Leiden/Boston, 301–313.
Householder, F. (1940), "The Mock Decrees in Lucian", *TAPhA* 71, 199–216.
How, W.W./Wells, J. (1928), *A Commentary on Herodotus*, Oxford.
Jones, C.P. (1986), *Culture and Society in Lucian*, Cambridge, MA.
Kim, L. (2010), *Homer between History and Fiction in Imperial Greek Literature*, Cambridge.
Kranz, W. (1961), "Sphragis: Ichform und Namensiegel als Eingangs- und Schlußmotiv antiker Dichtung", in: *RhM* 104, 3–46.
Lane Fox, R. (2010), "Thucydides and Documentary History", in: *CQ* 60, 11–29.
Macleod, M.D. (1979), "Lucian's activities as a ΜΙΣΑΛΑΖΩΝ", in: *Philologus* 123, 326–328.

Merkle, S. (1989), *Die Ephemeris belli Troiani des Diktys von Kreta*, Frankfurt am Main.
Möllendorff, P. von (2000), *Auf der Suche nach der verlogenen Wahrheit. Lukians Wahre Geschichten*, Tübingen.
Morgan, J.R. (2013), "Love from beyond the grave: the epistolary ghost-story in Phlegon of Tralles", in: O. Hodkinson/P.A. Rosenmeyer/E. Bracke (eds.), *Epistolary Narratives in Ancient Greek Literature*, Leiden/Boston, 293–322.
Mossman, J. (2006), "Travel Writing, History, and Biography", in: B. McGing/J. Mossman (eds.), *The Limits of Ancient Biography*, Swansea, 281–303.
ní Mheallaigh, K. (2008), "Pseudo-Documentarism and the Limits of Ancient Fiction", in: *AJPh* 129, 403–431.
ní Mheallaigh, K. (2014), *Reading Fiction with Lucian: Fakes, Freaks and Hyperreality*, Cambridge.
ní Mheallaigh, K. (2018), "Lucian's Alexander: Technoprophecy, Thaumatology and the Poetics of Wonder", in: M. Gerolemou (ed.), *Recognizing Miracles in Antiquity and Beyond*, Berlin/Boston, 225–256.
Nilsson, M.P. (1958), "Die babylonische Grundlage der griechischen Astrologie", *Eranos* 56, 1–11.
Oakley, S.P. (2013), "C. Licinius Macer", in: T.J. Cornell (ed.), *The Fragments of the Roman Historians*, vol. 1, Oxford, 320–331.
Ober, J. (1995), "Greek *Horoi*: Artifactual Texts and the Contingency of Meaning", in: D.B. Small (ed.), *Methods in the Mediterranean: Historical and Archaeological Views on Texts and Archaeology*, Leiden/New York, 91–123.
Partington, J.R. (1937–1938), "The Origins of the Planetary Symbols for the Metals", in: *Ambix* 1, 61–64.
Peirce, C.S. (1998), "What Is a Sign?" (*c.* 1894), in: The Peirce Edition Project (ed.), *The Essential Peirce: Selected Philosophical Writings*, vol. 2, Bloomington, 4–10.
Plantzos, D. (1999), *Hellenistic Engraved Gems*, New York.
Platt, V. (2006), "Making an Impression: Replication and the Ontology of the Graeco-Roman Seal Stone", in: *Art History* 29, 233–257.
Popescu, V. (2013), "Paradoxography and the Aesthetics of Paradox in Lucian's *Prolaliai*", in: *Nuntius Antiquus* 9(2), 57–86.
Romm, J. (1990), "Wax, Stone, and Promethean Clay: Lucian as Plastic Artist", in: *ClAnt* 9, 74–98.
Rutherford, I. (1998), "Island of the Extremity: Space, Language and Power in the Pilgrimage Traditions of Philae", in: D. Frankfurter (ed.), *Pilgrimage and Holy Space in Late Antique Egypt*, Leiden, 229–256.
Saïd, S. (1994), "Lucien ethnographe", in: A. Billault (ed.), *Lucien de Samosate. Actes du colloque international de Lyon organisé au Centre d'études romaines et gallo-romaines les 30 septembre–1er octobre 1993*, Lyon, 149–170.
Schmidt, T.S. (1999), *Plutarque et les barbares. La rhétorique d'une image*, Leuven.
Sironen, E. (2003), "The Role of Inscriptions in Greco-Roman Novels", in: S. Panayotakis/M. Zimmerman/W. Keulen (eds.), *The Ancient Novel and Beyond*, Leiden/Boston, 289–314.
Slater, N. (2009), "Reading Inscriptions in the Ancient Novel", in: M. Paschalis/S. Panayotakis/G. Schmeling (eds.), *Readers and Writers in the Ancient Novel*, Groningen, 64–78.
Speyer, W. (1970), *Bücherfunde in der Glaubenswerbung der Antike. Hypomnemata* 24, Göttingen.
Speyer, W. (1971), *Die literarische Fälschung im heidnischen und christlichen Altertum. Ein Versuch ihrer Deutung*, Munich.

Stengel, A. (1911), *De Luciani Veris historiis*, Berlin.
Stoneman, R. (1992), "Oriental Motifs in the *Alexander Romance*", in: *Antichthon* 26, 95–113.
Stoneman, R. (1995), "Riddles in Bronze and Stone: Monuments and Their Interpretation in the *Alexander Romance*", in: *Groningen Colloquia on the Novel* 6, 159–170.
Strohmaier, G. (1976), "Übersehenes zur Biographie Lukians", in: *Philologus* 120, 117–122.
Terrone, E. (2014), "Traces, Documents, and the Puzzle of 'Permanent Acts'," in: *The Monist* 97.2, 161–178.
Torrance, I. (2013), *Metapoetry in Euripides*, Oxford.
Walt, S. (1997), *Der Historiker C. Licinius Macer. Einleitung, Fragmente, Kommentar*, Stuttgart.
Whitmarsh, T. (2001), *Greek Literature and the Roman Empire: The Politics of Imitation*, Oxford.
Whitmarsh, T. (2002), "Alexander's Hellenism and Plutarch's Textualism", in: *CQ* 52, 174–192.
Williamson, C. (1987), "Monuments of Bronze: Roman Legal Documents on Bronze Tablets", in: *ClAnt* 6, 160–183.
Zadorojnyi, A.V. (2013), "Shuffling Surfaces: Epigraphy, Power, and Integrity in the Graeco-Roman Narratives", in: P. Liddel/P. Low (eds.), *Inscriptions and Their Uses in Greek and Latin Literature*, Oxford, 365–386.

Part II: **Documentary Communities and Landscapes**

Inger N.I. Kuin
Cities Full of Words: Illiteracy and Epigraphy in Lucian of Samosata

Abstract: Even as the ancient cityscape surrounded Greeks and Romans with texts, interactions with these texts and their authority varied based on the degree of literacy of the observer. Lucian's use of inscriptions, and the challenges that they present in his fictions, provide a starting point for reconstructing the lived experiences of illiterate individuals in the cities of the Greek-speaking Roman East. The differing receptions that realistic and fantastical inscriptions receive in the Lucianic corpus reveal a paradox in Lucian's documentary messaging: though illiteracy hardly marginalized Greek-speakers economically or politically, it did render them vulnerable to deceptions, since even those who could read had to learn to fear the snares and seductions of written records. Unease with (seemingly) authoritative, public writing is, for Lucian, justified and can be shared among those who cannot read by themselves and those who can.

The Trojan War started at the wedding of Thetis and Peleus. All the gods had been invited, except Eris. In revenge she threw a golden apple among the gods on which was written: "for the most beautiful goddess." Hera, Aphrodite, and Athena immediately started fighting over the apple, and Zeus decided to postpone and delegate the decision: Paris would award the apple at a later time, with all due consequences.

The story of the apple and the beauty contest of the goddesses is surely one of the greatest hits of classical mythology. Yet, despite its familiarity, the apple entered the Trojan narrative as beauty prize for the goddesses only late in the literary tradition — certainly not before the Hellenistic period — though it is attested in Greek art as early as the archaic period.[1] The first author to mention that the apple had writing on it is Lucian of Samosata, who lived and worked in

---

I would like to thank the anonymous reviewers of the press, my co-editors, and Karen ní Mheallaigh for their helpful comments and suggestions.

1 Foster 1899; see also Littlewood 1968. The judgment is engraved on an ivory comb found at the sanctuary of Artemis Orthia in Sparta, first published in Dawkins 1929. Ps.-Hyg. *Fab.* 92 and Ps.-Apollod. *Epit.* 3 both connect the elements of the goddess Eris, the apple, and the judgment of Paris, but the apple does not yet have writing on it.

https://doi.org/10.1515/9783110791914-005

the second century CE. Lucian mentions the inscribed apple in no fewer than three of his works. In *Dialogi marini* (*Dialogues of the Sea Gods*), a nymph describes to another nymph how Eris threw an apple of solid gold into the crowd at the wedding of Thetis and Peleus. The nymph adds that on it "was written 'Let the beautiful one take me'" (*Dial. mar. 7*).[2] In *Dearum iudicium* (*Judgment of the Goddesses*), after Hermes hands the apple to Paris, he reads the (identical) inscription out loud to himself — and responds with despair at having to decide who will get the prize (*Dear. iud. 7*). In *Symposium sive Lapithae* (*Banquet*), a letter from a slighted philosopher is read out loud by his servant at the dinner party to which he was not invited and causes a brawl among those who are in attendance (*Symp.* 21–33). The character Lycinus comments: "It seemed to me that Hetoimocles by throwing his letter into the middle just like some apple caused woes no smaller than those of the *Iliad*" (*Symp.* 35).[3]

It is quite possible that Lucian derived the idea of putting writing on the apple of Eris from elsewhere.[4] However, regardless of whether it was a borrowing or his own invention, adding text to the prize apple suited particularly well the author's broader preoccupation with writing, inscriptions, and the cognitive and social aspects of dealing with documents. Even without writing, the apple is a document in the sense that, like any prize, it is a record of the outcome of the competition: possession of the prize serves as proof of the victory.[5] By inscribing the apple in his rendition of the Eris story, Lucian emphasizes its documentary status: the apple is a beauty prize *because* it says so.

The comparison of the slighted philosopher's letter with the apple in *Symposium* suggests that, for Lucian, the element of writing was crucial to the story of the judgment of Paris: the letter becomes the apple when its text is read out loud by someone, and, just as in *Dearum Iudicium*, causes bitter conflict among those present. Writing, be it in a mythical setting on Mount Ida or at a typical dinner party of second-century CE intellectuals, affects life.

---

2 ἐπεγέγραπτο δὲ 'ἡ καλὴ λαβέτω'. Translations are my own throughout.
3 καὶ ὁ Ἑτοιμοκλῆς τοίνυν ἐδόκει μοι τὴν ἐπιστολὴν ἐμβαλὼν εἰς τὸ μέσον ὥσπερ τι μῆλον οὐ μείω τῆς Ἰλιάδος κακὰ ἐξεργάσασθαι.
4 Such borrowing could be either of the motif of an inscribed apple of Eris specifically, from a source now lost to us, or of a different inscribed apple, for instance from the story of Acontius and Cydippe, told in Ov. *Her.* 20.237–242; 21.103–128. For post-Lucianic iterations of the apple of Eris with writing on it see e.g., Philostratus' *Epistolae* 1.62, and the narration of Paris' abduction of Helen among Libanius' *Progymnasmata*, Gibson 2008, 30–31.
5 On "document" as a category, see Arthur-Montagne, DiGiulio, and Kuin in this volume and n. 7 below.

Ferraris's concept of documentality assumes that documents can range from spoken promises — as long as they are remembered — to DNA-carrying hairs at a crime scene (which, when they become evidence, become documents), to the legal texts producing and sustaining international governance and business. Against this background, to say that we live in a world shaped by documents is to insist on a false dichotomy: our world is constituted by memories, traces, and soon-to-be traces. Literary texts represent a special type of document, because they have the capability to create discrete, imagined worlds, which can be reflective of the real world, but cannot be contained by it.[6] When Lucian shows how writing affects life, he does this within the imagined worlds created by his literary works. In this chapter, I set out to investigate in what ways Lucian's representation of one specific group of documents — epigraphic objects — reflects how his contemporaries experienced such objects in real life.[7]

1 Reconstructing Illiteracy

While the first part of this volume has focused on the theoretical approach to documents, in the second part we turn to the lived experience of documentation in the Roman Empire. Likewise, whereas Karen ní Mheallaigh showed how Lucian places imagined epigraphic objects in the service of creating a fictitious landscape shaped by its engagement with both literary predecessors and contemporary documentary practices, my approach goes in the opposite direction, as it were, in trying to reconstruct attitudes and responses to documentary practices in the everyday life of urbanized Romans from his fictions. In this chapter I

---

[6] Ferraris 2012; see also Arthur-Montagne, DiGiulio, and Kuin in this volume. On documents and traces, see Terrone 2014; also Arthur-Montagne in this volume. Literary works like the writings of Lucian can be considered documents-as-social-acts in the sense that they were shared (orally and in writing); additionally, as scholars we turn them into documents by studying their contents to reconstruct elements of Greco-Roman intellectual, social, and cultural history. I agree with Hedrick's (2015) objections to the distinction between "literary" and "documentary" as categories to classify ancient texts, which is why this chapter emphasizes the documentary aspects of (our use of) literary texts, alongside Lucian's interest in employing the documentary register within his literary imagination.

[7] For this methodology compare Zadorojnyi 2013, 366–367: "The overt or implicit reflection on inscriptions by the Graeco-Roman literati gives, in turn, the insider's view of the communicative potentialities of epigraphy qua medium for sociocultural practices." Additionally, both Greek (Slater 1996) and Roman comedy (Marshall 2006, 197–202) have been used as sources for ancient attitudes towards literacy.

analyze Lucian's employment of epigraphic objects in an attempt to think through what it might have been like to be (partially) illiterate in the text-rich cityscapes inhabited by Lucian and his contemporaries. I will argue that Lucian's manipulation of epigraphic objects in his imaginary worlds indirectly shows us something about the everyday experience of living with such texts, both from the perspective of those who could read them, and from the perspective of those who could not. The choice for this circuitous approach is justified by the absence, to the best of my knowledge, of first-hand accounts of experiencing illiteracy — an absence, of course, that should not surprise us, given the overrepresentation in remaining ancient sources of the wealthy, the well-educated, and the powerful.

There are several reasons why Lucian is a particularly suitable author for an attempt to reconstruct the experience of (il)literacy through fiction. He lived and worked during the height of the so-called epigraphic habit: the high concentration of inscriptions that were set up during the first three centuries CE as compared to the overall Greek and Latin epigraphic "output" of the ancient Mediterranean.[8] As others have noted, Lucian showed remarkable interest in inscriptions, and in other types of written documents as well.[9] Additionally, numerous programmatic moments in his writing show, as I have argued elsewhere, that he wrote his pieces primarily with performance in mind, even if they would subsequently be circulated in written form. He wanted to reach non-elite audiences as much as elite audiences, and the content and style of his works indicate that he probably succeeded in doing so.[10] When Lucian alludes to any written text (epigraphic or not) in his performances, he does so knowing that many members in his audience would not themselves have been able to access such texts fully without assistance from others.

The remainder of this chapter will be organized as follows. In the second section I consider the difficult question of literacy levels in the ancient world, modern definitions of literacy, and the social consequences of illiteracy in Lucian's time, as far as those can be reconstructed. The third and fourth sections analyze the epigraphic objects that occur in Lucian's works. Epigraphic objects

---

8 Mrozek 1973, 1988; MacMullen 1982; Meyer 1990; Woolf 1996. See now Beltrán Lloris 2014 for a strong methodological critique of the notion of the "epigraphic habit."
9 Rosenmeyer 2001, 133–135. See also Sironen 2003; ní Mheallaigh 2008; ní Mheallaigh 2014, 171–183, 208–216, 250–258; ní Mheallaigh in this volume. If the information Lucian gives us about this is genuine, it may not be too far-fetched to connect the author's interest in inscriptions and other documents to his work as a legal secretary in the imperial service in Egypt: see Haensch 2008, 90–99; Nesselrath 2018, 184–186.
10 Kuin forthcoming.

are here defined as texts written on a hard surface, and are, for the reasons explained above, considered documents. In the third section I discuss realistic epigraphic objects, which, even if they may not strictly speaking be historical, could well have occurred in everyday life. In the fourth section I discuss unrealistic epigraphic objects, which are situated in fantastic settings far removed from everyday life. The reason for making this distinction is that Lucian the author has his narrators present these two groups of epigraphic objects differently: Realistic epigraphic objects are cast primarily as deceitful or fake within the narrative, while unrealistic ones typically go unquestioned, and are used by the narrator as proof of the validity of the fantasy world in which they occur. In the final section of the chapter I interpret this apparent paradox in how epigraphic objects are featured in Lucian's work as a reflection, on the author's part, on the experiences and challenges of his (partially) illiterate contemporaries living in cities that were full of writing.

2 The Experience of (Il)Literacy

What percentage of the population in antiquity was able to read and write? This question has been the topic of heated debate ever since the publication of William Harris's provocative 1989 book, *Ancient Literacy*, which argued that, across the Roman Empire, literacy was well under 20 percent, and locally as low as 5 percent. According to Harris, because economic and political systems did not require that most citizens be able to read and write, there was no organized school system, and writing materials were not cheaply and widely available, the vital preconditions for mass literacy were always absent in the Greco-Roman world.[11]

Challenges to Harris's argument have taken aim at his transposition of modern statistics to ancient contexts, and at his views about the cost of writing materials and the existence of schools.[12] Another strand of criticism has pointed to the different forms of literacies, semi-literacies, or functional literacies that existed in the ancient world. In antiquity, reading and writing often did not go together: many people could read, but not write, and Greg Woolf has argued

---

11 Harris 1989, 12.
12 On the use of modern statistics, see Corbier 1991. On writing materials, see Bowman 1991, 1994; Bowman and Thomas 1983–2011; Cribiore 2001, 147–159. On schools, see Cribiore 2001, 21–34.

that Harris was looking at the wrong kind of literacy altogether.[13] The vast majority of people did not need to be able to read and write, but were instead reliant on and conversant in certain graphic systems: numbers, symbols, and diagrams. Once literacy is defined as the ability to use the graphic systems necessary for everyday life, according to Woolf, practically everyone in antiquity was literate.

But even if most people were indeed able to navigate their daily lives using graphic systems other than writing and reading Greek or Latin, this tells just part of the story. The majority of the population in the Roman Empire was at most only orally proficient in the political, legal, and literary languages of the day. What was it like for individuals to live in an inscribed cityscape without being able to read the texts that surrounded them? Research has shown that, in most modern societies, not being able to read or write is typically experienced as embarrassing and isolating.[14] How does this compare to illiteracy in ancient contexts?

In the documentary papyri of Ptolemaic and Roman Egypt illiteracy is a recurring topic, when parties to the transaction are said not to have written or signed the document themselves, but through a proxy (either a professional scribe, a relative, or a business associate) on account of being unable to read and write. On the basis of these texts, Herbert Youtie concludes that in Egypt "the illiterate person was able to function in a broad variety of occupations, to be recognized as a respectable member of his class, to attain financial success, to hold public office, to associate on equal terms with his literate neighbors"; consequently, "illiteracy did not induce anxiety."[15] This situation has been contrasted favorably with modern conditions,[16] but also with the state of affairs in the ancient urban society of classical Greece and Rome, where literacy supposedly *was* a dividing line in terms of social status and wealth.[17]

Was Egypt indeed a special case, and was literacy only a strong social marker in cities outside Egypt? The unevenness in the types of sources that are

---

13 Corbier 1991; Lane Fox 1994; Johnson and Parker 2009; Woolf 2015. Recently published herders' graffiti from sixth century BCE Attica attest to rudimentary literacy among non-aristocratic communities at a very early date, Langdon 2015.
14 On the Netherlands, see Buisman and Houtkoop 2014; on Europe, see Desjardins and Schuller 2006; on Canada, see Canadian Council on Learning 2007.
15 Youtie 1975, 201, 221.
16 Youtie 1975, 201; see also Kraus 2000, 342.
17 Kraus 2000, 323 relies on passages from Greek philosophy and rhetoric, and from Latin rhetoric and historiography where literacy is connected to Greekness and Romanness respectively, and to human virtue in general.

available for Egypt as compared to the rest of the Roman Empire or (pre-Roman) Greece makes it all but impossible to answer this question in a satisfactory way. Records of everyday transactions like the ones preserved in large quantities among the Egyptian papyri are only sparsely available for other parts of the Roman Empire.[18] But even in Egypt illiteracy could still render individuals vulnerable, as is attested by the oft-cited papyrus *P.Oxy.* 71. In this text a fourth-century CE priest named Aurelius Demetrius complains to the prefect of Egypt about a *gymnasiarch* named Sotas, with whom he had deposited some money. Sotas, says Demetrius, had tried to cheat him out of his money, by abusing the fact that he, Demetrius, is illiterate.[19]

The story of Demetrius can be compared to a famous anecdote in Plutarch's *Life of Aristides*. Aristides son of Lysimachus was ostracized in 482 BCE.[20] Plutarch describes how "an illiterate and very rustic man" (τινα τῶν ἀγραμμάτων καὶ παντελῶς ἀγροίκων) asked the person sitting next to him to write the name "Aristides" on his ostracon. The neighbor turns out to be Aristides, but instead of revealing his identity he asks the illiterate man why he wants to ostracize Aristides. Even though the answer is superficial and irksome — the farmer says he is tired of hearing people call Aristides "the Just" all the time — Aristides dutifully writes his own name on the ostracon (Plut. *Arist.* 7).

Plutarch's anecdote may well be apocryphal, and we should be hesitant to draw any conclusions from it on the much-debated topic of ostracism as an indication of mass or high literacy in ancient Athens.[21] Nonetheless, the story is highly relevant for the question of how illiteracy was experienced. The anecdote functions like a joke where the reader's expectation is reversed. We are meant to think that Aristides will retaliate: he will deceive the man by putting a different name on the ostracon. The illiterate farmer would have no way of knowing whether or not Aristides acted in good faith. The punchline is that Aristides,

---

18 But, for an example from Herculaneum, see Bodel in this volume; for an example from Pompeii, see *TPSulp.* 46, with text and translation at Du Plessis 2012, 188, and also, in a bilingual Greek and Latin inscription, *AE* 1984, 0227; for an example from Syria, see *PLond.* 2.229. In all of these examples one of the parties to a contract is said to "not know *litteras.*" None of the texts provide further details on the illiterate party to the contract.
19 *P.Oxy.* I 71, col. 1, lines 9–11: ἐπ<ε>ιδὴ τοίνυν μετῄειν αὐτὸν τὰ χρήματα ἐπὶ τοῦ στρατηγήσαντος Ἥρωνος, ἐπ<ε>ιράθη μέν τινα κακουργίαν ἐπὶ ἀποστερέσι τῇ ἡμετέρᾳ ποιήσασθαι διὰ τὸ ἀγράμματόν με εἶναι ... See also Grenfell and Hunt 1898, 131–135; Youtie 1975, 206; Kraus 2000, 327.
20 Cf. [Arist.] *Ath. Pol.* 22.7. Over a hundred ostraca with his name have been found in the Agora and the Ceramicus: Sickinger 2017, 447.
21 Harris 1989, 53–55; Coulet 1996, 99; Missiou 2011, 58–70; Sickinger 2017, 460–463.

despite the man's ill will toward him, does write down his own name on the potsherd. The anecdote shows that Plutarch and his first-century CE audience members were keenly aware of the risks, dependencies, and vulnerabilities that were associated with being illiterate in a literate society.

Even if the vast majority of its members could not read or write in the traditional sense, I believe that the world of Plutarch and of Lucian can indeed be described as a literate society, because "it uses the written word in some of its vital functions."[22] The bureaucracy of the Empire relied on the written word, while (inscribed) texts also played a large role in other spheres, including religion.[23] Inscriptions and painted words in public spaces were texts that everybody was confronted with on a daily basis. Epigraphic literacy differed from being able to read generally, in that it "required skills (for instance, contextual decoding of abbreviations and scripts) that were both greater than and less than those required for 'literacy' in its normal sense."[24] Reading inscriptions demands a lower level of literacy skills than, say, reading the *Aeneid*, but it also requires additional, specialized knowledge.[25] In modern societies illiteracy is a marginal phenomenon, and this in large part contributes to the social stigma associated with it. It seems likely that, simply because illiteracy was far more widespread in the Roman world, in Egypt, and elsewhere, it would have affected people's status much less.[26] Yet, despite this important difference, two features are shared by modern and ancient illiterates. First, not being able to read and write in a literate society, as defined above, makes individuals vulnerable and dependent. Secondly, because of this vulnerability associated with the inaccessibility of text, written documents can appear alienating or intimidating to individuals who are mostly or entirely illiterate.[27] Lucian's complex represen-

---

22 Macdonald 2005, 49; see also Bagnall 2011, 2–3.
23 For the latter see, e.g., Barchiesi, Rüpke, and Stephens 2004.
24 Bodel 2015, 751.
25 One of Petronius' characters famously says that he may have little education, but that he *does* know inscribed, "stony letters"; *Sat.* 58: *Non didici geometrias, critica et alogias nenias, sed lapidarias litteras scio, partes centum dico ad aes, ad pondus, ad nummum.*
26 Among the competitive, cultured elites of the Roman cities, an insufficient knowledge of literature in comparison to one's peers was sometimes also understood as illiteracy. This kind of illiteracy did carry considerable stigma within the social context of the elite: see Youtie 1975; Kaster 1998, 35–50; Kraus 2000.
27 Attention has been drawn recently to the ability of inscriptions to communicate meaning through their non-textual features (layout, design, size, location, etc.) without being read, as well as the fact that locals would be able to learn the contents orally. See, e.g., Williamson 1987; Beard 1991; Linders 1992; Eastmond 2015; Kamphorst this volume. However, as Hedrick 1994 has pointed out, public written documents, especially those of a political nature, always

tation of epigraphic objects, to which we will now turn, is informed by and responding to precisely these kinds of vulnerabilities.

3 Realistic and Deceitful

As mentioned, Lucian of Samosata lived during the period in which scholars have located the peak of the epigraphic habit, and epigraphic objects occur regularly in his writings. He performed his works in front of a mixed audience — in terms of wealth, social status, and education — containing individuals who had no or limited proficiency in reading. There are several programmatic moments in his corpus that attest to this performance scenario, but probably the strongest evidence comes from *Apologia* (*Self-Defense*), which is a *recusatio* for another piece by Lucian, *De mercede conductis* (*On Hirelings in Great Houses*). The latter was performed first in front of a large audience consisting of non-elite and elite listeners. Subsequently, some learned Lucian fans decided to obtain a copy of the text to read at home.

In *Apologia* the following is said about *De mercede conductis* (*Apol.* 3):

> πάλαι μέν, ὦ φιλότης, ὡς εἰκός, εὐδοκίμηταί σοι τουτὶ τὸ σύγγραμμα καὶ ἐν πολλῷ πλήθει δειχθέν, ὡς οἱ τότε ἀκροασάμενοι διηγοῦντο, καὶ ἰδίᾳ παρὰ τοῖς πεπαιδευμένοις, ὁπόσοι ὁμιλεῖν αὐτῷ καὶ διὰ χειρὸς ἔχειν ἠξίωσαν.[28]

> My friend, this piece of yours, as is right, has long been admired, both when it was performed before a great crowd, as those who then heard it told me, and privately among educated people, who have chosen to read the work, and to hold onto it.

The sequence of events described here would have been similar *mutatis mutandis* for most if not all of Lucian's works.[29] Whenever Lucian refers to epigraphic

---

have an exclusionary effect: inscriptions set up in public spaces serve as a reminder of the distinction between those who can read them independently and those who cannot, which largely (though not fully) maps on to the distinction between those who are in positions of political power and those who are not.

28 Cf. Hafner 2017, 78–79. *Apologia* is an imagined dialogue between the first-person narrator, who is presented as also being the author of *De mercede conductis*, and his friend Sabinus, who is accusing the narrator of hypocrisy because he has taken on a position in the Roman service in Egypt despite his critique of Greeks working for Romans in *De mercede conductis*. In the passage cited, the narrator is quoting this Sabinus.

29 Compare the remarks in *Im.* 9, *Pro Im.* 14, and *Sat.* 23. On Lucianic performance, see Bellinger 1928; Ureña Bracero 1995; Kuin forthcoming.

objects or other types of documents in his performances he does so knowing that different groups among his audience would have different experiences with and attitudes toward such texts, depending on their level of reading proficiency, which could in turn affect their responses.

By far the most egregious user of realistic but deceitful epigraphic objects and other documents in Lucian's works is Alexander of Abonuteichus, the possibly historical holy man, whose life the author recounts in the dramatic biography and takedown *Alexander Pseudomantis* (*Alexander or the False Prophet*).[30] The work itself poses as a document, namely a letter to an Epicurean named Celsus, and features many instances of fake or misleading writing. The letter-writer and narrator is belatedly revealed as being named "Lucian" (*Alex.* 55), but he should by no means be identified with Lucian the author.[31] To prepare for his arrival in Abonuteichus, Alexander has bronze tablets inscribed, announcing that Asclepius and Apollo will take up residence in Abonuteichus soon, and buries them in the temple of Apollo in Chalcedon. These tablets — strongly reminiscent of Joseph Smith's tablets, which are considered scripture by Mormons[32] — are duly discovered and taken to be genuine by the locals, who immediately start building a temple (*Alex.* 10).

Alexander arranges for his arrival to coincide with the promulgation of two oracular texts, one of which purports to derive from the Sybilline books, affirming his divinity and healing powers. The oracles become the talk of the town, and significantly increase the buzz around the newly arrived prophet. The narrator emphasizes the importance of the oracular writings in the successful manipulation of the locals: "Those miserable Paphlagonians, although they knew (εἰδότες) that his parents were insignificant and humble, trusted (ἐπίστευον) the oracle" (*Alex.* 11). The people of Abonuteichus willfully ignore their own knowledge, allowing themselves to be convinced by the authority of written oracles (and fake inscribed tablets) instead.[33]

The focal point of Alexander's cult is its production of oracular responses to people's questions. Petitioners submit sealed questions that Alexander answers either in written form, penned on the outside of the sealed questions, or as autophones, that is, by ventriloquizing through his divine snake-with-puppet-

---

30 See now Bremmer 2017 for the debate over the historicity of Alexander.
31 Branham 1984; cf. Elm von der Osten 2006, 144–147; Van Nuffelen 2011, 186–188.
32 See Jones 1986, 136 n. 15; Victor 1997, 137. See ní Mheallaigh (2018, 229) for several ancient *comparanda*.
33 In *Alex.* 11 both texts are called "an oracle" (χρησμός), but the first one is also described as "speaking" (λέγων). See Hdt. 8.136 for another passage where λέγων describes a written oracular text.

head Glycon. The autophones were given only to rich and powerful people (*Alex.* 26). In both cases, Alexander and his assistants commit fraud by secretly unsealing and resealing the questions overnight. For the written answers, interpreters are at the ready who will read and decode the response received, albeit for a hefty fee.

The answers that the petitioners receive are so specific that, in their eyes, Alexander and Glycon have already proved their divinity by knowing the questions without opening them. The content of the answers, then, must be divinely inspired and true (*Alex.* 19–21). Just as with the tablets and oracles announcing his arrival, Alexander imitates existing traditions in oracular practice.³⁴ He successfully draws on the authority of written texts, whether on papyrus or on stone, that are made to seem divinely inspired in order to manipulate the petitioners.³⁵

The most harmful written text produced and circulated by Alexander was a one-verse oracle that he promised would ward off the plague that hit the Empire around 165 CE. It read: "Phoebus unshorn fends off the cloud of the plague" (*Alex.* 36).³⁶ Many people had the verse inscribed above their doors, but the narrator gleefully reports that the inscription had the opposite result. He assures us, lest we suspect him of some form of superstition, that the houses bearing the inscription were especially hard hit by the plague, either through chance, or for some practical reason. Perhaps the inhabitants of the inscribed houses behaved more carelessly, thinking themselves protected "by Phoebus shooting the plague with his arrows" (*Alex.* 36).³⁷

Alexander is, in the narrator's representation of him, the perfect villain. His use of epigraphic objects and other written documents is an extension of this villainy, and he employs them precisely because of the trust they embody. He appropriates the implied authority of the inscribed word in order to carry off his confabulations. Alexander of Abonuteichus could be as successful as he was in large part thanks to his clever use of pseudo-documents.³⁸

---

34 On the historical context, see ní Mheallaigh 2018, 233.
35 Cf. Zadorojnyi 2013, 368: "the most fundamental function of epigraphic writing [was] to assert and authorize facts, identities, power."
36 Φοῖβος ἀκειρεκόμης λοιμοῦ νεφέλην ἀπερύκει.
37 Φοῖβον ἀποτοξεύοντα τὸν λοιμόν.
38 By applying this term to deceitful documents used by characters within the narrative, rather than to narratives posing as documents (although the author Lucian also does this with his epistle-shaped work *Alexander Pseudomantis*), I am deliberately expanding William Hansen's understanding of the term (Hansen 2003).

In Lucian's *Quomodo historia conscribenda sit* (*On Writing History*) we also encounter someone tampering with inscribed text for selfish purposes, though perhaps not as egregiously as Alexander. The unnamed first-person narrator relates how the architect Sostratus of Cnidus built the famous lighthouse on Pharos, and, when it was complete, had a double inscription installed (*Hist. conscr.* 62):

> Οἰκοδομήσας οὖν τὸ ἔργον ἔνδοθεν μὲν κατὰ τῶν λίθων τὸ αὑτοῦ ὄνομα ἐπέγραψεν, ἐπιχρίσας δὲ τιτάνῳ καὶ ἐπικαλύψας ἐπέγραψε τοὔνομα τοῦ τότε βασιλεύοντος, εἰδώς, ὅπερ καὶ ἐγένετο, πάνυ ὀλίγου χρόνου συνεκπεσούμενα μὲν τῷ χρίσματι τὰ γράμματα, ἐκφανησόμενον δέ, "Σώστρατος Δεξιφάνους Κνίδιος θεοῖς σωτῆρσιν ὑπὲρ τῶν πλωϊζομένων."

> Having finished the building he wrote his name on the masonry inside. Then he concealed it with gypsum and wrote the name of the then ruling king, knowing that, as in fact happened, in a short time the letters and the plaster would together fall away to reveal the words: "Sostratus of Cnidus, son of Dexiphanes, to the savior gods, on behalf of those who sail."

It appears that Lucian has either invented or recorded an anecdote for his narrator that served to explain why the lighthouse on Pharos had an inscription listing Sostratus as dedicator. We know of two other such explanations, both of them different from Lucian's.[39] It was unusual for architects to have their names inscribed prominently on buildings of their design, an honor that was instead granted to the individual or group funding the structure, or to honorees designated by them.[40] Sostratus' cleverness allows him to be the exception.

Sostratus' double inscription belies expected features of inscribed, public texts, such as durability and legitimacy. The first inscription, instead of serving as a reminder of the king's generosity for the ages, degrades so quickly that the lighthouse outlives the official text by far. The second, clandestine inscription undercuts the official, sanctioned nature of public epigraphic writing: Sostratus has inserted his name into the official record illegally but successfully. Once the story of Sostratus' trick, if indeed it was true, was forgotten, the inscription alone would remain, and everybody who saw it would assume that Sostratus was the rightful, sanctioned dedicator of the lighthouse. The alternative ac-

---

39 Pliny relates that the king allowed Sostratus, the architect, to put his own name on the structure (*NH* 36.83). In Strabo (17.1.6) Sostratus is no longer the architect, but just a friend of the king, and *he* is said to have dedicated the lighthouse. In some manuscripts an inscription is then cited, identical to the one in *Hist. conscr.* 62, but Radt rejects this part of the text (Radt 2005 *ad loc.*).
40 Siwicki 2019.

counts of the inscription both assume that the text was indeed authorized by the king, but they predate Lucian's significantly. Most likely Lucian crafted a fictitious anecdote to undermine the existing accounts without having to disprove them.

It is tempting to connect this example of false epigraphy to literary production. In the context of *Historia* would-be writers are warned to prize enduring value over ephemeral celebrity, though more cynically one can also read the anecdote as a comment on the unreliability of historical sources and narratives. And Sostratus manages to hide in plain sight through his epigraphic ruse, much like Lucian the author does in his works, by including characters that share his name, or figures such as Lycinus and the Syrian.[41]

Even though the method used by Sostratus was an inscription, the illegitimate and subversive writing of his name on the lighthouse is reminiscent of a very different medium of writing: graffiti. In a recent article, Alexei Zadorojnyi characterizes ancient graffiti as the "antipode" to epigraphy; for the Greco-Roman imperial elite the latter was the bearer of "aesthetic and political prestige ... a medium of promoting one's own culture and authority," while the former were "dubious and ignoble texts."[42] We have already seen how Lucian deliberately subverts the prestige and authority of epigraphic writing in both *Alexander* and *Historia*. He represents the informal public writing of graffiti as being equally deceitful and dangerous, albeit transposed to a different social world in which illiteracy is explicitly shown as part of everyday life. In his witty *Dialogi meretricii* (*Dialogues of the Courtesans*) there are two moments where graffiti are used as means of deception: in one case a prostitute is the victim, in another, the perpetrator.

The prostitute Melitta is complaining to her friend, or perhaps procuress, Bacchis about her client Charinus, who has lost interest in her. She tells Bacchis that when she confronted Charinus he accused her of having an affair with one Hermotimus, because, he said, their names were written on a tombstone in the Ceramicus. Melitta denied everything, but Charinus could not be mollified. The next day, as Melitta tells Bacchis, she decided that she wanted to find out more about the graffiti (*Dial. meret.* 4.3):

ἔπεμψα οὖν Ἀκίδα κατασκεψομένην· ἡ δ' ἄλλο μὲν οὐδὲν εὗρε, τοῦτο δὲ μόνον ἐπιγεγραμμένον ἐσιόντων ἐπὶ τὰ δεξιὰ πρὸς τῷ Διπύλῳ, Μέλιττα φιλεῖ Ἑρμότιμον, καὶ μικρὸν αὖθις ὑποκάτω, Ὁ ναύκληρος Ἑρμότιμος φιλεῖ Μέλιτταν.

---

41 See Zadorojnyi 2013, 372; ní Mheallaigh 2014, 178–179.
42 Zadorojnyi 2018, 63.

> I sent Acis to look, but she found nothing other than this, written near the Dipylon gate on the right, "Melitta loves Hermotimus," and a little lower down, "The ship-owner Hermotimus loves Melitta."

It is likely that Melitta herself could not read;[43] this is why she sent her friend Acis to find out why Charinus got so jealous. Bacchis, in response, explains the graffiti to Melitta as a prank from some youngsters, who wanted to tease Charinus, knowing that he was the jealous type (*Dial. meret.* 4.3).

The likelihood of Bacchis' explanation for the graffiti about Melitta is confirmed later on in *Dialogi meretricii*, where we find another instance of slandering through graffiti, this time targeting a philosophy teacher. The prostitute Drosis talks about her client Cleinias with Chelidonium, another prostitute. Cleinias has stopped seeing Drosis because his teacher Aristaenetus, a philosopher, has forbidden it. Cleinias has sent a note to Drosis, which Chelidonium reads for her because she cannot read herself. In the letter he declares his love for Drosis, and he describes how Aristaenetus never lets him out of his sight (*Dial. meret.* 10.3). In revenge, and to get Cleinias' father to fire the philosopher, the prostitutes decide to spread the rumor that the teacher is having sexual relations with his pupil. A male friend will tell Cleinias' father, and Chelidonium volunteers to write the following on a wall in the Ceramicus: "Aristaenetus is corrupting Cleinias" (*Dial. meret.* 10.4).[44] When Drosis asks her how she will escape detection, Chelidonium says casually: "I will just go at night, and I will get some charcoal somewhere" (*Dial. meret.* 10.4).[45]

The two graffiti stories from *Dialogi meretricii* mirror each other almost perfectly. In the first case a prostitute who (most likely) cannot read is the victim of a false piece of public writing in the Ceramicus, which causes her to lose her client. In the second case an illiterate prostitute conspires with a colleague who can read and write to slander someone through a false piece of writing in the Ceramicus in order to get her client back. In turn, the graffiti share with the inscribed texts from *Alexander* and *Historia* the fact that they are intentionally deceitful. All three works, by featuring oracular writing, building inscriptions,

---

43 Taking into account the varying levels of literacy in different periods and areas, nonetheless "in all places women are less likely to be literate than men," Cole 1981, 129, with discussion of Luc. *Dial. meret.* at 143.
44 Ἀρισταίνετος διαφθείρει Κλεινίαν. For other literary prostitutes who read and write see book 4 (in the Loeb edition) of Alciphron's letters and Libanius' speech in character for a prostitute, Gibson 2008, 402–405.
45 τῆς νυκτός, ὦ Δροσί, ἄνθρακά ποθεν λαβοῦσα. Compare Mart. 12.61.7–10 for the use of charcoal in ancient graffiti; and see Keegan 2014, 23–24, 64.

and amorous graffiti respectively, incorporate common categories of Roman epigraphy that would have been familiar to everyone in the audience. In these Lucianic works the representation of writing in the everyday public space, inscribed and painted, breaks down the barrier between ignoble and authoritative texts, by framing both as equally unreliable. None of the featured texts are genuine, sanctioned, or true. But despite their falsity the writings still influence reality as if they were true, in large part because of their status as epigraphic objects in the world. Alexander's cult is successful, lovers are deceived, and visitors to Pharos might think that Sostratus dedicated the lighthouse instead of the king. The examples of the prostitutes' graffiti and the inscriptions used by Alexander, in particular, show that public texts independent of their veracity impact people's lives, both for those who can read them and for those who cannot. The story of Drosis from *Dialogi meretricii* illustrates how even someone who is illiterate can still use public writing to achieve their purpose by going through an intermediary. At the same time, Lucian underlines that Drosis and Melitta are both dependent on the kindness of their friends in navigating the informal, public writing that is an integral part of their lifeworld.

4 Unrealistic and Legitimizing

In Lucian's *Verae historiae* (*True Stories*), which is often grouped with the ancient novels, the narrator reports to the readers on inscriptions in space, inside a whale, on the Island of the Blessed, and on wine and cheese islands, respectively; of these five epigraphic objects two are cited in full.[46] In the previous chapter Karen ní Mheallaigh has masterfully shown how intricately several of these fictional inscriptions are intertwined with specific documentary practices from antiquity, such as boundary-marking, seal-making, treaty-inscriptions, funerary epigraphy, and the literary peritext. She concluded that the documents of *Verae historiae* "are thickly entangled in the ruses this most slippery of fictional texts, and are offered up for scrutiny under the most exacting metafictional eye"; according to ní Mheallaigh, Lucian the author presents these epigraphic objects to the audience of *Verae historiae* as a playful test within the

---

[46] It has been argued that *VH* in its current form was, as an outlier within Lucian's corpus, intended primarily for a reading audience, although the piece likely *was* performed in shorter portions: see Georgiadou and Larmour 1998, 51–59; cf. von Möllendorff 2000, 10 n. 22. On inscriptions in the ancient novel see Slater 2009.

context of the work's aim "as en exposé of specious truth-making".⁴⁷ The following analysis complements ní Mheallaigh's argument, by focusing specifically on how the internal narrator presents these inscriptions. Although, ultimately, Lucian the author trusts the audience to recognize that these epigraphic objects indeed have no existence outside the fiction of *Verae historiae*, within the narrative they are offered up as reliable.

The narrator of *Verae historiae* presents all five inscriptions featured as trustworthy, and uses them as legitimizing anchors of plausibility. As such, these epigraphic objects stand in sharp contrast to the ones discussed in the previous section. The texts used by Alexander, Sostratus, and the prostitutes (or texts like them) were possible or existed in the real world of the audience, but all of them were presented within the narrative as being deceitful. The inscriptions in *Verae historiae* are far removed from reality, but the narrator treats them as faithful witnesses to his account.

The first inscription that we encounter in *Verae historiae* is a bronze *stêlê* set up on the wine island, bearing Greek letters that are only faintly visible, with the implication being that the inscription is very old, and has been worn out by time — an ostentatious touch of realism on the part of the narrator. The text reads: "This is the furthest point that Heracles and Dionysus reached." Next to the inscription are two sets of footprints, one 100 feet long and one much smaller. The narrator infers that the former must belong to Heracles, the latter to Dionysus. The inscription, serving as a document, and the footprints, functioning as traces, together incontrovertibly establish a visit from the gods to the very place where the narrator now finds himself (*VH* 1.7).⁴⁸

The narrator of *Verae historiae* here evokes famous literary parallels for footprints as evidence for the earlier presence of now absent important figures, and, through the addition of the inscription, supersedes the motif.⁴⁹ By making the narrator double down on the documentary proof of the divine visit, Lucian (as noted by ní Mheallaigh in the previous chapter) shows himself acutely aware

---

47 ní Mheallaigh in this volume.
48 προελθόντες δὲ ὅσον σταδίους τρεῖς ἀπὸ τῆς θαλάσσης δι' ὕλης ὁρῶμέν τινα στήλην χαλκοῦ πεποιημένην, Ἑλληνικοῖς γράμμασιν καταγεγραμμένην, ἀμυδροῖς δὲ καὶ ἐκτετριμμένοις, λέγουσαν Ἄχρι: τούτων Ἡρακλῆς καὶ Διόνυσος ἀφίκοντο. ἦν δὲ καὶ ἴχνη δύο πλησίον ἐπὶ πέτρας, τὸ μὲν πλεθριαῖον, τὸ δὲ ἔλαττον - ἐμοὶ δοκεῖν, τὸ μὲν τοῦ Διονύσου, τὸ μικρότερον, θάτερον δὲ Ἡρακλέους.
49 E.g., the two-cubit-long footprint of Heracles in Scythia at Hdt. 4.82; Electra inferring her brother Orestes' return from a lock of hair and a set of footprints at Aesch. *Choe.* 164–229, with the parody at Eur. *El.* 508–537. Cf. Georgiadou and Larmour 1998, 72; von Möllendorff 2000, 79; ní Mheallaigh 2014, 210; ní Mheallaigh in this volume.

of the ways in which documents can be interdependent, and how they can collaboratively reproduce events of the past — even if this past is entirely made up.

In between the two quoted inscriptions of *Verae historiae*, the narrator mentions three inscriptions without citing their texts. All three are much more ordinary in terms of their content than the Dionysus and Heracles inscription, even if there is nothing ordinary about their respective locations. Of this subset of mentioned-but-unquoted inscriptions two are temple dedications: when the narrator is trapped in the stomach of a whale he finds a temple dedicated to Poseidon there (*VH* 1.32),[50] and similarly he finds a temple suitably dedicated to the milky nymph Galatea when he is stranded on an island of cheese (*VH* 2.3).[51] In both cases he implies that the audience would be justified to ask: "Well, how did you know whose temple it was?" His mention of a dedicatory inscription in each case provides the answer to this imagined question. By anticipating and answering such questions, as if this type of inquiry would have any hold over the unhinged world of *Verae historiae*, the narrator momentarily tricks the audience into believing that they are dealing with a reliable account of his recent travels.

Temples were expected to have dedicatory inscriptions, the contents of which were typically formulaic and predictable. Thus the narrator only has to allude to the document being there to sustain the realism of his narrative, as the audience would be able to fill in the rest. The third mentioned-but-unquoted text likewise belongs to a standard and formulaic category of inscriptions. Moreover, it is an inscription that has not yet been dedicated, which further explains why the narrator describes rather than quotes it. The anticipated epigraphic object is to be set up in space: The war between the inhabitants of the Moon and the Sun, as reported by the narrator, concludes with a peace treaty. One of the provisions of the treaty is that it shall be "inscribed on a slab of amber, which shall be placed in mid-air, on neutral territory" (*VH* 1.20).[52]

The narrator's summary of the treaty between the Sun-dwellers and the Moon-dwellers follows the formulaic language of peace treaties known to us

---

50 οὔπω δὲ πέντε ὅλους διελθὼν σταδίους εὗρον ἱερὸν Ποσειδῶνος, ὡς ἐδήλου ἡ ἐπιγραφή.
51 ἱερὸν δὲ ἐν μέσῃ τῇ νήσῳ ἀνῳκοδόμητο Γαλατείας τῆς Νηρηΐδος, ὡς ἐδήλου τὸ ἐπίγραμμα. *Epigraphe* and *epigramma* are nearly synonymous, though the former means "inscription" exclusively, while the latter can also refer to a literary epigram. On the term *epigraphe*, see now Kirk 2018.
52 ἐγγράψαι δὲ τὰς συνθήκας στήλῃ ἠλεκτρίνῃ καὶ ἀναστῆσαι ἐν μέσῳ τῷ ἀέρι ἐπὶ τοῖς μεθορίοις.

from the epigraphic record and from historiography.⁵³ Just as with the temple dedications we are dealing with a very common genre of inscriptions: the narrator can loosely allude to the contents of the document, and the audience is able to imagine easily what such a text would entail. The temple dedications and the (future) inscribed treaty represent "normal" inscriptions that have been transported to a completely fantastical context.

The most astonishing inscription in *Verae historiae* in terms of its contents is the couplet that the narrator has the shade of Homer compose for him before his untimely departure from the Island of the Blessed, to be carved in beryl and set up by the harbor (*VH* 2.28):

> Λουκιανὸς τάδε πάντα φίλος μακάρεσσι θεοῖσιν
> εἶδέ τε καὶ πάλιν ἦλθε φίλην ἐς πατρίδα γαῖαν.
>
> Lucian, dear to the blessed gods, saw all of this
> and went back again to his dear fatherland.

It is with these two hexameter lines that the audience finds out for the first time, just as late as in *Alexander Pseudomantis*, that the narrator is named "Lucian," just like the author. In a highly playful conceit the narrator presents some of the most unlikely information of his whole account in the shape of a tangible epigraphic object.⁵⁴ This text, which the narrator presents as evidence proving that he indeed went to the Island of the Blessed — the implication being that if one were to ever make it there, one could go and check the verses — is moreover written by Homer, "the maker of lies."⁵⁵

The Homeric lines mark, as ní Mheallaigh notes in the previous chapter, a pseudo-ending to the work as a whole. The narrator uses inscriptions as a structuring device: Almost at the beginning of his narrative, he treats the audience to the overly documented visit of Heracles and Dionysus, followed by mentions of three quotidian inscriptions in very non-quotidian locations, while the final inscription is again cited in full as it competes with the opening inscription as epigraphic marvel. Together the inscriptions of *Verae historiae* bear testimony

---

53 Thucydides in particular, as discussed by ní Mheallaigh in this volume. See Householder 1940 on other mock decrees in Lucian.
54 On this inscription, see also Saïd 1994, 161–162; ní Mheallaigh 2008, 419–422; ní Mheallaigh 2014, 254–258.
55 Georgiadou and Larmour 1998, 213. See Kim 2010, 140–156 for Lucian's frequent representation of Homer as a liar.

to how the epigraphic habit could seep into even the most outlandish corners of the literary imagination.

Lucian also uses inscriptions in fantastical scenarios other than those found in the *Verae historiae*. They are comparable in that in each case within the context of the narrative the inscriptions are presented as reliable, contributing to rendering plausible a narrative that as a whole is entirely implausible. Lucian's short piece *Dipsades* contains an inscribed funerary *stêlê* located in the mythical Libyan desert. The anonymous narrator tells us that his friend has seen the epitaph of a man who was killed by a snakebite that made him as thirsty as Tantalus. In a gesture of tongue-in-cheek realism, the narrator admits that he only remembers the first four lines of the funerary epigram, but those he cites in full.[56] Similarly, in *Scytha* (*Scythian*), a first-person narrator gives detailed directions to a grave monument in Athens of the fictional character Toxaris. Here the realistic element is the detailed description of the decay of the monument: the *stêlê* has fallen over, and both the inscription and the relief are worn out, with only parts of them remaining visible (*Scyth.* 2). Lucian has the narrator of *Scytha* access the same toolkit as the narrator of *Verae historiae*, who in his description of the *stêlê* supposedly set up by Heracles and Dionysus on the wine island also mentioned that the inscribed letters had worn out over time, and were barely legible.

Lucianic characters encounter inscriptions even on Mount Olympus. In *Deorum concilium* (*Parliament of the Gods*), the god Momus proposes a decree concerning foreign gods, reminiscent of the soon-to-be-inscribed peace treaty in *Verae historiae*. However, when Momus reads out the proposed law, he says it has already been inscribed (*Deor. conc.* 14).[57] Zeus forestalls a vote on the motion, when he realizes that the "foreigners" easily outnumber the other gods, and declares it carried. The result is that a decree that was not even voted on has been inscribed, and will, presumably, be displayed on Olympus *as if* it has been approved by the divine assembly (*Deor. conc.* 19).[58] In the *Saturnalia*, a

---

56 *Dips.* 6. On the fantastical, allegorical nature of the piece, see Leigh 2000.
57 ψήφισμά τι περὶ τούτων ἀναγνώσομαι ἤδη ξυγγεγραμμένον. One could argue that Momus is reading the decree out from a piece of papyrus, and that this is what he means when he says it "has already been written." This, however, would not be very remarkable, and not something Momus has to draw attention to. For the characterization of Momus as a god who is aggressively trying to "clean up" Olympus, which is his role throughout, it would be much more fitting if he means that the text actually has already been inscribed.
58 On the basis of the opening of the decree, Householder 1940, 201–205 argues convincingly that it was inspired by decrees from Ionian Magnesia. His point that Lucian presents the decree as being introduced and not yet passed is less convincing: Momus' intent is certainly to have

narrator who calls himself Cronosolon says that he has been instructed by the god Cronus to publicize new laws for the Saturnalia festival. After reciting these laws in full he says that every rich man must inscribe them on a bronze slab, and set up the slab in the center of their courtyard. The inscription will, according to Cronosolon, serve as protection against famine, plague, fire, and other evils (*Sat.* 13–18). At first glance this inscription-to-be is very similar to the protective inscription in *Alexander Pseudomantis* discussed in the previous section. But a major difference is that in the case of the latter the narrator emphatically tells the audience that the formula is fake and ineffective, while in *Saturnalia* the narrator insists that the text comes from Cronus directly. Observant audience members know that this cannot be so: the opening of the piece is a dialogue between Cronosolon and the god during which neither laws nor any other instructions get handed down (*Sat.* 1–9). The laws actually are Cronosolon's invention and not the god's.

Both the laws-to-be-inscribed from *Saturnalia* and the decree from *Deorum concilium*, through their form and through the way in which they are represented by the characters within the respective narratives, lay claim to a specific kind of legitimacy — divine sanction in the case of the laws, a democratic endorsement in the case of the decree — which on closer inspection turns out to be unwarranted. Lucian leaves it up to the audience to figure out that this is so.

Our final inscription comes from *De Dea Syria* (*On the Syrian Goddess*), perhaps the piece in Lucian's corpus for which it is most difficult to decide whether it is a realistic or an unrealistic setting. I follow Lightfoot in reading the piece as informed by Lucian's actual knowledge of (and even pride in) the temple at Hierapolis in his native Commagene, but written as an exoticizing Herodotean pastiche that renders the sanctuary nearly as fantastical as the places featured in *Verae historiae*, though not quite. The passage containing the inscription, however, is a moment, as Lightfoot acknowledges, where Lucian does push *De Dea Syria* fully into the realm of the fantastical.[59] The unnamed first person narrator of the piece is a pilgrim to the temple and a devotee who, in true Lucianic fashion, withholds the precise extent of his personal attachment to the goddess until the very last sentence (*DDS* 60).

After discarding several possible origin stories for the temple the narrator posits Dionysus as its founder, because, he says, two inscribed phalli stand at

---

the decree appear as a fait accompli, which is why he has already had it inscribed. At the very end of the decree, as at the beginning, it is referred to as a ψήφισμα, which often means "a measure passed by the assembly" (*LSJ* A; cf. Ar. *Ach.* 536).
59 Lightfoot 2003, 209–221.

the entrance, each of them 300 fathoms tall, which equals 1,800 feet or roughly 550 meters (*DDS* 28). He cites the inscription as follows: "I, Dionysus, dedicated these phalli to my stepmother Hera." The narrator says that together with other signs in the temple, such as "barbarian" clothes, Indian stones, and horns of ivory left there by Dionysus, the pillars "suffice" for him as evidence of Dionysus' founding, even though he can (and does) mention even further proofs (*DDS* 16).[60] The narrator's piling on of several types of documents, epigraphic and otherwise, closely resembles the efforts of the narrator of *Verae historiae* to prove the presence of Dionysus and Heracles on the wine island.[61] In both cases the inscription is presented by the respective narrators as the final, definitive punch that allows them to rest their case: Dionysus was here.

In *Verae historiae*, the narrator uses the medium of inscribed, public writing to present his fantastical travelogue as plausible, and to make himself seem reliable on account of his eye for detail. The inscriptions described by first-person narrators in *Dipsades* and *Scytha* function in a similar way. In *De Dea Syria* the pilgrim narrator marshals epigraphic objects precisely during the most far-fetched episode of his account, and shows himself fully committed to their evidentiary value. In *Saturnalia* and *Deorum concilium*, featured characters make use of (impending) epigraphic documents, imbuing them with unwarranted authority to serve their own purposes; their manipulations go unnoticed and unpunished by the other characters. Lucian the author expects the audience to see through such manipulations, and to admire the scaffolding (his!) underneath. Catching on to the deceptions of these swashbuckling narrators and interlocutors is part of understanding Lucian's characterization of them. In juxtaposition, however, with the quotidian epigraphic objects from the previous section, which are presented as unreliable from the get go, the fact that the legitimacy of these fantastical epigraphic objects remains inviolate within the narrative sends a message about dealing with written documents as such.

5 Epigraphy and Illiteracy

As social objects, documents rely on human subjects to come into existence, but they are not subjective: Once established they have a presence and power of

---

[60] "τούσδε φαλλοὺς Διόνυσος Ἥρῃ μητρυιῇ ἀνέθηκα." {τὸ} ἐμοὶ μέν νυν καὶ τάδε ἀρκέει...
[61] Cf. Lightfoot 2003, 363–373.

their own in the world, independent of our subjective experience of them.[62] From Lucian's depiction and appropriation of documents it becomes clear that he was keenly interested in the sway that documents hold over everyday life, as well as in their potential as building blocks of imaginary fantasy worlds outside everyday life. The juxtaposition of what I have termed realistic deceitful epigraphic objects and unrealistic legitimizing epigraphic objects works to fully expose the dangerous, potentially destructive power of such documents. Through the narrators of such pieces as *Verae historiae* and *De Dea Syria*, who co-opt the aura of legitimacy and authority of the medium of epigraphy as it is used in everyday life, Lucian showcases the power of faux-authoritative inscribed text to effectively conjure up impossible yet plausible fantasy worlds. But whatever is benign and playful in the hands of Lucian's narrators, becomes insidious in realistic settings in the hands of characters like Alexander or the youthful pranksters of *Dialogi meretricii*, causing distress, confusion, and disease. Lucian tells the audience that everyday life is full of individuals who will manipulate or invent epigraphic documents as blithely as his narrators, and, what's worse, without any regard for the real world consequences of their actions.

A problem for any argument that interprets several Lucianic pieces alongside each other, and attributes meaning to them together as a group, is the performance setting. Even if several pieces were performed consecutively at one event, there is — in most cases — no way of knowing which ones they were.[63] Still, even a single piece like *Alexander* or *Dialogi meretricii* already showcases the unreliability of documents in Lucian, while repeat audience members and readers of Lucianic works that were circulating would have been able to appreciate the fantastical documentary "proofs" of *Verae historiae* alongside the slandering of Alexander's entrepreneurial use of faked written oracles. Another caveat is that Lucian's treatment of epigraphic objects is not exclusively geared towards showing the potential dangers of relying on such documents, even if I argue that this is an important element. Lucian is likely also saying something about literature. As Karen ní Mheallaigh argued in the previous chapter, writing fictitious literary narratives is quite like inventing documents, rendering Lucian the author potentially as mendacious as Sostratus, Alexander or any of the "Lucian"-narrators. Nonetheless, the key difference between them remains that the

---

62 Ferraris 2012, 318.
63 Exceptions are the diptychs *Imagines* and *Pro imaginibus*, *De mercede conductis* and *Apologia*, and (perhaps) *Vitarum auctio* and *Bis accusatus*, which quite possibly would have been performed together, or at least in short succession.

author, just like the narrator of *Verae historiae*, is honest about his lying by confining himself to literature.

Lucian shows that whoever lives with documents can be seduced and therefore snared, sooner or later, by the semblance of authoritative text, no matter how flimsy it may be underneath. Secondly, epigraphic objects and other documents can impact our lives, whether they are real or fake, whether we can read them or not. The lifelike depiction of illiterate prostitutes relying on their friends in *Dialogi meretricii* shows that Lucian was cognizant of the challenges of being (partly) illiterate in the text-rich cities of the Roman Empire. The layered unreliability of inscriptions in Lucian can, therefore, be understood as a way of reaching out to audience members for whom textual objects were by definition unreliable because they had no way of independently testing their contents. The implication is not that being able to read and write is unimportant because people get duped by texts anyway, but rather that unease with (seemingly) authoritative, public writing is justified and can be shared among those who cannot read by themselves and those who can. Being illiterate in cities that were full of writing meant, as it does for Melitta and Drosis, having to trust others to verify texts that impact your life too. Lucian's representation of epigraphic objects in his works reflects on this experience by showing that in a fundamental sense documents are always duplicitous and unverifiable; all of us, literate and illiterate, have little choice but to trust their authority, rendering us profoundly vulnerable.

References

Bagnall, R.S. (2011), *Everyday Writing in the Graeco-Roman East*, Berkeley.
Barchiesi, A./Rüpke, J./Stephens, S.A. (eds.) (2004), *Rituals in Ink: A Conference on Religion and Literary Production in Ancient Rome Held at Stanford University in February 2002*, Stuttgart.
Beard, M. (1991), "The Function of the Written Word in Roman Religion", in: Humphrey (1991), 35–58.
Bellinger, A.R. (1928), *Lucian's Dramatic Technique*, New Haven.
Beltrán Lloris, F. (2014), "The 'Epigraphic Habit' in the Roman World", in: Bruun and Edmondson (2014), 131–146.
Bodel, J. (2015), "Inscriptions and Literacy", in: Bruun and Edmondson (2015), 745–763.
Bowman, A.K. (1991), "Literacy in the Roman Empire: Mass and Mode", in: Humphrey (1991), 119–132.
Bowman, A.K. (1994), "The Roman Imperial Army: Letters and Literacy on the Northern Frontier", in: Bowman and Woolf (1994), 109–125.

Bowman, A.K./Thomas, J.D. (eds.) (1983–2011), *Tabulae Vindolandenses*, 4 vols., Cambridge/London.
Bowman, A.K./Woolf, G. (eds.) (1994), *Literacy and Power in the Ancient World*, Cambridge.
Branham, R.B. (1984), "The comic as critic: Revenging Epicurus: A study of Lucian's art of comic narrative," in: *ClAnt* 3.2, 143–163.
Bremmer, J.N. (2017), "Lucian on Peregrinus and Alexander of Abonuteichos: A Skeptical View of Two Religious Entrepreneurs", in: R.L. Gordon/G. Petridou/J. Rüpke (eds.), *Beyond Priesthood: Religious Entrepreneurs and Innovators in the Roman Empire*, Berlin, 49–78.
Bruun, C./Edmondson, J. (eds.) (2015), *The Oxford Handbook of Roman Epigraphy*, Oxford.
Buisman, M./Houtkoop, W. (2014), *Laaggeletterdheid in kaart*, The Hague.
Canadian Council on Learning (2007), *State of Learning in Canada: No Time for Complacency*, Ottawa.
Cole, S.G. (1981), "Could Greek Women Read and Write?" in: H. Foley (ed.), *Women in Antiquity. Special Issue. Women's Studies* 8, New York, 129–155.
Corbier, M. (1991), "L'écriture en quête de lecteurs", in: Humphrey (1991), 99–118. Revised and reprinted 2006 in M. Corbier, *Donner à voir, donner à lire. Mémoire et communication dans la Rome ancienne*, Paris, 77–90.
Coulet, C. (1996), *Communiquer en Grèce ancienne*, Paris.
Cribiore, R. (2001), *Gymnastics of the Mind: Greek Education in Hellenistic and Roman Egypt*, Princeton.
Dawkins, R.M. (1929), *The Sanctuary of Artemis Orthia at Sparta. JHS Supplementary Paper 5*, London.
Desjardins, R./Schuller, T. (eds.) (2006), *Measuring the Effects of Education on Health and Civic Engagement*, Paris.
Du Plessis, P.J. (2012), *Letting and Hiring in Roman Legal Thought, 27 BCE–284 CE*, Leiden.
Eastmond, A. (2015), "Introduction: Viewing Inscriptions", in: A. Eastmond (ed.), *Viewing Inscriptions in the Late Antique and Medieval World*, Cambridge, 1–9.
Elm von der Osten, D. (2006), "Die Inszenierung des Betruges und seiner Entlarvung: Divination und ihre Kritiker in Lucians Schrift "Alexandros oder der Lügenprophet"', in: D. Elm von der Osten/J. Rüpke/K. Waldner (eds.), *Texte als Medium und Reflexion von Religion im römischen Reich*, Stuttgart, 141–157.
Ferraris, M. (2012), *Documentality: Why It Is Necessary to Leave Traces*, transl. R. Davies. New York: Fordham University Press. First published 2009 as *Documentalità. Perché è necessario lasciare tracce*, Rome.
Foster, B.O. (1899), "Notes on the Symbolism of the Apple in Classical Antiquity", in: *HSPh* 10, 39–55.
Georgiadou, A./Larmour, D.H.J. (1998), *Lucian's Science Fiction Novel, True Histories: Interpretation and Commentary*, Leiden.
Gibson, C.A. (2008), *Libanius's Progymnasmata: Model Exercises in Greek Prose Composition and Rhetoric*, Atlanta.
Grenfell, B.P./Hunt, A.S. (eds.) (1898), *The Oxyrhynchus Papyri Vol. I*, London.
Haensch, R. (2008), "Die Provinz Aegyptus: Kontinuitäten und Brüche zum ptolemäischen Ägypten. Das Beispiel des administrativen Personals", in: I. Piso, *Die römischen Provinzen. Begriff und Gründung*, Cluj-Napoca, 81–105.
Hafner, M. (ed. and transl.) (2017), *Lukians Apologie. Classica Monacensia* 50, Tübingen.
Hansen, W. (2003), "Strategies of Authentication in Ancient Popular Culture", in: Panayotakis et al. (2003), 301–314.

Harris, W.V. (1989), *Ancient Literacy*, Cambridge, MA.
Hedrick, C.W. (1994), "Writing, Reading, and Democracy", in: R. Osborne/S. Hornblower (eds.), *Ritual, Finance, Politics: Athenian Democratic Accounts Presented to David Lewis*, Oxford, 157–174.
Hedrick, C.W. (2015), "Written Media in Antiquity," in: D.L. Selden/P. Vasunia (eds.), *The Oxford Handbook of the Literatures of the Roman Empire*, Oxford Handbooks Online, doi.org/10.1093/oxfordhb/9780199699445.013.10.
Householder, F. (1940), "The Mock Decrees in Lucian", in: *TAPhA* 71, 199–216.
Humphrey, J.H. (ed.) (1991), *Literacy in the Roman World*. *JRA* Supplementary Series 3, Ann Arbor.
Johnson, W.A./Parker, H.N. (eds.) (2009), *Ancient Literacies: The Culture of Reading in Greece and Rome*, Oxford.
Jones, C.P. (1986), *Culture and Society in Lucian*, Cambridge, MA.
Kaster, R. (1988), *Guardians of Language: The Grammarian and Society in Late Antiquity*, Berkeley.
Keegan, P. (2014), *Graffiti in Antiquity*, London/New York.
Kim, L. (2010), *Homer between History and Fiction in Imperial Greek Literature*, Cambridge.
Kirk, A. (2018), "What is an ἐπιγραφή in Classical Greece?", in: Petrovic et al. (2018), 29–47.
Kraus, T.J. (2000), "(Il)literacy in Non-Literary Papyri from Graeco-Roman Egypt: Further Aspects of the Educational Ideal in Ancient Literary Sources and Modern Times", in: *Mnemosyne* 53, 322–342.
Kuin, I.N.I. (forthcoming), *Lucian's Laughing Gods: Religion, Philosophy, and Popular Culture in the Roman East*, Ann Arbor.
Lane Fox, R.J. (1994), "Literacy and Power in early Christianity", in: Bowman and Woolf (1994), 126–148.
Langdon, M.L. (2015), "Herders' Graffiti", in: A.P. Matthaiou/N. Papazarkadas (eds.), *AΞΩN: Studies in Honor of Ronald S. Stroud*, Athens, 49–58.
Leigh, M. (2000), "Lucan and the Libyan Tale", in: *JRS* 90, 95–109.
Lightfoot, J. (2003), *Lucian: On the Syrian Goddess*, Oxford.
Linders, T. (1992), "Inscriptions and Orality", in: *SO* 67, 27–40.
Littlewood, A.R. (1968), "The Symbolism of the Apple in Greek and Roman Literature", in: *HSPh* 72, 147–181.
Macdonald, M.C.A. (2005), "Literacy in an Oral Environment," in: P. Bienkowski/C. Mee/ E. Slater (eds.), *Writing and Ancient Near Eastern Society: Papers in Honour of Alan R. Millard*, New York, 49–118.
MacMullen, R. (1982), "The Epigraphic Habit in the Roman Empire", in: *AJPh* 103, 233–246.
Marshall, C.W. (2006), *The Stagecraft and Performance of Roman Comedy*, Cambridge.
Meyer, E.A. (1990), "Explaining the Epigraphic Habit in the Roman Empire: The Evidence of Epitaphs", in: *JRS* 80, 74–96.
ní Mheallaigh, K. (2008), "Pseudo-Documentarism and the Limits of Ancient Fiction", in: *AJPh* 129, 403–431.
ní Mheallaigh, K. (2014), *Reading Fiction with Lucian: Fakes, Freaks and Hyperreality*, Cambridge.
ní Mheallaigh, K. (2018), "Lucian's Alexander: Technoprophecy, Thaumatology and the Poetics of Wonder", in: M. Gerolemou (ed.), *Recognizing Miracles in Antiquity and Beyond*, Berlin/Boston, 225–256.
Missiou, A. (2011), *Literacy and Democracy in Fifth-Century Athens*, Cambridge.

Möllendorff, P. von (2000), *Auf der Suche nach der verlogenen Wahrheit. Lukians Wahre Geschichten*, Tübingen.
Mrozek, S. (1973), "À propos de la répartition chronologique des inscriptions latines dans le Haut-Empire", in: *Epigraphica* 35, 113–118.
Mrozek, S. (1988), "À propos de la répartition chronologique des inscriptions latines dans le Haut-Empire", in: *Epigraphica* 50, 61–64.
Nesselrath, H.G. (2018), "Lucian on Roman Officials", in: P. Bosman (ed.), *Intellectual and Empire in Greco-Roman Antiquity*, London, 178–188.
Nuffelen, P. Van (2011), *Rethinking the Gods: Philosophical Readings of Religion in the Post-Hellenistic Period*, Cambridge.
Panayotakis, S./Zimmerman, M./Keulen, W. (eds.) (2003), *The Ancient Novel and Beyond*, Leiden.
Petrovic, A./Petrovic, I./Thomas, E. (eds.) (2018), *The Materiality of Text: Placement, Perception, and Presence of Inscribed Texts in Classical Antiquity*, Leiden.
Radt. S. (2005), *Strabons Geographika Bd. 4. Buch XIV - XVII: Text und Übersetzung*, Göttingen.
Rosenmeyer, P. (2001), *Ancient Epistolary Fictions: The Letter in Greek Literature*, Cambridge.
Saïd, S. (1994), "Lucien ethnographe", in: A. Billault (ed.), *Lucien de Samosate. Actes du colloque international de Lyon organisé au Centre d'études romaines et gallo-romaines les 30 septembre–1er octobre 1993*, Lyon, 149–170.
Sickinger, J.P. (2017), "New Ostraka from the Athenian Agora", in: *Hesperia* 86, 443–508.
Sironen, E. (2003), "The Role of Inscriptions in Greco-Roman Novels", in: Panayotakis *et al.* (2003), 289–300.
Siwicki, C. (2019), "Roman Architects and the Struggle for Fame in an Unequal Society," in: C. Pieper/C. Damon (eds.), *Eris vs. Aemulatio: Competition in Classical Antiquity*, Leiden, 208–229.
Slater, N. (1996), "Literacy and Old Comedy", in: I. Worthington (ed.), *Voice into Text: Orality and Literacy in Ancient Greece*, Leiden, 99–112.
Slater, N. (2009), "Reading Inscriptions in the Ancient Novel", in: M. Paschalis/S. Panayotakis/G. Schmeling (eds.), *Readers and Writers in the Ancient Novel*, Groningen, 64–78.
Terrone, E. (2014), "Traces, Documents, and the Puzzle of 'Permanent Acts'", in: *The Monist* 97, 161–178.
Ureña Bracero, J. (1995), *El diálogo de Luciano*, Amsterdam.
Victor, U. (1997), *Alexandros oder der Lügenprophet*, Leiden.
Williamson, C. (1987), "Monuments of Bronze: Roman Legal Documents on Bronze Tablets", in: *ClAnt* 6, 160–183.
Woolf, G. (1996), "Monumental Writing and the Expansion of the Roman Society in the Early Empire", in: *JRS* 86, 22–39.
Woolf, G. (2015), "Ancient Illiteracy?", in: *BICS* 58(2), 31–42.
Youtie, H.C. (1975), "ὑπογραφεύς: The Social Impact of Illiteracy in Graeco-Roman Egypt", in: *ZPE* 17, 201–221.
Zadorojnyi, A.V. (2013), "Shuffling Surfaces: Epigraphy, Power, and Integrity in the Graeco-Roman Narratives", in: P. Liddel/P. Low (eds.), *Inscriptions and Their Uses in Greek and Latin Literature*, Oxford, 365–386.
Zadorojnyi, A.V. (2018), "The Aesthetics and Politics of Inscriptions in Imperial Greek Literature", in: Petrovic *et al.* (2018), 48–68.

Pierre Schneider
Documenting the *oikoumenê*: What "Documents" Supported the Description of the Inhabited World in the Hellenistic and Early Imperial Periods?

Abstract: This chapter investigates the collective attitude towards documentary evidence among ancient geographers by surveying geographical writing and descriptions of the *oikoumenê gê* from the Hellenistic period onward in order to discern attitudes towards documentary source materials. Ancient authors, in an effort to compile a robust body of geographical knowledge, employed even plants, animals, and objects as documentary material. Ferraris's theory of the document as social object is inadequate for understanding how the ancient geographers envisioned their sources. Instead, a fundamentally different way of knowing the world emerges from authors like Pliny, Diodorus Siculus, and others, dependent on an expansive, almost universal interpretation of what constitutes a document.

Historians are engaged constantly in the work of exploring and interpreting documents: unlike experimental sciences, where progress arises from an interplay between experiment and theory, "l'histoire se fait avec des documents" ("history is made by documents"), as the French historian Henri-Irénée Marrou puts it.[1] As a historian, however, I never really ask myself what documents are. Were I urged by someone to answer this question, I would probably give an intuitive definition. This might be similar to Marrou's, stating that any material used by historians to shed light on past times may be categorized as a document, be it written or not:

> A document is any source of information from which the historian can pull something for the purpose of knowing the human past, seen from the angle of the question put to him. It is obvious that it is impossible to say where the document starts or ends: little by little the definition grows and ends up encompassing texts, monuments, and observations of all kinds.[2]

---

1 On this method of constructing history, see Marrou 1975, 64–91.
2 Marrou 1975, 73: "Est un document toute source d'information dont l'historien sait tirer quelque chose pour la connaissance du passé humain, envisagé sous l'angle de la question qui lui a été posée. Il est bien évident qu'il est impossible de dire où commence et où finit le docu-

According to such an intuitive approach, the document is closely associated with the notion of "information," and undoubtedly with that of "proof." If, however, one embarks on a more thorough investigation of what information is, one may start to feel less secure.

A special issue of *The Monist* in 2014 addressed such questions of proof and information in response to the emerging theory of documents as social objects set forth in Ferraris's book, *Documentality: Why It Is Necessary to Leave Traces*.[3] One contributor, Michael Buckland, notes that Ferraris's theory of documentality correctly captures the social role that documents often play. But Buckland claims that Ferraris's book fails to account for a semiotic view of the document, in which documentary status might be conferred by the idiosyncratic perceptions of an individual, who could consider nearly anything as documentary information.[4] As Buckland rightly wrote in an earlier article, "determining what might be informative is a difficult task": trees, for instance, providing firewood for heating and lumber for building are not informative at first glance; however, "as representative trees they are informative about trees." In addition, the thickness of tree rings caused by annual variations in weather provides information for archaeologists and climatologists. This leads Buckland to the disappointing conclusion that "if anything is, or might be, informative, then everything is, or might well be, information. In which case calling something 'information' does little or nothing to define it. If everything is information, then being information is nothing special."[5] Subsequently if anything is, or may be, informative, everything is, or may be, a document.

My aim, through these introductory observations, is to illustrate briefly how complex the questions relating to documents and information are — and all the more so if one considers antiquity. In the face of such vast questions, focusing on a specific topic seems preferable. In the organizers' initial framing document for the conference that generated this volume, a very important subject was put forward in the form of a simple question: "What qualifies as a document?" This line of reasoning is further pursued in the Introduction to the present volume:

> [*Documentality*] initiates a fundamental conversation about the meaning of "document" in the Roman Empire ... On a more basic level still, our volume investigates whether Imperial readers and writers recognized the document as a coherent genre. Ancient Greek and Lat-

---

ment: de proche en proche, la notion s'élargit et finit par embrasser textes, monuments et observations de tous ordres." Translation by the editors of the volume.
3 Ferraris 2012.
4 Buckland 2014, 181.
5 For further discussion, see Buckland 1991, 356.

in possess robust vocabularies for letters, inscriptions, and contracts, but were these forms of writing classified together in the ancient imagination?[6]

Examining to what extent the document was perceived as a coherent genre bearing a specific name is the question on which this chapter focuses, except that it does not embrace the documents particularly studied by papyrologists and epigraphists: private and official letters, contracts, counts, decrees, etc. It is rather the informative material used by ancient geographers and authors occasionally dealing with geography (e.g., Diodorus of Sicily) on which I shall concentrate, in a *longue durée* approach: from the sixth century BCE onward ancient geography had continuously improved, with a climax between Alexander the Great's expedition and the time of Roman conquests. Indeed many remote regions were made (better) known to the Mediterranean people during this period: East Africa, South Arabia, India, the Erythraean Sea (i.e., the Indian Ocean), Britannia, Germania, Dacia, and other parts of the *oikoumenê gê* (inhabited earth). The first section of the chapter consists of a succinct presentation of the "documentary material" supporting ancient geographical knowledge.[7] The second section establishes that, according to modern criteria, this material falls within the category of "document." The last section addresses the issue that seems to me crucial: did ancient authors conceive of "documents" in the same way as us? My view is that, with respect to geographical knowledge, there is a disjunction between ancient and modern ideas about "documentary material."

1 What Were the Building Blocks of Ancient Geographical Knowledge?

To begin, let us consider the manner in which Strabo, writing in the early Roman Empire, describes regions far beyond its borders and the sources that underlay his accounts. Strabo's description of India is preceded by a long intro-

---

[6] Arthur-Montagne, DiGiulio, and Kuin in this volume.
[7] Regarding ancient geography, my field of expertise encompasses the southern and eastern edges of the *oikoumenê*. Thus I will mostly explore texts dealing with countries such as India, *Aithiopia* — which is not modern Ethiopia, but an area covering Nubia and the Horn of Africa — and Arabia. Although most of the Greek and Roman sources have not come down to us, a number of texts — e.g., regional monographs (such as *Indika*, *Aithiopika*, *Arabika*), the accounts composed by Alexander's companions — have been preserved as fragments. On these authors, see Pearson 1960 and Pédech 1984.

ductory section in which the author assesses the various sources of information at his disposal. First of all, in conformity with common conceptions of information in the ancient world, he distinguishes between two sources, sight (ὄψις) and hearsay (ἀκοή): "Not many of our people have seen it [India]; and even those who have seen it, have seen only parts of it, and the greater part of what they say is from hearsay" (Strabo 15.1.12).[8] Strabo then proceeds to list the sources he drew on with an appreciation of their respective value. The accounts (μνήμη) produced before Alexander's expedition are mostly obscure, or confusing (15.1.5). Those published (συγγράψαντες) by Alexander's companions in India are valued; regrettably, Strabo says, even though they were able to observe the country and its inhabitants, they contradict each other (15.1.2). Later authors composed treatises (συγγράψαντες) but failed to offer accurate information (15.1.3). The most recent data were provided by Alexandrian merchants — who "are of no use as regard the history of the places they have seen" — and by an embassy sent to Augustus by King Pandion. This detailed review makes it clear that written sources were the building blocks not only of Strabo's description of India, but also of almost all texts dealing with geographical matter.

Neither in this passage nor in other geographical texts do we come across a Latin or Greek word that could be rendered by "document" or "documentary material" (on this point, see further below). Instead, a variety of terms are used. Some point to a specific kind of text, such as "history" (ἱστορία), "speeches" (λόγοι), "account" (ἐξήγησις), "description of the earth" (περίοδος τῆς γῆς), and so forth. In general, these terms need contextualizing in order to be properly understood, as in the following example borrowed from Agatharchides of Cnidus, who flourished in the mid-second century BCE. Agatharchides wrote a treatise entitled *On the Erythraean Sea* — a description of the Indian Ocean countries. Like many other ancient authors, he does not find it essential to list the sources available to him. At one point, however, he explains why he was not able to complete his work:

> Τὰ μὲν οὖν ὑπὲρ τῶν ἐθνῶν τῶν ἐκκειμένων πρὸς μεσημβρίαν, ὡς ἦν ἐφ' ἡμῖν, ἐν πέντε βιβλίοις ἐπιμελῶς ἱστορήκαμεν· ὑπὲρ δὲ τῶν ἐν τῷ πελάγει νήσων ὕστερον τεθεωρημένων...ἡμεῖς μὲν παραιτησάμενοι τὴν ἐξήγησιν ἄρδην ἀπολελοίπαμεν, οὔτε τὸν πόνον τῆς ἡλικίας ὁμοίως ὑποφέρειν δυναμένης, πολλῶν ἡμῖν ὑπέρ τε τῆς Εὐρώπης καὶ τῆς Ἀσίας ἀναγεγραμμένων, οὔτε τῶν ὑπομνημάτων διὰ τὰς κατ' Αἴγυπτον ἀποστάσεις, ἀκριβῆ παραδιδόντων σκέψιν.

---

8 Translation Jones 1930. See also, e.g., Hdt. 2.29 and Strabo 2.5.11. With respect to the description of the *oikoumenê*, sight was higher ranked than hearsay, for observation was considered as the best source of information.

We have carefully recorded in five books the situation concerning the tribes located in the south as they were in our time. But we have entirely given up the idea of writing an account of the islands in the sea which were discovered later ... since our age is unable to bear the toil, particularly after we had written large works about Europe and Asia and because we have been unable to accurately examine the *hypomnêmata* as a result of the disturbances in Egypt.⁹

The *hypomnêmata* are referred to again elsewhere, with more details, when Agatharchides claims that he drew "upon the royal *hypomnêmata* preserved in Alexandria (τὰ μὲν ἐκ τῶν ἐν Ἀλεξανδρείᾳ βασιλικῶν ὑπομνημάτων)."¹⁰ But what were these *hypomnêmata*? The word possesses various meanings: "reminder," "memoranda," "note," "minutes," "publication," "treatise," "commentaries," and the like.¹¹ In the present context there is, however, little dispute: Agatharchides points to notes stored in the royal archives, such as the reports by Ptolemaic officials who explored the African coasts of the Red Sea in order to select sites for hunting elephants — for example Simmias, who made a thorough investigation (ἐξήτασε) of the African tribes lying along the southern Red Sea coast.¹²

Written sources are also often referred to with words as vague as the previous ones, e.g., "authors" (*auctores*), "historians" (οἱ ἵστορες), "writers" (οἱ συγγράψαντες), and the like. Let us quote, for instance, this excerpt from Pliny's *Natural History*, in which the most important trading ports of southwest India are listed:

> regnabat ibi, cum proderem haec, Caelobothras. alius utilior portus gentis Neacyndon, qui vocatur Becare; ibi regnabat Pandion, longe ab emporio in mediterraneo distante oppido quod vocatur Modura; regio autem ex qua piper monoxylis lintribus Becaren convehunt vocatur Cottonara. quae omnia gentium portuumve aut oppidorum nomina apud neminem priorum reperiuntur, quo apparet mutari locorum status.

> The King of Muziris, at the date of publication, was Caelobothras. There is another more serviceable port, belonging to the Neacyndi tribe, called Becare; this is where King Pandi-

---

9 Agatharchides of Cnidus, *Erythr.* 110 (Müller) = Photius, *Bibliotheca*, 460b, transl. Burstein 1989, 173. The last sentence has been misunderstood by Burstein; compare with R. Henry's translation: "parce que nos sources, à cause des troubles survenus en Égypte, ne nous fournissaient pas d'information exacte."
10 Agatharchides of Cnidus, *Erythr.* 79 (Müller) = Diod. Sic. 3.38.1. This sentence is attributed to Diodorus by some scholars, e.g., Peremans 1967.
11 Cf. *LSJ*, s.v. ὑπόμνημα.
12 Agatharchides of Cnidus, *Erythr.* 41 (Müller) = Diod. Sic. 3.18.4. Simmias explored the southern Red Sea area in the service of Ptolemy III.

on reigned, his capital being a town in the interior a long way from the port, called Modura; the district from which pepper is conveyed to Becare in canoes made of hollowed tree-trunks is called Cottonara. But all these names of tribes and ports or towns are to be found in none of the previous writers, which seems to show that the local conditions of the places are changing.[13]

Apparently Pliny takes pride in being the first one to report the names of Muziris, Becare, and Modura, from where precious commodities — namely pepper and pearls — were imported into the Roman Empire, but he does not disclose the names of his informants, nor does he tell us which *auctores* were unaware of this shift in the geography of exchanges.[14] This should come as no surprise, for most authors, as noted above, were silent on the sources they exploited.[15]

Besides literary sources that represented the bulk of the "documentary material," a certain amount of knowledge was obtained from non-written material, such as hearsay accounts.[16] For instance, Pliny the Elder updated his description of the Arab-Persian Gulf with information supplied by ambassadors and merchants, but how he found this information remains obscure:

> *primo afuit a litore stadios X et maritimum etiam ipsa portum habuit, Iuba vero prodente L̄ p.; nunc abesse a litore C̄X̄X̄ legati Arabum nostrique negotiatores qui inde venere adfirmant.*
>
> It [Charax[17]] was originally at a distance of 1¼ miles from the coast, and had a harbour of its own, but when Juba published his work it was 50 miles inland; its present distance from the coast is stated by Arab envoys and our own traders who have come from the place to be 120 miles.[18]

---

13 Plin. *HN* 6.105, edition and translation from Rackham 1942.
14 Pliny's listing of new regions is reflective of the Imperial project of incorporating new information into the Roman system; see Murphy 2004 and Naas 2011, 57–61. On Pliny's aims in cataloging such information in the *Historia naturalis*, see Doody 2010, 23–30.
15 While Pliny does list his primary authorities extensively at the end of the *summarium* and often includes citations in his discussion, especially when they are of comparable social standing to Pliny himself (Murphy 2004, 60–61), he does on occasion suppress those sources. On Pliny's use of sources, see Naas 2002, 145–170 and Smith 2007, 148–155; on the *summarium* generally, see Doody 2001 and Riggsby 2007, 93–98.
16 Non-literary written sources — e.g., inscriptions — played a very limited role in this matter. Among the few examples worth quoting there is Cosmas Indicopleustes, *Top. Christ.* 2.64 (the inscription of Adulis).
17 A city lying close to the Euphrates' mouth.
18 Plin. *HN* 6.139–140, edition and translation from Rackham 1942.

Pliny may refer to Roman or Italian merchants who were involved in long-distance business within the Indian Ocean area.[19] To take another instance, several centuries later — in the mid-sixth century CE — Cosmas Indicopleustes wrote his *Topographia Christiana*, a treatise partly based on his personal experience as a merchant in the western Indian Ocean. This position allowed him to personally visit various places and question locals, as shown by the following example: witnessing a trade circuit supplying the Huns Hephtalites — settled in India — with Egyptian emeralds, he endeavored to collect fresh information from reliable sources.[20]

Much more interesting, however, is the case of non-verbal material, for it occasionally played a role in geographical discussions. Coming to this topic, we can hardly ignore Alexander the Great's attempt to solve the question of the Nile source while leading his army in India. This question, along with that of the summer floods, was counted among the most important geographical problems to sort out. In 327 BCE Alexander, in the course of his Indian expedition, thought that the mystery had been solved:

πρότερον μέν γε ἐν τῷ Ἰνδῷ ποταμῷ κροκοδείλους ἰδών, μόνῳ τῶν ἄλλων ποταμῶν πλὴν Νείλου, πρὸς δὲ ταῖς ὄχθαις τοῦ Ἀκεσίνου κυάμους πεφυκότας ὁποίους ἡ γῆ ἐκφέρει ἡ Αἰγυπτία, καὶ [ὁ] ἀκούσας ὅτι ὁ Ἀκεσίνης ἐμβάλλει ἐς τὸν Ἰνδόν, ἔδοξεν ἐξευρηκέναι τοῦ Νείλου τὰς ἀρχάς, ὡς τὸν Νεῖλον ἐνθένδε ποθὲν ἐξ Ἰνδῶν ἀνίσχοντα καὶ δι' ἐρήμου πολλῆς γῆς ῥέοντα καὶ ταύτῃ ἀπολλύοντα τὸν Ἰνδὸν τὸ ὄνομα, ἔπειτα, ὁπόθεν ἄρχεται διὰ τῆς οἰκουμένης χώρας ῥεῖν, Νεῖλον ἤδη πρὸς Αἰθιόπων τε τῶν ταύτῃ καὶ Αἰγυπτίων καλούμενον...καὶ δὴ καὶ πρὸς Ὀλυμπιάδα γράφοντα ὑπὲρ τῶν Ἰνδῶν τῆς γῆς ἄλλα τε γράψαι καὶ ὅτι δοκοίη αὐτῷ ἐξευρηκέναι τοῦ Νείλου τὰς πηγάς, μικροῖς δή τισι καὶ φαύλοις ὑπὲρ τῶν τηλικούτων τεκμαιρόμενον. ἐπεὶ μέντοι ἀτρεκέστερον ἐξήλεγξε τὰ ἀμφὶ τῷ ποταμῷ τῷ Ἰνδῷ, οὕτω δὴ μαθεῖν παρὰ τῶν ἐπιχωρίων τὸν μὲν Ὑδάσπην τῷ Ἀκεσίνῃ, τὸν Ἀκεσίνην δὲ τῷ Ἰνδῷ τό τε ὕδωρ ξυμβάλλοντας καὶ τῷ ὀνόματι ξυγχωροῦντας, τὸν Ἰνδὸν δὲ ἐκδιδόντα ἤδη ἐς τὴν μεγάλην θάλασσαν, δίστομον τὸν Ἰνδὸν ὄντα, οὐδέ‹ν› τι αὐτῷ προσῆκον τῆς γῆς τῆς Αἰγυπτίας· τηνικαῦτα δὲ τῆς ἐπιστολῆς τῆς πρὸς τὴν μητέρα τοῦτο ‹τὸ› ἀμφὶ τῷ Νείλῳ γραφὲν ἀφελεῖν.

---

19 See also Plin. *HN* 6.149: "Juba omits to mention Batrasavave, the town of the Omani, and the town of Omana which previous writers have made out to be a famous port of Carmania, and also Homna and Attana, towns said by our traders (*nostri negotiatores*) to be now the most frequented ports in the Persian Gulf," transl. Rackham 1942. While merchants and foreign writers are included, as a rule Pliny prefers military sources and considers them to be the most reliable; see Beagon 1992, 188–189.
20 Cosmas Indicopleustes, *Top. Christ.* 11.21: "Some things I have narrated and written down after learning them through experience, others I have told after I learned them accurately by being close to the places" (τὰ μὲν πείρᾳ μαθὼν ἐξηγησάμην καὶ διέγραψα, τὰ δὲ καὶ ἐγγὺς τῶν τόπων γενόμενος ἀκριβῶς μεμαθηκὼς ἐξεῖπον).

He had already seen crocodiles on the Indus, as on no other river except the Nile, and beans [i.e. lotus seeds] growing on the banks of the Acesines of the same sort as the land of Egypt produces and, having heard that the Acesines runs into the Indus, he thought he had found the origin of the Nile; his idea was that the Nile rose somewhere in India, flowed through a great expanse of desert, and there lost the name of Indus, and then, where it began to flow through inhabited country, got the name of Nile from the Ethiopians in those parts and the Egyptians .... In fact it is reported that, when writing to Olympias about the Indian country, Alexander wrote among other things that he thought he had discovered the springs of the Nile, drawing a conclusion about matters of so much importance from very slender indications; but that, when he had more accurately investigated the geography of the river Indus, he learnt from the inhabitants that the Hydaspes joins its stream to the Acesines and the Acesines to the Indus, and that they resign their names, while the Indus then flows out into the Great Sea by two mouths and has nothing whatever to do with Egypt, and as a result he cancelled the part of the letter to his mother which dealt with the Nile.[21]

Irrespective of Alexander's mistake, it must be noted that his geographical reasoning was supported less by written material than by the living creatures that he could observe, namely crocodiles and "beans" which had not been found outside Egypt until this time. These were regarded as substantial proofs until he was confronted with contradictory information provided by the locals. In fact, Alexander was not alone in doing so. His companions also regarded plants and animals as apt pieces of evidence: the parallel they established between India and *Aithiopia*[22] — especially with regard to "climate" (ἀήρ, or κρᾶσις τῶν ἀέρων) — in order to emphasize the similarities between the two areas was backed by such reasoning.[23] Dark-skinned people, remarkable animals and marvelous plants served as proofs that these countries were equally fertile:

ἔχειν δὲ καὶ κιννάμωμον καὶ νάρδον καὶ τὰ ἄλλα ἀρώματα τὴν νότιον γῆν τὴν Ἰνδικὴν ὁμοίως ὥσπερ τὴν Ἀραβίαν καὶ τὴν Αἰθιοπίαν ἔχουσάν τι ἐμφερὲς ἐκείναις κατὰ τοὺς ἡλίους· διαφέρειν δὲ τῷ πλεονασμῷ τῶν ὑδάτων ὥστ' ἔνικμον εἶναι τὸν ἀέρα καὶ τροφιμώτερον παρὰ τοῦτο καὶ γόνιμον μᾶλλον, ὡς δ' αὕτως καὶ τὴν γῆν καὶ τὸ ὕδωρ, ἤδη καὶ μείζω τά τε χερσαῖα τῶν ζῴων καὶ τὰ καθ' ὕδατος τὰ ἐν Ἰνδοῖς τῶν παρ' ἄλλοις εὑρίσκεσθαι.

And he [Aristobulus] says that the southern land of India, like Arabia and *Aithiopia*, bears cinnamon, nard, and other aromatic products, being similar to those countries in the effect of the rays of the sun, although it surpasses them in the copiousness of its waters; and

---

21 Arr. *Anab.* 6.1.2–6, edition and translation from Brunt 1983.
22 Arabia and Egypt were also part of this scheme.
23 See, e.g., Strabo 16.1.13 = Onesicritus, *FGrH* 134 F7. The main point was that India and *Aithiopia*/Egypt, receiving a comparable amount of solar heat, shared the same ἀήρ, even though the former benefited from a greater amount of rain than the latter.

that therefore its air is humid and proportionately more nourishing and more productive; and that this applies both to land and to the water, and therefore, of course, both land and water animals in India are found to be larger than those in other countries.[24]

The idea that living or stuffed animals, fresh or dried plants, stones, and the like could be employed as material supporting, or enhancing, the body of geographical knowledge is less unusual than it may seem at first glance. Let us, for instance, recall King Ptolemy II and the so-called Alexandrian zoo. This ruler had wild animals hunted in *Aithiopia* and brought back to Alexandria for exhibition. Likewise, a vivid account of the capture of a giant snake in *Aithiopia*, preserved by Agatharchides of Cnidus, illustrates how unique this enterprise was. To close the story he reports that Ptolemy gave the hunters a suitable reward and kept the snake as a marvelous exhibit for visitors to his kingdom. How animals and geographical knowledge could relate to each other is made explicit by Agatharchides of Cnidus in this conclusion:

> ὁ δὲ Πτολεμαῖος ... τὸνδ' ὄφιν ἔτρεφε τετιθασευμένον καὶ τοῖς εἰς τὴν βασιλείαν παραβάλλουσι ξένοις μέγιστον παρεχόμενον καὶ παραδοξότατον θέαμα. Διόπερ τηλικούτου μεγέθους ὄφεως εἰς ὄψιν κοινὴν κατηντηκότος οὐκ ἄξιον ἀπιστεῖν τοῖς Αἰθίοψιν οὐδὲ μῦθον ὑπολαμβάνειν τὸ θρυλούμενον ὑπ' αὐτῶν. ἀποφαίνονται γὰρ ὁρᾶσθαι κατὰ τὴν χώραν αὐτῶν ὄφεις τηλικούτους τὸ μέγεθος ...
>
> As for Ptolemy ... he kept and fed the snake which had now been tamed and afforded the greatest and most astonishing sight for the strangers who visited his kingdom. Consequently, in view of the fact that a snake of so great a size has been exposed to the public gaze, it is not fair to doubt the word of the Ethiopians or to assume that the report which they circulated far and wide is mere fiction. For they state that there are to be seen in their country snakes so great in size ...[25]

Interestingly, this living snake being exhibited to ordinary people (ὄφεως εἰς ὄψιν κοινὴν κατηντηκότος) partly answers a question raised by Daniela Dueck. At the end of her history of ancient geography, Dueck poses the question of "popular geographical knowledge." She wonders how common people could get geographical information and how much they could know of remote and

---

24 Strabo 15.1.22 (ed. Meineke 1877) = Onesicritus, *FGrH* 134 F22 (the bulk of this passage was believed by Jacoby to go back to this person). Translation Jones 1930.
25 Diod. Sic. 3.37.8–9, ed. Vogel 1888 (transl. Oldfather 1935). Cf. Diod. Sic. 3.36.3: "The second Ptolemy ... brought to the knowledge of the Greeks (ἐποίησεν εἰς γνῶσιν ἐλθεῖν τοῖς Ἕλλησι) other [i.e. than elephants] kinds of animals which had never before been seen and were objects of amazement," transl. Oldfather 1935.

exotic places.²⁶ In this regard, Ptolemy II's zoo no doubt provided a better picture (φαντασία)²⁷ of distant *Aithiopia* to those who could afford a trip to Alexandria.²⁸

Thus, ancient geographical knowledge was based on, and improved by various types of evidence: written texts recording all kinds of data and stored in various places, hearsay accounts, and finally non-verbal pieces of information. The question is whether, or to what extent, this material may be defined as "documents," starting from the modern perspective.

2 Was Ancient Geographical Knowledge Based on "Documents"? The Modern Point of View

Any attempt to answer this question requires us to clarify the meaning of "document" and "documentary material." A first step leads us to language dictionaries, which offer basic definitions, such as the following one: "A piece of written, printed, or electronic matter that provides information or evidence or that serves as an official record."²⁹ Turning more specifically to the ancient world, the *Encyclopedia of the Ancient World* has an entry on "documents and archives." Here a slightly different conception of document shows up:

> Although in the Greek states and in Rome literacy was less widespread and oral communication was more important than it is in the more developed parts of the modern world, businesses — both of states and of individuals or groups of individuals — generated documents, which were stored and published in various ways.³⁰

---

26 Dueck 2012, 118–121.
27 This word — meaning here "representation of appearances or images, primarily derived from sensation" (*LSJ*) — appears in an interesting passage from Strabo (2.5.1), where a distinction is established between the uneducated (ἀπαίδευτος) man and the πολιτικός regarding their respective level of geographical knowledge.
28 On Ptolemy's "zoo," and animals in Egypt more broadly, see now McDonald 2014.
29 *Oxford Dictionaries* (https://en.oxforddictionaries.com/definition/document, accessed March 31, 2022). This definition comes with a variety of examples: "The originals of several documents handed in as evidence also appeared to form part of the file"; "Information can take the form of certificates, documents and other written evidence"; "Most of what I write is actually just cut and paste stuff from official documents, but I seem to get away with it," etc.
30 Rhodes 2012.

In Rhodes's eyes, the document relates to businesses (contracts, testimonies, annual praetors' edicts, accounts, etc.), meaning that literary texts fall outside the scope of documentary material. Given that a considerable quantity of data was brought to geographers by literary texts, as seen above, this approach is not satisfactory, for it would lead to the conclusion that ancient geography was not based on documents. As the chapters of DiGiulio and Fournet in the final section of this volume reveal, the text world of the Roman Empire admits a far greater degree of overlap between the boundaries of literary and documentary writing than the modern historian might. Texts which the *Encyclopedia* might differentiate as strictly documents or literature could "exist alongside one another as part of the same archive of knowledge."[31]

The International Organization for Standardization (ISO) operates with a broader definition, according to which information stored on a specific support is regarded as a document.[32] Here, information must be understood as a set of data which produces something intelligible: texts printed on books, music recorded on CDs, pictures stored on DVDs, and emailed texts, all being information stored on support, are equally documents.[33] From this contemporary perspective, most types of evidence that I have listed in the previous section fall within the category of document: the *hypomnêmata* used by Agatharchides; Juba's *Arabika* read by Pliny, and the like. Similarly, hearsay accounts become documents as soon as they are recorded and stored: one may compare the reports by the *nostri negotiatores* mentioned by Pliny the Elder and preserved in his *Natural History*. These kinds of recorded accounts, as Bodel describes in his analysis of signatory witnesses, were valuable not as proofs but as a "more permanent form [of] oral testimony that could later be verified" and reveal that Rome "never fully emerged from the oral stage of documentary development."[34] Conversely, hearsay information that has not been recorded disappears, and accordingly cannot be categorized as documentary material.

A difficulty arises, however, with the case of living animals exhibited in zoos, or plants displayed in sanctuaries: the giant Ethiopian snake proudly shown to Greek visitors at Alexandria is by no means information stored on a

---

31 DiGiulio in this volume.
32 International Organization for Standardization/Technical Committee 46 (Information and Documentation), with various guidelines available at https://www.iso.org/committee/48750.html, accessed March 21, 2022.
33 Compare this with the definition provided by the French Union of Documentation Organizations: documents are "all bases of materially fixed knowledge, and capable of being used for consultation, study, and proof" (Briet 2006, 10).
34 Bodel in this volume.

support; nor is the Arabian frankincense tree transplanted into an Asian temple by kings of Asia Minor. Like Ptolemy II, these kings aimed at making an emblematic Arabian tree visible to a broad public.³⁵ In reality, this difficulty is solved if we adopt Michael Buckland's approach to the question of "documentality." His analysis is in turn based on the research of two twentieth-century European documentalists, Paul Otlet and Suzanne Briet. To begin with, Buckland states that the most prevalent use of the word "information" includes any material thing or presentation — such as a radio announcement or television documentary — perceived as instructive. In this sense, "information" becomes a synonym for a broad view of "document." Then, according to what he calls the conventional, or material view, several types of documents can be identified:

> Documents are graphic records, usually of textual form, inscribed or displayed on a flat surface (clay tablet, paper, microfilm, computer screen) that are material, local, and, generally, transportable. These objects are made as documents. The limits of inclusion are unclear. Some have argued, for example, for the inclusion of terrestrial globes and of sculptures under this heading.

He goes on to say:

> On this view almost anything can be made to serve as a document, to signify something, to be held up as constituting evidence of some sort. Models, educational toys, natural history collections, and archaeological traces can be considered in this category. Briet's classic discussion of documentality in her manifesto "Qu'est-ce que la documentation?" famously asserted that a specimen of a newly discovered species of antelope, when positioned in a taxonomy and in a cage, was made to serve as a document.³⁶

From this point of view, any source of information, in material form, capable of being used for reference, or study, or as an authority is a document. Bodel identifies this understanding as a common line of thinking between Roman jurists and modern epigraphists: "material and the medium are irrelevant."³⁷ This view would also appear to substantiate Arthur-Montagne's analysis of school texts as documents to be studied and transferred to the wax tablets of the mind.³⁸

Otlet was, in fact, the first to point out that objects themselves — natural objects, artifacts, objects bearing traces of human activity such as archaeological finds, explanatory models, works of art, etc. — can be regarded as "documents"

---

35 See Theophr. *Hist. pl.* 9.4.8–9 and Plin. *HN* 12.56–57.
36 Buckland 2014, 179–180; compare Briet 2006, 10–11. Conversely the animal in the wild must not be regarded as a document.
37 Bodel in this volume.
38 Arthur-Montagne in this volume.

if we are informed by observation of them.³⁹ Briet, however, went further, offering the most accurate — and, she adds, the less intuitive and accessible — definition of document:

> Any concrete or symbolic indexical sign (*indice*), preserved or recorded towards the ends of representing, of reconstituting, or of proving a physical or intellectual phenomenon. Is a star a document? Is a pebble a document? Is a living animal a document? No. But the photographs and the catalogues of stars, the stones in a museum of mineralogy, and the animals that are catalogued and shown in a zoo, are documents.⁴⁰

This modern view properly accounts for the "non-verbal" material used by Greek and Romans to build on and expand their knowledge of the *oikoumenê*: an animal offered to observation and study — such as the python at Alexandria's zoo — was actually made into a document. Even though very little is known to us about cataloging in antiquity, this creature was a "concrete sign" preserved for the goal of representing natural phenomena. The "documentary status" of captured and exhibited animals is proved by a passage where Strabo discusses and emends the description of the rhinoceros published by Artemidorus some decades earlier. The latter could see a specimen in Alexandria (καίπερ ἑωρακέναι φήσας ἐν Ἀλεξανδρείᾳ), while the former also observed one in an unspecified place (ἀπὸ γε τοῦ ὑφ' ἡμῶν ὁραθέντος).⁴¹

To conclude, on the basis of these modern definitions of the document, it seems clear that ancient geographical knowledge was based on documents.⁴² But what about the Greek and Roman point of view? Did ancient geographers regard written accounts, living creatures, literary texts, and so on as "documents"? Did they even conceive of "documents"? In other words, is the modern concept of document relevant to ancient geography, or somehow anachronistic?

---

39 Buckland 1991, 354–355.
40 Briet 2006, 10.
41 Strabo 16.4.15. This discussion takes place in Strabo's presentation of *Aithiopia*.
42 Ferraris's theory of documents — in which intention and recording are strongly tied — is of little interest in the present discussion when compared to Buckland's approach. See, however, the editors' Introduction in the present volume, and also the important preliminary observations of Bodel in this volume.

3 Was Ancient Geographical Knowledge Based on Documents? The Ancient Point of View

As seen in the first section, the modern expression "documentary material" or "document" lacks an equivalent in Greek or Latin. Instead, various words such as *logoi* (e.g., *Aiguptioi logoi*, *Indikoi logoi*), *anagraphai*, *hypomnêmata*, *historia*, and *auctores* turn up in Agatharchides, Strabo, Eratosthenes, Polybius, Pliny the Elder, and others. Each of them points to a more or less particular type of written evidence. For instance, *anagraphê* applies to the treatise, record, or description. This meaning certainly overlaps with the modern concept of document as defined earlier, but there is by no means strict correspondence between the two. As the editors of this volume rightly point out: "The relevant Greek terms can be divided into, on one hand, words that emphasize the act that created the document (typically the act of writing [γράφειν]) and, on the other hand, words that emphasize the function of the document [μνήματα; σημεῖα; γνωρίσματα])."[43]

Considering the Latin vocabulary, from which our own word "document" derives, the term *liber* does not match our modern "document." Neither does *documentum*, a term that refers to a lesson, an example, or a proof, as in the following sentence by Cicero: "Publius Rutilius was a model of virtue, antiquity, and prudence for our men" (*P. Rutilius documentum fuit hominibus nostris virtutis, antiquitatis, prudentiae*; Cic. *Rab. Post.* 10.27). In fact, *documentum* and *exemplum* are closely related. This point is clearly established in the Introduction to the present volume: "*documenta* contain lessons, and within Livy's historical narrative they link the historical events that they describe with the present and future generations for whom these lessons are intended." In contrast, it is not until the late eighteenth century that the French word *document* (meaning "information" or a "piece of information") appears in written evidence. Let us quote, for instance, this excerpt from the narrative by La Pérouse, a naval officer who was appointed in 1785 by Louis XVI to lead an expedition around the world. Interestingly, *documens* turns up in the context of geographical knowledge: "The island Sainte-Catherine ... is a Portuguese settlement, which, for seventy years, has not been visited much by European vessels other than

---

43 Arthur-Montagne, DiGiulio, and Kuin in this volume (Greek words added by me).

ones from that country; this is why there is little hope of getting information (*documens*) from travelers' accounts."⁴⁴

The gap between modern and ancient lexica seems to me so important that one may wonder whether, or to what extent, our concept of "document" and "documentation" existed in antiquity — at least in the making of ancient geography. In my opinion, our ideas could hardly exist in antiquity, for the following main reason. As Briet recalls when reflecting on the profession of documentalist, the notion of documentation is historically related to the never-ending increase in knowledge that characterizes modern and contemporary times:

> Little by little, the theory of documentation has grown since the great period of the typographical explosion that began in the third quarter of the nineteenth century, which corresponds to the development of the historical sciences as the progress of techniques. Otlet had been its magus, the international leader, with his Institute of Bibliography, his universal decimal classification etc. ... Gutenberg's invention has created such a voluminous and intense typographical production, especially in the last one hundred years, that the problem of the conservation and utilization of graphic documents became acute. Since the seventeenth century, the abundance of written documents has required a scientific method of prospecting and of classifying books and manuscripts: bibliography.⁴⁵

Thus, while obviously ancient geography was based on documents from our point of view, ancient geographers could hardly regard the material they used as documents, since this concept did not exist. In these circumstances, it is worth trying to clarify their ideas about the "documentary material" supporting their scientific activities. The prologue of Arrian's *Anabasis* clearly helps us dissect ancient geographers' attitude, even if he refers to historians instead of geographers:

> Πτολεμαῖος ὁ Λάγου καὶ Ἀριστόβουλος ὁ Ἀριστοβούλου ὅσα μὲν ταὐτὰ ἄμφω περὶ Ἀλεξάνδρου τοῦ Φιλίππου συνέγραψαν, ταῦτα ἐγὼ ὡς πάντῃ ἀληθῆ ἀναγράφω, ὅσα δὲ οὐ ταὐτά, τούτων τὰ πιστότερα ἐμοὶ φαινόμενα καὶ ἅμα ἀξιαφηγητότερα ἐπιλεξάμενος. ἄλλοι μὲν δὴ ἄλλα ὑπὲρ Ἀλεξάνδρου ἀνέγραψαν, οὐδ' ἔστιν ὑπὲρ ὅτου πλείονες ἢ ἀξυμφωνότεροι ἐς ἀλλήλους· ἀλλ' ἐμοὶ Πτολεμαῖός τε καὶ Ἀριστόβουλος πιστότεροι ἔδοξαν ἐς τὴν ἀφήγησιν, ὁ μὲν ὅτι συνεστράτευσε βασιλεῖ Ἀλεξάνδρῳ, Ἀριστόβουλος, Πτολεμαῖος δὲ πρὸς τῷ ξυστρατεῦσαι ὅτι καὶ αὐτῷ βασιλεῖ ὄντι αἰσχρότερον ἤ τῳ ἄλλῳ ψεύσασθαι ἦν· ἄμφω δέ, ὅτι τετελευτηκότος ἤδη Ἀλεξάνδρου ξυγγράφουσιν [ὅτε] αὐτοῖς ἥ τε ἀνάγκη καὶ ὁ μισθὸς τοῦ

---

44 Milet-Mureau 1797, 90: "L'île Sainte-Catherine ... est un établissement portugais, qui, depuis soixante-dix ans, n'a été que très-peu visité par les vaisseaux européens autres que ceux de cette nation; il y a donc peu de documens à espérer des relations des voyageurs." Translation by the editors of the volume.
45 Briet 2006, 12.

ἄλλως τι ἢ ὡς συνηνέχθη ξυγγράψαι ἀπῆν. ἔστι δὲ ἃ καὶ πρὸς ἄλλων ξυγγεγραμμένα, ὅτι καὶ αὐτὰ ἀξιαφήγητά τέ μοι ἔδοξε καὶ οὐ πάντη ἄπιστα, ὡς λεγόμενα μόνον ὑπὲρ Ἀλεξάνδρου ἀνέγραψα.

Wherever Ptolemy son of Lagus and Aristobulus son of Aristobulus have both given the same accounts of Alexander son of Philip, it is my practice to record what they say as completely true, but where they differ, to select the version I regard as more trustworthy and also better worth telling. In fact other writers have given a variety of accounts of Alexander, nor is there any other figure of whom there are more historians who are more contradictory of each other, but in my view Ptolemy and Aristobulus are more trustworthy in their narrative, since Aristobulus took part in King Alexander's expedition, and Ptolemy not only did the same, but as he himself was a king, mendacity would have been more dishonourable for him than for anyone else; again, both wrote when Alexander was dead and neither was under any constraint or hope of gain to make him set down anything but what actually happened. However, I have also recorded some statements made in the accounts of others, when I thought them worth mention and not entirely untrustworthy, but only as tales told of Alexander.[46]

Assessing the value of his sources before starting his narrative, Arrian explains why, among Alexander's companions, Ptolemy and Aristobulus stand out of all other authorities. The latter, having taken part in the expedition, could personally observe what he described (i.e., his account is based on what he saw), while the former was not only an observer but, as a king (he founded the Ptolemaic Empire), he could not lie. In addition, having composed their works after Alexander died, both were prevented from flattering the king, that is to say distorting the truth, in order to obtain a better position. In sum, Arrian does not draw on informative texts — or what we would call "documentary material" — but on trustworthy authors.

Similarly, ancient geographers emphasized those who provided geographical information, instead of information itself: what really mattered were the sources and their authors' intentions. Let us return to Strabo's review of the "documentary material" relating to India. Like Arrian, Strabo praises reliable authors, namely Alexander's friends, even if they happen to occasionally differ from each other, and even if they may have distorted some geographical facts because they wanted to flatter the king — here Strabo hints at the Caucasus, which was placed in India (Hindu Kush) so that Alexander could equal Heracles (15.1.8–9). In spite of this faulty attitude, Strabo says, they deserve confidence for having been first-hand "observers" (αὐτόπται); as such their descriptions of

---

[46] Arr. *Anab.* 1.1.1–3, edition and translation from Brunt 1976. On differentiating between ancient Greek geographers and historians, particularly in the context of Strabo's approach, see Clarke 1999, 193–336.

Indian regions and tribes are likely to convey true facts. Megasthenes, who stayed in India, is also regarded as a serious author, even if he sometimes gives credence to mythical stories conveyed by poets — here Strabo explicitly refers to Euripides, according to whom Dionysus visited the whole of Asia. In contrast, poets — except Homer — are blamed for inventing stories for the sake of giving pleasure to their audience. They use "tales" (μῦθος), which are a form of "deceit" (ψευδές). Besides poets, other authors such as Ctesias — who did not visit India — and, to some extent, the same Megasthenes come under suspicion, mainly because of the "incredible marvels" (τὸ θαυμαστόν; τερατολογία) that they reported: to Strabo's eyes, they were liars inventing "fiction" (πλάσμα) to entertain their audience.[47] Strabo is not alone in thinking so: such ideas are more or less ubiquitous.[48]

Thus, ancient geographers did not share the "neutral" conception of documents as a certain quantity of information recorded and stored, because — as noted above — this analytical and epistemological tool was not formulated until modern times. The sources they used, whatever their nature may be, were assigned a certain degree of truth and reliability.[49] If an author is considered prone to "truth" (τἀληθές, 15.1.28), then his text, being reliable (τὸ ἐγγυτάτω πίστεως, μνήμης ἄξια, 15.1.9–10 and 15.1.28) and having informative value, may be compared to a "document."[50] In contrast, a text composed by an ignorant author reporting "things that do not exist" (μὴ λέγοντος δὲ τὰ ὄντα, ἀλλὰ τὰ μὴ ὄντα ὡς ὄντα κατ' ἄγνοιαν, 1.2.35) is deprived of informative value. In other words, the status of "documentary material" depends on a subjective "appreciation" (δίαιτα) by the reader (15.1.10). Therefore, the same authority — e.g., Homer —

---

47 Strabo 1.2.35; 15.1.5–9 and 15.1.28. Note that another important distinction was made between private individuals and officials. Why, for instance, did Agatharchides use the accounts composed by the explorers dispatched to the Red Sea area by Ptolemy II? Because people serving a king — that is to say, having been chosen by a king — were far more reliable than individuals sailing back and forth on the Red Sea — i.e., merchants. Being motivated by their own private interests, the latter could not be regarded as *histores* — i.e., people aiming at improving geography.

48 See, in particular, Lucian, *Hist. conscr.* On Lucian's approach to epigraphic documents in particular, see Kuin and Ní Mheallaigh in this volume. On what she calls "wonder-culture" in the Roman Empire more broadly, see Ní Mheallaigh 2014, 261–277.

49 This, of course, is not to deny that we moderns also have categories of good and bad information. Historians, in particular, must systematically question and assess the reliability of their sources. On the philosophical underpinnings of Strabo's methodology and his approach to his sources, see Roseman 2005.

50 The same reasoning applies to "proofs" (τεκμήριον). See, for instance, Strabo 11.7.4; 13.3.2; 15.1.9; 16.2.23, etc.

could be highly esteemed by some geographers and strongly rejected by other scholars:

> καὶ πρῶτον ὅτι ὀρθῶς ὑπειλήφαμεν καὶ ἡμεῖς καὶ οἱ πρὸ ἡμῶν, ὧν ἐστι καὶ Ἵππαρχος, ἀρχηγέτην εἶναι τῆς γεωγραφικῆς ἐμπειρίας Ὅμηρον· ὃς οὐ μόνον ἐν τῇ κατὰ τὴν ποίησιν ἀρετῇ πάντας ὑπερβέβληται τοὺς πάλαι καὶ τοὺς ὕστερον, ἀλλὰ σχεδόν τι καὶ τῇ κατὰ τὸν βίον ἐμπειρίᾳ τὸν πολιτικόν, ἀφ' ἧς οὐ μόνον περὶ τὰς πράξεις ἐσπούδασεν ἐκεῖνος, ὅπως ὅτι πλείστας γνοίη καὶ παραδώσει τοῖς ὕστερον ἐσομένοις, ἀλλὰ καὶ τὰ περὶ τοὺς τόπους τούς τε καθ' ἕκαστα καὶ τοὺς κατὰ σύμπασαν τὴν οἰκουμένην, γῆν...

> First, I say that both I and my predecessors, one of whom was Hipparchus himself, are right in regarding Homer as the founder of the science of geography; for Homer has surpassed all men, both of ancient and modern times, not only in the excellence of his poetry, but also, I might say, in his acquaintance with all that pertains to public life. And this acquaintance made him busy himself not only about public activities, to the end that he might learn of as many of them as possible and give an account of them to posterity, but also about the geography both of the individual countries and of the inhabited world ...[51]

> τοῦτο μὲν δὴ ὀρθῶς ἂν λέγοις, ὦ Ἐρατόσθενες· ἐκεῖνα δ' οὐκ ὀρθῶς, ἀφαιρούμενος αὐτὸν τὴν τοσαύτην πολυμάθειαν καὶ τὴν ποιητικὴν γραώδη μυθολογίαν ἀποφαίνων, ᾗ δέδοται πλάττειν, φής, ὃ ἂν αὐτῇ φαίνηται ψυχαγωγίας οἰκεῖον. ἆρα γὰρ οὐδὲ τοῖς ἀκροωμένοις τῶν ποιητῶν οὐδὲν συμβάλλεται πρὸς ἀρετήν; λέγω δὲ τὸ πολλῶν ὑπάρξαι τόπων ἔμπειρον ἢ στρατηγίας ἢ γεωργίας.

> You may be right, Eratosthenes, on that point, but you are wrong when you deny to Homer the possession of vast learning, and go on to declare that poetry is a fable-prating old wife, who has been permitted to "invent" (as you call it) whatever she deems suitable for purposes of entertainment. What, then? Is no contribution made, either, to the excellence of him who hears the poets recited? I again refer to the poet's being an expert in generalship or geography.[52]

In sum, I tend to believe that "documentality" did not exist among ancient geographers, in that they did not regard their sources as "documents." Rather they concentrated on the reliability of those who produced information, often expressing a strong disapproval of their statements.[53] Conversely, we regard anything that can signify something, anything that can be held up as constituting evidence of some sort, as a document, whoever produced it, whatever its nature.

---

51 Strabo 1.1.2, edition and translation from Jones 1917.
52 Strabo 1.2.3.
53 See, among many examples, Curt. 9.1.31–34: *equidem plura transcribo quam credo* ("As for myself, I report more things than I believe," transl. Rolfe 1946).

References

Beagon, M. (1992), *Roman Nature: The Thought of Pliny the Elder*, Oxford.
Briet, S. (2006), *What Is Documentation?*, ed. and transl. R.E. Day and L. Martinet, with H.G.B. Anghelescu, Lanham, MD.
Brunt, P.A. (ed. and transl.) (1976), *Arrian: Anabasis, Books 1-4*, Loeb Classical Library 236, Cambridge, MA.
Brunt, P.A. (ed. and transl.) (1983), *Arrian: Anabasis, Books 5-7 Indica*, Loeb Classical Library 269, Cambridge, MA.
Buckland, M.K. (1991), "Information as Thing", in: *Journal of the American Society of Information Science* 42, 351–360.
Buckland, M.K. (2014), "Documentality beyond Documents", in: *The Monist* 97, 179–186.
Burstein, S.M. (ed.) (1989), *Agatharchides of Cnidus: On the Erythraean Sea*, London.
Clarke, K. (1999), *Between Geography and History: Hellenistic Constructions of the Roman World*, Oxford.
Doody, A. (2001), "Finding Facts in Pliny's Encyclopedia: The *Summarivm* of the *Natural History*", in: *Ramus* 30, 1–22.
Doody, A. (2010), *Pliny's Encyclopedia: The Reception of the Natural History*, Cambridge.
Dueck, D. (2012), *Geography in Classical Antiquity*, Cambridge.
Ferraris, M. (2012), *Documentality: Why It Is Necessary to Leave Traces*, transl. R. Davies, New York.
Jones, H.L. (ed. and transl.) (1917), *Strabo: Geography, Books 1-2*, Loeb Classical Library 49, Cambridge, MA.
Jones, H.L. (ed. and transl.) (1930), *Strabo: Geography, Books 15–16*, Loeb Classical Library 241, Cambridge, MA.
Marrou, H.-I. (1975), *De la connaissance historique*, 6th edn., Paris.
McDonald, A. (2014), "Animals in Egypt", in: G.L. Campbell (ed.), *The Oxford Handbook of Animals in Classical Thought and Life*, Oxford, 441–457.
Meineke, A. (ed.) (1877), *Strabonis Geographica*, Leipzig.
Milet-Mureau, L.A. (1797), *Voyage de la Pérouse autour du monde publié conformément au décret du 22 avril 1791*, Vol. 4, Paris.
Murphy, T. (2004), *Pliny the Elder's Natural History: The Empire in the Encyclopedia*, Oxford.
Naas, V. (2002), *Le projet encyclopédique de Pline l'ancien*, Rome.
Naas, V. (2011), "Imperialism, *Mirabilia* and Knowledge: Some Paradoxes in the *Historia Naturalis*", in: R. Gibson/R. Morello (eds.), *Pliny the Elder: Themes and Contexts*, Leiden, 57–70.
Ní Mheallaigh, K. (2014), *Reading Fiction with Lucian: Fakes, Freaks and Hyperreality*, Cambridge.
Pearson, L. (1960), *The Lost Histories of Alexander the Great*, New York.
Pédech, P. (1984), *Historiens compagnons d'Alexandre. Callisthène, Onésicrite, Néarque, Ptolémée, Aristobule*, Paris.
Peremans, W. (1967), "Diodore de Sicile et Agatharchide de Cnide", in: *Historia* 16, 432–455.
Oldfather, C.H. (ed. and transl.) (1935), *Diodorus Siculus: Library of History, Volume II: Books 2.35–4.58*, Loeb Classical Library 303, Cambridge, MA.
Rackham, H. (ed. and transl.) (1942), *Pliny: Natural History, Books 3–7*, Loeb Classical Library 352, Cambridge, MA.

Rhodes, P.J. (2012), "Documents and Archives", *The Encyclopedia of Ancient History*, doi.org/10.1002/9781444338386.wbeah08052.
Riggsby, A.M. (2007), "Guides to the Wor(l)d", in: T. Whitmarsh/J. König (eds.), *Ordering Knowledge in the Roman Empire*, Cambridge, 88–107.
Rolfe, J.C. (ed. and transl.) (1946), *Quintus Curtius: History of Alexander, Books 6-10*, Loeb Classical Library 369, Cambridge, MA.
Roseman, C.H. (2005), "Reflections of Philosophy: Strabo and Geographical Sources", in: D. Dueck/H. Lindsay/S. Pothecary (eds.), *Strabo's Cultural Geography: The Making of a Kolossourgia*, Cambridge, 27–41.
Smith, C. (2007), "Pliny the Elder and Archaic Rome", in: E. Bispham/G. Rowe/E. Matthews (eds.), *Vita Vigilia Est: Essays in Honour of Barbara Levick*, *BICS* Suppl. 100, London, 147–170.
Vogel, F. (ed.) (1888), *Diodori Bibliotheca historica*, Leipzig.

Sjoukje M. Kamphorst
A Community Set in Stone? Monumental Decrees as Instruments of Greek Interactions

Abstract: This chapter evaluates civic inscriptions in Greek cities as media for coordinating cooperation during the late Hellenistic and early Imperial periods. J.L. Austin's notion of "speech act theory" and Michael Chwe's concept of "rational rituals" serve as foils to Ferraris's understanding of documents as the material representations of social acts. The prevalence of inscribed civic documents to record inter-city relations suggests their role in documenting and performing community-building in Hellenistic and Roman Greece. In the transition to Empire, civil decrees may have lost their agency to foster diplomacy between *poleis*, but nonetheless remained "informational beacons" within communities about their relationship with Rome.

Greek cities had the custom of inscribing decrees and other civic documents on stone, resulting in the display of monumentalized documents in the most visible spaces of the city. Ferraris proposes to study documents as records of social acts or "social objects," with their own agency to (intentionally or unintentionally) shape realities.[1] In this light, the materiality and conspicuous display of inscribed official documents in the Greek city draws attention to their special significance as objects that had an effect on social reality. In this chapter, I investigate the social agency of inscribed decrees in interactions between cities, and what changing inscribing strategies can tell us about how this agency developed from the Hellenistic to the early Imperial period.

Although the function or "point" of inscribing in Greco-Roman society has long been the subject of research, most studies focus on the role of inscribed texts within a single Greek city (often Athens), or within the administrative unity of the Roman Empire.[2] The function of inscribed decrees in the communication *between* polities has however not received a great deal of attention.[3]

---

[1] Ferraris 2012, esp. 120–174; Ferraris 2014.
[2] On epigraphic culture generally, see Robert 1961. On Roman (public and funerary) epigraphy, see MacMullen 1982; Beard 1985; Corbier 1987 (which also offers extensive bibliography); C. Williamson 1987; Meyer 1990; Corbier 2006; Meyer 2012. On Athenian decrees, see Thomas 1989, 68–83; Hedrick 1999; Sickinger 1999, 2009; Lambert 2011, 2012; Meyer 2013. For Greek

This is remarkable, since a large proportion of documents inscribed by Greek cities were concerned with external contacts. All over the Greek world we find inscribed records documenting interactions between cities: collaborative agreements such as *sympoliteia* or *isopoliteia*; records of inter-city arbitrations; decrees granting *proxenia* or other official honors to foreigners and to their *poleis*; letters recognizing the *asylia* (inviolability) of sanctuaries or the panhellenic status of festivals; and various other types of documents. Most of these texts, whether they ultimately document letters, records, or agreements, are presented in a decree-like structure. Therefore, they are for the purpose of this chapter grouped together under the term "decrees recording inter-city interactions."

At the absolute height of the Greek practice of inscribing civic documents, in the second century BCE (see Figure 2), decrees recording inter-*polis* interaction may represent more than half of our evidence.[4] This observation deserves further exploration. A closer examination of decrees recording inter-city interactions should lead to a better understanding of why the Greeks inscribed civic documents at all, why this became particularly important in the Hellenistic era, and why the practice declined again in the Imperial period.

---

cities and *koina* in general, see Rhodes with Lewis 1997; Rhodes 2001a, 2001b. The materiality of texts in antiquity has likewise become a popular subject recently: see e.g., Berti *et al.* 2017; Petrovic *et al.* 2018.

3 The importance of inscribed documents in inter-*polis* contacts was hinted at in Ma 2003. See also Culasso Gastaldi 2014; Mack 2015 (on institutional aspects).

4 In Figure 2, decrees were categorized per 50-year period using a quantitative probability distribution, excluding all those decrees for which no (approximate) date is given, as laid out by Wilson 2009, 219–227 (this method is also employed for inscriptions in Mack 2015, 234–236). In the numbers labeled 'Greek States', I have included all entries listed as separate decrees in Rhodes with Lewis 1997. Rhodes and Lewis focus on documentary formulas, and therefore do not include all known decrees. Due to their stylistic uniformity and abbreviated nature, proxeny grants and other honorific texts may often have been omitted. The graph is thus by no means meant to represent hard data, but rather offers an indication of the development of Greek documentary epigraphic culture. I have compared this general development to graphs presented in Mack 2015, 237 and 268, recording respectively the number of decrees for *proxenoi* and for foreign judges. In the timeframe 249–200 BCE, my graph peaks around 850 decrees in total. Mack's proxeny graph also peaks here, at *c.* 660, and we can add roughly another twenty-five foreign judges' decrees. Combining this with estimated numbers of other texts recording inter-city relationships, such as *asylia*, festival travel, etc., indicates that they make up an enormous proportion (likely more than half) of the total decree material.

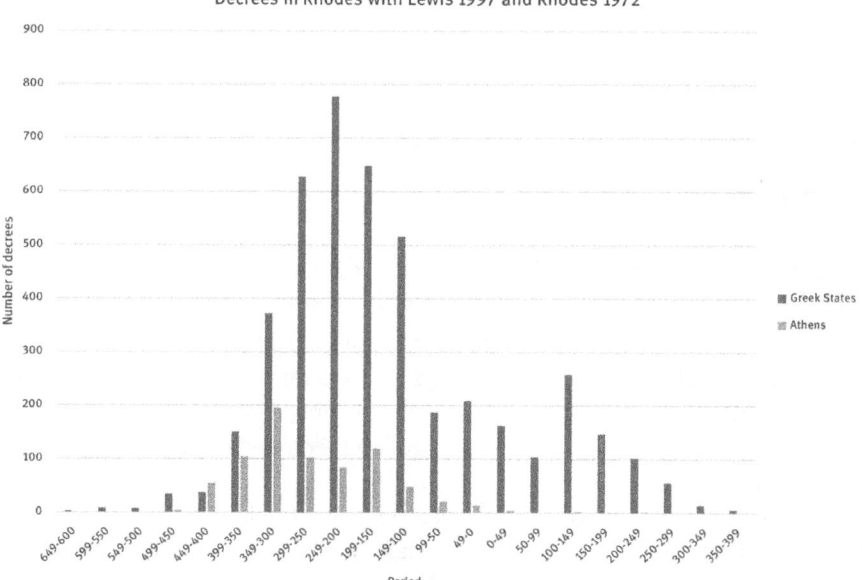

Fig. 2: This graph shows the chronological distribution of all decrees listed in the inventory in Rhodes with Lewis 1997, and in the appendices of Rhodes 1972.

Against the backdrop of these large questions, I argue here that it is imperative to approach inscribed decrees as constituent elements of the relationships between cities. First, I use speech act theory and a model of common knowledge creation from game theory to find out what social acts inscribed decrees represent, helping us understand their agency (section 1). I then apply this theoretical framework to a Hellenistic example of an honorific decree for foreign judges (section 2). Focusing on publication strategies employed to promote the contents of the decree, I here aim to show how an inscribed document's agency could extend over more than one city. Finally, I offer a comparison with the strategies involved in the publication of a Mytilenean decree from the very start of the Imperial age (section 3).

The contrast between the strategies used is indicative of changes in the Greek practice of inscribing civic documents over time, but also of the transformation of Greek connectivity and large-scale community formation in this period. This comparative case study reveals how important it is to consider monumentalized documents not just as sources, but as social objects, if we want to understand not just the Greek epigraphic culture, but also Mediterranean connectivity.

1 Inscriptions as Performance of Community-building

Ferraris proposes to look at what documents do rather than at how they present themselves.[5] To understand what inscribed decrees do in Hellenistic *polis* society, we can try to find out what social acts these inscriptions represent. The texts under investigation here are decrees, in essence rendering the transactions of council and/or assembly meetings. In this section, I argue that inscribed decrees represent both the decisions recorded in them, and the creation of a sense of community in the *polis*.

One of the ways in which inscribed decrees function as social objects becomes apparent when we consider the language used in them in light of J.L. Austin's speech-act theory.[6] Many of the things said at public meetings in the Hellenistic *polis* were more than just informative statements: they contained what Austin would call powerful "performative utterances." The confirmations of decisions, enacted by expressions like "it is decided that *x*" or "the assembly votes *y*," are such performative phrases.[7] More than just stating facts, the very uttering of such phrases (combined with the non-verbal utterances involved in voting) equals the performance of a social act, in this case the making of the decision.[8]

These social acts are preserved in inscribed decrees as (variations of) the phrase ἔδοξε τῇ βουλῇ καὶ τῷ δήμῳ, "the council and assembly resolve that." It is in the retention of the performative force of the language used at meetings that the capacity of these documents as social objects in Ferraris's sense is most recognizable.[9] With their undeniable and perpetual materiality, inscribed decrees were powerful physical anchors for the agency of civic gatherings to

---

5 Ferraris 2012 *passim* and see also the Introduction to this volume.
6 Austin 1962.
7 Austin 1962, 5–6.
8 See Ferraris 2012, 238–240 on speech acts as social acts.
9 See esp. Ferraris 2014 and also Terrone 2014 on documents as "permanent speech acts." Ceccarelli 2018, 147–149 also considers inscribed letters and decrees as performative utterances.

change aspects of the real world. Their presence in the city formed a constant iteration of ephemeral decision-making events.[10]

But council or assembly meetings were more than just decision-making events. Josiah Ober has argued that such meetings were essential in creating a particular kind of "common knowledge."[11] In its technical sense, common knowledge is more than shared knowledge: it is the mutual awareness of the possession of specific knowledge in a group. As such, it helps those willing to cooperate to coordinate their actions. If everyone is aware of a common plan, and is aware that all others are aware of it, individual group members may decide what they will do to execute it, because they are able to predict what other participants are going to do.

According to the political scientist Michael Chwe, a key element in creating such common knowledge is the participation in "rational rituals."[12] These include the public and repetitive presentation of informational content, as well as the use of inward-facing circles while doing so. Being positioned in an inward-facing circle, each looking at the other participants, promotes the awareness that others are present to take in the information. Repetition of the information presented underscores that even those who were not paying close attention must also have gotten the message.[13] Of course, the resulting common knowledge of norms, values, rules, and plans of action makes for much more than an effective organizational tool: it is an important aspect of community formation.

This consolidation of the community is a second type of social act performed by public meetings in the Greek *polis*. Decrees, then, do not just record *polis* decisions: by documenting the whole process that led to decision-making – the presentation of proposals, appeals by embassies from abroad, the issues put to a vote, sometimes even the number of votes cast in favour and against – they also represent the common knowledge and the sense of community generated through this process. Inscribed decrees served as beacons or focal points for the continued generation and renewal of that sense of community. They could per-

---

10 Ma 1999, 149; Ma 2012, 155 on Greek public inscriptions as iterations of speech-acts, or authoritative re-enactments of public transactions.
11 See Ober 2008, 168–210; cf. Chwe 2001. This understanding of common knowledge is a concept from game theory. For the use of Chwe's work in the interpretation of Greco-Roman group coordination, I also draw on C.G. Williamson 2013; C.G. Williamson 2021; van Nijf 2012, esp. 60–70; van Nijf 2013, 324–325.
12 Chwe 2001.
13 Chwe 2001, 28, 30–36. See e.g., also Chaniotis 2011 (and elsewhere), who focuses on the emotional component of ritual as a catalyst of community formation.

form this function of iterating both decisions and community formation even if the inscribed text was not read with regularity.[14] Inscribed decrees were placed prominently in the *epiphanestatoi topoi* (most conspicuous places) of the city and had an impressive material presence, executed in marble, often decorated with pediments, moldings, and sometimes even reliefs and textual headers (which are more easily legible).[15] It is therefore likely that people could link the monuments to specific decisions without reading them.[16] All inscribed decrees, of course, were representative of the community formation process that took place at civic meetings. In this way, the simple presence of monumentalized decrees helped to integrate the decisions reached at public meetings, and the sense of community and coordination generated in the process into *polis* society.

The connection between the inscriptions and the events at which these social acts were performed could be reinforced by subsequent rituals at festivals or other occasions. A good example is the announcement of public honors, voted in meetings, at a festival. The locations where inscriptions were erected – the monumental environments of sanctuaries, agoras, theaters, and other cultural and political hotspots – in turn played a central part. In their striking appearance inscriptions shaped public spaces and thus influenced the experience of the people inhabiting them. Through the activities that took place there, and through the high concentration of monuments with significance to the community, these locations already brought the shared experiences and knowledge of the *polis* to the forefront of the civic mind.[17] The public character of the environment furthermore promoted the idea that anyone could be seen

---

14 See Kuin in this volume on the authority of epigraphic texts to literate and illiterate people. See also Bodel in this volume on the interdependence of oral and written documentary testimony in the Roman Empire.

15 See for instance Petrovic *et al.* 2019, 1–20; Berti *et al.* 2017, 1–9; and both throughout on the importance of the materiality of inscribed texts.

16 Conversely, in the words of Ferraris 2012, 239, "it is enough if the words are registered in the minds of those present" for a social act to have meaning; "it is not strictly necessary that there be writing on paper or some other medium for there to be an inscription," he goes on – the "inscription" here being the consolidation of an act in social reality, not a literal inscribed text.

17 Ober 2008, 197 points to the potential coordinating function of prominent public monuments (even those without text), which can provide focal points for common knowledge: "As carriers of readily accessible informational content, public monuments may present spectators with a commonly available, relatively clear, and therefore "unitary" account of some aspect of shared culture or history." See esp. C.G. Williamson 2013, 140–144 on the significance of the environment of inscribed monuments for common knowledge generation.

taking in the information presented by a decree, in itself a condition for common knowledge generation.

As we have seen, in the Hellenistic period the practice of inscribing decrees became popular throughout the Greek world. Understanding these inscribed documents as social objects, monumentalized to enhance their impact on society, helps us understand how they had agency in community-building. Since there was a rise in the inscribing of documents pertaining to inter-city relationships specifically, this model is used below to interpret two examples from that domain.

2 The Hellenistic Period: Coordinating Reciprocal Relations

The surge in inscribed decrees observed above coincides with the demise of the tumultuous reign of Alexander and the subsequent installation of the Successor Kingdoms. These developments impacted the Greek world of cities in various ways. New cities were founded across what was briefly Alexander's empire. Pre-existing Greek settlements too, notably on the coast of Asia Minor and on the Greek mainland, found themselves confronted with a new reality. The eastern Mediterranean now fell under the sway of fiercely competing kings, whose spheres of influence and changing alliances were new factors in interregional politics and inter-city competition.

At the same time, the Greek cultural sphere was larger than ever before. Greek features of monumental architecture and urban planning, such as temples, theaters, gymnasia, stoas, agoras, and sacred roads, flourished throughout the Hellenistic kingdoms. Similarly, political and cultural institutions based on Classical Greek examples were widespread. Cities all over the region issued decrees in the name of councils and assemblies, organized agonistic festivals, and trained their youths in ephebic or similar civic institutions. These cultural and political similarities are indicative of the formation of a Greek cultural community, even across the borders of the Successor Kingdoms. The spread of the practice of inscribing decrees throughout the Greek world is part of this development of cultural convergence.

I now turn to an example of a decree recording inter-city interaction to connect these last two observations. To do so, I argue that inscriptions recording contacts between cities, as social objects that iterated the performance of social acts in inter-city relationships, were an integral part of creating a sense of community between the cities of the Hellenistic world.

An inscription found in Priene, on the Ionian coast, records a decree of the late fourth or early third century BCE.[18] It concerns the activities of a total of nine judges from Phokaia, Astypalaia, and Nisyros, who had been invited to Priene to settle local disputes.[19] The start of the decree recounts how the Prieneans had invited the judges, and how well they had performed their duties (2–12). The three cities are honored with golden crowns, as are the judges, who also receive honorific titles and privileges (12–42). After the long enumeration of honors, the text presents us with a substantial publication clause, which shows the multitude of ways in which the honors were publicized:

38–43 In order that the disposition of the people [of Priene] may be clear to all, [the disposition] which is worthy of good and excellent men, and in order that those who benefit the *polis* are remembered for all time, [it has been decided] to inscribe this decree on a stone *stêlê* and to set it up in the sanctuary of Athena; and that the *neôpoiês* provides the expenses.

43–49 And [it has been decided] that an ambassador must be chosen from all the citizens, one man for each *polis*, who, having arrived in the place that he was chosen for, shall deliver the decree and the crown for the panel of judges, and who shall ask the council and the people to give announcement of the crown at the Dionysia during the contest of the tragedies, as the Prieneans have decreed [to do] also in their own city;

49–52 and [they shall ask] to inscribe this decree on a stone *stêlê* and to set it up in the sanctuary, where it seems to be fitting to those cities who have sent the judges.

52–57 And for each *polis*, there shall be assigned thirty Alexander-*drachmai* for the *stêlê* and the inscription; the *neôpoiês* Theogeiton shall provide for these [expenses], and for the crowns voted for each of the panels of judges, and he shall give these to the chosen ambassadors, in order that they can take care of their task.

---

18 See the lemma at *IK.Priene* 107. The inscription was dated to c. 328/7 by Hiller 1906 (his no. 8), but to 286/5 by Crowther 1996.
19 Phokaia was a city further up the Ionian coast, c. 130 kilometers north-northwest, and part of the Ionian *koinon*, like Priene. Nisyros and Astypalaia are islands in the Dodecanese, about as far by sea; the journeys undertaken (by the judges themselves as well as by envoys conveying requests and honors) were thus substantial. On the exchange of judges and the epigraphic conventions surrounding it, see Robert 1973; Crowther 1992, 1993, 1994, 1995, 1996, 1999, 2006; Gauthier 1994. Scafuro 2013 lists a more complete recent bibliography.

57–59 The ambassadors chosen: to Phokaia, Pausanias; to Nisyros and for Astypalaia, Poseidonios.[20]

First of all, an inscribed version of the decree is to be erected in Priene. Provisions are furthermore made for multiple performances of the honor in the cities that sent the judges. Ambassadors are to bring the text of the decree to Phokaia, Nisyros, and Astypalaia, and must convince the citizens of those *poleis* to include the judges they had sent to Priene in their yearly public honorific ceremony during the Dionysian games.[21] In the ceremony, announcements are to be made of the crowns for the judges and the *poleis* as a whole. Crucially, this event takes place during the tragic contests, when a mass of people would have gathered in the theater to celebrate a civic festival and to enjoy the best entertainment of the year. An earlier section of the decree (26–29) stipulates that this ceremony must also take place in Priene (referenced in line 49), and that the announcement should include the reasons for which the crowns are awarded. Although it is not explicitly stated here, in many cities these announcements were subject to yearly repetition for as long as the honorands were alive, underscoring the long-term validity of the honor.[22] Finally, in addition to the inscription of the decree in Priene, the three honored *poleis* must be convinced to also inscribe the decree and to erect it at a sanctuary that they feel is fitting for this purpose.[23]

The act of honoring is thus made an integral part of the physical architecture of both cities and is incorporated in civic events in both *poleis*. Such extensive provisions for the broadcasting of honor are commonly found in honorific decrees, especially for prominent foreign benefactors and particularly in such

---

20 *IK.Priene* 107.38–59. Translation by the author. Greek text in Appendix 1.
21 This was standard honorific practice in most Hellenistic cities. Honors (especially from other *poleis*, for individuals or for the city as a whole) were often announced at the Dionysia, or at another prominent festival. For a description of this ceremony in Athens, see Goldhill 1987, 62–66. Other examples abound in Hellenistic honorific decrees: see, e.g., Smyrna: *IK.Smyrna* 579 (judges from Kaunos) lines 14–17, 20–25; Kos, *IG* XII 4.1.142 (Halikarnassos honors a Koan doctor) lines 31–35; and many others.
22 E.g. *IK.Knidos* 231 (Smyrna honors Knidian judges), line 25.
23 Typically, every city had a sanctuary where such honors were habitually publicized. Astypalaia and Nisyros have not left sufficient epigraphic traces to determine where they would have erected such texts; for Phokaia, the one foreign decree in honor of judges recovered there (*IK.Tralleis* 23) does not mention a specific location either, and its precise findspot is unknown. For other cities we have more information: in early Hellenistic Priene the proper spot was the sanctuary of Athena Polias, as seen in this and other decrees; in Iasos it was the sanctuary of Artemis; on Kos it was the Asklepieion; on Samos it was the Heraion; etc.

cases of invited judges. The amount of attention paid to this aspect is understandable, considering that publicity is an integral part of honor.[24] What stands out in this type of honorific decree is the attention paid to advertisement of the honor in both the receiving and the granting cities. The people of Priene are clearly committed to making the honor granted to the judges and the cities who sent them as important to the recipients as it is to themselves. They even send money with their ambassadors to pay for the expenses of publicizing the honor. The copies of the text commissioned by Priene in the other cities do not survive, but other inscriptions testify that it was common for the cities that had provided judges to inscribe the decrees honoring them.[25]

Here, it is important to draw attention to the fact that the inscriptions do more than just honor individuals: they are also part of a relationship between cities. Not only the judges themselves but also the cities that sent them are honored. In the first few lines of the decree, there is furthermore reference to the goodwill existing between Priene and the consulted cities (ὑπαρχούσηι εὐνοίαι, line 6), which has led them to fulfill the request for judges. This publicity circus, then, not only establishes and maintains the fame of Phokaia, Nisyros, and Astypalaia and their judges, but also reproduces the good relations between the cities.

If we interpret these elaborate oral and monumental performances of honor in the model that I proposed in the previous section, another effect becomes apparent. All monuments and events that refer to the decree can be considered iterations of the original social act, the honoring of the judges and their cities by Priene. This is accentuated by the performative formulation of the inscriptions and the announcement at the honorific ceremony. For the Prieneans, these performances refer to the initial meeting at which the honors were voted, for the members of the other *poleis* they refer to the meeting at which the ambassadors first presented the Prienean decree. In both cases, the events referred to in the decree evoke the presence of the other city also in a physical sense. In the hon-

---

24 Lambert 2011, 200: "insofar as honour is an abstract quality to do with the opinion of others it cannot exist in a vacuum; by definition it depends to an extent on people knowing about it." See especially Rubinstein 2013 on the role of oral performance of honor in inter-city relations (and in other contexts).
25 See, for instance, the Phokaian copy of an honorific decree for judges sent to Seleukeia/Tralleis, which survives (*IK*.Tralleis 23, referenced in note 20 above and Mack 2015, 268). Mack's bar graph of honorific decrees issued to foreign judges shows about as many honorific decrees surviving in the honoring communities as in the home communities of judges. Priene itself is a good example: besides this one decree honoring foreign judges, up to twenty-four decrees from other cities honoring foreign courts from Priene survive (*IK.Priene* 108–131).

ored *poleis* the Prienean ambassadors are in attendance, in Priene the judges are still present either in person or possibly by proxy of the front seats reserved for them at festivals (προεδρ[ί]α[ν] ἐν το[ῖ]ς ἀγῶ[σ]ι l.35).

As a result the common knowledge created at such events exceeds the borders of the *polis*. The presence of ambassadors and/or judges emphasizes that the other cities will take in or have taken in the same information, witnessing the same honorific act. The reciprocal exchange (honor for services) between cities is thus explicitly and continuously re-enacted in the honoring ceremonies, always presented as both beneficial and heartfelt. In this way, common knowledge and a sense of community are created not just within the *polis*, but *between cities*.

In both directions, the display of honor for individuals serves as a vessel for the perpetuation of the idea that the cities share common experiences and knowledge about each other.[26] They can be considered as an *imagined community*: the cities may be several days of travel removed from one another and the majority of their members cannot be expected to ever meet in real life, but through this ritual communication of information about their exchanges, they nevertheless feel connected.[27]

Inscriptions perpetuate the presence of the other city in the minds of the people, by including it in the physical and monumental urban environment. In the example above, an exact copy of the Prienean decree is to be inscribed in each of the judge-providing cities.[28] These twin documents would not only refer to the event of honoring, but also to their direct counterpart in Priene, creating an experience of synchronicity between the cities.[29] The idea that someone else, miles away, might at that very moment be observing the exact same text, evokes the feeling that at least part of reality is experienced in the same way in that other community.[30] The copies of the text form a powerful physical anchor for

---

26 See also Ma 2003, 21–22.
27 Anderson 1983, 6.
28 Such decrees do not always ask for copies of inscriptions to be erected in the contacted cities, but other examples abound, e.g., *IG* XII 4.1.131 (lines 20–29). This Samian decree (end of fourth century BCE), found in the Koan Asklepieion, honors Koan judges and was to be inscribed in two sanctuaries on Samos as well.
29 Ma 2003, 21 has called this "here-and-thereness." Although it is not certain that commissioned copies were always erected, there is no particular reason to doubt that this happened either, especially in this case, where Priene provided the money for *stêlê* and inscription. See also note 23 above.
30 Not dissimilar to the idea of "simultaneity" in Anderson's model of imagined community, there exemplified with the common ritual of reading newspapers in the morning: we do not

the carefully nurtured relationship, and a beacon for the imagined community with another city.

This mirrored publication of public decisions, through rituals as well as inscriptions, is a feature of numerous honorific exchanges, treaties, oaths, intercity arbitrations, and other interactions between Hellenistic cities.[31] It seems clear from the example presented above that in the complicated Hellenistic politics of kings and cities, mirrored rituals could help to create and enhance lasting bonds between *poleis* on regional or even supra-regional levels. Mirrored inscribed decrees were fixed focal points for the alignment of this common experience, and thus of participation in the larger Greek world. As monumentalized social acts, they presented tangible and lasting references, anchors of shared knowledge and practices.

3 The Imperial Period: A New Kind of Community

From the second century BCE onward, Roman influence expanded quickly over the Hellenistic world. It is at this time, too, that we can observe a decline in Greek public epigraphic activity in general, and in the recording of inter-city contacts in inscriptions in particular. This phenomenon can be explained in part by the centralized administration of Rome taking over the practical purpose of many of the institutions of Hellenistic inter-city interactions. Moreover, as William Mack has recently argued, favor bestowed by Rome as the central hub of power became the primary source of cities' regional prestige and authority.[32] This plausibly diminished the importance of ties with neighboring cities, since the necessity to stick together amid ever-changing royal hegemonies and large-scale power relations fell away.

This can however not fully explain the disappearance of epigraphic records of interaction. Mack for instance points out that the start of the decline in inscriptions recording proxeny precedes Roman primacy. The decline in in-

---

need to see others doing it to know that they are performing a similar ritual and taking in the same information. Anderson 1983, 22–36.

31 See esp. C.G. Williamson 2013 on oath inscriptions and ceremonies as an example of common knowledge creation. For multiple publication of other types of decrees (also at interregional sanctuaries), see, e.g., *FDelphes* III.4 355: arbitration decree to be inscribed in Larisa, Halos, Thebes, and Delphi; *IG* IX.1 97: Phokian League acknowledges *asylia* of temple of Poseidon and Amphitrite on Tenos, found in Elatea, also to be inscribed in Delphi and Kranai.
32 Mack 2015, 242–281.

scribed decrees recording interactions is moreover noticeable across the full range of inter-city relationships and consequently seems to tell a story of its own. I argue that looking at publication strategies and how their use transformed over time can provide deeper insight into what had changed for the Greek city in the tumultuous transition to empire, and why inscribing eventually became less desirable. A case study of an early Augustan era decree from the city of Mytilene serves as an example.

A well-known decree from Mytilene, inscribed on the front and adjoining narrow side of a single reused dark marble *stêlê*, concerns the installation of a major Mytilenean festival in honor of Augustus, venerating him as a god.[33] The celebrations would, among other things, include theatrical contests, a hymn, and sacrifices. The decree is usually dated between 27 BCE by its mention of the name Augustus or Σεβαστός granted in that year, and 11 BCE, by the death of the emperor's sister Octavia, who is referenced in the decree.[34]

Although fragmentary, the decree has traditionally sparked interest because it offers early evidence of imperial cult practices, and of how the cities of the larger Greek world related to the new imperial power in Rome.[35] For our current purpose, the most interesting passages are lines 10–14 of fragment A and lines 15–20 of fragment B, which detail how and where Mytileneans envisioned inscribed traces of their festival decree to be left behind:

fr. A

... [text fragmentary]
10 [it has been decided to send?] announcements of the first [contests] that will be held [...] to the most famous cities, and to set up plaques [or *stêlai* bearing copies of this decree in the temple?] that is being prepared for him by Asia in Pergamon and [in ...] and in Actium and in Brindisium and in Tarraco and in Ma[ssalia and in ... and in An]tioch near Daphne.
... [etc.]

fr. B

15 That they [the envoys] call on him to allow a plaque to be put up in his home and, in the Capitolium, a plaque or a *stêlê* bearing a copy of this decree.

---

33 Text editions: *CIG* II, add. 2167d (not 2167a, as referenced in *IG* fr. B alone); Conze 1865, table VII with p. 13; Cichorius 1888, 30–41; *IG* XII 2 58; *OGIS* 456; *IGR* IV.39. See also esp. Labarre 1996, 285–287, no. 21 (and references there); Rowe 2002, 130–135.
34 Respectively lines 15 fr. A, 28 fr. B. For the date, see notes in the various publications of, and commentaries on the text.
35 See, for instance, Price 1984, 55–56, 127–128, and esp. 217–219.

21 That the envoys offer thanks concerning him to the Senate and the vestal virgins and his wife, Julia [sic], and his sister, Octavia, and his children and relatives and friends.
27 That a crown be sent of two thousand gold pieces, which should be presented by the envoys.
30 That the envoys properly in his presence offer thanks to the Senate for having conducted itself most sympathetically toward the city and for its traditional kindness.[36]

The passage in fragment A informs us about heralds to be sent out to announce the festival, as was customary throughout the Hellenistic period. Besides presumably making oral announcements, the heralds were to leave inscribed documents in the places where they went, in addition to the inscription in Mytilene that has survived. If the supplement of line 12 is indeed correct, we are dealing with integral copies of the decree, inscribed on plaques and perhaps on *stêlai* or similar monuments.[37] This makes the text of prime interest for studying the function of inscribing documents in an inter-city context.

The fragment preserves the names of at least six cities where the heralds were to make their announcement and where they were to have the decree inscribed: they went from Mytilene to Pergamon, via Actium and Brundisium, through Tarraco on the Iberian coast to Massalia in modern France, back to Antioch on the farthest eastern shore of the Mediterranean (see Figure 3). Strikingly, the preserved list of cities circles the Mediterranean, probably reflecting the itinerary of the ambassadors (although Tarraco and Massalia are in reverse order). In the currently accepted reading, there is furthermore room for a number of additional cities in this already grand tour.[38]

It is important that the decree denotes the cities that the heralds should visit as ἐπισημοτάταις (11), "most famous." The specific criteria for selection are

---

[36] *IGR* IV.39 (=*IG* XII 2.58) A lines 10–14, B lines 15–20. Translation modified from Rowe 2002. Greek text in Appendix 2.

[37] Cichorius 1888, 31–41; see also the Greek text in Appendix 2. The supplement is rather elaborate, setting the width of the text at a minimum of 90 characters, while the largest preserved width is only 36. It is based on the similarity of the phrasing with lines 15–20 of fragment B, where δέλτοι or plaques are also concerned, here too in conjunction with the infinitive ἀναθεῖναι. The supplement therefore seems plausible and has not been disputed thus far.

[38] Possibly these would include cities in northern Africa, conspicuously absent in the preserved text. Cichorius 1888, 36 offers some suggestions: "es kann wohl als sicher gelten, dass darunter waren: Athen, Ephesus (vielleicht zu Z. 13 ['Εφέc]ῳ), Korinth, Alexandria; dann vielleicht auch noch Lugdunum, Carthago, Rhodos, Ankyra, Nikomedia, Sardes, Byzantion." His reasoning behind these suggestions is, however, not clear. The inclusion of Lugdunum, for instance, seems unlikely: would the ambassadors venture so far inland? The names preserved in the text surely suggest that the envoys' tour of at least the western Mediterranean was predominantly by sea.

illuminated by the inclusion of Actium, which was a rather insignificant place in its own right were it not for Augustus' great victory over Marcus Antonius and Cleopatra there.[39] Upon closer consideration, it becomes clear that all the places chosen for publication represent some kind of link between the emperor and the Greek world.

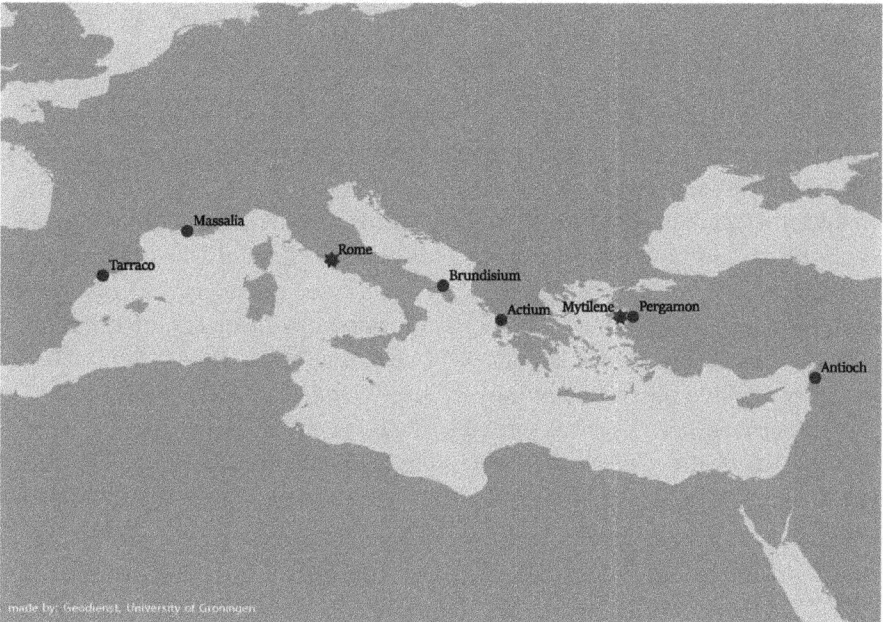

Fig. 3: This map shows the locations of the cities mentioned in *IGR* IV.39 (=*IG* XII 2.58).

The choice of Pergamon is perhaps the clearest example: one of the leading cultural centers of the Hellenistic world, this city was at that time building a

---

39 The ideological significance of the cities has been hinted at before. See remarks by Paton in *IG*: "*Non erant urbes provinciarum capita; locos fuisse, ubi iam extabant templa vel area Augusti, coniicere vix licet. Sunt potius loci vel per se vel propter praeclara ipsius Augusti facinora celeberrimi*"; Labarre 1996, 278: "Des tablettes ou des stèles portant la copie de ce décret seront placées ... dans un grand nombre de cités importantes de l'Empire (liées à Auguste par l'histoire ou le culte)"; Rowe 2002, 134–135. However, the significance of publication in these places does not seem to have been thoroughly examined.

splendid temple for Augustus. Actium of course represented a strong link through its location on the coast of the Greek heartland and Augustus' great victory.[40] Brundisium originated as a Greek settlement as early as the seventh century BCE, and was also significant for Augustan ideology: here, as well as in Rome, an arch was erected in 29 BCE to commemorate the victory at Actium.[41] Massalia, in recent history, had set the scene for an early victory of Julius Caesar, Augustus' adoptive father, in the Civil War — and even before this event it had certainly been the most prominent early Greek colony in the far west of the Mediterranean.[42] Making a leap back to the east, Syrian Antioch, as the former Seleucid capital, could also be considered a Greek cultural center. Augustus had already visited the city in 31–30 BCE (and would do so again in 20). He had been quick to recognize the strategic importance of Syria and its capital, granting it the rank of Imperial province.[43]

For Tarraco, though situated in a region with multiple early Greek colonies, no strong connection to the Greek world is readily apparent. The link to Augustus is, however, immediately clear: the emperor spent two years of his Iberian campaign (26–25 BCE) there in illness, and (possibly in that same period) the city had erected an altar in his name.[44] Depending on the dating of the Mytilenean decree, it is possible that the city was included as a place of publication purely because the ambassadors went there to meet the emperor himself.[45] Whether the Mytilenean envoys met the emperor in Tarraco or in Rome is uncertain (though it is likely that they did indeed visit Rome, if only for an audience

---

[40] Actium had a long Greek history as a natural harbor of strategic importance, and was furthermore home to a well-established Apollo cult of more than regional importance. For Actium as strategic landmark in Greek history, see, e.g., Thuc. 1.29.3; Polyb. 4.63.4; Liv. 44.1.2. The Apollo sanctuary at Actium was, incidentally, for a long time the place where the Acarnanian *koinon* publicized its treaties with other polities, as well as other official documents: see, e.g., IG IX, 1² 1.3; IG IX, 1² 2.208, 209, 582, 588.

[41] Cass. Dio 51.19.1. See Chelotti 2011 on the ideological significance of Brundisium for Augustus.

[42] On Caesar's victory in 49 BCE, see Caes. B Civ. 1.34–36, 56–58; 2.1–16, 22.

[43] Downey 1963, 80–88. The imperial family's recognition and appreciation of the city is furthermore clear from the elaborate public building programs set up there from the Augustan era onwards.

[44] The altar is mentioned in Quint. *Inst.* 6.3.77. Some argue that the Mytilenean embassy inspired the erection of the altar: see n. 45 below.

[45] The jury is however still out on the date of embassy and decree: recent studies argue for a later date, possibly between 17 and 11 BCE. See Chelotti 2011, 102–104, after Étienne 1974, 365–370 and Fishwick 1987, 171–173. A later date, as they point out, could still find Augustus at Tarraco: he resided in Spain in 16–13 BCE as well, but it remains uncertain whether the ambassadors necessarily went to Tarraco to meet with him there.

with the Senate, as described in fragment B 21–24). Most importantly for our current purpose, they were to make a case to the emperor for publication of the text in the imperial city: they would ask to put up a copy of the text in his own house, and on the Capitoline Hill as well (15–20).

Making arrangements for two inscriptions in the city that is the actual addressee of the embassy was not uncommon in the Hellenistic tradition of inscribing decrees recording interactions. The choice of the Capitoline Hill is not surprising either: it was customary for *senatus consulta* as well as treaties to be displayed here.[46] What is noteworthy is the request for the publication of the text in Augustus' house. Although the *domus* functioned to some extent as public space, the specific request underscores that the focus of the ambassadors' entire venture is the emperor himself, as the embodiment of Rome as a political entity.

The intended mode of publication is reminiscent of the Hellenistic tradition of having multiple copies of the decree inscribed, in combination with repeated oral announcement. It seems natural for Mytilene to broadcast the momentous occasion of the festival, and to have this announcement inscribed in numerous cities. But at the same time, the practice has changed: there is no mention of inviting cities to the festival, as was common in the Hellenistic period. Likewise, the places of publication are not chosen for the *poleis*' potential as allies or even for their value as promotional space. Rather, the emperor and his relationship to the Greek world appear as the common denominator throughout the publication scheme outlined in the text. Whereas strategies of inscribing multiple copies of a document previously served the purpose of fostering relationships between individual cities, here this mode of publication is explicitly used to cultivate a relationship with Rome and the emperor.

To come back to the question posed at the start of this section, this specific decree shows that it did not necessarily become less important to inscribe intercity relationships. On the contrary, for Mytilene it appears to have been very important. By leaving documentary traces of its new festival for Augustus in a diverse array of cities around the Mediterranean, the *polis* aimed to showcase itself as a prominent member of this new Rome-centric world. The inclusion of cities with firm roots in the Greek world *and* a connection to the emperor could be constructed as an attempt to show Mytilene's commitment, as a Greek city, to

---

[46] See Kajava 2008. An earlier alliance of the Mytileneans with Julius Caesar is likewise reported to have been posted here on a bronze plaque: *IG* XII 2.35 (= *IGR* 4.33; also Labarre 1996, 277–284, no. 20; Sherk 1969, 146 ff., no. 26); see lines 17–23.

becoming a constituent part of the new imagined community of the Greco-Roman Mediterranean.

What did change, was the effect of the intended strategy within the new parameters of interaction. No longer did inscribing a document like the one from Mytilene create common knowledge of things shared between individual cities. Rather, it pointed to the emperor as an external unifying principle. This also means that the advantage of inscribing such a text for the communities that were approached probably diminished. No other copies of the text were found. While this by no means guarantees that they were never inscribed, it does raise the question of whether Actium, Brundisium, Antioch, and the other cities would have found it useful to display the document. Possibly, they had their own ways of maintaining ties to the emperor, and little to gain by helping the Mytileneans promote theirs.

4 Conclusion

In this chapter, I have proposed to interpret monumentalized documents, specifically inscribed decrees, as iterations of the social acts of decision-making and common-knowledge-creation at civic meetings. The examples I have used show that inscribed decrees also had this iterative agency in the coordination of interactions between cities. Within institutions of inter-city interaction, inscriptions and events were mirrored to maximize the iteration effect and to extend both the results of decisions and of community formation over cities. As highly visible social objects, inscribed decrees were focal points for the alignment of the cities' experiences of the relationship.

In a fragmented world of kings and cities, inscribing connections between individual cities was useful because monumentalized decrees strengthened the sense of community by creating common knowledge within and between *poleis* about the relationships between them. When the central Roman administration superseded Hellenistic institutions of interaction, *poleis* no longer needed to rely on each other to solve local problems and to gather prestige and standing in the wider world. The Mytilenean decree for Augustus is a case in point for how this is reflected in the Greek documentary epigraphic culture. Reminiscent of the Hellenistic mode of interaction, the publication strategy employed still shows a desire to reach out to other cities. One of the ways this worked best in the past was by broadly publicizing texts representing city-to-city links. The point of alignment between these cities, however, is no longer an experience shared between them, but the external factor of the emperor.

The Mytilenean decree thus provides a key to unifying two seemingly contrary developments: the "new documentary consciousness" of the Imperial period observed in the Introduction to this volume, and the declining Greek practice of inscribing decrees noted at the start of this chapter. Inscribing decrees, as shown by Mytilene's elaborate publication strategy, remained of paramount importance. The resulting monuments did not necessarily lose their agency as iterations of decision-making events, or as informational beacons within communities. Their role as instruments for fostering common knowledge and a sense of community between cities, however, was lost with the changing role of the institutions of inter-city relationships. As Rome and the emperor started to function as the point of alignment for the dispersed communities of the Mediterranean world, the imagined community expressed in inscribed decrees vanished, making way for new representations of empire.

Appendix 1: Text of *IK.Priene* 107, Honorific Decree by Priene for Judges from Phokaia, Nisyros, and Astypalaia

A.1 [ἐπὶ] στεφανηφόρου Κλείτου μηνὸς Μεταγειτν[ιῶνος,]
[γνώ]μη [τ]ιμούχων· ἐπειδὴ ὁ δῆμο[ς] ὅ τε Φωκαι[έ]ων κα[ὶ]
[Νισ]υ[ρ]ίων καὶ Ἀστυπαλαιέων αἰτησαμένων ἡμῶ[ν δι]-
καστήρι[ο]ν ἐπὶ τὰ συμβόλαια τά τε κοινὰ καὶ τὰ ἴδια ἀ[πέ]-
5   [στε]ιλεν ἡμῖν ἄνδρας καλοὺς καὶ ἀγαθοὺς ἀκόλουθα πρ[άτ]-
[των τ]ῆι πρὸς τὸν δῆμον αὑτῶι ὑπαρχούσηι εὐνοίαι, οἵ τ[ε]
[παραγε]νόμενοι δικασταὶ πᾶσαν παρέσχοντο φιλοτιμ[ί]-
[αν] πρ[ὸ]ς τὸ διαλύειν τοὺς ἐν τοῖς ἐγκλήμασιν ὄντας, [καὶ]
[τὰ]ς μὲν ἐδίκασαν τῶν δικῶν τῆι ψήφ[ω]ι κατὰ τοὺς νό-
10 [μου]ς, τὰς δὲ [δ]ιῄτησαν ἴσω[ς] καὶ δικαίως, εἰς ὁμόνοιαν
[καὶ φι]λίαμ προαιρούμενοι τ[ὸν δ]ῆμον τὸμ Πριηνέων κ[α]-
[ταστῆσ]αι, δεδόχθαι τῆι βουλῆι καὶ τῶι δήμωι· ὅπως ἄ[ν]
[γένηται φ]αν[ε]ρὸ[ν] ὅ[τι ὁ δῆ]μος ὁ Πριηνέω⟨ν⟩ ἐπίσταται τοὺς
[καλοὺς καὶ ἀγαθ]οὺς ἄνδρας καὶ αὐτ[ῶι χ]ρε[ία]ς π[α]ρα-
B.15 σχομέν[ους τιμᾶν, τὰς ἀξία]ς ἑκά[στωι χάρ]ιτας ἀποδ[ι]δοὺς τῶν
εὐεργετημ[άτων, ἐπαινέσαι τόν τε Φωκ]αιέων καὶ [Ν]ις[υρί]-
ων καὶ Ἀστυπα[λαιέων δῆμον ἀρετῆς ἕνεκα καὶ εὐνοί]
ας ἣν ἔχων ἐξαπ[έστειλεν τοὺς δικαστὰς πρὸς τὸν δῆμον]
τὸμ Πρ[ι]ηνέων· ἐπαι[νέσαι δὲ καὶ τοὺς δικαστὰς τοὺς ἐξαπο]-
20 σταλέντας Φωκαιέωμ μ[ὲν— — — — — — — — —]
[Ἡγ]ήσιδος?, Θράσυλλον Ἀθη[ν— — — — Νισυρίων δὲ]
[. .]Ν[.] Ναυ[λ]ίδου?, Καλλίαν Ἀρισ[τί]μου, Α[— — Ἀστυπαλαιέ]-

ῳν δὲ Νόσσον Ἐλπινίκου, Νίκωνα Ν[— — — — — — —]
Τελεσάρχου ἀρετῆς ἕνεκα καὶ δικαιοσ[ύνης ἧς πεποίηνται]
25 περὶ τὰς κρίσεις, καὶ στεφανῶσαι ἕκαστον α[ὐτων ἑκάστην]
τε πόλιν στεφάνωι χρυσέωι τῶι ἐκ τοῦ νόμ[ου· τῆς δὲ ἀναγγε]-
λίας τοῦ στεφάνου τὴν ἐπιμέλειαμ ποιήσασθαι [τὸν ἀγωνο]-
θέτην τοῖς πρώτ[οι]ς Δ[ιο]νυσίοις τραγωιδῶ[ν τ]ῶ[ι ἀγῶνι, δη]-
λοῦντα διὰ τῆς ἀναγ[γελ]ίας τὰς αἰτίας [δι'] ἃ[ς στεφανοῦνται·]
30 εἶναι δὲ αὐτοὺς καὶ προ[ξ]ένους καὶ εὐεργέ[τα]ς το[ῦ δήμου]
τοῦ Πριηνέων· δεδόσθαι δὲ αὐτοῖς καὶ ἀτέλειαν ὧ[ν ἂν εἰσά]-
[γω]νται ἢ ἐξάγωνται εἰς τὸν ἴδιον οἶκον καὶ εἴσπλου[ν καὶ ἔκ]-
[π]λουν ἀσυλεὶ καὶ ἀσπονδεὶ καὶ ἐμ πολέμωι καὶ ἐν εἰρήνηι κ[αὶ]
[ἔφο]δον ἐπὶ τὴν βο[υ]λὴν [καὶ] τὸν δῆμον ἐά[ν] του δέωνται π[ρώτοις]
35 [μ]ετὰ τὰ ἱερὰ καὶ προεδρ[ί]α[ν] ἐν το[ῖ]ς ἀγῶ[σ]ι καὶ ἐμ πρυτανε[ίωι]
[κ]αὶ ἐμ Πανιωνίω[ι] σίτ[η]σιν κα[ὶ] γ[ῆς κ]αὶ οἰκίας ἔγκτησιν καὶ ἱερῶν
[κ]αὶ ἀρχείωμ μετουσίαν ὧ[γ κ]αὶ [οἱ Πρ]ιηνεῖς μετέχουσιν· ταῦτα δὲ
ὑπάρχειν καὶ αὐτοῖς καὶ ἐκγό[ν]οι[ς·] ὅπως δ' ἂν ἦι φανερὰ πᾶσιν
ἥ τε τοῦ δήμου προαίρεσις ἣν ἔχει κατα[ξί]ως καλῶν καὶ ἀγ[α]-
40 θῶν ἀνδρῶν, καὶ οἱ εὐεργετοῦντες τὴμ πόλιν εἰς ἅπαν[τα]
[τ]ὸγ χρόνομ μνημονεύωνται, ἀναγράψαι τὸ ψήφισμα τόδ[ε]
[ε]ἰς στήλην λιθίνην, καὶ στῆσαι ἐν τῶι ἱε[ρ]ῶ[ι τ]ῆς Ἀθηνᾶ[ς·]
τὸ δὲ ἀνάλωμα ὑπηρετῆσαι τὸν νεωποίην· ἑλέσθαι δὲ
καὶ πρεσβευτὴν ἐξ ἁπάντων τῶμ πολιτῶν εἰς ἑκάστη[ν]
45 πόλιν ἄνδρα ἕνα, ὅστις παραγενόμενος οὗ ἂν αἱρεθῆι τό
τε ψήφισμα ἀποδώσει καὶ τὸν στέφανον τῶι δικαστηρίω[ι]
καὶ αἰτήσεται τὴμ βουλὴν καὶ τ[ὸ]ν δῆμον ἀναγγελίαν τοῦ
στεφάνου δοῦναι Διον[υ]σίοις ἐν τῶι ἀγ[ῶ]νι τῶν τραγωιδ[ῶ]ν,
καθότι καὶ Πριηνεῖς παρ' αὐτοῖς ἐψηφι[σμ]έ[ν]οι εἰσίν· καὶ τὸ [ψή]-
50 φισμα τόδε ἀναγράψαι εἰς στήλ[η]ν λ[ιθί]νην καὶ στῆσαι εἰς [τὸ]
ἱερόν, οὗ ἂν τῶι δήμωι τῶι ἀποστείλαντι [τ]οὺ[ς] δικαστὰς ἐπ[ι]-
τήδειον εἶναι φαίνηται· τετάχθ[αι δ]ὲ ἑκ[αστηι] πόλει εἰς τε
τὴν στήλην καὶ τὴν ἀναγραφὴν Ἀλ[εξανδρείας] δραχμὰ[ς]
τριάκοντα· ὑπερετῆσαι δὲ καὶ εἰς ταῦτ[α καὶ εἰς τον] στέφανο[ν]
55 τὸν ἑκάστωι τῶν δι[κα]στηρίων ἐψη[φισμένον τὸ]ν νεω[ποί]
ην Θεογείτονα καὶ δοῦναι ταῦτ[α] καὶ τοῖς αἱρεθεῖ]σι πρεσ-
[β]ευταῖς ὅπ[ω]ς τὴν ἐπιμέλε[ια]γ ποιήσω[ν]τα[ι. Ἡιρέθη]σ[α]ν
[πρ]εσβευταὶ εἰς Φώκαιαν Πα[υ]σα[νί]ας, ε[ἰς Ν]ί[συρον καὶ] εἰς
[Ἀστ]υπάλαιαν δὲ [Π]οσειδωνί[ος].

Appendix 2: Text of IGR IV.39 (=*IG* XII 2.58), Mytilenean Decree on a Festival for Augustus

```
A.1  — — — — — — — — — — — — — — — — — — — —ν δὲ κα-
     — — — — — — — — — — — — — — — — — — —ιάδας ἱερὰ
     — — — — — — — — — — — — — — — —εσθαι ἐν τε-
     — — — — — — — — — — — — — — — γραψόντων εἰς α-
5    [— — — — — — — — — — — — —]ηθέντα ὕμνου ὑπὸ
     [— — — — — — — — — — — ἐ]ν ταῖς γινομέναις θέαις
     [— — — — — — — — τιθέναι δὲ κατὰ πενταετηρ]ίδα ἀγῶνας θυμελικοὺς
     [— — — — — — — — — — τοῖς νικήσ]ασιν ἆθλα ὅσα ὁ Διακὸς νόμος πε-
     [ριέχει — — — — — — — — —]άνων καὶ τοῦ ἀρχιερέως καὶ τοῦ στεφανη-
10   [φόρου — — — — — — — — —]ς καταγγελεῖς τῶν πρώτων ἀ(χ)θησο-
     [μένων ἀγώνων — — — — — ταῖς ἐπισ]ημοτάταις πόλεσιν, ἀναθεῖναι δὲ δέλτου-
     [ς ἢ στήλας τοῦδε τοῦ ψηφίσματος ἐχούσας τὸ ἀντίγραφον ἐν τῷ ναῷ τῷ
     κατασ]κευαζομένῳ αὐτῷ ὑπὸ τῆς Ἀσίας ἐν Περγάμῳ κα-
     [ὶ — — — — — — — —]ῳ καὶ Ἀκτίῳ καὶ Βρεντεσίῳ καὶ Ταρραχῶνι καὶ Μα[σ]-
     [σαλίᾳ καὶ — — — — — — καὶ Ἀν]τιοχήᾳ τῇ πρὸς τῇ Δάφνῃ. Τὰς δὲ κατ' ἐνιαυτὸν
15   [θυσίας — — — — ἐν τῷ ναῷ τοῦ Διὸ]ς καὶ ἐν τῷ τοῦ Σεβαστοῦ. Ὅρκον δὲ εἶναι τῶν δι-
     [καστῶν — — — — — — — — —]ομένων σὺν τοῖς πατρίοις θεοῖς καὶ τὸν Σεβασ-
     [τόν. — — — — ἐν τῷ ναῷ τῆς Ἀφροδί]της τὴν εἰκόνα τοῦ θεοῦ. Τὰς δὲ τῶν γανων [sic]
     — — — — — — — — — — — — τεμένους εἶναι καὶ τἆλλα δίκαια καὶ τίμι[α]
     [— — — — — — — — — — κ]ατὰ δύναμιν τὴν ἑαυτοῦ. Ἱερῶν δὲ ἐπὶ [τ]ράπε-
20   [ζαν — — — — — — — — — κατ]ὰ μῆνα ἐν τῇ γενεθλίῳ αὐτοῦ ἡμέρᾳ καὶ π[α]-
     [ριστάναι — — — — — — — τῶν] αὐτῶν θυσιῶν ὡς καὶ τῷ Διΐ παρίσταται. Τρέ-
     [φεσθαι δὲ — — — — — —βοῦς λευκοὺ]ς ἐφελιωμένους ὡς καλλίστους καὶ με[γ]-
     [ίστους — — — — μὲν ὑπὸ τῶν κατ' ἐνια]υτὸν στρατηγ⟨ῶ⟩ν, δύο δὲ ὑπὸ τῶν [ἐπ]ι[σ]-
     [τατῶν — — — — — — —] δὲ ὑπὸ τῶν ἀγορανόμων, τρία δὲ ὑπὸ τοῦ ἀρχιερέως
25   [— — — — — — — δίδοσθαι δὲ ἐκ τοῦ] δημοσίου δραχμὰς ἑκάστῳ τετρα-
     [κοσίας — — — — — — — — δ]είκνυσθαι δὲ τοὺς τραφέντας
     [— — — — — — — — ἐν τ]οῖς ἀγῶσιν τρέφεσθαι τὸν ἴσο[ν]
     [χρόνον — — — — — — — — —] τὴν γενέθλιον ἡμέραν αὐτο[ῦ]
     — — — — — — — — — — — — μηδενὶ διδομένου
30   [— — — — — — — — — — — — τῷ σ]τεφανηφόρῳ καὶ τ[ῷ]
     [— — — — — — — — — — — καθ'] ἕκαστον ἔτος ἐν
     — — — — — — — — — — — —αι τίθεσθαι ἐπ[ὶ]
     — — — — — — — — — — — — —ενα— — —
     (vac.?)

B.1  εὐεργεσιῶν νομισ — — εὐχα-
     ριστίαν. Ἐπιλογίσασθαι δὲ τῆς
     οἰκείας μεγαλοφροσύνης ὅτ[ι]
     τοῖς οὐρανίου τετε[υ]χόσι δό-
5    ξης καὶ θεῶν ὑπεροχὴν καὶ
     κράτος ἔχουσιν οὐδέποτε δύ-
```

ναται συνεξισωθῆναι τὰ καὶ
τῇ τύχῃ ταπ(ε)ινότερα καὶ τῇ φύ-
σει. Εἰ δέ τι τούτων ἐπικυδέσ-
10 τερον τοῖς μετέπειτα χρό-
νοις εὑρεθήσεται, πρὸς μη[δὲ]-
[ν] τῶν θεοποιεῖν αὐτὸν ἐπὶ [πλέ]-
ον δυνησομένων ἐλλείψει[ν]
τὴν τῆς πόλεως προθυμίαν
15 καὶ εὐσέβειαν. **Παρακαλεῖν
δὲ αὐτὸν συγχωρῆσαι ἐν τῇ [οἰ]-
κίᾳ αὐτοῦ δέλτον ἀναθεῖνα[ι]
καὶ ἐν τῷ Καπετωλίῳ δέ[λτον]
ἢ στήλην τοῦδε τοῦ ψηφ[ίσμα]-**
20 **τος ἔχουσαν τὸ ἀντίγραφ[ον].**
Εὐχαριστῆσαι δὲ περὶ αὐτο[ῦ]
τοὺς πρέσβεις τῇ τε συγ[κλή]-
τῳ καὶ ταῖς ἱερήαις τῆς Ἑσ[τί]-
ας καὶ Ἰουλίᾳ τῇ γυναικὶ αὐτοῦ
25 καὶ Ὀκταΐᾳ τῇ ἀδελφῇ καὶ τοῖς
τέκνοις καὶ συγγενέσι καὶ φίλοις. Πεμφθῆναι δὲ καὶ στέφανον ἀπὸ χρυσῶν δισχιλίων, ὃν
καὶ ἀναδοθῆναι ὑπὸ τῶν πρέσ-
30 βεων. Εὐχαριστῆσαι δὲ ἐπ' αὐτοῦ καὶ τῇ συγκλήτῳ τοὺς πρέσβεις προσενηνεγμένης αὐτῆς
τῇ πόλει συμπαθέστατα καὶ
τῆς πατρίου χρηστότητος
35 οἰκείως.

References

Anderson, B. (1983), *Imagined Communities: Reflections on the Origin and Spread of Nationalism*, London.
Austin, J.L. (1962), *How to Do Things with Words*, Cambridge, MA.
Beard, M. (1985), "Writing and Ritual: A Study of Diversity and Expansion in the Arval Acta", in: *PBSR* 53, 114–162.
Berti, I./Bolle, K./Opdenhoff, F./Stroth, F. (eds.) (2017), *Writing Matters: Presenting and Perceiving Monumental Inscriptions in Antiquity and the Middle Ages*, Berlin.
Ceccarelli, P. (2018), "Letters and Decrees: Diplomatic Protocols in the Hellenistic Period", in: P. Ceccarelli/L. Doering/T. Fögen/I. Gildenhard (eds.), *Letters and Communities: Studies in the Socio-Political Dimensions of Ancient Epistolography*, Oxford, 147–183.

Chaniotis, A. (2011), "Emotional Community through Ritual: Initiates, Citizens, and Pilgrims as Emotional Communities in the Greek World", in: A. Chaniotis (ed.), *Ritual Dynamics in the Ancient Mediterranean: Agency, Emotion, Gender, Reception*, Stuttgart, 264–290.

Chelotti, M. (2011), "Brindisi e Augusto", in: S. Cagnazzi et al. (eds), *Scritti di storia per Mario Pani*, Bari, 101–109.

Chwe, M. (2001), *Rational Ritual: Culture, Coordination, and Common Knowledge*, Princeton.

Cichorius, C. (1888), *Rom und Mytilene*, Leipzig.

Conze, A. (1865), *Reise auf der Insel Lesbos*, Hannover.

Corbier, M. (1987), "L'écriture dans l'espace public romain", in: *L'urbs. Espace urbain et histoire (Ier siècle av. J.-C.–IIe siècle ap. J.-C.). Actes du colloque international organisé par le Centre national de la recherche scientifique et l'École française de Rome (Rome, 8–12 Mai 1985)*, Rome, 27–60.

Corbier, M. (2006), *Donner à voir, donner à lire. Mémoire et communication dans la Rome ancienne*, Paris.

Crowther, C.V. (1992), "The Decline of Greek Democracy?", in: *JAC* 7, 13–48.

Crowther, C.V. (1993), "Foreign Judges in Seleucid Cities", in: *JAC* 8, 40–77.

Crowther, C.V. (1994), "Foreign Courts on Kalymna in the Third Century BC", in: *JAC* 9, 33–55.

Crowther, C.V. (1995), "Iasos in the Second Century BC III: Foreign Judges from Priene", in: *BICS* 40, 91–138.

Crowther, C.V. (1996), "I. Priene 8 and the History of Priene in the Early Hellenistic Period", in: *Chiron* 26, 195–250.

Crowther, C.V. (1999), "Aus Der Arbeit der 'Inscriptiones Graecae' IV: Koan Decrees for Foreign Judges", in: *Chiron* 29, 251–320.

Crowther, C.V. (2006), "Foreign Judges in Thessaly in the Hellenistic Period: A Second Century Phenomenon?", in: G.A. Pikoulas (ed.), *Inscriptions and History of Thessaly: New Evidence: Proceedings of the International Symposium in Honor of Professor Christian Habicht*, Volos, 31–48.

Culasso Gastaldi, E. (2014), "'To Destroy the Stele,' 'To Remain Faithful to the Stele': Epigraphic Text as Guarantee of Political Decision", in: *AIO Papers* 3, 1–13.

Downey, G. (1963), *Ancient Antioch*, Princeton.

Étienne, R. (1974), *Le culte impérial dans la péninsule ibérique d'Auguste à Dioclétien*, Paris.

Ferraris, M. (2012), *Documentality: Why It Is Necessary to Leave Traces*, transl. R. Davies, New York.

Ferraris, M. (2014), "Total Mobilization", in: *The Monist* 97, 200–221.

Fishwick, D. (1987), *The Imperial Cult in the Latin West: Studies in the Ruler Cult of the Western Provinces of the Roman Empire*, vol. 1, pt 1, Leiden.

Gauthier, P. (1994), "Les rois hellénistiques et les juges étrangers: à propos de décrets de Kimôlos et de Laodicée du Lykos", in: *JS* 2, 165–195.

Goldhill, S. (1987), "The Great Dionysia and Civic Ideology", in: *JHS* 107, 58–76.

Hedrick, C.W., Jr. (1999), "Democracy and the Athenian Epigraphical Habit", in: *Hesperia* 68, 387–439.

Hiller von Gaertringen, F. (1906), *Inschriften von Priene*, Berlin.

Kajava, M. (2008), "Alcune note sulle Deltoi, Capitoline e altre", in: M.L. Caldelli et al. (eds.), *Epigrafia 2006. Atti della XIVe rencontre sur l'épigraphie in onore di Silvio Panciera con altri contributi di colleghi, allievi e collaborator*, Rome, 115–120.

Labarre, G. (1996), *Les cités de Lesbos aux époques hellénistique et impériale*, Lyon.

Lambert, S.D. (2011), "What Was the Point of Inscribed Honorific Decrees in Classical Athens?", in: S.D. Lambert (ed.), *Sociable Man: Essays on Ancient Greek Social Behaviour in Honour of Nick Fisher*, Swansea, 193–214.

Lambert, S.D. (2012), *Inscribed Athenian Laws and Decrees 352/1–322/1 BC: Epigraphical Essays*, Leiden.

Ma, J. (1999), *Antiochos III and the Cities of Western Asia Minor*, Oxford.

Ma, J. (2003), "Peer Polity Interaction in the Hellenistic Age", in: *P&P* 180, 9–39.

Ma, J. (2012), "Epigraphy and the Display of Authority", in: J. Davies/J. Wilkes (eds.), *Epigraphy and the Historical Sciences*, Oxford, 133–158.

Mack, W. (2015), *Proxeny and Polis: Institutional Networks in the Ancient Greek World*, Oxford.

MacMullen, R. (1982), "The Epigraphic Habit in the Roman Empire", in: *AJPh* 103, 233–246.

Meyer, E.A. (1990), "Explaining the Epigraphic Habit in the Roman Empire: The Evidence of Epitaphs", in: *JRS* 80, 74–96.

Meyer, E.A. (2012), "Epigraphy and Communication", in: M. Peachin (ed.), *The Oxford Handbook of Social Relations in the Roman World*, Oxford, 191–226.

Meyer, E.A. (2013), "Inscriptions as Honors and the Athenian Epigraphic Habit", in: *Historia* 62, 453–505.

Nijf, O.M. van (2012), "Political Games", in: K. Coleman/J. Nélis-Clément (eds.), *L'organisation des spectacles dans le monde romain*, Vandoeuvres, 47–95.

Nijf, O.M. van (2013), "Ceremonies, Athletics and the City: Some Remarks on the Social Imaginary of the Greek City of the Hellenistic Period", in: E. Stavrianopoulou (ed.), *Shifting Social Imaginaries in the Hellenistic Period. Narrations, Practices, and Images*, Leiden, 311–338.

Ober, J. (2008), *Democracy and Knowledge: Innovation and Learning in Classical Athens*, Princeton.

Petrovic, A./Petrovic, I./Thomas, E. (eds.) (2018), *The Materiality of Text: Placement, Perception, and Presence of Inscribed Texts in Classical Antiquity*, Leiden.

Price, S.R.F. (1984), *Rituals and Power: The Roman Imperial Cult in Asia Minor*, Cambridge.

Rhodes, P.J. (1972), *The Athenian Boule*, Oxford.

Rhodes, P.J. (2001a), "Public Documents in the Greek States: Archives and Inscriptions, Part I", in: *G&R* 48, 33–44.

Rhodes, P.J. (2001b), "Public Documents in the Greek States: Archives and Inscriptions, Part II", in: *G&R* 48, 136–153.

Rhodes, P.J. with Lewis, D.M. (1997), *The Decrees of the Greek States*, Oxford.

Robert, L. (1961), "Épigraphie", in: C. Samaran (ed.), *L'histoire et ses méthodes*, Paris, 453–497.

Robert, L. (1973), "Les juges étrangers dans la cité grecque", in: E. von Caemmerer (ed.), *Xenion. Festschrift für Pan. J. Zepos anlässlich seines 65. Geburtstages am 1. Dezember 1973*, Athens, 765–782.

Rowe, G. (2002), *Princes and Political Cultures: The New Tiberian Senatorial Decrees*, Ann Arbor.

Rubinstein, L. (2013), "Spoken Words, Written Submissions, and Diplomatic Conventions: The Importance and Impact of Oral Performance in Hellenistic Inter-Polis Relations", in: C. Kremmydas/K. Tempest (eds.), *Hellenistic Oratory: Continuity and Change*, Oxford, 45–66.

Scafuro, A.C. (2013), "Decrees for Foreign Judges: Judging Conventions — or Epigraphic Habits?", in: *Symposion* 24, 365–395.

Sherk, R.K. (1969), *Roman Documents from the Greek East: Senatus Consulta and Epistulae to the Age of Augustus*, Baltimore.

Sickinger, J.P. (1999), *Public Records and Archives in Classical Athens*, Chapel Hill, NC.

Sickinger, J.P. (2009), "Nothing to Do with Democracy: 'Formulae of Disclosure' and the Athenian Epigraphic Habit", in: L. Mitchell/L. Rubinstein (eds.), *Greek History and Epigraphy: Essays in Honour of P. J. Rhodes*, Swansea, 87–102.

Terrone, E. (2014), "Traces, Documents, and the "Puzzle of Permanent Acts"", in: *The Monist* 97, 161–178.

Thomas, R. (1989), *Oral Tradition and Written Record in Classical Athens*, Cambridge.

Williamson, C. (1987), "Monuments of Bronze: Roman Legal Documents on Bronze Tablets", in: *ClAnt* 6, 160–183.

Williamson, C.G. (2013), "As God Is My Witness: Civic Oaths in Ritual Space as a Means towards Rational Cooperation in the Hellenistic Polis", in: R. Alston/O.M. van Nijf (eds.), *Cults, Creeds and Identities in the Greek City after the Classical Age*, Leuven, 119–174.

Williamson, C.G. (2021), *Urban Rituals in Sacred Landscapes in Hellenistic Asia Minor*, Leiden.

Wilson, A. (2009), "Approaches to Quantifying Roman Trade", in: A. Bowman/A. Wilson (eds.), *Quantifying the Roman Economy: Methods and Problems*, Oxford, 213–249.

Part III: **Between Documents and Literature**

Scott J. DiGiulio
Dead Letters, Documentality, and the *Noctes Atticae* of Aulus Gellius

Abstract: Amidst the explosive proliferation of written texts in the latter half of the second century CE, Aulus Gellius' miscellany, the *Noctes Atticae* (*NA*), offers a critical lens for understanding how at least one ancient reader approached reading different material in the Roman Empire. This chapter examines Gellius' use of texts that would be conventionally termed "documentary" and argues that he sees them as more analogous to the literary works quoted throughout the *NA* than we might initially assume. While his narratives discussing the treatment of official documents suggest that some material had privileged status, his citations from the letters of Cicero and Augustus, as well as his discussions of public inscriptions, reveal that the divide between the documentary and the literary was more permeable than we might otherwise imagine. In his hands, literary works and documents stand together as authoritative evidence for Latin language and style within the broader text-world of his miscellany.

Spanning a wide range of time, genres, and languages, the literary landscape of the Antonine era represented a vast archive, with all forms of writing, including what we might conventionally consider documentary material, finding a home in the physical libraries that proliferated throughout the first and second centuries CE.[1] The cultural prominence of these institutions had literary effects as well, including the development of the loose genre of compiled or miscellanistic texts, which gather troves of information and streamline them; the resultant books digest the essential elements of other works so that a reader might have

---

I am indebted to audiences at the DocuMentality conference and Fordham University and to the anonymous reviewers for their comments on versions of this chapter. Unless noted, all translations are my own.

---

[1] On the place of the library in imperial culture, see Too 2010; on the library as a metaphor for cultural knowledge and performance of the canon specifically, see Too 2000. On the storage of legal and other official texts no longer in force in libraries, which she terms "documents morts," see Moatti 2003, 38–39.

easy access to them in a text of readable length.² Within discussions of miscellanistic literature, Aulus Gellius and his sole surviving work, the *Noctes Atticae* (hereafter *NA*), loom large. As a miscellanist, Gellius deftly assembles a range of textual material into a single work, ostensibly for the education of his young sons as he notes in the extant opening of the preface (*NA praef*.1), and the breadth of sources included for this purpose is considerable. Across the nearly four hundred entries that make up the *NA* one can find excerpts from Aesop's fables standing cheek by jowl with fragments of Republican poetry, Claudius Quadrigarius alongside discussions about word usage in Plautus, and readings of Homer juxtaposed with analysis of Epicurus' language.

Despite its heterogeneity, Gellius' endeavor is unified by the act of reading itself: the *NA* is a work that challenges his audience to cultivate a specific reading practice in order to help them negotiate their contemporary textual landscape.³ In his preface, Gellius coaches his audience in the habits of reading that he believes are necessary to navigate the world he envisions: namely, one in which an educated Roman must demonstrate mastery of the Greek and Latin culture, especially as this manifests in literary texts. He labels his work a "storehouse of literature" (*litterarum penus*, *NA praef*.2), and offers Aristophanes' *Clouds* as a shibboleth near the end of the preface (*praef*.20–21), coding the work as literary-minded despite the inclusion of legal, philosophical, and other material. Within this generic diversity, Gellius includes numerous accounts of reading and interacting with the written word, especially literary works broadly defined; in this respect, the *NA* is a *liber librorum* — "a book of books."⁴ In this, his representation of his reading and social interactions appears to align with Ferraris's conceptions of social acts, as Gellius' record of his conversations and

---

2 Perhaps more than any other literary form, the miscellany rose to prominence in the second century during the period known as the Second Sophistic. These texts, written in both Latin and Greek, are characterized by their collecting of a range of brief entries on diverse topics, a (frequently explicit) lack of order, and their focus on helping to situate a range of knowledge into a broader performative or cultural context. Nevertheless, despite commonalities, there is no single ancient term for these sorts of works, and the term "miscellany" is itself an anachronism, first used in this way by the Renaissance humanists. On the genre generally, see Oikonomopoulou 2017 (with bibliography); on approaching their disorder and structure, see König 2007; Paulas 2012; Xenophontos 2012; Jacob 2013.
3 Several new studies of the *NA* have appeared in recent years, building on the seminal Holford-Strevens 2003 and exploring cultural and literary elements of the work: Gunderson 2009; Keulen 2009; Rust 2009; Heusch 2011; Howley 2018 (especially focused on critical reading and the cultural knowledge in the *NA*).
4 Gunderson 2009 uses *libri librorum* as the title of his sixth chapter, in which he discusses the unavoidable presence of books and texts throughout the *NA*.

readings expresses the social entanglements inherent in the literature culture of second-century CE Rome. Given the ostensible purpose of the excerpts that Gellius gathered into the *NA* (to teach his children and, by extension, his audience) and their diversity of material, perhaps it is better to speak of the work as a *documentum documentorum* ("a document of documents") rather than a *liber librorum*.[5]

Gellius does not confine himself merely to citations of literary works in a strict sense throughout the *NA*, instead including a significant amount of material that is "documentary" from a modern historiographical perspective, ranging from records of conversations, to letters, to inscriptions. However, an important question that is too infrequently asked is whether he envisions any significant differences between the kinds of texts in his miscellany. In this chapter, I focus on Gellius' usage of sources that would be considered documentary from the modern perspective and assess whether he sees them as somehow distinct within the reading environment that he constructs. While he refers to a range of material that we might term documents, his use of two specific sets of such texts in the *NA* is illustrative: letters and a limited number of inscriptions.

What emerges is a fundamental blurring of the line between "documentary" and "literary" throughout. In this respect Gellius appears not to privilege a specific category of "documentary" texts, and his approach appears in line with other contemporary forms of research, as Schneider argues in his chapter on geography in the Imperial period.[6] The evidence of this second-century miscellany in many cases suggests a different understanding of an ancient "document" than the model proposed by Ferraris. While certain elements are shared between the two (in particular, a need for collective intention and consensus that gives documentary force to a text), Gellius does not primarily see the texts he cites as revelatory of social reality; his focus is rather on what his audience may learn from the material he has collected and how. He further problematizes the question of whether authority resides with one or the other form of text, as he draws extensively on both documents and literary works, often in the same context. Each can, and frequently does, shed light on the other in his anecdotes,

---

5 As Gellius states in the preface, the purpose of the text is to educate his children; as such, his work falls squarely within a didactic tradition, akin to Cicero's *De officiis*, Seneca's *Epistulae morales*, etc. Its constituent parts might best be termed *documenta*, following Varro's derivation of the word (*Ling.* 6.62: *ab eodem principio documenta, quae exempla docendi causa dicuntur*, "*documenta*, which are examples said for the sake of instructing, come from the same starting element"). On Gellius' educational purpose, see Morgan 2004, 188–191.
6 Something similar may be observed in ethnographic texts in eastern parts of the empire; for one example, see Andrade 2020.

but neither is singularly authoritative. In his reading, Gellius utilizes both forms of evidence as complements to one another that require the same critical approach.[7] These textual forms all illuminate questions of style and eloquence: within the *NA* the central concern when adducing texts, irrespective of their genre and form, is to document *eloquentia* (eloquence) for Gellius' audience and to illustrate the proper use of the resources of the Latin language.[8]

1 Epistolary Authority, Epistolary Eloquence

How and when do letters appear in the *NA*? They are quoted or otherwise referenced in thirty-two of Gellius' *commentarii* (conventionally translated as "chapters"), and he intersperses citations to numerous letters from prominent historical figures including Cicero and Augustus, among others.[9] Additionally, he includes letters of less certain authenticity, such as those purportedly authored by the Macedonian royal family, which are almost certainly the kinds of fabrications produced as part of the imperial Greek educational curriculum.[10] Gellius gravitates toward non-literary letters — that is to say, those letters written to specific addressees and which were primarily intended to serve as private communicative acts, in contrast with those epistles that have been composed either in prose or verse for public consumption or written solely with a popular audience in mind — and largely demurs from engaging epistolary predecessors such as Horace, Pliny the Younger, or Seneca the Younger.[11] Nevertheless, practically

---

7 On reading approaches inscribed within the *NA*, see DiGiulio 2020.
8 In this respect Gellius appears not to privilege a specific category of "documentary" texts, focusing instead on those texts that can enhance his presentation of *eloquentia*; the approach appears in line with other forms of research in the same period (cf. Schneider in this volume).
9 *NA* 1.22, 2.10, 4.7, 4.9, 5.21, 6.3, 6.10, 9.3, 10.1, 10.11, 10.24, 10.26, 10.27, 12.2, 12.3, 12.13, 13.12, 14.7, 14.8, 15.5, 15.7, 15.13, 16.9, 17.2, 17.9, 20.5; this list includes references to general corpora, such as Julius Caesar's letters, as well as more properly literary collections, such as Seneca's *Epistulae morales* and Varro's *Epistolicae quaestiones*.
10 Holford-Strevens 2003, 40, 255 n. 67, observing that Gellius cites the letters ostensibly for points of style or wit, with the majority of these letters being fictitious. Pseudonymous letters attributed to famous political or philosophical figures from the past abound in the Imperial period, in part thanks to the connection between such letter-writing and the practice of *ethopoiia*, which was central to rhetorical education in the Imperial period; see Rosenmeyer 2001, 193–233; Malosse 2005. On letters of Alexander in the Imperial period, see Whitmarsh 2013.
11 On the first nine books of Pliny's letters as a deliberately assembled, self-consciously literary collection composed with the reading public in mind, see among others Marchesi 2008,

all these letters, whether private communications or pseudonymous school exercises, are quoted with a view to illustrating their good style, usage, or cleverness, as in the case of exchanges between Alexander and Aristotle: "in the letter of each there was the slenderest thread of especially fine brevity" (*an autem prosus in utriusque epistula brevitatis elegantissimae filum †tenuissimum†, NA* 20.5.10). In this regard, Gellius appears not to distinguish between genuine and inauthentic or otherwise literary letters, which already produces one kind of elision and leads us to question whether he conceived of epistles as documents in the same way that modern historians might. His discussions throughout the *NA*, as well as ancient epistolary theory with which he would have been familiar and the evidence of his near contemporaries, suggest that letters were considered literary works first and documentary texts (in the modern sense) second, if at all.

The treatment of Cicero's *Letters* is illustrative in this respect; while these epistles were not originally intended for public consumption, and thus represent private "documents," Gellius does not afford them any special status as such.[12] In fact, his handling of the *Letters* does more to obscure the differences between what we term "documents" and "literary texts" from the modern perspective than to mark them off as distinct genres or sources.[13] At least in part, this may stem from the *Letters*' status as personal texts and the putative distinctions that Gellius had inherited from the earlier tradition. While the Latin episto-

---

Gibson and Morello 2012, Marchesi 2015, Whitton 2019; on Seneca's *EM*, see e.g. Henderson 2004, Schafer 2011, For Greek literary letters see Rosenmeyer 2001, Ceccarelli 2013. The process of editorial excerption may also transform a set of originally documentary letters into a literary collection, irrespective of those epistles' original communicative intent. For the case of Cicero, see Beard 2002 and Grillo 2015; on their "epistoliterarity," see the essays collected in Martelli 2016. For further discussion of the line between literary and documentary letters, including how they distinction was understood in Late Antiquity, see Amory in this volume.

12 Cicero's letters circulated in antiquity in books organized by correspondent, and Gellius' citations indicate that that was the form in which he knew them (e.g. 1.22.19, "in the book of letters of Marcus Cicero addressed to Lucius Plancus"; *in libro epistularum M. Ciceronis ad L. Plancum*). The *Epistulae ad familiares* were likely published by Tiro, with the first citations in Seneca the Elder; the *Epistulae ad Atticum* are first mentioned by Seneca the Younger, indicating that they may have appeared later. On the arrangement and publication of the letters, see Shackleton Bailey 1965, 59–76; Shackleton Bailey 1977, 20–24; Trapp 2003, 13–14. On the ancient availability of the letters, especially those to Atticus, see Beard 2002, 116–119.

13 In many cases the attitude that letters represented historical testimony has at least partly been imposed by modern editors who chronologically reordered epistolary collections into something akin to biographies or histories. Chronological organization was the exception rather than the norm and, however much is made of the organization of Cic. *Att.*, it remains in the minority; see Gibson 2012; Gibson 2013.

lary form had evolved by Gellius' time to include artistically fashioned collections such Pliny the Younger's *Epistles*, Cicero himself envisioned a distinction between public records and private letters, as he details in the *Pro Flacco*: "the one who did the deed is not here, he who is said to have paid the money has not been brought here, no private letters are produced, the public records remain in the power of the prosecutors" (*qui gessit non adest, qui numerasse dicitur non est deductus; privatae litterae nullae proferuntur, publicae retentae sunt in accusatorum potestate*, Cic. *Flac*. 23).[14] While Cicero makes finer distinctions between the different types of letter in his correspondence, notably at *Fam*. 2.4 and *Fam*. 4.13,[15] the fact that he included these forms of public and private writing in the same forensic context conveys his sense that the two are different forms of documents preserving parallel sets of information. With respect to private letters, Cicero may even have shared Cornelius Nepos' claim that one could reconstruct Roman history from Cicero's own letters: "eleven rolls of letters sent to Atticus continuously from his consulship to the very end which, should someone read them, he would have little need of a continuous history of those times" (*undecim volumina epistularum ab consulatu eius usque ad extremum tempus ad Atticum missarum: quae qui legat, non multum desideret historiam contextam eorum temporum*, Nep. *Att*. 16.3).[16] Regardless of the problems raised by this passage, at the very least it demonstrates that by Cicero's time the notion was established that letters could represent records of historical events, and thus possess a privileged status as a document in the modern sense.

Elsewhere, Cicero's discussions of the epistolary form more closely echo the ideals of the theoreticians, such as Demetrius, reflecting the idea that letters are two portions of a dialogue (Demetr. *Eloc*. 223); as such, each illuminates the character, and the soul, of the other (*Eloc*. 227). The letter thus replaces direct oral communication between absent parties and evokes the connection between writer and addressee; in this sense, there is nevertheless awareness that the act

---

14 Cf. Cic. *Flac*. 37. On the two passages and their insights into Cicero's conception of letters as a form, see Fögen 2018, 48, 55–60; on the distinction between public and private, see Trapp 2003, 4–5. Beyond letters, the category of texts that might fall under the rubric of "public document" was broad in antiquity; compare Bodel in this volume for examples in Roman law.

15 Morello 2013; Fögen 2018, 56–57. For Cicero it was critical to match style with his correspondent and reason for writing; while his letters frequently have conversational elements interleaved throughout, their registers are nevertheless calibrated to the specific situation for writing.

16 On Nepos' claim and several of the problems raised by the passage, including the relation of his "eleven books" (*undecim libri*) to the extant sixteen books of letters to Atticus, see Gibson 2012, 56–57.

of writing the conversation transforms those words into something more permanent.[17] This awareness of both writer and addressee suggests something akin to Ferraris's collective intentionality, which is a prerequisite for moving from utterance to document: the letters are the textual remnants of the social networks and interactions of Cicero's time.[18] Independent of their function within the social reality of the Late Republic, at their core the corpus of letters are the surviving traces of the two halves of a conversation between Cicero and his correspondents. Whether such dialogue produces a document in the ancient mind, as Ferraris might suggest, this intensely interpersonal quality of epistles is central to Cicero's own composition, and it is indubitably this element, and not the historical detail that could be gleaned, which draws Gellius to the letters he chooses to cite. They provide a glimpse of the letter-writer's character and his literary style, which may be seen as an extension of the former: *qualis vita, talis oratio*.

The *Letters* are among the least-cited Ciceronian texts in the *NA*, as Gellius has a clear preference for the rhetorical, and to a lesser extent the philosophical, works throughout. Of nearly eighty direct references to Cicero's works, the *Letters* appear only three times, and when he does cite the *Letters* it is almost always in the service of a philological or stylistic point.[19] For instance, in the *Letters*' first appearance (*NA* 1.22.19), Gellius introduces an epistle near the end of his discussion to highlight an extended meaning of *superesse*. The letter there is part of a broader nexus of citations deployed to answer the question at hand, with each piece of evidence carrying the same weight regardless of the genre from which it derives; thus, Cicero's *Letters* can be cited in the same breath as Vergil, Sallust, Plautus, and Varro's Menippean satires. Gellius appears to maintain fairly fluid generic divides, and all of these varied texts work together in

---

17 As Amory discusses elsewhere in this volume, this conception continued into Late Antiquity and even expanded to include the messenger of the letter, who was considered a "living letter" (ἔμψυχος ἐπιστολή) and effectively became a third party in the conversation. The assimilation of speaker and written text appears in miscellanistic discourse as well, including figures termed "living libraries" (βιβλιοθήκη ἔμψυχος), as in Eunap. *VS* 456; see Too 2010, 83–115.

18 On collective intentionality and the establishment of utterances as social objects (and hence documents), see Ferraris 2012, 146–174. Letters, as theorized in the ancient context, are a step removed from Ferraris's concerns about establishing social reality; they are inherently more ephemeral, given their putative status as representations of a conversation. Yet, even in the ancient rhetoricians, such letters are records of the social interactions that they represent, and, following Ferraris, may help constitute the social existence of writer and addressee.

19 Cicero is a chief linguistic authority for Gellius, frequently quoted to support Gellius' own word choices, in addition to being one of the pillars of good style; see Santini 2006, esp. the conclusions at 100–104.

service of his broader philological point. Similarly, at *NA* 4.9, Gellius cites *Att.* 9.5.2 to explore the meaning of *religiosus* that was proposed by Nigidius Figulus and to illustrate the proper usage of the term (*NA* 4.9.6); however, in the very next sentence, he cites Cicero again (the fragmentary *De accusatore constituendo*) to illustrate the opposite meaning. Gellius provides no other comment on the distinction between the two, and continues to introduce other sources for his discussion. It is notable that he does not feel any need to distinguish between Cicero's letters and his rhetoric — for the purposes of Gellius' analysis, the words of Cicero carry the same authority, regardless of putative genre.[20]

The final citation of Cicero's *Letters* looks very similar to the first two — a source for understanding language. *NA* 12.13 begins from a simple question: does the phrase *intra Kalendas* include the day of the Kalends itself? Gellius poses the question to his friend and teacher Sulpicius Apollinaris, who, after some protestation, provides a lengthy discussion of the underlying semantics of the phrase, supporting his discussion with citation of Cicero's *Third Verrine* (II 3.207 = *NA* 12.13.17). Gellius initially accepts Sulpicius' answer, that *intra* includes the day itself. However, this answer is nearly undone when Gellius later encounters Cicero using the word with a different meaning at *Fam.* 4.4.4: "but afterwards I found 'within the measure' was said in the book of Marcus Tullius' *Letters to Servius Sulpicius*, just as people say 'within the Kalends' when they wish to say 'before the Kalends'" (*set postea in libro M. Tullii* Epistularum ad Servium Sulpicium *sic dictum esse invenimus "intra modum" ut "intra Kalendas" dicunt qui dicere "citra Kalendas" volunt*, *NA* 12.13.21); in like manner, Gellius notes that Cicero's usage at *Pro Sestio* 58 disagrees with Sulpicius (12.13.25). Once again, epistles and speeches are juxtaposed by Gellius in order to reach a deeper understanding of how language works. He is able to combine these two citations into his ultimate answer, and has it both ways: "According therefore to the analogy of the words of Marcus Tullius may not one who is bidden to make a decision 'within the Kalends' lawfully make it before the Kalends and on the Kalends themselves?" (*num igitur secundum istam verborum M. Tullii similtudinem, qui iubetur "intra Kalendas" pronuntiare, is et ante Kalendas et ipsis Kalendis iure pronuntiare potest*, 12.13.29). For Gellius' specific purpose, neither genre of writing is more appropriate than the other, nor is one more authoritative —

---

[20] Central to Gellian notions of *auctoritas* is a canonical set of predominantly Republican authors who represent proper Latinity; an individual's intimate knowledge of these authors serves as a demonstration of his own authority. See Holford-Strevens 2003, 172–179; Gunderson 2009, 59–68.

they possess the same evidentiary force when it comes to assessing linguistic usage.

This fact aligns well with Gellius' use of Cicero throughout the *NA*, and the orator's reputation in the archaist movement in which Gellius participates. Indeed, Fronto appears to classify the *Letters* in much the same way in one of his own letters to the emperor Antoninus Pius. Fronto notes that, while ill,

> memini me excerpisse de Ciceronis epistulis ea dumtaxat, quibus inesset aliqua de eloquentia vel philosophia vel de re p(ublica) disputatio; praeterea si quid elegantius aut verbo notabli dictum videretur, excerpsi.
> (Fronto 104.6–9 VdH = *Ep. ad Ant.* 3.8.2)

> I recall that I had excerpted from the letters of Cicero in which there was some discussion about eloquence or philosophy or the state; I especially made an excerpt if anything seemed rather elegantly said, or made use of a noteworthy word.

Like Gellius, Fronto reads the *Letters* with an eye toward style and notable turns of phrase; even as he claims to have excerpted material from different passages of interest for their content, his primary criterion is stylistic. Similarly, he includes the *Letters* alongside the speeches as part of the same corpus as he urges his addressee to read the epistles: "but I consider all the letters of Cicero as things that should be read, in my opinion even more than all his speeches: there is nothing more perfect than the letters of Cicero" (*omnes autem Ciceronis epistulas legendas censeo, mea sententia vel magis quam omnis eius orationes: epistulis Ciceronis nihil est perfectius*; Fronto 104.12–14 VdH = *Ep. ad Ant.* 3.8.2).

Gellius' use of Cicero's *Letters*, then, is in line with other contemporary attitudes to the epistolary corpus and appears no different than his citations of other Ciceronian texts throughout the *NA*, where these writings provide examples of correct, or otherwise elegant, usage. In this regard, Gellius' employment of Cicero blurs the distinctions between literary and documentary. His use of the *Letters* alongside the other parts of the Ciceronian corpus erodes any potential barriers between documentary and literary, contrary to any expectations that modern scholars might have, given our own use of the corpus. Indeed, as Amory suggests elsewhere in this volume, such slippage between the two forms continued into Late Antiquity, oscillating between informative and performative modes. Even letters that might appear informative might nevertheless focus upon their literary aesthetics, with the informative function assigned to the letter-carrier. Fournet in this volume likewise notes a similar purpose in the early transposition of various documents, like petitions and letters, into literary compilations. However, over time the mutual pull that documents and literary texts exerted on one another increasingly muddied the waters between the two, as the process of "documentarization" — that is, of documents increasingly finding a natural home in more ostensibly literary works to the extent that divisions between the two forms of writing increasingly eroded — caused contemporary readers to see relatively limited divisions between these forms and instead recognize their capacity for mutual enrichment. Indeed, one might suggest that Gellius' use of Cicero might provide evidence for an early stage in the process of Fournet's "documentarization."

The Antonine treatment of Cicero's *Letters* suggests that at least one set of ancient readers understood these personal missives to be artistic constructions, even if they included some historical detail. In fact, while much modern scholarship on Cicero's *Letters* views them as essential documents for the history, social and otherwise, of the Late Republic, Gellius and Fronto both suggest that, in the Antonine era, the *Letters* were texts to be read and considered alongside the speeches and philosophical works as part of a single Ciceronian literary corpus. If their value for historians today is the contemporaneous testimony to historical events that they provide, for authors of the Antonine era their primary importance was their testimony about elegant Latin usage and style.

What of the other letters that appear in the *NA*? Does Gellius take steps to distinguish them as documents in any way? In a discussion of the perils of the sixty-third year of life, Gellius quotes in its entirety a brief letter from the emperor Augustus to his grandson Gaius (*NA* 15.7.3 = Aug. *Ep.* fr. 22). The brief letter provides a clear window into Augustus' personal life.[21] However, Gellius' purpose in reading the letter had little to do either with its reference to the details of old age contained in it, or with the historical moment that is reflected in the document. Instead, his aim was explicitly literary (*NA* 15.7.3):

> *Nocte quoque ista proxima superiore, cum librum Epistularum divi Augusti, quas ad Gaium nepotem suum scripsit legeremus, duceremurque elegantia orationis neque morosa neque anxia, sed facili hercle et simplici, id ipsum in quadam epistula super eodem anno scriptum offendimus.*

On the night immediately before, when I was reading the book of the *Letters* of the Divine Augustus, which he had written to his grandson Gaius, and I was drawn by the elegance

---

21 While our surviving fragments of Augustus' personal letters derive from intermediate sources (especially Suetonius, but also Quintilian, Gellius, and Macrobius, among others), by the late first century at least some letters were publicly available (including the autographs: Plin. *NH* 18.94, 18.139, 21.9; Quint. 1.7.22), and by Gellius' time the letters were collected into books apparently organized by correspondent. On the letters and the image of the emperor that emerges from them, see Bourne 1918; Giordano 2000; Mastrorosa 2012.

of his style that was neither fraught nor anxious, but straightforward and direct, I encountered that very [word] in a certain letter written in the same year.

Gellius' primary stated interest in reading the letter is its style; while the content of the letter may support Gellius' point about the perils of the sixty-third year of life, his only description of how he came to be reading it notes that he was interested in the artistry of the language. Augustus' confirmation of the conventional anxiety about the sixty-third year is incidental, even if this detail furnishes Gellius with raw material for his argument.

It is perhaps striking that Gellius provides the entirety of this letter, which constitutes nearly half of the entire *commentarius*. Augustus is a stylistic authority here, so in that regard providing the entirety of the letter makes sense, even given the relatively trivial content of the letter itself, and this pattern recurs in further citations of these texts. The emperor's letters appear in two other instances, in relatively close proximity to one another in Book 10, and, like Cicero's letters, both explain the meanings of specific words. Gellius reports Augustus' use of the Greek motto σπεῦδε βραδέως in his letters to support his own interpretation of the meaning of the adverb *mature* ("at the right moment," *NA* 10.11.5 = Aug. *Ep.* fr. 50):

> *Illud vero Nigidianum rei atque verbi temperamentum Divos Augustus duobus Graecis verbis elegantissime exprimebat. Nam et dicere in sermonibus et scribere in epistulis solitum esse aiunt* σπεῦδε βραδέως, *per quod monebat, ut ad rem agendam simul adhiberetur et industriae celeritas et diligentiae tarditas, ex quibus duobus contrariis fit maturitas.*

> Indeed, the divine Augustus most elegantly expressed Nigidius' balance of its meaning, and of the word, in two Greek words; for they say that he was accustomed to say in conversation and write in his letters "hasten slowly," through which he cautioned that, to accomplish a task, the swiftness of diligence and the slowness of scrupulousness are to be applied at the same time, out of which pairing of opposites *maturitas* arises.

Augustus is again celebrated as an exemplar of *elegantia*: the cleverness of his Greek phrase showcases his style, while affording Gellius the opportunity to support his overarching point about how to interpret *mature*.

Similarly, in a discussion of the correct usage of *diepristini*, *diecrastini*, and similar forms at 10.24, Gellius again turns to Augustus as an authority for proper diction. He does not provide any specific passage, merely asserting that Augustus' common usage supports the previous claim: "likewise the divine Augustus, who was not ignorant about the Latin language and an adherent of his father's fine style in his speech, oftentimes in his letters used that means of marking the days" (*Divus etiam Augustus, linguae Latinae non nescius munditiarumque patris sui in sermonibus sectator, in epistulis plurifariam significatione ista dierum non aliter usus est*, 10.24.2). Gellius praises Augustus' style, noting that he follows Caesar in his directness, and the *lemma* of the chapter itself reinforces this interpretation: "That *diepristini, diecrastini, diequarti,* and *diequinti* are used by *those who speak elegantly,* and not the words which are now in common use" (*"Diepristini," "diecrastini" et "diequarti" et "diequinti," qui elegantius locuti sint dixisse, non ut ea nunc volgo dicuntur,* 10.24.lem). Augustus possesses authority as both emperor and litterateur, and Gellius' citations access both levels of authority. By incorporating Augustus' words into his narrative, Gellius imbues the *NA* with their weight, with the result that we look favorably on Gellius' cultural authority and see his project as cleaving closely to the ideals of the Early Principate. Augustus' inclusion demonstrates Gellius' own weight as a researcher, superior to the other miscellanists that abounded in the Imperial period who had less access to such material; it therefore further elevates Gellius' own authority in the competitive intellectual culture of second-century Rome.

Yet, there is a subtle irony here: in these two instances, Gellius barely provides Augustus' *ipsissima verba*, even as he holds up Augustus as an authority on style — it is only at 15.7 that an excerpt from Augustus is provided. The difference between these references is one of content: while Gellius uses the authority of Augustus alone to support his claims elsewhere, in citing the entirety of a rather personal letter, Gellius offers a voyeuristic view of the *princeps*. Not only do we see his simple eloquence and his learning, but we are also given an intimate glimpse of Augustus the man, as Gellius coopts the emperor's words. We might even see Gellius operating in parallel fashion to the messengers that conveyed letters and delivered part of those documents' contents in the late antique world, as Amory suggests elsewhere in this volume: by presenting the letter he implicates himself within its communicative dynamics and positions himself as a trusted intermediary of the emperor. Even more, as he presents the epistle's words and enmeshes them within the text of the *NA* we momentarily lose sight of the division between Gellius' work and Augustus' letter, and Gellius thus reinforces the implicit equation of his cultural authority to that of the *princeps*. By so thoroughly incorporating letters in this way in the *NA*, his book becomes a document of Roman culture, with all the weight and validity that the letters carry.

We can contrast Gellius' use of Augustus' letters with Suetonius' use of the same corpus of material in his biography of the first emperor.[22] Suetonius makes ample use of letters that can be attributed to Augustus, though most letters are

---

[22] On Suetonius' use of sources generally, see Wallace-Hadrill 1983, 87–96 (on Augustus specifically, 91–95); on material attributable to Augustus in the *Augustus*, see Wardle 2014, 25–28.

cited less for their historical value and more for what they reveal about Augustus' personal life.²³ He cites three letters in succession at *Aug.* 76 to comment upon Augustus eating habits, and a further three letters are included at *Aug.* 71 to demonstrate his taste for playing dice; both sets of letters comment upon the emperor's morals by giving us privileged access to his character.²⁴ Indeed, at least one of the letters — a private one to his daughter (*Aug.* 71.4 = Aug. *Ep.* fr. 5) — must certainly have come from the imperial archives.²⁵ These inclusions appear to run counter to the way that Gellius employs the letters, with their clear interest in the character of the biographical subject and their use as evidence for the morals and interior qualities of the emperor.²⁶

In this case, the difference in genre may account for the different approaches, with Suetonius fleshing out his character sketch with otherwise inaccessible personal detail. But his comments on Augustus' epistolary habits reveal an interest in the lexicographical and stylistic points that attracted Gellius. After a lengthy discussion of Augustus' style in formal genres like oratory, Suetonius notes that "letters written in his own hand show that he rather frequently and notably made use of certain words from everyday speech" (*cotidiano sermone quaedam frequentius et notabiliter usurpasse eum litterae ipsius autographae ostentant, Aug.* 87.1), listing many examples before discussing the quirks of Augustus' orthography at length (*Aug.* 88). The letters were thus a valuable source for Suetonius about Augustus the litterateur, perhaps even more than they were about Augustus the emperor: they provide an insider's view not only of Augustus' character but also the quirks of his writing, which is ranked highly by his biographer.²⁷ While closer to what scholars would consider documentary,

---

23 Wardle 2014, 25–26 notes that twelve references can plausibly be assigned to the letters; of these, ten relate to Augustus' personal life and only a single letter definitively addresses political matters.
24 On playing dice in Rome and its moral complexity, see Purcell 1995. Dicing was also a particular interest of Suetonius throughout the *Lives* as a window onto the moral character of his subjects (Wardle 2014, 449–450).
25 Suetonius' access to the archives, thanks to his status as an imperial secretary (*ab epistulis*) to Hadrian, provided significant sources of information for his *Lives* in several instances; see Wallace-Hadrill 1983, 88–91. However, his inclusion of documentary material declines over the course of the collection; Geue 2020, 214–220 suggests that Suetonius ceases to trust letters closer to his own time as actually reflective of the emperors and their characters.
26 Suetonius does not cite the letters uncritically and occasionally constructs intratextual relationships between them to ironic effect; see Damon 2014, 55–56.
27 Suetonius offers high praise for Augustus as a Latin literary stylist across a range of genres and notes his clarity and restraint (*Aug.* 85–86), especially when compared to the Caesars that

Suetonius' use of the letters nevertheless suggests that, like Gellius, he understood them as lying within the literary spectrum and of special interest for what their language reveals.

One last example of how Gellius makes use of these texts confirms the literary role he sees for such texts. At *NA* 12.2, Gellius provides a sustained critique of Seneca the Younger as both a stylist and a critic in which he focuses narrowly on Seneca's stylistic evaluations of Ennius, Cicero, and Vergil. He lambasts his predecessor for concentrating on trivial elements and his failure to appreciate the style of Republican authors. He accomplishes his polemical attack primarily by citing directly from an otherwise unknown letter from the twenty-second book of the *Epistulae morales*.[28] What is striking about this letter, though, is the manner in which Gellius' treatment extends beyond the text: the passages that he chooses to cite all allude to other prominent passages of imperial literary criticism, and their evaluations of Seneca and his time.[29] This polemic also draws on Quintilian, who likewise disapproved of Seneca, but there is another element to this critique that is owed to Quintilian beyond the condemnation of Seneca's judgment. Gellius' attack on Seneca is conducted in the main through direct quotation of the *Epistulae morales*, with limited editorial analysis or interjection on his part, save for his harsh description of Seneca's pronouncements to which he chooses to draw critical attention.

This is very much in line with the way that Quintilian refashions *Ep. mor.* 114's critique of Maecenas as a stylist into a challenge of Seneca.[30] Gellius takes this rhetorical strategy one step further — instead of alluding to the *Epistulae morales*, he goes straight to the source and quotes Seneca's own words in order that their lack of judgment be manifest. Why cite this specific letter then? Gellius appears to use it as a strategy to expose Seneca, to allow his own words to undermine his authority. If the other letters mentioned above appear in order to establish their (and Gellius') linguistic *bona fides*, this epistle has the opposite goal. It serves as a *documentum* that illustrates how *not* to read, and is a teach-

---

come after. For Augustus as a paradigm against which the other emperors should be compared see, e.g., Langlands 2014.

28 Reynolds 1965, v.

29 Gellius' framing of Seneca's critique has strong commonalities with arguments presented in Quint. *Inst.* 10.1.129 as well as Tac. *Dial.* 16–23 (Aper's second speech and the defense of modernism); while Gellius may not draw directly on these works, he is nevertheless working within the mainstream of literary criticism of his time. On Gellius' critical tendencies, see Jensen 1997; Holford-Strevens 2003, 220–222.

30 On Quintilian's reworking of *Ep. mor.* 114's critique of Maecenas, see Taoka 2011, 126–131.

ing moment. But by incorporating it into the broader tradition of criticism against Seneca, Gellius seems less interested in the text as a document *per se*.

For all that Gellius' treatment of letters within the *NA* suggests no real distinction from the literary texts that he cites, one piece of external evidence must be addressed. In a letter to Claudius Julianus, dated to sometime around the year 160 CE, Fronto comments to his friend on activities that he has heard a certain Gellius has undertaken: "I did not know that my words were being sought very annoyingly by Gellius; you can be sure that I warned him about publishing them, as I write letters most reluctantly" (*non agnovi ista mea ab Gellio pessime quaeri: credideris admonuisse se edere. ego epistulas invitissime scribo*, Fronto, 182.5–7 VdH = *Ep. ad amicos* 1.19).[31] Gellius seeks Fronto's letters, which the latter notes he was loath to write in the first place, as potential fodder for his own enterprise; in Gellius' hands, there is potential for distortion, or other transformation, of Fronto's words and character.[32] To be sure, Gellius' memorialization of Fronto within the *NA* does appear to take liberties in his representation of the imperial tutor, satirizing Fronto's literary attitudes even as he establishes him as an authoritative critic.[33] While we cannot be certain of Gellius' precise motivations solely on the basis of this testimony, in seeking out Fronto's letters Gellius appears to recognize that those letters provide a degree of intimate access to Fronto's thought. Without Gellius' interaction with the letters preserved in the *NA*, however, we can only conjecture as to why they had a special appeal to him and what his purpose in seeking them out was. Fronto's own reaction sheds little light on the question: while Gellius supposedly sought out his letters, possibly for inclusion in the *NA*, we are left to puzzle over exactly why Fronto believed that Gellius was acting *pessime* — whether because of his methodology, or simply because he failed to secure permission first.

---

[31] On the date of the letter, see Champlin 1974, 152; Holford-Strevens 2003, 138. Holford-Strevens 2003, 138 n. 48 argues for identifying the Gellius here with the author of the *NA* rather than L. Gellius Menander, suggested by Marshall 1963.

[32] Holford-Strevens 2003, 138–139, discussing the interpretation of *pessime* and its implications for Gellius' activity and Fronto's disapprobation; cf. Keulen 2009, 38–39, noting that *pessime* may indicate Gellius' satirical intent.

[33] On the subversion of Fronto in the *NA* generally, see Keulen 2009, 39–46.

2 Language Set in Stone

So much, then, for letters in the *NA*. What of other documentary texts, such as inscriptions, that Gellius employs? If letters are comparatively infrequent in the *NA*, inscriptions are a precious rarity, figuring prominently in just two of Gellius' discussions, but, as with the letters, Gellius draws on these texts primarily to philological ends.[34] At the beginning of Book 10, he notes that, in an exchange of his letters with a friend, the question arose of whether *tertium* or *tertio* was the proper form for the number of a consulship. In answering the question, Gellius draws on Varro's and Tullius Tiro's accounts of the dedicatory inscription of Pompey's theater, in which this very question was sidestepped thanks to Cicero's suggestion: writing TERT instead of choosing one form or the other. Nevertheless in Gellius' day the original inscription was not extant, and the restored text further avoids the question: "For many years later when the stage-building which had fallen was restored, the number of the third consulship was indicated not as before with the first letters, but with just three carved lines" (*nam cum multis annis postea scaena, quae prociderat, refecta esset, numerus tertii consulatus non uti initio primoribus litteris, sed tribus tantum lineolis incisis significatus est*, 10.1.9). Ultimately, neither past nor present inscription provides any help in his inquiry, leaving Gellius to continue exploring the literary tradition to find his ultimate answer. He builds up the reliability of his response over the course of his narrative: both Varro and Tiro vouch for the account (even if the latter's authority is problematic), and Cicero originally provided the diplomatic solution.[35] However, both inscriptions deliberately avoided resolving the linguistic question, which represents a significant shortcoming, and Gellius must situate his inquiry within the world of literary texts as a result. In this respect the inscription has failed to document the Latin language.

---

34 In addition to the building inscriptions discussed below, Gellius reports the funerary epitaphs of the poets Naevius, Plautus, and Pacuvius; his stated reason for including those three texts is purely philological ("I decided that they should be recorded in these *commentarii* because of their excellence and charm," *nobilitatis eorum gratia et venustatis scribenda in his commentariis esse duxi*, *NA* 1.24.1). On the other hand, Gellius discusses a single inscription purportedly set up by Hesiod (*Anth. Pal.* 8.53), which had been cited by Varro to support the claim that Hesiod and Homer lived at the same time (*NA* 3.11). Varro's documentary research is treated as a methodologically distinct, and necessary, corrective to the errors appearing in Accius' reckoning of Homer and Hesiod's time period; see DiGiulio 2018, 326–327.
35 Gellius frequently challenges Tiro's intellectual authority, seeing him as uncivilized and lacking true Romanness; see Keulen 2009, 259–264.

That is not to say that there were no documentary *comparanda* available to Gellius. He undoubtedly would have known the prominent inscription on the Pantheon, restored by Hadrian in the mid-120s.[36] Its omission as supporting evidence seems glaring, given the close parallels between the inscriptions and the relative physical proximity of the two structures. Moreover, given Hadrian's antiquarian interests, it is more than likely that the emperor's choice to word his Pantheon inscription as he did represents an intervention in precisely the grammatical debate which Gellius discusses.[37] The inscriptions are in clear dialogue with one another, and Gellius' commentary almost certainly applies to both buildings. He uses the (literary) narratives surrounding Pompey's inscription to interrogate the propriety of not only the text on Pompey's theater but also that of the Pantheon. Through the prominent figures of the Republican past that he has cited, he subtly imposes his own intellectual authority on the Imperial present.

Moreover, Gellius has apparently seen the theater inscription — he knows that it no longer bears the original solution. Asserting his firsthand knowledge puts him in the physical space of the Campus Martius and establishes his value as an eyewitness. Further, by being in the space, Gellius evokes its connection to the authority of the Principate. In fact, by evoking his presence in the Imperial center, Gellius confirms his own reliability for the reader, in a way typical of the second century. Indeed, as Kuin and ní Mheallaigh note in this volume, such eyewitness boasts were so commonplace that Lucian could satirically undermine this trope throughout his corpus. We might even compare the "unreality effect" of the inscriptions encountered in the *True Stories* discussed in their chapters as Lucian deliberately raises his audience's suspicion about the reliability and veracity of those texts. Gellius' claims to be an eyewitness have similar literary purpose: his comments on the theater of Pompey reflect their instability as witnesses to the Latin language and simultaneously demonstrate his own mastery of the discourse used on these buildings, implicitly positioning him as an authority on Imperial culture.

On the surface, the other central appearance of an inscription in the text serves a similar role: as the launching point for an extended philological in-

---

[36] *CIL* VI 896: *M(arcus) Agrippa L(uci) f(ilius) co(n)s(ul) tertium fecit*. On the inscription generally, see Boatwright 2013. Hetland 2007, based on a reexamination of the brick stamps, argues that the restoration had begun under Trajan, though, as Boatwright suggests, this need not preclude Hadrian's ultimate (and indeed likely) influence on the style of the inscription.

[37] Boatwright 2013, 23–25, in discussing how deliberately archaizing word choices in the inscription are suggestive of Hadrianic authorship, notes the connection between the emperor's reputation for antiquarian interest and Gellius' discussion of Pompey's theater here.

quiry. At *NA* 13.25, Gellius describes an encounter along with Favorinus and several others in the Forum Traiani, in which Favorinus calls attention to a large inscription beneath the monuments commemorating Trajan's victories in Dacia (*NA* 13.25.1–2):

> *In fastigiis fori Traiani simulacra sunt sita circum undique inaurata equorum atque signorum militarium, subscriptumque est: "ex manubiis" Quaerebat Favorinus, cum in area fori ambularet et amicum suum consulem opperiretur causas pro tribunali cognoscentem nosque tunc eum sectaremur, quaerebat, inquam, quid nobis videretur significare proprie "manubiarum" illa inscriptio.*

> Gilded representations of horses and military standards are situated in the pediments and all around the Forum of Trajan, and "from the loot" is written underneath. Favorinus asked, when he was walking in the open area of the forum and was waiting for a friend of his, a consul that was hearing cases at the tribunal, and at that time we were accompanying him, he asked, I say, what that word *manubiae* properly seemed to mean to us.

However, after Favorinus' companion notes that *ex manubiis* effectively means *ex praedis*, the inscription has played its role and fades from view. The topic shifts into an extended discussion of pleonasm and its operation, as Favorinus attempts to explain why some people erroneously conflate *manubiae* and *praeda*; the conclusion is to take care when encountering pleonasm, since there are often subtle differences between the two words.[38] In Favorinus' articulation, two synonyms are not paired together without reason ("two words meaning the same thing are not placed next to one another to no purpose," *verba idem duo significantia non frustra posita esse* ἐκ παραλλήλων, 13.25.21), and in fact there are subtle differences between these two which are ignored by the careless at their peril (13.25.31).[39] Much of the actual content of the chapter consists of Favorinus' exploration of how such synonyms are used in Homer, Cicero, and others. His exegesis is grounded in his reading of literary texts, through which he illustrates that such juxtapositions require the reader to explore the interstices between the two parts in order to access the meaning of each. Notably, none of those texts are included in the lemma summarizing the chapter ("What

---

38 Howley 2018, 55. The choice to have Favorinus discuss pleonasm is to an extent a metacommentary on Favorinus' own archaizing style, in which doublets and triplets are common: see Beall 2001, 98–100.

39 Gellius tackles a similar topic *in propria persona* earlier in the same book at 13.3 (distinguishing between the meaning of *necessitas* and *necessitudo*, as he attempts to explain their differing semantic fields). However, he does not provide a similar theorizing conclusion to that of Favorinus at 13.25, though his discussion anticipates several of Favorinus' methodological choices.

manubiae are is inquired and treated and there certain things are said about the reason for using more words meaning the same thing," *Quaesitum tractatumque quid sint "manubiae"; atque inibi dicta quaedam de ratione utendi verbis pluribus idem significantibus*, 13.25.lem), which itself is a kind of pleonastic synonym for Gellius' discussion. The ultimate lesson is thus true of the table of contents entries as much as, if not more than, Gellius' *commentarii* themselves.[40]

What does Gellius accomplish by using the inscription as a framing device for his narrative? On the one hand, by focusing on the gaze of Favorinus and his companions, Gellius represents the physical world around him as another text for his characters to read — indeed, he synecdochally expands the Bibliotheca Ulpia to include the entirety of the Forum, thus making the whole available to read and interpret.[41] At the same time, he plays off the connections that he draws between the building inscription and his own enterprise. In citing the inscription here, Gellius locates his own work at the physical center of Roman cultural authority, and in so doing he coopts some of that authority for his own book, transforming it into a similar monument of Imperial learning and power. In this regard, this is a rare instance in which Gellius' citation of a documentary text extends beyond a philological point: by locating his text at the physical Imperial center, and especially one of the centers of culture, Gellius positions himself as an authoritative exegete of Roman knowledge for his readers. Additionally, by including this Imperial inscription, he effectively asserts that his own words carry the same weight as the text that he has included here.[42]

For all of the distinctiveness of the treatment of the Forum Traiani inscription, perhaps Gellius' quotation shares at least one function with the use of Cicero's *Letters* earlier: Gellius subsumes the authority of each into his own work. Effectively, by citing these authoritative documentary texts, Gellius raises the *NA* to their status — he becomes an arbiter of the Latin language and of

---

[40] The table of contents may be seen as a kind of document in that it serves as an external validation of the *commentarii*, providing an authoritative listing which includes their contents and their order. In this respect, the existence of a table of contents can be seen as analogous to archival deposit copies, which were utilized to validate secondary copies, disprove forgeries, etc. See Williamson 1995, 244–248; Moatti 2003, 32. Just as with discrepancies between the table of contents and the *commentarii* themselves, there was no expectation in the Roman world that the copies be exact transcriptions; see Moatti 2003, 32.
[41] Keulen 2009, 238–241.
[42] Keulen 2009, 241: "In this way, the inscription on the imperial monument becomes an authenticator of Gellius' own cultural authority, raising his writing to the same level as the inscription."

imperial culture, and his book acquires the same level of authority as the Bibliotheca Ulpia.

3 Documents Beyond the Page?

The manner in which Gellius incorporates documentary material as a source largely aligns with his broader compositional methodology. However, the narratives themselves can offer another avenue to understanding how documents fit into the work, and Gellius' broader attitude toward documents. One salient episode is Scipio Africanus' reaction to being called to account for loot taken in the Roman–Seleucid War (*NA* 4.18). Resentful of the indictment brought forth by the tribunes, Scipio prominently displayed a scroll containing the record of the loot, before tearing it up it in full view of the Senate (4.18.9–12):

> *Ibi Scipio exsurgit et prolato e sinu togae libro rationes in eo scriptas esse dixit omnis pecuniae omnisque praedae; illatum, ut palam recitaretur et ad aerarium deferretur. "Sed enim id iam non faciam" inquit "nec me ipse afficiam contumelia," eumque librum statim coram discidit suis manibus et concerpsit aegre passus quod, cui salus imperii ac rei publicae accepta ferri deberet, rationem pecuniae praedaticiae posceretur.*

> Then Scipio rose and, after he produced a book-roll out of the fold of his toga, said that the accounts of all of the money and booty were written in it; that he had brought it so that it might be read openly and deposited at the treasury. "But I will not do that now," he said, "nor will I debase myself," and he immediately tore up that book-roll before everyone with his own hands and rent it to bits, incensed that he was required to provide an account of the money taken as loot, he to whom the prosperity of the Republic and its power ought to be credited.

Gellius depicts not only the use but also the destruction of documentary material, expressly disallowing its entry into the public record, representing a moment in which official material is handled in a radical fashion. While he treats the other documentary material in the *NA* as sources that can be compiled for the purpose of making a broader argument about style and language, the Scipio episode demonstrates that the destruction of official records is transgressive.[43] Moreover, it is the (admittedly unread) contents of that book-roll that matter here, not how they were written, as the narrative drives home. The destruction of the scroll is shocking, partly because of the context in which it is destroyed,

---

[43] On the episode within the context of book-burning and the destruction of written material, see Howley 2017, 231–232.

and partly because of the nature of the text that it contains. Moments such as this one betray an understanding that at least one class of documents may exist that is closer to Ferraris's conception. The book-roll destroyed by Scipio is a document in that it is notionally a record of a social act (the depositing of war loot into the treasury); by destroying it, Scipio produces outrage because his act violates the social bonds that give that document its meaning.

And yet, while Gellius depicts Scipio's treatment of the document within the narrative in a way that appears distinct from his own usage of documents, the conclusions that he draws about the episode undercut some of the differences. As he caps the passage, Gellius remarks that Scipio destroyed the document because he felt it a travesty that someone who had done so much for the state should be called to make an account. But this is expressed by Gellius with a play on words: he claims that Scipio need not provide an account of the money because his heroism on behalf of the Republic has already been entered into the ledgers (with *accepta ferri* being the technical bookkeeping terminology for entering as a credit).[44] The destruction of the accounts in front of the Senate enriches the dramatic narrative, while opening the possibility for Gellius' linguistic cleverness.[45]

As I have suggested in this brief survey of documentary texts in the *NA*, Gellius approaches them with a certain degree of ambivalence. On the one hand, he treats them as sources indistinct from the vast array of literature that he cites alongside them, and he happily deploys them to support his philological, antiquarian, and other inquiries. On the other hand, he acknowledges that documents possess a specific authorizing force, which he frequently attempts to coopt for his own purpose. Gellius' careful selection of these documents enables him to represent himself as an authority on Roman culture at the highest levels, as in the case of the Forum Traiani inscription. Central to this mastery of Roman culture is language: indeed, the fact that Gellius uses documents primarily as sources for philological discussion confirms this notion. His insistence on the *elegantia* of the authors of these texts reinforces this point. Language is a central pillar of cultural authority within the worldview promulgated in the *NA*, and the value of documents lies in their status as stylistic exemplars.

---

44 *TLL* 1.0.314.13–49, 1.0.321.56–1.0.322.21 s.v. *accipio*.
45 The destruction seems quite similar to other similar scenes in the *NA*, namely the burning of the Sibylline Books (1.19) and the (accidental) destruction of the Library at Alexandria (7.17). In each case Gellius uses the drama of destruction, an unexpected and almost perverse act, to color his own narrative, while having precious little to say about the destruction of the material itself. See Howley 2017, 231 n. 102.

Returning to one of Gellius' chapters mentioned briefly earlier, we can further explore the implications of this last point, especially about the intersection of documents and language. In 12.13, as Gellius explores the proper meaning of *intra Kalendas*, his first recourse is to ask the grammarian Sulpicius Apollinaris for his advice; Sulpicius replies that, though he may speak with authority as a grammarian, nevertheless the meaning of words frequently changes over time as a result of common usage. Indeed, he suggests that even the law may lose its meaning because of popular neglect: "For the true and proper meanings of common words are not only changed through longer uses, but also the orders of the laws themselves are erased by a silent agreement" (*non enim verborum tantum communium verae atque propriae significationes longiore usu mutantur, sed legum quoque ipsarum iussa consensu tacito oblitterantur, NA* 12.13.5). At least in part, the law is eroded when the populace is silent, whether out of malice or through simple illiteracy.[46]

A similar phenomenon may be observed at 11.18.4, where the laws of Draco "were allowed to lapse because of a silent and undocumented consensus of the Athenians" (*tacito inlitteratoque Atheniensium consensu oblitteratae sunt*), rather than any official act of the *boule*.[47] The Athenians elected to ignore the letter of the law, reflecting an evolution of the legal tradition to suit their contemporary needs, as well as introducing an etymological play for Gellius: they could not understand its letter because of their illiteracy/lack of reading (*inlitterato*).[48] The Athenians elected to allow their law to become a dead letter — that is, they

---

[46] Cf. Gunderson 2009, 81: "The unwritten unwrites with the silent consent of illiteracy ... Similarly, the unspoken unwrites in 12.13.5, where laws again lose their meanings: *consensu tacito oblitterantur* ['they were erased by a silent agreement']. This same legal association is also leveraged in a metaphorical passage: the fundamental elements of filial piety are effaced and abolished when children are handed over to wet nurses (*oblitteratis et abolitis nativae pietatis elementis* ['with the elements of filial piety forgotten and abolished']; 12.1.23). The breast-feeding chapter is reaching a political crescendo."

[47] Gellius focuses in particular on the laws related to theft, juxtaposing Draco's laws with the Twelve Tables, which offer a range of punishments. He further appeals to the jurists, arriving at a definition of theft that seems to apply not so much to the theft of actual objects, but has more in common with the discourse of plagiarism in antiquity; see generally McGill 2012. Gellius' account may be colored by the rhetoric of plagiarism, even if he needs no reason for discussing the laws other than his own genuine interest in Roman law (on which see generally Holford-Strevens 2003, 294–301; Howley 2013 interprets Gellius' interest in the jurists as part of a broader strategy for understanding the Latin language and Roman culture) and the comparison of Greek and Roman cultural systems.

[48] Gunderson 2009, 81. Keulen 2009, 107 n. 27 observes the further play between *inlitteratoque* and *oblitterae*.

collectively decided upon a new legal standard (which Ferraris would term a social act). In this respect, Gellius appears to think that laws, like Scipio's ledger, constitute a different category of texts.

Even the Twelve Tables, the foundational documents of Roman law, are not immune to such changes as Gellius suggests at 20.10, where he attempts to identify the meaning of the legal phrase "lay hands on according to the law" (*ex iure manum consertum*), only to find that the practice fell into disuse (20.10.9).[49] Both points about which Sulpicius had warned Gellius are evident here: not only does the unnamed grammarian initially plead his inability to help because he knows about the poets rather than the law, but a law derived from Rome's foundational code has been ignored as contemporary custom has dictated. The central texts of Roman law have lost the authority they once possessed. These changes seem relatively benign at first: it is suggested that it is a natural process, as laws, like language, change over time. However, Gellius' examples indicate that this transformation is symptomatic of a broader cultural illiteracy, as a result of which the authority of language and mores can degrade. The opening chapter of Book 20 suggests as much, where it is claimed that any obscurities in the laws of the Twelve Tables are owed entirely to the ignorance of those who are unable to understand them ("Let us not assign their obscurities to the fault of those writing [the laws] but to the ignorance of those that were not following them," *Obscuritates ... non adsignemus culpae scribentium, sed inscitiae non adsequentium*, 20.1.5).[50]

Documents require a degree of complicity between reader and writer in order to have authoritative force.[51] What Gellius suggests here, and throughout his treatment of such evidence in the *NA*, is the instability of these documents: without the reader's proper knowledge of and training in language, even supposedly authoritative documents lose that authority. In this regard, then, Gellius appears to see all written text as a source for understanding language, including texts that modern historical interest would term documentary, like letters or building inscriptions. We might even be tempted to claim that a process analogous to the "documentarization" that Fournet proposes elsewhere in this volume is already beginning to take place: documentary texts are increas-

---

49 He discovers that, although the Twelve Tables prescribe laying hands on objects upon which a litigant is making a claim in the presence of a praetor, as the empire grew this practice fell into disuse ("it was established contrary to the Twelve Tables by a silent agreement," *institutum est contra duodecim tabulas tacito consensu*, *NA* 20.10.9).
50 Gunderson 2009, 80.
51 See Ferraris 2012, 148–154 on collective intentionality.

ingly at home in texts like the *NA*, and the eagerness with which Gellius discusses them suggests their place within the same literary spectrum in the latter second century CE.

The Gellian conception of a document thus diverges from the modern historian, but also from the model proposed by Ferraris. While I have suggested in several instances that Gellius appears to envision different classes of texts based on their social function, which aligns with Ferraris's conception of a document, nevertheless his interests suggest a fundamentally different understanding of the value of such texts. As opposed to Ferraris's interpretation of the written word as essential for constructing social reality, Gellius' concerns are more narrowly focused upon his own text-world, in which all genres exist alongside one another as part of the same archive of knowledge.

Indeed, when we see certain documents examined in their archival setting at *NA* 11.17.1, it is striking that these records are housed in the Bibliotheca Ulpia: "the edicts of the old praetors fell into my hands while I happened to be sitting in the library of the temple of Trajan and was looking for something else" (*edicta veterum praetorum sedentibus forte nobis in bibliotheca templi Traiani et aliud quid requirentibus cum in manus incidissent*). Documents are part of the written fabric of Gellius' world, situated in a library alongside famous authors. They represent a cultural and linguistic source equal to the great Republican authors so prized by Gellius as stylistic authorities. Indeed, if his sources are documents in the sense of providing evidence, what they document is the Latin language. If the *NA* is then a collection of evidence designed to foster knowledge of Latin, and by extension to cultivate a breed of educated Roman citizens, Gellius' compilatory work becomes less a *liber librorum*, and more a *documentum documentorum*.

References

Andrade, N. (2020), "Bardaisan's Disciples and Ethnographic Knowledge in the Roman Empire", in: A. König/R. Langlands/J. Uden (eds.), *Literature and Culture in the Roman Empire, 96–235: Cross-Cultural Interactions*, Cambridge, 291–308.

Beall, S.M. (2001), "Homo Fandi Dulcissimus: The Role of Favorinus in the 'Attic Nights' of Aulus Gellius", in: *AJPh* 122, 87–106.

Beard, M. (2002), "Ciceronian Correspondences: Making a Book Out of Letters", in: T.P. Wiseman (ed.), *Classics in Progress: Essays on Ancient Greece and Rome*, Oxford, 103–144.

Boatwright, M.T. (2013), "Hadrian and the Agrippa Inscription of the Pantheon", in: T. Opper (ed.), *Hadrian: Art, Politics and Economy*, London, 19–30.

Bourne, E. (1918), "Augustus as a Letter-Writer", in: *TAPhA* 49, 53–66.

Ceccarelli, P. (2013), *Ancient Greek Letter Writing: A Cultural History (600–150 BC)*, Oxford.

Champlin, E. (1974), "The Chronology of Fronto", in: *JRS* 64, 136–159.
Damon, C. (2014), "Suetonius the Ventriloquist", in: T. Power/R.K. Gibson (eds.), *Suetonius the Biographer: Studies in Roman Lives*, Oxford, 38–57.
DiGiulio, S.J. (2018), "*Monumenta rerum ac disciplinarum*: Varro's Literary Role in Gellius Noctes Atticae Book 3", in: *AJPh* 139, 311–341.
DiGiulio, S.J. (2020), "Gellius' Strategies of Reading (Gellius): Miscellany and the Active Reader in *Noctes Atticae* Book 2", in: *CPh* 115, 242–264.
Ferraris, M. (2012), *Documentality: Why It Is Necessary to Leave Traces*, transl. R. Davies, New York.
Fögen, T. (2018), "Ancient Approaches to Letter-Writing and the Configuration of Communities through Epistles", in: P. Ceccarelli/L. Doering/T. Fögen/I. Gildenhard (eds.), *Letters and Communities: Studies in the Socio-Political Dimensions of Ancient Epistolography*, Oxford, 43–79.
Geue, T. (2020), "Keeping/Losing Records, Keeping/Losing Faith: Suetonius and Justin Do the Document", in: A. König/R. Langlands/J. Uden (eds.), *Literature and Culture in the Roman Empire, 96–235: Cross-Cultural Interactions*, Cambridge, 203–222.
Gibson, R. (2012), "On the Nature of Ancient Letter Collections", in: *JRS* 102, 56–78.
Gibson, R. (2013), "Letters into Autobiography: The Generic Mobility of the Ancient Letter Collection", in: T.D. Papanghelis/S.J. Harrison/S. Frangoulidis (eds.), *Generic Interfaces in Latin Literature: Encounters, Interactions and Transformations*, Berlin/Boston, 387–416.
Gibson, R./Morello, R. (2012), *Reading the Letters of Pliny the Younger: An Introduction*, Cambridge.
Giordano, L. (2000), "Ottaviano Augusto scrittore: le lettere private", in: *MAT* 24, 3–52.
Grillo, L. (2015), "Reading Cicero's *Ad Familiares* I as a Collection", in: *CQ* 65.2, 655–668.
Gunderson, E. (2009), *Nox Philologiae: Aulus Gellius and the Fantasy of the Roman Library*, Madison.
Henderson, J. (2004), *Morals and Villas in Seneca's Letters: Places to Dwell*, Cambridge.
Hetland, L.M. (2007), "Dating the Pantheon", in: *JRA* 20, 95–112.
Heusch, C. (2011), *Die Macht der Memoria. Die "Noctes Atticae" des Aulus Gellius im Licht der Erinnerungskultur des 2. Jahrhunderts n. Chr.*, Berlin.
Holford-Strevens, L. (2003), *Aulus Gellius: An Antonine Scholar and his Achievement*, rev. edn., Oxford.
Howley, J.A. (2013), "Why Read the Jurists? Aulus Gellius on Reading Across Disciplines", in: P.J. du Plessis (ed.), *New Frontiers: Law and Society in the Roman World*, Edinburgh, 9–30.
Howley, J.A. (2017), "Book-Burning and the Uses of Writing in Ancient Rome: Destructive Practice between Literature and Document", in: *JRS* 107, 213–236.
Howley, J.A. (2018), *Aulus Gellius and Roman Reading Culture: Text, Presence, and Imperial Knowledge in the* Noctes Atticae, Cambridge.
Jacob, C. (2013), *The Web of Athenaeus*, transl. A. Papaconstantinou, Washington, DC.
Jensen, J.P. (1997), "Aulus Gellius als Literaturkritiker: Impressionist oder Systematiker? Versuch einer Aufstellung seiner literaturkritischen Werttypologie", in: *C&M* 48, 359–389.
Keulen, W. (2009), *Gellius the Satirist: Roman Cultural Authority in* Attic Nights, Leiden.
König, J. (2007), "Fragmentation and Coherence in Plutarch's *Sympotic Questions*", in: J. König/T. Whitmarsh (eds.), *Ordering Knowledge in the Roman Empire*, Cambridge, 43–68.
Langlands, R. (2014), "Exemplary Influences and Augustus' Pernicious Moral Legacy", in: T. Power/R.K. Gibson (eds.), *Suetonius the Biographer: Studies in Roman Lives*, Oxford, 111–129.

Malosse, P.-L. (2005), "Ethopée et fiction épistolaire", in: E. Amato/J. Schamp (eds.), Ἐθοποιία. La représentation de caractères entre fiction scolaire et réalité vivante à l'époque impériale et tardive, Salerno, 61–78.
Marchesi, I. (2008), *The Art of Pliny's Letters: A Poetics of Allusion in the Private Correspondence*, Cambridge.
Marchesi, I. (ed.) (2015), *Pliny the Book-Maker: Betting on Posterity in the Epistles*, Oxford.
Marshall, P.K. (1963), "The Date of Birth of Aulus Gellius", in: *CPh* 58.3, 143–149.
Martelli, F. (ed.) (2016), *Envois: New Readings in Cicero's Letters*, special issue of *Arethusa* 49.3, Baltimore.
Mastrorosa, I.G. (2012), "Préoccupations familiales et stratégies dynastiques dans la correspondance d'Auguste", in: F. Guillaumont/P. Laurence (eds.), *La présence de l'histoire dans l'épistolaire*, Tours, 403–417.
McGill, S. (2012), *Plagiarism in Latin Literature*, Cambridge.
Moatti, C. (2003), "Les archives romaines: réflexions méthodologiques", in: A.M. Biraschi *et al.* (eds.), *L'uso dei documenti nella storiografia antica*, Naples, 27–43.
Morello, R. (2013), "Writer and Addressee in Cicero's Letters", in: C. Steel (ed.), *The Cambridge Companion to Cicero*, Cambridge, 196–214.
Morgan, T. (2004), "Educational Values", in: L. Holford-Strevens/A.D. Vardi (eds.), *The Worlds of Aulus Gellius*, Oxford, 187–205.
Oikonomopoulou, K. (2017), "Miscellanies", in: W.A. Johnson/D. Richter (eds.), *The Oxford Handbook of the Second Sophistic*, Oxford, 447–462.
Paulas, J. (2012), "How to Read Athenaeus' *Deipnosophists*", in: *AJPh* 133, 403–439.
Purcell, N. (1995), "Literate Games: Roman Urban Society and the Game of *Alea*", in: *P&P* 147, 3–37.
Reynolds, L.D. (ed.) (1965), *L. Annaei Senecae Ad Lucilium Epistulae Morales*, Oxford.
Rosenmeyer, P.A. (2001), *Ancient Epistolary Fictions: The Letter in Greek Literature*, Cambridge.
Rust, E.M. (2009), "*Ex Angulis Secretisque Librorum*: Reading, Writing, and Using Miscellaneous Knowledge in the *Noctes Atticae*", unpublished PhD thesis, University of Southern California.
Santini, P. (2006), *L'auctoritas linguistica di Cicerone nelle "Notti Attiche" di Aulo Gellio*, Naples.
Schafer, J. (2011), "Seneca's *Epistulae Morales* as Dramatized Education", in: *CPh* 106.1, 32–52.
Shackleton Bailey, D.R. (ed.) (1965), *Cicero Letters to Atticus*, Cambridge.
Shackleton Bailey, D.R. (ed.) (1977), *Cicero Epistulae ad Familiares*, Cambridge.
Taoka, Y. (2011), "Quintilian, Seneca, *Imitatio*: Re-Reading *Institutio Oratoria* 10.1.125–31", in: *Arethusa* 44, 123–137.
Too, Y.L. (2000), "The Walking Library: The Performance of Cultural Memories", in: D. Braund/J. Wilkins (eds.), *Athenaeus and His World: Reading Greek Culture in the Roman Empire*, Exeter, 111–123.
Too, Y.L. (2010), *The Idea of the Library in the Ancient World*, Oxford.
Trapp, M. (ed.) (2003), *Greek and Latin Letters: An Anthology, with Translation*, Cambridge.
Wallace-Hadrill, A. (1983), *Suetonius: The Scholar and His Caesars*, London.
Wardle, D. (ed.) (2014), *Suetonius: Life of Augustus*, Oxford.
Whitmarsh, T. (2013), "Addressing Power: Fictional Letters between Alexander and Darius", in: O. Hodkinson/P.A. Rosenmeyer/E. Bracke (eds.), *Epistolary Narratives in Ancient Greek Literature*, Leiden, 169–186.

Whitton, C. (2019), *The Arts of Imitation in Latin Prose: Pliny's Epistles/Quintilian in Brief*, Cambridge.

Williamson, C. (1995), "The Display of Law and Archival Practice", in: H. Solin/O. Salomies/U.-M. Liertz (eds.), *Colloquium Epigraphicum Latinum. Acta Colloquii Epigraphici Latini Helsingiae 3–6 sept. 1991 habiti*, Helsinki, 239–251.

Xenophontos, S.A. (2012), "Plutarch's Compositional Technique in the *An seni respublica gerenda sit*: Clusters vs. Patterns", in: *AJPh* 133, 61–91.

Jean-Luc Fournet

The Relationship between Documents and Literature in Late Antiquity: The Case of the Petition, between Document, Adaptation and Literary Creation

Abstract: The realm of documents and that of literature are not as hermetic to each other as one would like to believe. The influence of documents has strongly marked the literary works, especially during the late antiquity: one started to compose letters or petitions in verse or to include real or fictitious documents in less circumstantial works; one developed patriographical rhapsodies or hagiographic collections, for example, by transmuting documentary material into literature. This chapter evaluates the phenomenon of "documentarization" with the case of late antique petitions by comparing the authentic petitions known by papyri, those transmitted by the literary sources (with some modifications) and those forged for literary purposes. The relationships, sometimes conflicting, sometimes complementary, always informative, between documents and literature are well illustrated by this documentary genre, which shows the difficulty of drawing a dividing line between "literature" and "document" in the later Roman Empire.

For the papyrologist, the relationship between documents and literature raises a complex issue, relatively unexplored because of the interdisciplinary treatment it requires. Papyrologists are accustomed to working on either documents or literature, but independently, without ever crossing the two types of sources. They are indeed accustomed to regarding the papyrological documentation as consisting of two blocks impermeable to each other, covered by different fields and methods. The first block is that of documents (over 60,000 edited Greek and Latin papyri): texts of manifold genres (letters, contracts, receipts, accounts, etc.), which have to do with history inasmuch as they concern the family, professional, religious, or administrative daily life of individuals. The second block is that of literary papyri, the ancient books which preserved Greek and Latin authors read by the ancients (over 10,000 published Greek and Latin papyri)

I would like to thank Antonio Ricciardetto for proofreading this paper and the anonymous peer reviewers for their suggestions.

https://doi.org/10.1515/9783110791914-009

and which belong to the field of philology or history of literature. These two blocks represent two types of papyrology which, because they cover different areas and require very specific knowledge, tend to form two separate branches of papyrology. Scholars generally specialize in one or the other.

A priori, the difference between a document and a literary book is epistemologically founded. What, for example, do a lease and an edition of Homer have in common? The two types belong to different activities (professional work and *otium*), normally take very different forms (the handwriting of documents is ostensibly different from the calligraphy of literary productions), and follow channels of dissemination that have nothing to do with each other (literature is the subject of a tradition that documents did not experience). Yet, if we look more closely, the boundary between the two is more fluid than is commonly believed. The polarity between documents and literature was initially not so clear-cut for the ancients — even if the use of different handwriting styles shows that they were felt to be of different natures.[1] The ancients used the same name, *bibliothêkê*, to designate a library of books (in the modern sense) and public archives; at home, they stored their books and documents in the same space; lastly, they did not hesitate to mingle books and documents on the same sheet of papyrus (by reusing a document to copy a literary text in the remaining blank portions or vice versa), which shows a much deeper permeability between these two types of text than our modern conceptions lead us to believe. Moreover, in practice, the same professionals could be asked to produce both types, meaning that contamination could occur between them.

These contaminations were even encouraged by the cultural trends that developed during the Early Roman Empire and culminated in late antiquity. A dual phenomenon occurred. The first is what might be called the "literarization" of documents. More and more clearly, from the late third century CE, documents — relating to everyday writing or practice, as opposed to literary texts — showed, by their writing, vocabulary, and rhetoric, the influence not only of Christian literature (as we would expect at this time) but more surprisingly of profane literature. They contain more and more literary quotations, their vocabulary is more and more deeply marked by Atticism as well as poetry, and they are more and more often introduced by a very rhetorical preamble intended as a piece of literature justifying the more down-to-earth text that follows.[2] In the other direction, papyrological sources show us a phenomenon that I will call

---

[1] See the case of Horapollo's petition (*P.Cair.Masp.* III 67295, I–II, below) which, copied as a literary text a century after the original document, is written with a literary script.
[2] Fournet 2016, 77–81 (§ 37–38 in the English edition).

the "documentarization" of literature. In some milieus at least, the literary patrimony was often given a practical function. Far from having the sole purpose of initiating and sustaining the pleasure of reading regarded as a gratuitous act, some authors produced practical manuals of eloquence or guides to writing documents. Not only did the literary corpus change its nature and function, but it also underwent a redefinition of its boundaries by opening itself to genres that belonged to the world of documents. For example, collections of letters became fashionable. These texts, originally ephemeral documents, enjoyed a second life by acquiring the status of a literary text, disseminated as manuscripts of literature to readers who could reuse them as models for writing documents. Contemporary literary works in general were also influenced by documents: one might write documents in verse (letters, and even complaints, as we shall see), or include real or fictional documents in less circumstantial works of a literary nature. Patriographic rhapsodies or hagiographic collections, for instance, were developed by transmuting purely documentary material into literature.³

It is this phenomenon of "documentarization" of literature that I would like to illustrate here through a case study of the petition, one of the best-attested documentary genres in our papyrological sources. The petition was a complaint that an individual or a group of individuals addressed to an authority to complain about an injustice that they suffered and to initiate legal proceedings to obtain compensation. Nearly 2,000 petitions on papyrus have survived (about 500 for the Ptolemaic period, 900 for the Early Roman period, and 450 for the Late period). An example dating from 425–430 CE, a petition addressed by the Bishop of Syene to Emperor Theodosius II, will give an idea of what interests me here about the shape and structure of this documentary genre:

Τοῖς γῆς καὶ θαλάσσης καὶ παντὸς ἀνθρώπων ἔθν[ου]ς καὶ γένους [δ]εσπόταις
   Φ[λ(αουίοις)] Θεοδοσίῳ καὶ Βαλεντινιανῷ τοῖς [αἰ]ωνίοις Αὐγού[στοι]ς
δέησις καὶ ἱκεσία παρ[ὰ] Ἀππίωνος ἐπισκόπου λεγεοῶνος Συήνης καὶ Κεν.. Σ[υ]ήνης
   καὶ Ἐλεφαντίνης ἐπαρχίας τῆς ὑμετέρας Ἄνω Θ[η]βαείδος.
Εἴωθεν ἡ ὑμετέρα φ[ι]λανθρωπία πᾶσειν τοῖς δεομένοις χεῖρα δεξιὰν ὀρέγειν, [ὅ]θεν
   κἀγὼ τοῦτο σαφῶς μεμαθηκὼς ἐπὶ τάσδε τὰς δεήσεις
5 ἐλήλυθα τοῦ πράγμα[το]ς ὄντος ἐν τούτοις. Ἐγ μέσῳ τῶν ἀλιτηρίων βαρβάρω[ν]
   με[τ]ὰ τῶν ἐμῶν ἐκκλησιῶν τυγχάνων τῶν τε Βλεννύω[ν]
μεταξὺ καὶ Ἀνν[ο]υβάδων πολ[λ]ὰς παρ' ἐκείγων ὡς [ἐ]ξ ἀφα[ν]οῦς κ[ατ]αδρομ[ὰς
   ὑπ]ομένομεν οὐδενὸς στρατιώτου προειστ[α]μένου τῶν
ἡμετέρων τόπων. Ἐκ τούτου τῷν ὑπ' ἐμὲ ταπιν[ου]μέν[ω]γ ἐκκλησιῶ[ν] καὶ μὴ
   δυ[ν]αμένων μήτε τοῖς αὐταῖς προσφεύγουσειν ἐπαμύνειν
προσπίπτω προκυλινδούμενος τῶν θείων ὑμῶν καὶ ἀχράγ[των] ἰχνῷ[ν ὥστ]ε

---

3 Fournet 2016, 82–83 (§ 40–41 in the English edition).

κα[τ]αξιῶσαι θεσπίσαι φρουρεῖσ[θ]αι τὰ[ς ὑπ' ἐμὲ (?)]
ἁγίας ἐκκλησίας ὑπὸ τῶν παρ' ἡμεῖν στρατιωτῶν κ[αὶ] πίθεσθ[αι] [αὐτο]ὺς ἐμο[ὶ καὶ
ὑ]πακούειν περὶ πάντων καθὼς οἱ ἐγ Φιλῶν οὕτω
10 καλουμένου φρουρίῳ τῆς ὑμετέρας Ἄνω Θηβαε[ί]δο[ς] κατα[σταθέντες] στρατι[ῶτα]ι
ὑπουργοῦσειν ταῖς ἐν Φιλῶ(ν) ἁγίαις τοῦ Θεο[ῦ]
ἐκκλησίαις. οὕτω γὰρ δυνησ[ό]μεθα ἀδε[ῶς ζῶ]ντες [- - -] . . . . [. . .] .σκας μετειέναι
νομοθεσίας . . .[- - -]
βαρυτάτης ὁριζομένης κατὰ τῶν παραβάγ[των] . . . . [. . .] .ν τὰ [θειω]δῶς παρ' ὑμῶν
θεσπισθέντα, πάσης
συναρπαγῆς τοῦ δι' ἐναντίας μέρους γενομ[ένη]ς ἢ μελ[λούσ]ης γενέ[σθαι]
σχολαζούσης, θείας ὑμῶν κε . . . . .
ἰδικῆς χάριτος περὶ τούτου φοιτώσης πρ[ὸ]ς τὸν μεγαλοπρεπέστατον καὶ
περίβλεπ[τον] κόμιτα καὶ δοῦκα
15 τοῦ Θηβαϊκοῦ λιμίτου· καὶ τούτου τυχὼν τὰς συνήθεις εὐχ[ὰς] ἀ[ναπ]έ[μψ]ω τῷ Θεῷ
ὑπὲρ τοῦ αἰωνίου [ὑ]μῶ[ν] κρ[άτου]ς
διὰ παντός.†††[4]

[*Praescriptio* ("prescript"): (a) *inscriptio*] To the masters of land and sea and every nation of humankind, Flavii Theodosius and Valentinianus, the eternal Augusti, petition and supplication [(b) *intitulatio*] from Appion, bishop of the legion of Syene and of Contra Syene and of Elephantine, in your province of Upper Thebaid.

[*Prooimion* ("preamble")] Your Benevolence is accustomed to stretch out a right hand to all who are in need. Therefore I too, having learned this clearly, have come to these petitions, the matter being thus:

[*Narratio* ("facts of the case")] Situated with my churches in the midst of the sinful Barbarians, the Blemmyes and the Nobadae, we are subject to many stealthy attacks by them, with no soldier protecting our places.

[*Precatio* ("request")] Therefore, since the churches under me have been humbled and are unable to protect the very ones who flee to them, I prostrate myself, rolling on the ground before your divine and immaculate footsteps so that you deem it right to decree that the holy churches under me be guarded by the soldiers among us, and that they obey me and heed me in all matters, just as the soldiers stationed in the fortress so-called "of Philae" in your Upper Thebaid will be at the service of the holy churches of God in Philae.

For thus we will be able to live without fear [...] and follow [...] most stern decree [...] being issued against those who have transgressed [...] what has been divinely ordained by you, every deceit of an opposing party, past or future, being null and void, with your divine [...] and special grace in this matter being addressed to the most magnificent and conspicuous count and duke of the frontier district of the Thebaid.

And having obtained this, I shall send up to God the customary prayers for your eternal power for all (time).[5]

---

4 *SB* XX 14606.
5 Translated by Porten *et al.* 1996, 441–442 (D 19), with some changes.

Over the nearly thousand years of its history in Egypt, the petition demonstrates a very strict and relatively stable form and formulary despite mutations during late antiquity under the influence of rhetoric and a more literary approach to written culture.[6] What interests me here is how and under what conditions this documentary genre entered the field of literature. These conditions depend on the type of literature or literary sources we deal with.

We have first to begin with questions about the ambiguous concept of "literature" or "literary sources": a document is usually considered the opposite of literature, but the latter can be defined in various ways depending on the point of view that is adopted: essentially — to simplify things — transmission or content. From the perspective of transmission, literary sources designate texts that are subject to edition and tradition/transmission: that is, texts intended for publication, subject to an editorial process and intentionally given to copyists for a wide dissemination that is not limited to a single professional category or to a short period (which excludes, for example, an administrative circular copied several times but disseminated to a group of individuals that is professionally and temporally well defined). From this point of view, literary sources contrast with documents that are issued in one or more copies (for the parties of a contract or for an appropriate archival repository, etc.), but are not intended to become part of a flow of transmission over several generations.

1 *Acta*

Literary sources contrast with documents but are not necessarily different in terms of content. Documents can, in fact, be collected and edited, as happened with the *Acta Conciliorum Œcumenicorum* (*ACO*), which gathered the proceedings of the sessions of the ecumenical councils, from the Council of Ephesus onwards (431 CE), in which all the bishops congregated to settle doctrinal, liturgical, or canonical issues. Such proceedings are full of documents presented at the synods, such as letters, reports, or petitions. Nothing in and of itself distinguishes these petitions transmitted by "literary sources" from the originals, which belong strictly speaking to the category of documents. Nothing, that is, except the editorial work they underwent, which could lead to alterations of the form of the original document (for example, by removing or modifying the prescript and deleting the subscriptions). The original documents are above all

---

6 Fournet 2019.

altered by the intentions and biases of those who collected and edited these texts, which led them to remove certain documents or, even worse, to change the content or the order of some of them. For example, the *acta* of the Council of Ephesus (431 CE), which opposed Nestorius and his follower Bishop John of Antioch to Cyril, Bishop of Alexandria, were preserved by the so-called *Collectio Vaticana*, "which was composed in praise of Cyril of Alexandria,"[7] indicating a selection or a partisan rearrangement of the documents.

Studying the petitions of the *ACO* some years ago, I was nevertheless convinced that they are generally very similar to the original documents.[8] Here, for example, is the petition submitted by Eusebius, Bishop of Dorylaeum, to the emperors Marcian and Valentinian at the Council of Chalcedon in 451 CE:

> Τοῖς φιλοχρίστοις καὶ εὐσεβεστάτοις βασιλεῦσιν ἡμῶν Φλαβίοις Βαλεντινιανῶι καὶ Μαρκιανῶι τοῖς αἰωνίοις αὐγούστοις παρὰ Εὐσεβίου τοῦ ἐλαχίστου ἐπισκόπου Δορυλαίου ποιουμένου τὸν λόγον ὑπέρ τε ἑαυτοῦ καὶ τῆς ὀρθοδόξου πίστεως καὶ ὑπὲρ τοῦ ἐν ὁσίοις Φλαβιανοῦ τοῦ γενομένου ἐπισκόπου Κωνσταντινουπόλεως.
>
> Σκοπὸς τῶι ὑμετέρωι κράτει ἁπάντων μὲν τῶν ὑπηκόων προνοεῖν καὶ χεῖρα ὀρέγειν ἅπασιν τοῖς ἀδικουμένοις, μάλιστα δὲ τῶν εἰς ἱερωσύνην τελούντων, καὶ ἐν τούτωι τὸ θεῖον θεραπεύοντες, παρ' οὗ τὸ βασιλεύειν ὑμῖν καὶ κρατεῖν τῶν ὑφ' ἡλίωι δεδώρηται. Ἐπεὶ οὖν πολλὰ καὶ δεινὰ καὶ παρὰ πᾶσαν ἀκολουθίαν ἡ εἰς Χριστὸν πίστις καὶ ἡμεῖς πεπόνθαμεν παρὰ Διοσκόρου τοῦ εὐλαβεστάτου ἐπισκόπου τῆς Ἀλεξανδρέων μεγαλοπόλεως, πρόσιμεν τῆι ὑμετέραι εὐσεβείαι τῶν δικαίων ἀξιοῦντες τυχεῖν. Τὰ δὲ τοῦ πράγματος ἐν τούτοις.
>
> Ἐπὶ τῆς ἔναγχος γενομένης συνόδου ἐν τῆι Ἐφεσίων μητροπόλει, ἣν ὄφελόν γε ἦν μὴ γενέσθαι, ἵνα μὴ κακῶν καὶ ταραχῆς τὴν οἰκουμένην ἐμπλήσηι, ὁ χρηστὸς Διόσκορος παρ' οὐδὲν θέμενος τὸν τοῦ δικαίου λόγον καὶ τὸν τοῦ θεοῦ φόβον, ὁμόδοξος ὢν καὶ ὁμόφρων Εὐτυχοῦς τοῦ ματαιόφρονος καὶ αἱρετικοῦ, λανθάνων δὲ τοὺς πολλούς, ὡς ὕστερον ἑαυτὸν ἐφανέρωσεν, εὑρὼν καιρὸν τὴν γεγενημένην παρ' ἐμοῦ κατὰ Εὐτυχοῦς τοῦ ὁμοδόξου αὐτοῦ κατηγορίαν καὶ τὴν ἐπ' αὐτῶι ἐξενεχθεῖσαν ψῆφον παρὰ τοῦ τῆς ὁσίας μνήμης Φλαβιανοῦ τοῦ ἐπισκόπου, πλῆθος ἀτάκτων ὄχλων συναγαγὼν καὶ δυναστείαν ἑαυτῶι διὰ χρημάτων πορισάμενος, τήν τε εὐσεβῆ θρησκείαν τῶν ὀρθοδόξων τό γε ἧκον εἰς αὐτὸν ἐλυμήνατο καὶ τὴν κακοδοξίαν Εὐτυχοῦς τοῦ μονάζοντος, ἥτις ἄνωθεν καὶ ἐξ ἀρχῆς παρὰ τῶν ἁγίων πατέρων ἀπεκηρύχθη, ἐβεβαίωσεν.
>
> Ἐπεὶ οὖν οὐ μικρὰ τὰ τετολμημένα αὐτῶι κατά τε τῆς εἰς Χριστὸν πίστεως καὶ καθ' ἡμῶν, δεόμεθα καὶ προσπίπτομεν τῶι ὑμετέρωι κράτει θεσπίσαι τὸν εὐλαβέστατον ἐπίσκοπον Διόσκορον ἀπολογήσασθαι τοῖς παρ' ἡμῶν αὐτῶι ἐπαγομένοις, δηλαδὴ τῶν παρ' αὐτοῦ καθ' ἡμῶν πεπραγμένων ὑπομνημάτων ἀναγινωσκομένων ἐπὶ τῆς ἁγίας συνόδου, δι' ὧν δυνάμεθα ἀποδεῖξαι αὐτὸν καὶ ἀλλότριον ὄντα τῆς ὀρθοδόξου πίστεως καὶ αἵρεσιν ἀσεβείας πεπληρωμένην κρατύναντα καὶ ἀδίκως ἡμᾶς καθελόντα καὶ τὰ δεινὰ ἡμᾶς κατεργασάμενον, θείων καὶ προσκυνουμένων ὑμῶν μανδάτων καταπεμπομένων τῆι ἁγίαι καὶ

---

7 Festugière 1982, 11: "qui a été composée à la gloire de Cyrille d'Alexandrie."
8 See Fournet 2010, 61–79.

οἰκουμενικῆι συνόδωι τῶν θεοφιλεστάτων ἐπισκόπων, ἐφ' ὧι τε ἡμῶν καὶ τοῦ προειρημένου Διοσκόρου διακοῦσαι καὶ ἀνενεγκεῖν εἰς γνῶσιν τῆς ὑμετέρας εὐσεβείας πάντα τὰ πραττόμενα πρὸς τὸ παριστάμενον τῆι ἀθανάτωι ὑμῶν κορυφῆι. Καὶ τούτου τυχόντες ἀδιαλείπτους εὐχὰς ἀναπέμψομεν ὑπὲρ τοῦ αἰωνίου ὑμῶν κράτους, θειότατοι βασιλεῖς.[9]

To our Christ-loving and most pious emperors Flavius Valentinian and Flavius Marcian perpetual Augusti from Eusebius the most insignificant bishop of Dorylaeum, speaking on behalf of himself, of the orthodox faith, and of Flavian, [now] among the saints, late bishop of Constantinople.

It is the concern of your authority to provide for all your subjects, and to extend a hand to all who are wronged, especially those enrolled in the priesthood; in this you serve the Godhead from whom you have received rule and authority over what is under the sun. Since the Christian faith and we ourselves have suffered many outrages, contrary to all good order, at the hands of Dioscorus the most devout bishop of the great city of Alexandria, we come to your piety to ask for justice. The facts of the case are as follows.

At the recent council in the metropolis of Ephesus — would that it had never taken place and had not filled the world with trouble and confusion! — this admirable Dioscorus set at naught both considerations of justice and the fear of God. Sharing the doctrines and views of the vain and heretical Eutyches, and deceiving the many, as he revealed himself later, he found his opportunity in the accusation which I had brought against the likeminded Eutyches and in the sentence which Bishop Flavian of sacred memory had delivered against him. Gathering a huge and disorderly mob and using money to procure power, he did as much damage as he could to the pious religion of the orthodox and confirmed the heresy of the monk Eutyches, which had previously and from the first been condemned by the holy fathers.

Since his offences against the Christian faith and against us are far from trivial, we beg and petition your authority to decree that the most devout Bishop Dioscorus must answer the charges we have brought against him, with, of course, the reading before the holy council of the minutes of his proceedings against us; these will enable us to prove that he is a stranger to the orthodox faith and has given his support to heresy steeped in impiety, and that he deposed us unjustly and did terrible things to us. May you send divine and venerable instructions to the holy and ecumenical council of most God-beloved bishops, that they are to hear the case between the aforesaid Dioscorus and us and bring all the proceedings to the knowledge of your piety, according to the will of your immortal head. If we obtain this, we shall offer up ceaseless prayers for your everlasting reign, O most divine emperors.[10]

---

9 *ACO* II/1: 66, line 23–67, line 17 (text).
10 Translated by Price/Gaddis 2005, 131–132.

2 Historical Works

Fortunately, we know this petition from another literary source: Evagrius' *Ecclesiastical History*, which covers the years 431–593 CE and focuses on the discussions of the Council of Chalcedon, decisive for the Eastern Church. Evagrius used original documents to write his history, and the text of Eusebius' petition he gives presents no fundamental differences from that transmitted by the *ACO* (I indicate the few textual differences in bold):

[*inscriptio* om.] Παρὰ Εὐσεβίου τοῦ ἐλαχίστου ἐπισκόπου Δορυλαίου, ποιουμένου τὸν λόγον ὑπέρ τε ἑαυτοῦ καὶ τῆς ὀρθοδόξου πίστεως, καὶ ὑπὲρ τοῦ ἐν **ἁγίοις** Φλαβιανοῦ τοῦ γενομένου ἐπισκόπου Κωνσταντινουπόλεως.
  Σκοπὸς τῷ ὑμετέρῳ κράτει ἁπάντων μὲν τῶν ὑπηκόων προνοεῖν καὶ χεῖρα ὀρέγειν ἅπασι τοῖς ἀδικουμένοις, μάλιστα δὲ **τοῖς** εἰς ἱερωσύνην **τελοῦσι**. Καὶ ἐν τούτῳ τὸ θεῖον θεραπεύοντες, παρ' οὗ τὸ βασιλεύειν ὑμῖν καὶ κρατεῖν τῶν ὑφ' ἥλι**ον** δεδώρηται. Ἐπεὶ οὖν πολλὰ καὶ δεινὰ [**καὶ** om.] παρὰ πᾶσαν ἀκολουθίαν ἡ εἰς Χριστὸν πίστις καὶ ἡμεῖς πεπόνθαμεν παρὰ Διοσκόρου τοῦ εὐλαβεστάτου ἐπισκόπου τῆς Ἀλεξανδρέων μεγαλοπόλεως, πρόσιμεν τῇ ὑμετέρᾳ εὐσεβείᾳ τῶν δικαίων ἀξιοῦντες τυχεῖν.
  Τὰ δὲ τοῦ πράγματος ἐν τούτοις· ἐπὶ τῆς ἐναγχος γενομένης συνόδου ἐν τῇ Ἐφεσίων μητροπόλει—ἣν ὄφελόν γε ἦν μὴ γενέσθαι, ἵνα μὴ κακῶν καὶ ταραχῆς τὴν οἰκουμένην ἐμπλήσῃ—ὁ χρηστὸς Διόσκορος παρ' οὐδὲν θέμενος τὸν τοῦ δικαίου λόγον καὶ τὸν τοῦ θεοῦ φόβον, ὁμόδοξος ὢν καὶ ὁμόφρων Εὐτυχοῦς τοῦ ματαιόφρονος καὶ αἱρετικοῦ, λανθάνων δὲ τοὺς πολλούς, ὡς ὕστερον ἑαυτὸν ἐφανέρωσεν, εὑρὼν καιρὸν τὴν γεγενημένην παρ' ἐμοῦ κατὰ Εὐτυχοῦς [**τοῦ** om.] ὁμοδόξου αὐτοῦ κατηγορίαν καὶ τὴν ἐπ' αὐτῷ ἐξενεχθεῖσαν ψῆφον παρὰ τοῦ τῆς ὁσίας **λήξεως** Φλαβιανοῦ [**τοῦ** om.] ἐπισκόπου, πλῆθος ἀτάκτων ὄχλων συναγαγὼν καὶ δυναστείαν ἑαυτῷ διὰ χρημάτων πορισάμενος, τὴν [**τε** om.] εὐσεβῆ θρησκείαν τῶν ὀρθοδόξων τό γε ἧκον εἰς αὐτὸν ἐλυμήνατο, καὶ τὴν κακοδοξίαν Εὐτυχοῦς τοῦ μονάζοντος, ἥτις ἄνωθεν καὶ ἐξ ἀρχῆς παρὰ τῶν ἁγίων πατέρων ἀπεκηρύχθη, ἐβεβαίωσεν. Ἐπεὶ οὖν οὐ μικρὰ τὰ τετολμημένα αὐτῷ κατά τε τῆς εἰς Χριστὸν πίστεως καὶ καθ' ἡμῶν, δεόμεθα καὶ προσπίπτομεν τῷ ὑμετέρῳ κράτει θεσπίσαι τὸν αὐτὸν εὐλαβέστατον ἐπίσκοπον Διόσκορον ἀπολογήσασθαι τοῖς παρ' ἡμῶν αὐτῷ ἐπαγομένοις· δηλαδὴ τῶν παρ' αὐτοῦ καθ' ἡμῶν πεπραγμένων ὑπομνημάτων ἀναγινωσκομένων ἐπὶ τῆς ἁγίας συνόδου, δι' ὧν δυνάμεθα ἀποδεῖξαι αὐτὸν καὶ ἀλλότριον [**ὄντα** om.] τῆς ὀρθοδόξου πίστεως, καὶ αἵρεσιν ἀσεβείας πεπληρωμένην κρατύναντα, καὶ ἀδίκως ἡμᾶς καθελόντα καὶ τὰ δεινὰ ἡμᾶς **κατειργασμένον**· θείων καὶ προσκυνουμένων ὑμῶν μανδάτων καταπεμπομένων τῇ ἁγίᾳ καὶ οἰκουμενικῇ συνόδῳ τῶν θεοφιλεστάτων ἐπισκόπων, ἐφ' ᾧ τε ἡμῶν καὶ τοῦ προειρημένου Διοσκόρου διακοῦσαι, καὶ ἀνενεγκεῖν εἰς γνῶσιν τῆς ὑμετέρας εὐσεβείας πάντα τὰ πραττόμενα πρὸς τὸ παριστάμενον τῇ ἀθανάτῳ ὑμῶν κορυφῇ. Καὶ τούτου τυχόντες ἀδιαλείπτους εὐχὰς ἀναπέμψομεν ὑπὲρ τοῦ αἰωνίου ὑμῶν κράτους, θειότατοι βασιλεῖς.[11]

---

[11] Evagrius, *Ecclesiastical History*, 2.18 (Bidez/Parmentier 1898, 68, line 11–69, line 22).

From Eusebius, the lowliest bishop of Dorylaeum, who is making the speech on behalf of himself, and of the orthodox faith and of Flavian, the former bishop of Constantinople, who is with the saints.

It is an objective of your might to take forethought for all subjects and to stretch out a hand to all who are wronged, but especially to those who minister in the priesthood. For in this indeed is served the Divinity by whom the imperial power and rule over human affairs is granted to you. Accordingly, since the faith in Christ and we ourselves have suffered many outrages contrary to all due order from Dioscorus, the most devout bishop of the metropolis of the Alexandrians, we are approaching your piety asking to obtain justice.

The facts of the matter are as follows: at the Synod which recently occurred at the metropolis of the Ephesians — would indeed that it had never occurred, so that it did not fill the whole world with evils and confusion! — the good Dioscorus, setting at nought consideration of justice and fear of God, being of the same doctrine and the same mind as the foolish-minded and heretical Eutyches, as he subsequently revealed himself, but being undetected by the multitude, using as an opportunity the accusation made by me against Eutyches, his fellow in doctrine, and the sentence brought against him by Bishop Flavian of holy estate, after assembling a multitude of unruly crowds and furnishing strength for himself through money, he polluted the pious worship of the orthodox, as far as was in his power, and corroborated the false doctrine of Eutyches the monk, which had from before and from the beginning been repudiated by the holy Fathers. Accordingly, since his affronts against the faith in Christ and against us are not minor, we request and prostrate ourselves before your might to decree that the same most devout Bishop Dioscorus should make a defence against our accusations against him: namely that when the records of what had been done by him against us are read out at the holy Synod, by means of these we can reveal that he is indeed alienated from the orthodox faith, that he fortified a heresy which is filled with impiety, and that he unjustly deposed us and ejected terrible things on us; we will do this once your sacred and adored instructions are sent to the holy and ecumenical Synod of the bishops, most beloved by God, to the effect that they should listen carefully to us and the aforesaid Dioscorus, and refer all the transactions to the cognizance of your piety, in accordance with the opinion of your immortal supremacy. And if we obtain this we shall send up incessant prayers on behalf of your eternal might, most sacred emperors.[12]

As we can see, the variants are minimal:
– Omission of the *inscriptio* from the prescript, which Evagrius did not see fit to retain insofar as he says above that it is addressed to the emperor (τὰς ἐπιδεδομένας παρ' αὐτοῦ τῇ βασιλείᾳ δεήσεις[13]): only the *intitulatio* declaring the identity and quality of the petitioner is deemed important and is retained;

---

12 Translated by Whitby 2000, 66–68.
13 Whitby 2000, 68, lines 4–5.

– Morphological (κατεργασάμενον / κατειργασμένον), lexical (μνήμης / λήξεως), and syntactic variants (εἰς ἱερωσύνην τελούντων / τοῖς εἰς ἱερωσύνην τελοῦσι, omission of ὄντα) that do not alter the general sense;
 – Omissions of particles or articles that are unimportant.

These differences are due either to the different models, or to Evagrius, or to copyists who transmitted the texts.

With Evagrius and other historians, we turn to another type of literary source, which is defined as a literary source not only by the way it was transmitted, but also by its contents.[14] Indeed, we are dealing with a literary work composed by an author which contrasts with raw materials, even if it has recourse to them. We enter, strictly speaking, the domain of literature, which provides a wide range of genres whose degree of "literary creativity" varies according to their relationship with the world of documents. These range from historical works that use documents they are supposed to include with fidelity to works of pure literary creation which twist documents for artistic purposes, including works occupying intermediate positions (such as hagiographic texts) where real documents play a dramatic role by serving the intention of the author. Let's review these cases.

3 Hagiographical Works

I distinguish hagiographic works from historical works in the name of a rationalism which the ancients would not have understood and would certainly not have approved of. While hagiographies were considered historical works, it is nevertheless clear that the biases of the former (supporting religious claims) are generally more visible and affect more deeply the whole construction of the work than in the latter. But I recognize that this distinction is often only a matter of degree and that it depends on the author's personality: it can happen that a historian has less reliable information or a more deficient critical sense than a hagiographer.[15] I will give an example of this later on.

---

14 Examples from other historians include Zacharias the Scholastic, *Ecclesiastical History*, 9.5 (Brooks 1924, 79, line 21–84, line 14), who cites a petition addressed by monophysite bishops to Justinian in 531. The same document is cited by Michael the Syrian in his *Chronicle*, 9.22 (Chabot 1901, 196–203). This petition is included in Feissel's list of imperial petitions in Feissel 2004, 48–49, reprinted in Feissel 2010, 379, no. 14.

15 On the question of degree, see Odorico/Agapitos 2004 and Toneatto 2004.

Aiming at creating a historical work, the author of a life of a saint did not hesitate to use documents in order to sustain the veracity of his account or to give it a semblance of veracity. For the first case, let us consider Cyril of Scythopolis (c. 525–after 559 CE), who, in his *Life of St. Sabas*, cites several petitions made by the Palestinian monk Sabas (d. 532 CE); one, addressed to Emperor Anastasius in 517 CE, is even reproduced in full despite its length.[16] This displays all the formal characteristics of a petition to the emperor and there is no reason to doubt its authenticity, especially since Cyril is known for the quality of his information, not hesitating to use archival documents in addition to oral testimonies. Extensive excerpts of this petition are also quoted by Theodorus of Petra in his *Life of St. Theodosius* (sixth century CE).[17]

In contrast, there may be serious doubts about the veracity of the petition cited by Leontius of Neapolis (sixth century CE) in his *Life of John the Almsgiver* (or *Eleemon*) (written in the 640s CE) when narrating the Persian invasion in 619 CE, at which time John was Bishop of Alexandria and a famine struck Alexandria, crowded with all the people trying to escape the Persians.[18] In this critical situation, John received a petition from a rich landowner, Cosmas, who offered to give him all his wealth in exchange for the post of deacon:[19]

Τῷ παναγίῳ καὶ τρισμακαρίστῳ πατρὶ πατέρων, ἀρχιερεῖ ἀρχιερέων, διδασκάλῳ διδασκάλων, ποιμένι ποιμένων Ἰωάννῃ τοποτηρητῇ τοῦ Χριστοῦ δέησις καὶ ἱκεσία παρὰ Κοσμᾶ ἀναξίου δούλου τῶν δούλων τῆς σῆς παναγιστείας. — Μεμαθηκώς, πανάγιε κῦρι, τὴν περιέχουσαν τὴν τιμίαν σου κεφαλὴν κατὰ συγχώρησιν θεοῦ, μᾶλλον δὲ ἐξ ἡμετέρων ἁμαρτιῶν στενοχωρίαν, οὐχ ὅσιον ἡγησάμην ὁ δοῦλός σου ἐν ἀνέσει διάγειν τοῦ δεσπότου μου ἐν στενώσει διάγοντος. Ἔστιν οὖν τῷ ἀναξίῳ σου δούλῳ σίτου μοδίων διακόσιαι χιλιάδες καὶ χρυσίου λίτραι ἑκατὸν ὀγδοήκοντα, ἅστινας δοῦναι παρακαλῶ τῷ Χριστῷ διὰ τοῦ κυροῦ. Μόνον ἵνα ὁ ἀνάξιος τῆς αὐτοῦ διακονίας ἐν ἀπολαύσει γένωμαι, ἵνα διὰ τῆς τοιαύτης

---

16 Cyril of Scythopolis, *Life of St. Sabas* (Schwartz 1939, 152, line 21–157, line 23), translated by Price 1991, 162–167. I give here just the prescript: Βασιλεῖ θεοφιλεστάτωι καὶ εὐσεβεστάτωι ἐκ θεοῦ αὐγούστωι καὶ αὐτοκράτορι Φλαβίωι Ἀναστασίωι τῶι φιλοχρίστωι **δέησις καὶ ἱκεσία** παρὰ Θεοδοσίου καὶ Σάβα τῶν ἀρχιμανδριτῶν καὶ λοιπῶν ἡγουμένων καὶ μοναχῶν ἁπάντων τῶν τὴν ἁγίαν τοῦ θεοῦ πόλιν καὶ πᾶσαν τὴν περὶ αὐτὴν ἔρημον καὶ τὸν Ἰορδάνην κατοικούντων ("To the most dear to God and most pious emperor, by God's will Augustus and Imperator, Flavius Anastasius the lover of Christ, a petition and supplication from the archimandrites Theodosius and Sabas, other superiors, and all the monks inhabiting the holy city of God, the whole desert round it and the Jordan"). On Cyril, see Flusin 1983.
17 Usener 1890, 56–60 (*BHG* 1176). See also Festugière 1963, 133f.
18 On Leontius, see especially Mango 1995. For the date of the *Life*, see Déroche 2016, 152–153, who proposes 642–649 CE.
19 Leontius of Neapolis, *Life of John the Almsgiver*, 11, ed. and trans. by Festugière 1974, 358 with Rydén (text).

σὺν τῷ κυρῷ τοῦ θυσιαστηρίου τοῦ ἁγίου παραστάσεως καθαρισθῶ τῆς τῶν ἁμαρτιῶν μου ἀσωτίας. Εἴρηται γάρ, θεοκῆρυξ ἀληθινέ, διὰ τοῦ συμμαθητοῦ σου Παύλου ὅτι "ἐξ ἀνάγκης καὶ νόμου μετάθεσις γίνεται."

To the most holy and thrice-blessed father of fathers, high priest of the high priests, teacher of the teachers, shepherd of the shepherds, John the deputy of Christ, the request and petition of Cosmas, an unworthy servant of the servants of thy Holiness. Having learnt, most holy Sir, of the shortage in food which oppresses thy honourable person by the permission of God, or rather in consequence of our sins, I, thy servant, do not consider it just to live at my ease whilst my master abides in continual need. Your unworthy servant has two hundred thousand bushels of corn, and one hundred and eighty pounds of gold; these I beg that I may offer to Christ through you, my lord. Only let me, unworthy though I am, enjoy the post of deacon under you, so that by standing beside my lord at the holy altar I may be cleansed from the profligacy of my sins. For, true herald of God, it has been said by the holy apostle Paul that "There is made of necessity a change also of the law."[20]

The saint refused this form of blackmail and preferred to manage without the financial manna promised by Cosmas instead of selling an ecclesiastical office.

The text of the petition raises questions. First it is surprising that Cosmas' petition is sent and not submitted in person as said in the text.[21] This anomaly is certainly justified by the fact that Cosmas felt ashamed to "express such a request to his face."[22] Technically, from a procedural point of view, we are dealing with a letter and not a petition. But why did Cosmas imitate a petition (with its rigid protocol τῷ δεῖνι δέησις καὶ ἱκεσία παρὰ τοῦ δεῖνος, "petition to so-and-so from so-and-so") while addressing to John a letter that did not request reparation (that being the role of a petition)? Maybe he did so deliberately to accentuate the hierarchical difference between the bishop and himself (no doubt an important person) and amplify the imploring tonality of his missive, accentuated by a rhetoric of self-humiliation and pathetic effects characteristic of petitions.[23] It could well be a kind of drama staged by Cosmas for the purpose of gaining John's goodwill. It could also be a drama staged by Leontius to give more strength to the story: the diegetic role of this petition is all the stronger as

---

20 Translated by Dawes/Baynes 1977, 222, with changes. The biblical quotation is from Hebrews 7:12.
21 Σὺ ὁ τὴν δέησιν ἡμῖν διὰ τοῦ σοῦ νοταρίου καὶ υἱοῦ ἀποστείλας ("You who sent us your petition through your clerk").
22 Κατὰ πρόσωπον γὰρ οὐκ ἐτόλμα τι τοιοῦτον πρὸς αὐτὸν φθέγξασθαι.
23 Ἀναξίου δούλου τῶν δούλων ("unworthy servant of the servants"); τῷ ἀναξίῳ σου δούλῳ ("your unworthy servant"); ὁ ἀνάξιος ("unworthy though I am"); καθαρισθῶ τῆς τῶν ἁμαρτιῶν μου ἀσωτίας ("I may be cleansed from the profligacy of my sins"). We have other papyrological examples of letters influenced by the phraseology of petitions.

it provokes an unexpected reaction. John's negative answer actually generates surprise, because of the attractive proposition made by Cosmas. By resisting the most eloquent and pathetic solicitations and attaching more importance to principles than to his personal interests, John proves to be a Christian hero. In short, there is every reason to doubt the veracity of this petition, which contributes to the narrative construction and serves the edifying function of hagiography.

4 Collections of Letters

Among the literary works bearing a similarity to documents are the collections of letters by the illustrious figures of the intellectual and religious world, which multiplied from the fourth century CE onwards. The letters of an individual were gathered for an edition, which implies, if not reworking, at least selection, classification, and formatting to create a "literary" work in itself: for instance, overly formal elements such as the prescript, the salutation formula — when it exists — and the endorsement are deleted.[24] We have many collections of letters and letter-writing manuals with series of examples,[25] but we do not have collections of petitions or guides to writing petitions. The reasons are obvious: the letter implies an exchange of ideas and feelings between two people bearing witness to their character, personality, and history which is absent from petitions, these being too dependent on the formal framework of legal proceedings. The petition could not claim the same status as the letter, which could more easily be isolated later on from the original conditions of its drafting to become a literary work in itself. Moreover, the intellectuals whose memory was thought to be deserving of being kept alive through their epistolary production, did not necessarily leave enough petitions to make collections.

Nevertheless, petitions may have crept into epistolary collections. This is the case of a "letter" that Saint Basil wrote in 372 CE to the praetorian prefect Modestus in order to request the continuation of the tax exemption enjoyed by clerics.[26]

---

24 On letters, see DiGiulio and Amory in this volume.
25 The latter are collected and translated by Malherbe 1988.
26 See Gascou 1997, 189–204, repr. in Gascou 2008, 417–429, no. 19.

ΜΟΔΕΣΤΩ ΕΠΑΡΧΩ

Αὐτὸ τὸ γράφειν πρὸς ἄνδρα τοσοῦτον, κἂν μηδεμία πρόφασις ἑτέρα προσῇ, μέγιστόν ἐστι τῶν εἰς τιμὴν φερόντων τοῖς αἰσθανομένοις, διότι αἱ πρὸς τοὺς παμπληθὲς τῶν λοιπῶν ὑπερέχοντας ὁμιλίαι μεγίστην τοῖς ἀξιουμένοις τὴν περιφάνειαν προξενοῦσιν. Ἐμοὶ δ' ὑπὲρ πατρίδος πάσης ἀγωνιῶντι ἀναγκαία πρὸς τὴν σὴν μεγαλόνοιαν ἡ ἔντευξις, δι' ἧς ἱκετεύω πράως καὶ κατὰ τὸν σεαυτοῦ τρόπον ἀνασχέσθαι καὶ χεῖρα ὀρέξαι τῇ πατρίδι ἡμῶν εἰς γόνυ ἤδη κλιθείσῃ. Ἔστι δὲ ὑπὲρ οὗ ἱκετεύομέν σε τὸ πρᾶγμα τοιοῦτον. Τοὺς τῷ Θεῷ ἡμῶν ἱερωμένους, πρεσβυτέρους καὶ διακόνους, ὁ παλαιὸς κῆνσος ἀτελεῖς ἀφῆκεν. Οἱ δὲ νῦν ἀπογραψάμενοι, ὡς οὐ λαβόντες παρὰ τῆς ὑπερφυοῦς σου ἐξουσίας πρόσταγμα, ἀπεγράψαντο, πλὴν εἴ πού τινες ἄλλως εἶχον ὑπὸ τῆς ἡλικίας τὴν ἄφεσιν. Δεόμεθα γοῦν μνημόσυνον τῆς σῆς εὐεργεσίας τοῦτο ἡμῖν ἐναφεθῆναι παντὶ τῷ ἐπιόντι χρόνῳ ἀγαθὴν περὶ σοῦ μνήμην διαφυλάττον καὶ συγχωρηθῆναι κατὰ τὸν παλαιὸν νόμον τῆς συντελείας τοὺς ἱερατεύοντας, καὶ μὴ εἰς πρόσωπον τῶν νῦν καταλαμβανομένων γενέσθαι τὴν ἄφεσιν (οὕτω γὰρ εἰς τοὺς διαδόχους ἡ χάρις μεταβήσεται οὓς οὐ πάντως συμβαίνει τοῦ ἱερατεύειν ἀξίους εἶναι), ἀλλὰ κατὰ τὸν ἐν τῇ ἐλευθέρᾳ ἀπογραφῇ τύπον κοινήν τινα συγχώρησιν κληρικῶν γενέσθαι, ὥστε ὑπὸ τῶν οἰκονομούντων τὰς Ἐκκλησίας τοῖς ἑκάστοτε λειτουργοῦσι τὴν ἀτέλειαν δίδοσθαι. Ταῦτα καὶ τῇ σῇ μεγαλοφυΐᾳ ἀθάνατον τὴν ἐπὶ τοῖς ἀγαθοῖς δόξαν διαφυλάξει καὶ τῷ βασιλικῷ οἴκῳ πολλοὺς τοὺς ὑπερευχομένους παρασκευάσει καὶ αὐτοῖς τοῖς δημοσίοις μέγα παρέξει ὄφελος, ἡμῶν οὐ πάντως τοῖς κληρικοῖς, ἀλλὰ τοῖς ἀεὶ καταπονουμένοις τὴν ἀπὸ τῆς ἀτελείας παραμυθίαν παρεχομένων, ὅπερ οὖν καὶ ἐπὶ τῆς ἐλευθερίας ποιοῦμεν, ὡς ἔξεστι γνῶναι τῷ βουλομένῳ.[27]

TO THE PREFECT MODESTUS

The very act of writing to so great a man, even if there be no other excuse, is most conducive to honour in the eyes of the discerning; for intercourse with men who are overwhelmingly superior to the rest of mankind affords the greatest distinction to such as are deemed worthy of it. As for me, as I strive earnestly for my country as a whole, I must needs address to your Magnanimity this petition (which I entreat you to suffer calmly even according to your character), that you stretch forth a helping hand to our fatherland now bowed to its knees. And the matter regarding which we seek your help is this.

Those who are consecrated to our God, that is presbyters and deacons, the earlier census left immune from taxation. But the present registrars, alleging that they had received no authorization from your high Lordship, have enrolled them, with the exception perhaps of some who are otherwise exempt because of old age. Therefore we ask that this exemption be granted us as a memorial of your beneficence, which will protect your good name for all future time, and that according to the old law those who act as priests be exempt from contribution, and that the exemption be not granted to the persons of those who now receive it (for in that case the favour would pass to their heirs, who might not be at all worthy of priestly duties), but that a general concession be granted the clergy according to the draft of the open register, so that exemption may be given by those who regulate the affairs of the churches to such as on each occasion are in the service.

This will not only keep the glory of the good deeds of your great Lordship immortal, but it will also increase the number of those who pray for the imperial house, and will con-

---

[27] Basil, *Letters*, 104 (Courtonne 1961, 4–5).

fer a great benefit even upon the public revenues, since we give the relief which is derived from our immunity from taxation, not altogether to the clergy, but to those who are at any time in distress; indeed, this is just what we do when we are free to do so, as anyone who wishes may find out.[28]

According to its formulary, this letter is actually a petition. There are other examples of petitions that found their way into epistolary collections.[29] The fact that the two genres, letter and petition, tended to influence each other during late antiquity and had recourse to the same phraseology may account for these mistakes. Moreover, the strong rhetorical tonality of petitions at that time and its more and more literary nature (poetic words, sophisticated expressions, quotations) may explain why they were considered worthy testimonies to an author's writing skills, deserving to appear in the midst of his epistolary production. These collections were above all regarded as samples or models directly usable by their owners. The letter and the petition were the two basic modes of communication at that time, one in the private sphere, the other in dealing with the authorities. These collections were therefore used as manuals.

This practical dimension is confirmed by a papyrus found in the library of a lawyer and amateur poet, Dioscorus of Aphrodite (sixth century CE). The *P.Cair.Masp.* III 67295 is a roll in which Dioscorus copied a petition (cols. I–II) by the philosopher Horapollo from the fifth century CE (known as the author of the *Hieroglyphika*) and at least two deeply rhetorical letters with Homeric quotations (col. III), one addressed to a bishop, the other written by an "erudite (ἐμπαίδευτος) *notarios*" to a colleague.[30] These texts were copied with a very literary script, indicating that this roll was not considered a simple copy of documents but a collection of models, falling under the category of literary papyri.[31]

---

28 Translated by Deferrari 1928, 195–197.
29 See the ἀναφορά petition by Simeon Stylites to Justin II (or Justinian shortly before his death according to van den Ven 1957, 2–3) against the Samaritans from Porphyreôn in Phoenicia, in which Simeon requested an investigation and sanctions (*Letters*, 5, PG LXXXVI/2, cols. 3216C–3220A). On ἀναφορά, see also Fournet 2010, 67–71. Note that the genre of certain documents was not always identified by the editors of such collections: for instance, Letter 36 by Cyril (*PG* LXXVII, cols. 165B–168B) is presented as a λίβελλος (= petition) in the title that was subsequently inserted.
30 Another hand copied a letter (?) addressed to a count ἐξπελλευτής (col. IV), but it is too damaged to be transcribed. Maspero does not edit it.
31 Dioscorus used Horapollo's petition to write his own petitions: the most obvious evidence is the reuse of the phrase ἀνορυχαὶ καὶ ἀνασκαφαί (*P.Cair.Masp.* III 67295, II, 5) in *P.Cair.Masp.* III 67283, I, 16 (540–544/5): ἀνορυχαῖς καὶ ἀνασκαφαῖς. In the same petition, note the use of εὐζωΐα "well-living" (I, 8: cf. *P.Cair.Masp.* III 67295, I, 19) and of σ]χολὴν ἄγειν (I, 12; cf. *P.Cair.Masp.* III 67295, I, 13).

5 Patria

The case I would like to discuss now will bring us back to historians but, with it, we will definitively leave historical reality to enter the domain of literary invention. John Malalas, in his *Chronographia*, 10.12, quotes a petition addressed by a certain Veronica to King Herod (borrowed subsequently by John of Damascus, in his *Orationes de imaginibus tres*, who says he has taken it directly from Malalas[32]). Veronica, who was cured of severe bleeding by Christ, decided to erect a statue of him in her city and asked Herod for the permission to do it by submitting a petition:

1   Σεβαστῷ Ἡρώδῃ τοπάρχῃ καὶ θεσμοδότῃ Ἰουδαίων τε καὶ Ἑλλήνων, Βασιλεῖ τῆς Τραχωνί-
    τιδος χώρας, δέησις καὶ ἱκεσία παρὰ Βερονίκης ἀξιωματικῆς πόλεως Πανεάδος. Δικαιοσύνη
    καὶ φιλανθρωπία καὶ αἱ λοιπαὶ τῶν ἀρετῶν πασῶν περιστέφουσι τὴν ὑμετέραν θείαν κο-
    ρυφήν. Ὅθεν κἀγὼ τοῦτο εἰδυῖα ἧκον σὺν ἀγαθαῖς ταῖς ἐλπίσιν πάντως τῶν αἰτουμένων
    τευξομένη. Τίς δὲ ἡ τοῦ παρόντος προοιμίου κρηπὶς
5   προϊὼν ὁ λόγος σε διδάξει. Ἐκ παιδόθεν ληφθεῖσα πάθει αἱμορροίας ὀχετῶν εἰς ἰατροὺς
    κατανάλωσά
    μου τὸν βίον καὶ τὸν πλοῦτον, καὶ ἴασιν οὐχ ηὗρον. Ἀκηκουῖα δὲ τοῦ θαυμαζομένου Χρι-
    στοῦ τὰ ἰάματα,
    ὡς νεκροὺς ἐξανίστησιν καὶ τυφλοὺς πάλιν εἰς φάος ἕλκων καὶ δαίμονας ἐκ βροτῶν ἀπε-
    λαύνων καὶ
    πάντας τοὺς ἐν νόσοις μαραινομένους λόγῳ θεραπεύει, πρὸς αὐτὸν [οὖν] κἀγὼ ὡς πρὸς
    θεὸν ἔδραμον.
    Καὶ προσεσχηκυῖα τὸ περιέχον αὐτὸν πλῆθος, δειλιάσασα δὲ ἐξειπεῖν αὐτῷ καὶ τὴν ἀήττη-
    τόν μου νόσον,
10 μή πως τὸν μολυσμὸν τοῦ πάθους ἀποστρεφόμενος ὀργισθῇ κατ' ἐμοῦ καὶ πλέον μοι ἐπέλ-
    θῃ ἡ πληγὴ τῆς νόσου, καθ' ἑαυτὴν ἐλογισάμην, ὅτι εἰ δυνηθείην ἅψασθαι τοῦ κρασπέδου
    τοῦ ἱματίου αὐτοῦ, πάντως ἰαθήσομαι· καὶ λάθρα εἰς τὸ περὶ αὐτὸν εἰσδύνασα πλῆθος ἐσύ-
    λησα τὴν ἴασιν, τοῦ κρασπέδου αὐτοῦ ἁψαμένη· καὶ σταλείσης μου τῆς πηγῆς τοῦ αἵματος
    γέγονα παραχρῆμα ὑγιής. Αὐτὸς δὲ μᾶλλον, ὡς προγνοὺς τῆς ἐμῆς καρδίας τὸ βούλευμα,
    ἀνέκραξε· 'τίς μου ἥψατο; δύναμις γὰρ ἐξῆλθεν ἀπ' ἐμοῦ.' Ἐγὼ
15 δὲ ὠχριῶσα καὶ στένουσα τὴν νόσον θρασυτέραν ὑποστρέφειν ἐπ' ἐμὲ λογιζομένη, προ
    σπεσοῦσα αὐτῷ
    τὴν γῆν ἐπλήρωσα δακρύων, τὴν τόλμαν ἐξειποῦσα. Ὁ δὲ ὡς ἀγαθὸς σπλαγχνισθεὶς ἐπ' ἐμὲ
    ἐπεσφράγισέν μοι τὴν ἴασιν, εἰρηκώς· 'θάρσει, θύγατερ, ἡ πίστις σου σέσωκέ σε· πορεύου
    εἰς εἰρήνην.' Οὕτως καὶ ὑμεῖς, σεβαστοί, τὴν δέησιν ἀξίαν τῇ δεομένῃ παράσχετε.[33]

---

32 John of Damascus, *Orationes de imaginibus tres*, 3.68.12–35 (Kotter 1975). The text is introduced in the following way: Ἐκ τῆς χρονογραφίας Ἰωάννου Ἀντιοχείας τοῦ καὶ Μαλάλα περὶ τῆς αἱμορροούσης καί, ἧς ἐποίησε τῷ σωτῆρι Χριστῷ, στήλης· κτλ.
33 John Malalas, *Chronographia*, 10.12 (Thurn 2000, 35). I give the text with an apparatus criticus comparing John Malalas' text (JM) with that of John of Damascus (JD).

2 δέησις καὶ ἱκεσία JD : ἱκεσίας δεήσεις JM(O) ‖ Βερονίκης JM(O)· Βερνίκης JD ‖ **2–3** αἱ λοιπαὶ τῶν ἀρετῶν πασῶν JM : τὰ λοιπὰ τῶν ἀρετῶν JD ‖ **3** θείαν om. JD ‖ ἦκον JM(O Sl) : om. JD ‖ **4** πάντως τῶν αἰτουμένων τευξομένη JM(O) : πάντων τῶν τευξομένων JD ‖ **4–5** τίς δὲ ἡ τοῦ παρόντος προοιμίου κρηπὶς προϊῶν JM : ἥτις ἡ τοῦ παρόντος προοιμίου κρηπίς· προϊῶν γάρ JD ‖ **5** ἐκ παιδόθεν JM : ἐκ παιδῶν JD ‖ πάθει JM(O) : πάθη JD ‖ κατανάλωσά JM : ἀναλώσασά JD ‖ **6** τὸν om. JD ‖ ὡς JD : ὃς JM(O) ‖ **7** ἐξανίστησιν JM : ἐξανίστησι JD ‖ καὶ τυφλοὺς om. JD ‖ φάος JM(O) : φῶς JD ‖ **8** νόσοις JM(O) : νόσῳ JD ‖ θεραπεύει JM(O Sl) : θεραπεύων JD ‖ οὖν secludo ‖ πρὸς αὐτὸν οὖν κἀγώ JM : κἀγὼ πρὸς αὐτόν JD ‖ **9** τὸ περιέχον αὐτὸν πλῆθος JM : τῷ περιέχοντι αὐτὸν πλήθει JD ‖ **9–10** δὲ ἐξειπεῖν αὐτῷ καὶ τὴν ἀήττητόν μου νόσον, μή JM : μή πως JD ‖ **10** μολυσμὸν τοῦ πάθους JM : ἐκ τοῦ πάθους μολυσμόν JD ‖ πλέον JM(O) : πλείων JD ‖ **11** εἰ JM : ἐὰν JD ‖ πάντως ἰαθήσομαι JM : σωθήσομαι JD ‖ **11–13** καὶ λάθρα εἰς τὸ περὶ αὐτὸν εἰσδύνασα πλῆθος ἐσύλησα τὴν ἴασιν, τοῦ κρασπέδου αὐτοῦ ἁψαμένη· καὶ σταλείσης JM : οὖ καὶ ἁψαμένη καὶ σταθείσης JD ‖ **14** τὸ βούλευμα JM : τὰ βουλεύματα JD ‖ γὰρ ἐξῆλθεν ἀπ' ἐμοῦ JM : ἀπ' ἐμοῦ ἐξῆλθεν JD ‖ **15** ὑποστρέφειν JM(O) : ἀποστρέφειν JD ‖ **16** ὁ δέ JM : αὐτὸς δέ JD ‖ ἐπεσφράγισέν μοι JM : ἐπεσφράγιζέ μου JD ‖ **18** ἀξίαν τῇ δεομένῃ edidi secundum JD : ὀξεῖαν τῇ δεομένῃ JM, τῇ δεομένῃ ἀξίαν JD.

To the august toparch Herod, lawgiver to Jews and Hellenes, emperor of the land of Trachonitis, a petition and supplication from Veronica, a dignitary of the city of Paneas. Justice and benevolence and all the other virtues crown your highness's sacred head. Thus, since I know this, I have come with every confidence that I shall certainly obtain my requests. My words as they progress will reveal to you what foundation there is for this present preamble. From my childhood I have been smitten with the affliction of an internal hemorrhage; I spent all my livelihood and wealth on doctors but found no cure. When I heard of the cures which Christ performs with his miracles, who raises the dead, restores the blind to sight, drives demons out of men and heals with a word all those wasting away from disease,[34] I too ran to him as to God. I noticed the crowd surrounding him and I was afraid to tell him of my incurable disease in case he should recoil from the pollution of my affliction and be angry with me and the violence of the disease should strike me even more. I reasoned to myself that, if I were able to touch the hem of his garment, I would certainly be healed.[35] I crept secretly into the crowd around him and I won my cure by touching his hem.[36] The flow of blood was stopped and immediately I was healed. He, however, as though he knew in advance my heart's purpose, cried out, "Who has touched me? For power has gone out of me." I went white with terror and lamented, thinking that the disease would return to me with greater force, and I fell before him covering the ground with tears. I told him of my boldness. Out of his goodness he took pity on me and

---

34 The text of John of Damascus is different here: "[having heard] that he raised up the dead by bringing them back to the light, driving demons out of [the body of] men and healing by his words all those wasting away from disease."
35 "Saved" (John of Damascus).
36 Sentence absent in John of Damascus, except "touching," which goes with the following sentence.

confirmed my cure, saying, "Be of good courage, my daughter — your faith has saved you. Go your way in peace." So, your highness, grant your suppliant this urgent[37] petition.[38]

Herod, struck by this miracle and regretting having ordered the beheading of John the Baptist in spite of his wife's entreaties (a story that Malalas tells us just before), gave her permission and

> immediately Veronica ... set up in the middle of her city of Paneas a bronze statue of beaten bronze, mixing it with a small quantity of gold and silver, to our Lord God Jesus Christ. This statue remains in the city of Paneas to the present day, having been moved many years ago from the place where it stood in the middle of the city to a holy chapel.

The document that John Malalas quotes has all the characteristics of a petition except that the object of the request (setting up a statue) is not expressed (Veronica simply says in conclusion "grant your suppliant this just request").[39] This is a first anomaly. But there is something worse: this petition looks like a real petition, but one from the Byzantine period. Indeed, the use of δέησις καὶ ἱκεσία within the prescript (typical of petitions addressed to the emperor) appears only in the fourth century CE, that is to say, four centuries after the time when this petition is supposed to have been written.[40] Moreover, it starts with an introductory sentence of encomiastic nature ("Justice and benevolence and all the other virtues crown your highness's sacred head," lines 2–3), a phenomenon that appears only in the second century CE.[41]

There is no doubt that this text is a Byzantine forgery. If we are to believe John Malalas, he is not the forger, since he says that he had "found this document (*hypomnema*) in the city of Paneas in the house of a man called Bassus, a Jew who had become Christian." He adds that it was accompanied by "lives of all the emperors who had formerly reigned over the land of Judaea."[42] This piece of information gives us the key to the nature of the petition. In fact, it was not

---

37 Better "just" (ἀξίαν) than "urgent" (ὀξεῖαν).
38 Translation from Jeffreys/Jeffreys/Scott 1986, 126–127 with one change.
39 Its structure is typical of a petition: (1) the *praescriptio* with δέησις καὶ ἱκεσία (lines 1–2); (2) the *prooimion* with a compliment of an encomiastic nature (lines 2–3); (3) a transitional sentence between the *prooimion* and the *narratio* (lines 3–5), beginning with ὅθεν κἀγὼ τοῦτο εἰδυῖα; (4) the *narratio* (lines 5–17), introduced by the verb διδάσκω; (5) the *precatio* (line 18), with the vocative referring to the recipient (σεβαστοί).
40 See Fournet 2010, 61–63, 74.
41 On the first *prooimia*, see *P.Berl.Frisk* 81–91.
42 Ὅπερ ὑπόμνημα ηὗρον ἐν τῇ αὐτῇ Πανεάδι πόλει παρὰ Βάσσῳ τινὶ γενομένῳ ἀπὸ Ἰουδαίων χριστιανῷ. Ἐν οἷς ὑπῆρχεν ὁ Βίος πάντων τῶν Βασιλέων τῶν Βασιλευσάντων πρῴην τῆς Ἰουδαϊκῆς χώρας.

the document itself or a copy of it that Bassus kept but a collection of *Lives* of the local rulers, including various pieces of more or less authenticity. So we are dealing with a patriographic text. *Patria* were stories related to a city and are typical of the late antique literary production. They often incorporated a documentary basis distorted or reinterpreted in such a way as to serve the interests of the city which was the subject of the *patria*. Thus this is a petition forged to restore the figure of the Tetrarch Herod, tarnished by the beheading of John the Baptist; Veronica's petition to which he gave its agreement in some sense absolves his previous crime by showing his remorse. The subliminal message of this text is that Herod finally accepted and favored Christianity.

6 Petitions in Verse or "Literarized" Petitions

I will conclude this study with an example of completely "literarized" petitions: that is to say, petitions that have become pieces of literature in the strict sense. In the works of Dioscorus of Aphrodite (sixth century CE), a poet I mentioned above, among the many encomia of high officials (emperor, governors, etc.), we find "poems of petition" or, more exactly, eulogies with the function of a petition.[43] Here is an example, a poem addressed perhaps to the prefect of the city:

1   Ὦ πτολίαρχε μέγιστε βοηθόε πᾶσιν ἀνάγκης,
    κλῦθι πονιομένου Παφίης χθονὸς ἐνναετῆρος,
    δέξεο 'μῆς γενιῆς τὰ δυσίμερα δάκρυα μόχθων·
    πολλά μοι ἐν γραφίδεσσι χαράγματα οἴκοθεν ἤχθη,
5   ὅττι καὶ Γαβριήλις χερείονα τῶν πρὶν ἔερξεν
    Πενταπολίτης Θεόδωρος ἀτάσθαλα ἔργα καὶ αὐτὸς
    ἡμετέρων σφετέρισσεν ἀλωῶν καρπὸν ἀπούρας.
    Χῶρον ἅπαντα θέριζε μελισταγέων σταφυλάων.
    Θρέμματα ἠδὲ βόας πόρεν Ἀρσᾷ κτήματα πάντα,
10 οὕνεκεν ἐνδεκάτης Θεοδόσσιος ὧν λάβε χρυσῶν,
    [ἡμετ]έρης γενιῆς βιοτήσιον. Νῦν δὲ φαεινῶν
    [σοῦ πρ]οκυλ[ι]νδόμενος πόδας ἰχνῶν, ὕψος ἄρειον[44]

---

43 See Fournet 1999, vol. 1, 373–408 (= *P.Aphrod.Lit.* IV). In this edition, I made a distinction between pure petitions and petition-like *encomia*, where the encomiastic elements are strongly developed. The first include *P.Aphrod.Lit.* IV 1–3; the second *P.Aphrod.Lit.* IV 4–16. The other poems, even though their primary function is different (*adventus*, birthday, marriage, etc.), similarly retain the function of a petition.
44 *P.Aphrod.Lit.* IV 1 (c. 551 CE).

> O greatest ruler of the city, general assistance against distress, listen to an inhabitant of land of the Paphian [= the village of Aphrodite] in his suffering. Receive the sad tears of pain from my family. I have brought from home many documents testifying that Gabriel has committed worse crimes than the acts of violence formerly accomplished by Theodorus of Pentapolis: he himself stole and appropriated the fruit from our threshing floors; he reaped entirely the honey-dripping grapes of our vineyard. Flocks, cattle, our entire property he gave to Arsas, because of the sums of gold due for the eleventh indiction, which Theodosius had stolen from us, the resources of our family. And at present, knelt at your radiant feet, O martial highness ... [the ending was never written].

Like a petition, this poem presents a complaint (4–11), preceded by a preamble or *prooimion* (1–3), and followed by a prostration formula (11–12), which was supposed to introduce the request to issue a decree in favor of the petitioner (which Dioscorus never composed, leaving his poem unfinished). A comparison of Dioscorus' "petition poems" with the many prose petitions he drafted shows that they have the same structure, phraseology, and vocabulary.[45] It seems that in most cases these versified petitions were submitted to the authorities along with the petitions in prose, the only ones valid from a legal point of view. In other words, these are true petitions (from the perspective of their function) but they take a totally literary form following the precepts of the encomiastic rhetoric so popular during late antiquity. These petitions contributed to making the authorities more favorably disposed to the prose petitions that were simultaneously presented, while providing a demonstration of the writer's literary talents.

Was Dioscorus a unique case? The lack of originality evidenced by his poetic production makes me suspect that he was not the inventor of the versified petition. There is at least another example in Latin literature: Sidonius Apollinaris' poem 8 in which the poet asks Emperor Majorian for tax relief.[46] On the Greek side, it would be possible to identify as a versified petition the τραγῳδία περὶ τοῦ δημοσίου τοῦ καλουμένου χρυσαργύρου ("*tragodia* on the tax call *chrysargyron*") addressed to Emperor Anastasius (491–518 CE), a lost work of the poet and grammarian Timothy of Gaza, in which the author probably asked the emperor for the abolition of the *chrysargyron* (a tax affecting traders and crafts-

---

[45] The best example is *P.Aphrod.Lit.* IV 12.
[46] See, for instance, lines 19–22: *Geryones nos esse puta monstrumque tributum: / Hinc capita, ut vivam, tu mihi tolle tria. / Has supplex famulus preces dicavit / responsum opperiens pium ac salubre* (Loyen 1960). Poem 5 by the same poet also ends with a request (574–603), but it is included in a eulogy and the primary function of the poem is to celebrate the coming of Emperor Majorian, who had newly acceded to the throne.

men); but the term *tragodia*⁴⁷ is problematic and the collective nature of this request suggests instead that it is a kind of "embassy discourse" (*presbeutikos logos*).⁴⁸

7 Conclusion

Marked by literature, the petition came in turn to mark literature. In certain historical and hagiographic works, it became an ornament of the story, even acquiring a diegetic function. When included in collections of letters, it was treated as a piece of literature and disseminated under the same conditions as literary works. First regarded as evidence of the style and eloquence of various great writers, these samples of documents might in turn become models for following generations. Some writers went so far as to compose false petitions for ideological purposes, such as Veronica's petition, or real petitions with a purely literary form, the versified "petition poem" — a new literary genre that needs to be recognized. These are borderline cases, but they show how the boundaries between documents and literature could be blurred in late antiquity.

References

Aujac, G. (ed. and trans.) (1991), *Denys d'Halicarnasse. Opuscules rhétoriques. IV. Thucydide*, Paris.
Bidez, J./Parmentier, L. (eds.) (1898), *The Ecclesiastical History of Evagrius with the Scholia*, London.
Brooks, E.W. (ed.) (1924), *Historia ecclesiastica Zachariae Rhetori vulgo adscripta*, vol. 2, Corpus Scriptorum Christianorum Orientalium 88, Leuven.
Chabot, J.-B. (ed. and trans.) (1901), *Chronique de Michel le Syrien, patriarche jacobite d'Antioche, 1166–1199*, vol. 2, Paris.
Courtonne, Y. (ed. and trans.) (1961), *Saint Basile. Lettres*, vol. 2, Paris.
Dawes, E./Baynes, N.H. (trans.) (1977), *Three Byzantine Saints: Contemporary Biographies*, 2nd edn., London.
Deferrari, R.J. (ed. and trans.) (1928), *Basil. Letters*, vol. 2, Cambridge, MA.

---

47 Glucker 1987, 52 interprets it as "apparently simply a long poem rather than a dramatic tragedy." If it is not to be taken in a dramatic sense, the term seems rather to designate a pompous speech (see Aujac 1991, 152, commenting on 3.66).
48 In Fournet 2004, 61–67, I show that the petition was very close in style to the *presbeutikos logos* as defined by Menander Rhetor.

Déroche, V. (2016), "Notes sur le VIIe siècle", in: O. Delouis/S. Métivier/P. Pagès (eds.), *Le saint, le moine et le paysan. Mélanges d'histoire byzantine offerts à Michel Kaplan*, Byzantina sorbonensia 29, Paris, 139–153.

Feissel, D. (2004), "Pétitions aux empereurs et formes du rescrit dans les sources documentaires du IVe au VIe siècle", in: D. Feissel/J. Gascou (eds.), *La pétition à Byzance. Actes de la Table ronde, tenue à Paris, le 24 août 2001, à l'occasion du XXe Congrès international des études byzantines, 19–25 août 2001*, Paris, 33–52.

Feissel, D. (2010), *Documents, droit, diplomatique de l'Empire romain tardif*, Bilans de recherche 7, Paris.

Festugière, A.J. (trans.) (1963), *Les moines d'Orient*, vol. 3, pt. 3: *Les moines de Palestine*, Paris.

Festugière, A.J. (trans.) (1974), *Vie de Syméon le fou et vie de Jean de Chypre*, Paris.

Festugière, A.J. (trans.) (1982), *Éphèse et Chalcédoine. Actes des conciles*, Textes, dossiers, documents 6, Paris.

Flusin, B. (1983), *Miracle et histoire dans l'œuvre de Cyrille de Scythopolis*, Paris.

Fournet, J.-L. (1999), *Hellénisme dans l'Égypte du VIe siècle. La bibliothèque et l'œuvre de Dioscore d'Aphrodité*, MIFAO 115, Cairo.

Fournet, J.-L. (2004), "Entre document et littérature: la pétition dans l'Antiquité tardive", in: D. Feissel/J. Gascou (eds.), *La pétition à Byzance. Actes de la Table ronde, tenue à Paris, à l'occasion du XXe Congrès international des études byzantines, 19–25 août 2001*, Paris, 61–7.

Fournet, J.-L. (2010), "Les pétitions des *Acta Conciliorum Œcumenicorum* comparées à celles de la documentation papyrologique (V[e]–VIe s.): libelle, *didaskalia* et *anaphora*", in: C. Gastgeber (ed.), *Quellen zur byzantinischen Rechtspraxis. Aspekte der Textüberlieferung, Paläographie und Diplomatik. Akten des internationalen Symposiums Wien, 5.–7. 11. 2007*, Veröffentlichungen zur Byzanzforschung 25, Vienna, 61–79.

Fournet, J.-L. (2016), *Ces lambeaux, gardiens de la mémoire des hommes. Papyrus et culture de l'Antiquité tardive*, Paris (English edition available at: https://books.openedition.org/cdf/5832, accessed March 21, 2022).

Fournet, J.-L. (2019), "Anatomie d'un genre en mutation: la pétition de l'Antiquité tardive", in: A. Nodar/S. Torallas Tovar (eds.), *Proceedings of the 28th Congress of Papyrology Barcelona, 1–6 August 2016*, Scripta Orientalia 3, Barcelona, 571–590.

Gascou, J. (1997), "Les privilèges du clergé d'après la 'Lettre' 104 de s. Basile", in: *RSR* 71, 189–204.

Gascou, J. (2008), *Fiscalité et société en Égypte byzantine*, Bilans de recherche 4, Paris.

Glucker, C.A.M. (1987), *The City of Gaza in the Roman and Byzantine Periods*, BAR International Series 325, Oxford.

Jeffreys, E./Jeffreys, M./Scott, R. (trans.) (1986), *The Chronicle of John Malalas*, Byzantina Australiensia 4, Melbourne.

Kotter, B. (ed.) (1975), *Die Schriften des Johannes von Damaskos*, vol. 3. Patristische Texte und Studien 17, Berlin.

Loyen, A. (ed. and trans.) (1960), *Sidoine Apollinaire*, 3 vols., Paris.

Malherbe, A.J. (comp. and trans.) (1988), *Ancient Epistolary Theorists*, Sources for Biblical Study 19, Atlanta.

Mango, C. (1984), "A Byzantine Hagiographer at Work: Leontios of Neapolis", in: I. Hutter/H. Hunger (eds.), *Byzanz und der Westen. Studien zur Kunst des europäischen Mittelalters*, Vienna, 25–41.

Odorico, P./Agapitos, P.A. (eds.) (2004), *Les Vies des saints à Byzance. Genre littéraire ou biographie historique? Actes du IIe Colloque international philologique "EPMHNEIA", Paris, 6–7–8 juin 2002*, Dossiers byzantins 4, Paris.

Porten, B. *et al.* (1996), *The Elephantine Papyri in English: Three Millennia of Cross-Cultural Continuity and Change*, Documenta et monumenta orientis antiqui 22, Leiden.

Price, R./Gaddis, M. (trans.) (2005), *The Acts of the Council of Chalcedon*, vol. 1, Liverpool.

Price, R.M. (trans.) (1991), *Cyril of Scythopolis: The Lives of the Monks of Palestine*. Kalamazoo, MI.

Schwartz, E. (ed.) (1939), *Kyrillos von Skythopolis*, Texte und Untersuchungen 49.2, Leipzig.

Thurn, I. (ed.) (2000), *Ioannis Malalae Chronographia*. Corpus Fontium Historiae Byzantinae, Series Berolinensis 35, Berlin.

Toneatto, V. (2004), "Le récit hagiographique: réinterprétation de l'histoire et construction idéologique. Le cas des vies d'Euthyme et de Sabas par Cyrille de Scythopolis", in: Odorico/Agapitos (2004), 137–159.

Usener, H. (ed.) (1890), *Der heilige Theodosios. Schriften des Theodoros und Kyrillos*, Leipzig.

Van den Ven, P. (1957), "Les écrits de S. Syméon Stylite le Jeune avec trois sermons inédits", in: *Muséon* 70, 1–57.

Whitby, M. (trans.) (2000), *The Ecclesiastical History of Evagrius Scholasticus*, Liverpool.

Yasmine Amory
When the Letter Speaks Up: Living and Lifeless Letters

Abstract: This chapter uncovers the oral elements of the ancient epistolary experience by considering the role of late antique letter-carriers, who would animate written letters by reading them aloud and conveying personal messages from sender to recipient. This emphasis on epistolary performances and the personification of the letter-writer by the messenger underscores that written text was not necessarily perceived as the most authoritative medium in ancient record-keeping. Simultaneously, this evidence demonstrates the utility of Ferraris's notion that social acts can be inscribed as immaterial documents in memory, to be passed on subsequently via the messenger's oral utterances. Late Antiquity's "living letters" reflect our still-evolving understanding of the Graeco-Roman epistolary habit.

One of the main postulates of Maurizio Ferraris's theory of documentality states that "the constitute law of social objects is object = recorded act".[1] And, in a certain way, ancient texts have always been considered as such: that is, a document is a written act. The definition could be debatable, however, since labels are more blurred than that; they evolve and adapt over time and along with social changes.[2] I will attempt to show this by taking into account the documentary letter and its development in late antiquity. By examining the role of such letters, which were written on perishable materials by individuals who lived in antiquity, and of literary letters, which were also written by real individuals but

---

I would like to thank Jacqueline Arthur-Montagne, Scott DiGiulio, and Inger Kuin for the organization and their thoughtfulness, as well as the anonymous reviewers for their comments. This paper relates to my PhD research at the École pratique des hautes études (2014–18). The study, titled "Communiquer par écrit dans l'Égypte de l'Antiquité tardive: les lettres grecques des archives de Dioscore d'Aphrodité (Égypte, VIe siècle apr. J.-C.)," was supervised by Prof. Jean-Luc Fournet (Collège de France) and was funded by heSam Université. Papyri are cited according to Oates 2001. An up-to-date version is available online at http://www.papyri.info/docs/checklist, accessed March 31, 2022. Translations are my own unless otherwise specified.

1 Ferraris 2015, 425.
2 See, for example, the contribution of Fournet in this volume on the "literarization" of the petition.

were later published in epistolary collections for a broader public, I intend to contemplate the classical conception of the letter in its dual forms and as a written act.[3] Elsewhere in this volume, DiGiulio debates the function and the understanding of the letter as a document once it is included in a literary piece, thus exposing the blurred line between "documentary" and "literary". Here, I want to discuss the risks and limits of taking into consideration only the written modalities of the ancient letter, despite its performative and multimodal nature.

Two definitions — one contemporary, the other ancient; one general, the other specific — will introduce my considerations. The first is the definition of the "social object," as given by Ferraris. Ferraris states that "a social object is the result of a social act (involving at least two people, or a machine delegate and a person) which is characterized by being recorded on a piece of paper, a computer file or even simply in the heads of the people implicated in the act."[4] The second is the famous definition of the letter given by Pseudo-Libanius. Mentioning it might appear too obvious but, since it offers an answer to some of the key questions we are interrogating, such as "What is a document?" and "What is the function of a document?", I think it is worth recalling. Pseudo-Libanius tells us: "A letter, then, is a kind of written conversation with someone from whom one is separated, and it fulfils a definite need. One will speak in it as though one were in the company of the absent person."[5]

These definitions share the assertion that a document such as a letter exists simultaneously as a material object and as a result of a relationship between two people. Before reconsidering this pronouncement, it might be helpful to raise some logistical problems that we encounter when we approach the study of letters. I will then examine a particular aspect of the epistolary process in documentary and literary letters: the role of the letter-bearer, who was sometimes entrusted to carry an oral message. Finally, I will investigate the function of this document when its primary aim — that is, the informative purpose — is transferred to the messenger: in other words, what a letter becomes when it loses its concreteness, the practical contents.

---

[3] I do not consider in my analysis the "fictitious letter," the correspondents of which are imaginary. I use here the division made in Luiselli 2008, 678.
[4] Ferraris 2013, 59.
[5] Ps.-Lib. *Epist. Charact.* 2 (Weichert): Ἐπιστολὴ μὲν οὖν ἐστιν ὁμιλία τις ἐγγράμματος ἀπόντος πρὸς ἀπόντα γινομένη καὶ χρειώδη σκοπὸν ἐκπληροῦσα. Ἐρεῖ δέ τις ἐν αὐτῇ ὥσπερ παρών τις πρὸς παρόντα. Translated by Malherbe 1988, 67.

1 The Letter, a Trace of Communication

To reiterate Ferraris's theory, a letter is a social act that reflects a specific common practice. Yet, it only represents a record of this practice: as explained by Demetrius, who reports the thoughts of Artemon, the assumed editor of Aristotle's letters, the epistolary form was ideally suited to serve as one of the two halves of a dialogue.[6] In addition, in most cases we possess only half of the correspondence between two individuals. For this reason, the papyrologist Adam Bülow-Jacobsen has observed: "Such letters, and private letters on papyrus as well, always give us half of the correspondence between individuals. Questions, but no answers, or answers to questions we do not know."[7]

These words allow us to appreciate the rarity of *P.Thomas* 8 and 9, two letters from the Roman period containing a message from Longinus to Numerius and the corresponding answer by Numerius, which was probably never sent. Normally we would never find such related letters together.[8] More often, but still rarely, manuscripts may contain information permitting us to reconstruct the contents of a lost text. In letters, it may happen when the sender summarizes or repeats the contents of a lost message while writing to someone else. This is the case for *P.Cair.Zen.* III 59308:

> Zenon to Axates, greetings! I wrote to you once about Kollythes, the priest of the goddess Thoeris of Philadelphia, asking you to regularly pay him what is due to him by the priest of Thoeris for the maintenance of Philadelphia sanctuary. You answered to me that he is entitled to an annual allowance of 12 drachmas.[9]

---

6 Demetr. *Eloc.* 223.3–6 (Chiron): Ἀρτέμων μὲν οὖν ὁ τὰς Ἀριστοτέλους ἀναγράψας ἐπιστολὰς φησιν ὅτι δεῖ ἐν τῷ αὐτῷ τρόπῳ διάλογόν τε γράφειν καὶ ἐπιστολάς· εἶναι γὰρ τὴν ἐπιστολὴν οἷον τὸ ἕτερον μέρος τοῦ διαλόγου.
7 Bülow-Jacobsen 2001, 119.
8 Beside *P.Thomas* 8 and 9, only one other case is known in the papyrological documentation, the Roman letter from Longinus to Niger and its answer (O.Dios inv. 636 and O.Xer. inv. 858), published in Elmaghrabi 2013. Several letters preserve on the same papyrus the whole correspondence, for instance *P.Leid.Inst.* 42 (Philadelphia, second century CE) and *SB* XXVI 16686–16687 (= *P.Benaki* 4–5; Arsinoites, fourth century CE), which occurs when the addressee decides to reply on the back or at the end of the same sheet; see Bagnall and Cribiore 2006, 36.
9 *P.Cair.Zen.* III 59308, 1–5 (Philadelphia?; 250 BCE): Ζήνων Ἀξάτηι χαίρειν. Ἐγράψαμέν σοι καὶ πρότερον | περὶ Κολλύθου τοῦ ἱερέως τῆς Θοήριος τῆς Φιλαδελφείας ἀποδίδοσθαι | αὐτῶι τὸ γινόμενον παρὰ τοῦ ἱερέως τῆς Θοήριος εἰς τὸ ἱερὸν τὸ ἐμ (l. ἐν) Φι|λαδελφείαι, σὺ δέ μοι ἀντέγραψας ὅτι γείνοιτο αὐτῶι εἰς τὸν ἐνι|αυτὸν (δραχμαὶ) ιβ.

Nevertheless, these circumstances are uncommon. We usually have to shed light on veiled references and obscure expressions relating to subjects already mentioned in letters previously received. These expressions rank among what White labeled as "informational formulas."[10] They can be introduced by περί plus the genitive, when they refer to a specific matter, or be phrased in a sentence like "as you wrote to me, or as you ordered me."

But it is not only the complementary part of a correspondence that we usually find missing. Various non-textual elements are also lost: in fact, as suggested by Andrew Gillett, "we miss the complement to the written letter, the non-textual components, be they verbal or semiotic: 'half the letter, the living half, is automatically missing ... [a letter] was written, oral, material, visual.'"[11] In particular, one commonly neglected factor should be considered when investigating ancient epistolography: the unavoidable loss of the oral message that frequently accompanied the written text. Even though P.M. Head has already noted some attestations of this procedure in his paper on the letter-carrier among the Oxyrhynchus Papyri, I would like to explore some more papyrological examples which were not taken into account, and to correlate the practice with late antique literary letters.[12]

While the delivery of administrative correspondence was provided by an official postal service in Roman and late antique times, common citizens needed to find other ways to deliver their letters, by entrusting them to an acquaintance or a trader who happened to be heading in the right direction.[13] When the messenger was someone trusted, it was not uncommon to ask them to deliver some goods or a verbal message. The bearer of the letter, who is named in papyri by terms such as ὁ τὴν ἐπιστολὴν φέρων, or simply by the substantive ἐπιστολαφόρος (during the Roman imperial period) or γραμματηφόρος (in the late antique period), is then sometimes characterized by the adjectives πιστός ("trusty"), πιστικός ("faithful"), and ἀσφαλής ("unfailing").[14]

---

10 White 1986, 207.
11 Gillett 2012, 824, citing Mullett 1990, 183. The assertion refers to late antique literary letters, but it is also applicable to documentary letters.
12 Head's analysis is in fact focused on personal letters belonging to the *P.Oxy.* volumes and chronologically limited to the period between 200 BCE and 200 CE. These constitute a basis of comparison with Pauline practice (see Head 2009).
13 On the postal service in Egypt and its mode of operation, see Sarri 2018, 12–13, esp. 12 nn. 50 and 51 for further bibliography.
14 See Morelli 2007, 351–354, for the designation of *grammatephoros*, and Sarri 2018, 18–19 for the other standard terms used for letter-carriers. See Daris 2015 on the trustworthiness of the letter-bearers and for examples in papyri, along with Richards 2004, 183–184, who also pro-

2 The Messenger, "a Living Letter"

Since a letter could be intercepted, writers often avoided writing down significant, particularly confidential details, preferring to relay them through the bearer. Some documents give evidence of this habit: at the end of the letter *P.Col.* III 6, Simale writes: "Learn the rest from who is bringing you the letter, as he is not a stranger to us."[15] In the same way, at the end of *P.Iand.Zen.* 24 we read: "the one who is bringing you the letter will tell the rest."[16] The practice was more widespread than we think, as a short scene depicting the delivery of a letter and the oral message one might have entrusted to the messenger even appears in the *Colloquium Harleianum*, a bilingual educational text from the Imperial period containing dialogues that model everyday interactions.[17]

Some letters attest to the fact that the messenger could occasionally return to the sender with an oral message from the recipient. The sender of *P.Berl.Sarisch.* 16 complained about having neither received a written message nor being informed of his friend's health by either a servant or a boy;[18] the sender of *SB* I 4323 had to send a messenger in order to be informed of his lord's health.[19] In these two documents, the verb σημαίνω, "indicate, declare, tell, speak" (*LSJ*, s.v. σημαίνω) is used to express the idea of delivering an oral message. Other letters seem to indicate that information could be delivered either written or verbally. Aurelius Demareus writes to his sister not to send his allow-

---

vides attestations in Cicero. For the various roles of the bearer of business in Roman Egypt, see more generally Schubert 2021.
15 *P.Col.* III 6, 14–15 (?; October 3, 257 BCE): τὰ δὲ λοιπὰ | πυνθάνου τοῦ φέροντός σοι τὰ γράμματα. Οὐ γὰρ ἀλλότριος ἡμῖν ἐστιν.
16 *P.Iand.Zen.* 24, 10 (Philadelphia; 248 BCE): τὰ δὲ ἄλλα ὁ φέρων σοι τὴν ἐπιστολὴν ἐρ\ε/ῖ.
17 On this text, see Dickey 2015, 1–80. See especially the scene at paragraph 28e-h (Goetz): Πάντα καλῶς; Ἔδωκέν μοι ἐπιστολήν. Καὶ ὅπου ἐστίν; (Οὐκ ἔστιν ὧδε.) Ὧδέ ἐστιν. Δὸς αὐτήν, ἵνα καὶ ἴδω τί μοι ἔγραψεν. οὐδέν σοι εἶπεν; Οὐδέν, *Omnia bene? Dedit mihi epistulam. Et ubi est? (Non est hic.) Hic est. Da illam, ut et videam <quid> mihi scripserit. nihil tibi dixit? Nihil*, "'[Is] everything all right?' 'He gave me a letter.' 'And where is it?' ('It's not here.') 'Here it is.' 'Give it [to me], so that I may also see what he wrote to me. Didn't he say anything to you?' 'Nothing.'" Translated by Dickey 2015, 37.
18 *P.Berl.Sarish.* 16, 1–3 (Hermopolis; end sixth century–early seventh century CE): οὐκ οἶδα δὲ πόθεν ἡμέλησας γράψαι καὶ σημᾶναί μοι τὴ[ν ταχίστην -ca.?-] | ἢ δι' ἀνθρώπου ἢ \διὰ/ παιδός τινος τοῦ σχολαστικοῦ ἀνερχομέν[ου πρὸς ἡμᾶς -ca.?-] | τὴν ὑγιείαν σου.
19 *SB* I 4323, 1–4 (?; fourth century CE): ᵱ ἔγνων παρὰ τῆς δούλης ὑμῶν, τῆς γυναικός μου, ὡς ὁ θεοφιλέστατος κοινὸς | δεσπότης, ὁ πατὴρ ἡμῶν, ὀλίγον ἀηδίζεται καὶ ἐφρόντισα οὐ μετρίως ὥστ' ἐμὲ | ἀναγκασθῆναι πέμψαι τὸν γραμματηφόρον πρὸς τὴν ὑμετέραν ἀδελφικὴν εὐλάβειαν, | ἵνα δι' αὐτοῦ σημᾶναί μοι περὶ τῆς ὑγιείας αὐτοῦ, ἧς οὐδέν μοι τιμιώτερον.

ance until he lets her know or he writes to her again about it.[20] The sender of *P.Mich.* VIII 492 informs Thaisarion to give Coprous all the details by mouth, in order to instruct her.[21] Ptolemaios complains that his mother reproaches him for his behavior through letters and through men (the latter probably slaves used to deliver messages). He then explains why he did not send what was asked, even if he did hear the request, probably from the messengers. Finally, he takes the opportunity to blame his mother for not having asked for news while he was ill, either in letters or verbally.[22]

To summarize, in documentary texts the messenger usually carried a written missive. He might also be responsible for providing information not included in the letter, entrusted to him by the sender, provided that he was considered reliable. Occasionally, if an individual did not receive any news, he could send somebody to be informed of another person's health. The messenger might also in some cases represent the sender himself, when the latter was not able to reach the addressee.[23]

The choice of the messenger was subject to different criteria in literary letters. During his study on the role of ideology and ceremony in Byzantine epistolography, Karlsson noticed that the theme of the messenger's double role, as bearer of both written and oral communications, was also well attested in the literary correspondence of that time, where this person is called ἔμψυχος ἐπιστολή, "living, animated letter."[24] This is how Synesius, a bishop and writer who lived between the fourth and fifth centuries CE, designated his friend Gerontius in a letter to his brother:

> Receive, along with the living letter, the lifeless letter, along with the venerable Gerontius, receive this letter, that comes more from custom than to the need to speak with you. Because the memory of you accompanies our lives, and this young man can explain it to you in person much more clearly than a myriad of letters.[25]

---

20 *P.Oxy.* VII 1070, 45–46 (Alexandria?; third century CE): μηδέν μοι ἐν τῷ παρόντι ⟦δι⟧ ἐπιμηνιδίων διαπεπέμψησθαι (l. διαπέμψησθε) ἔστ' ἂν ὑμεῖν (l. ὑμῖν) πε|ρὶ τούτου δηλώσω ἢ καὶ γράψω.
21 *P.Mich.* VIII 492, 19–20 (Alexandria; second century CE): εἴρηκα καὶ Κοπροῦτι ταῦτα πάντα ἀπὸ λόγου εἶνα (l. ἵνα) σοι ⟦πα⟧ | εἴπῃ.
22 *SB* XVIII 13867, 7–8 (?; mid second century CE): μέμφεσθαι (l. μέμφεσθε) διὰ γραμμάτων κ[αὶ] διὰ | ἀνθρώπων; 13–14: εἰ ὀργή τις ἔνη (l. ἔνι) ἐν τῷ με [μηδὲν] | παραπ[έμ]ψασθαι ἀκούσαντ[α; 17–19: μέμφομαι δὲ ὑμᾶς ὅτ[ι] | οὔτε δ[ιὰ λ]όγων οὔτε διὰ γραμμ[ά]|των ἐ[πε]σκέψαστέ (l. ἐπεσκέψασθέ) με. See Sarischouli 1997 for the use of ἄνθρωπος in papyri to designate slaves.
23 See Arzt-Grabner 2009, 229–231 for examples of this circumstance.
24 Karlsson 1962, 17–21.
25 Synes. *Ep.* 85 (Garzya 1983, 232): Δέδεξο μετὰ τῆς ἐμψύχου καὶ τὴν ἄψυχον ἐπιστολήν, μετὰ τοῦ θαυμαστοῦ Γεροντίου ταῦτα τὰ γράμματα, νόμῳ τὸ πλέον ἢ τῇ χρείᾳ τοῦ προσειπεῖν σε

This testimony highlights the more advantageous aspect of the messenger, namely that he can immediately give more information if needed, unlike a fixed text. The same metaphor can be found elsewhere in authors mostly from the fourth and the fifth centuries CE, as in letter 205 from Basil to Bishop Elpidius. Written in 375 CE, it reports: "Yet having judged it to be proper for ourselves to greet you through such men as can by their own words easily supply what is lacking in the letter, and, as it were, can act as a living epistle both to him who writes and to him who receives."[26] As we see, the idea that a messenger could replace a letter is still present in this last excerpt. It is taken to the extreme in the second letter of Saint Paul to the Corinthians. At the beginning of the third chapter, Paul asserts that he does not need to send the Corinthians a letter of commendation, because they themselves constitute a letter, which has been written in their hearts, "known and read of all men."[27] Bishop Theodoret of Cyrus, who composed a commentary on the epistles of the apostle in the first half of the fifth century CE, glossed this verse with the following words: "We do not need a letter, since the facts themselves bear witness to us, and we have a living letter, which recommend us to you, your faith, which is praised by all the land and sea."[28]

In the biblical tradition, the role of the messenger is no longer defined by the written message he bears, but by the message that the believer brings with him and inside him. The believer does not need to deliver a written text, because he himself represents the word of God; he is "the epistle of Christ ministered by us, written not with ink, but with the Spirit of the living God; not in

---

γενόμενα. Ὅτι γὰρ ἡμεῖς συζῶμεν τῇ περὶ σοῦ μνήμῃ, μυρίων ἐπιστολῶν μακρῷ μεγαλοφωνότερον ὁ νεανίσκος ἂν διηγήσαιτο.

26 Bas. *Ep.* 205.5–9 (Courtonne 1973, 181): ὅμως καὶ ἡμῖν αὐτοῖς πρέπον εἶναι κρίνοντες διὰ τοιούτων προσφθέγγεσθαί σε, τῶν δυναμένων ὅσα διαφεύγει τὸ γράμμα παρ' ἑαυτῶν ῥᾳδίως ἀναπληρῶσαι καὶ οἱονεὶ ἀντ' ἐπιστολῆς ἐμψύχου γενέσθαι τῷ τε γράφοντι καὶ τῷ δεχομένῳ (trans. Deferrari 1953, 176–177). For other evidence of the messenger as intermediary of an oral message in the letters of Basil, see Courtonne 1973, 24–30.

27 2 Cor. 3:1–2: ἦ μὴ χρῄζομεν ὥς τινες συστατικῶν ἐπιστολῶν πρὸς ὑμᾶς ἢ ἐξ ὑμῶν; | ἡ ἐπιστολὴ ἡμῶν ὑμεῖς ἐστε, ἐγγεγραμμένη ἐν ταῖς καρδίαις ἡμῶν, γινωσκομένη καὶ ἀναγινωσκομένη ὑπὸ πάντων ἀνθρώπων.

28 Thdt. *II Ep. Paul. Cor.* 3.2, PG 82.392C: Ἡμεῖς οὐ δεόμεθα γραμμάτων· αὐτὰ γὰρ ἡμῖν τὰ πράγματα μαρτυρεῖ· καὶ ἐπιστολὴν ἔμψυχον ἔχομεν τὰ καθ' ἡμᾶς συνιστῶσαν ὑμῖν, τὴν πίστιν τὴν ὑμετέραν, τὴν πανταχοῦ γῆς καὶ θαλάττης ἀδομένην. A new edition of Theodoret of Cyrus's exegesis of the *Pauline Epistles* has recently been published (Perretti 2017), but I was not able to consult it.

tablets of stone, but in fleshy tablets of the heart."²⁹ The believer is a living letter of Christ and the written trace becomes superfluous. Finally, the latest testimony to this literary image appears to be in one letter of Maximus Planudes, a Byzantine scholar of the thirteenth century, to Melchizedek.³⁰

The notion of ἔμψυχος ἐπιστολή also occurs in Latin literature, though less frequently, under the expression *epistula vivens*. Letter 186 of Augustine and Alypius to Paulinus of Nola, written in 417 CE, begins with these sentences:

> At long last God has provided us with a most reliable bearer for our letter, Brother Januarius, who is rightly very dear to us all. Even if we did not write, Your Sincerity could know everything about us by means of him as if he were a living and intelligent letter.³¹

Once again, we find the idea that a messenger alone can replace a letter, since he personifies the letter. The representation of the messenger as a letter with a soul appears in Letter 31 too (395–396): "But we read this letter of yours, namely, the soul of the brothers, in conversation with them."³² The letter then recalls the abovementioned words of Paul, as it says that the philosopher has transcribed the message in his heart.³³

Leaving aside the specifically Christian conception of the messenger as unique bearer of the word of God, the binary notion of the letter-bearer was widespread for centuries. Late antique epistolographers mainly drew attention to the eloquence of the messenger, who could converse with the recipient. Thanks to this ability, the choice of messenger was sometimes very important: elite writers did not just require someone they trusted to bear the message, like

---

29 2 Cor. 3:3: ἐπιστολὴ Χριστοῦ διακονηθεῖσα ὑφ᾽ ἡμῶν, ἐγγεγραμμένη οὐ μέλανι ἀλλὰ πνεύματι θεοῦ ζῶντος, οὐκ ἐν πλαξὶν λιθίναις ἀλλ᾽ ἐν πλαξὶν καρδίαις σαρκίναις.
30 Maximus Planudes *Ep.* 85 (Leone 1991: 128–129): Καὶ δὴ τὸν ἐμὸν ὡς ὑμᾶς ἀπέστειλα παῖδα, ἔμψυχον ἐπιστολὴν μετὰ πολλὰς τὰς προλαβούσας ἀψύχους, ἵν᾽ ἅμα μὲν ὑμῖν τὰ ἡμέτερα, ἅμα δὲ κἀμοὶ τὰ καθ᾽ ὑμᾶς αὖθις ἐπανιὼν διηγήσαιτο, ὅσα δηλαδὴ μῆκος ἐπιστολῆς οὐκ ἂν χωρεῖν οἷόν τε γένοιτο ("I also send to you my boy, a living letter after the many lifeless letters you have received, in order that he may tell you my news, and, once he has come back, he may tell me yours, such as the length of a letter is obviously unable to contain"). A selection of Maximus Planudes' letters, with an Italian translation, is offered in Pascale 2007; for Letter 85, see 34–41.
31 August. *Ep.* 186.1.1, PL 33.815–816: *Tandem aliquando providit Deus nobis litterarum fidelissimum perlatorem, omnium nostrum merito charissimum fratrem Januarium; per quem, etiamsi non scriberemus, omnia quae circa nos sunt possit Sinceritas tua tanquam per viventem atque intelligentem epistolam noscere* (trans. Teske 2004, 209).
32 August. *Ep.* 31.2, PL 33.122: *Hanc autem epistolam vestram, fraternam scilicet animam, sic in eorum colloquio legebamus.* (trans. Teske 2001, 104).
33 August. *Ep.* 31.2, PL 33.122: *Itaque illam ad eiusdem beatitatis imitationem, studiosissime de vobis omnia percunctando in nostra corda transcripsimus.*

a relative, as was the case for the average citizen, but they looked for someone with keen intelligence. Basil waited for a long time to send his letter before finding someone appropriate to converse with Bishop Theophilus.[34] Augustine pointed out the virtues of his bearer by distinguishing him as a living letter as much as an intelligent person.[35] And it seems that Paul was seeking in his messengers those who could also explain his teachings.[36] William Doty has even suggested that Paul's letters were simple sketches which would have served as a canvas for the messengers, who were supposed to develop the doctrine verbally.[37] Thus, the messenger had to live up to the written message, which was a representation of the sender and of the relationship between the correspondents. Moreover, as a living letter he shared the characteristics of the lifeless letter: just as one of the most frequent epistolary *topoi* was that of discussing the events narrated in the letter as if the recipient was physically there,[38] the account of the messenger Olympius to Paulinus of Nola about recent events is said to have made Paulinus believe he had seen them with his own eyes.[39]

3 The Evolution of Private Epistles: From the Informative to the Gift Letter

While at first a letter might seem to be one of the most straightforward documents to understand, it conceals a series of difficulties because it shows only half of an exchange between two individuals. Its contents are always allusive, as the correspondents talk about something they have already discussed and on which they do not need to go into detail. Lastly, a letter can be accompanied by an ephemeral verbal message. A letter, which might be described as a "known

---

34 See Bas. *Ep.* 245.1–8. On the need for a smart *tabellarius* in the correspondence between Basile and Paulinus of Nola, see Gorce 1925, 214–215.
35 See above note 32. The importance in choosing a suitable messenger for Augustine's correspondence is pointed out in Paoli-Lafaye 2002, 242–243. For other examples illustrating the well-considered choice of the letter-carrier in Greek and Latin letters and how this could impact the addressee at the reception of the message, see Allen and Neil 2020, 104–107 (for Late Antiquity) and Bernard 2020, 309–311 (for the Byzantine period).
36 See Richards 2004, 202–204; and the discussion in Head 2009, 279–282. On the identity and role of Paul's letter-carriers, see also Harmon 2014.
37 Doty 1973, 45–46.
38 Thraede 1970, 79, 150–151.
39 On this episode, see Gorce 1925, 215.

known," is connected with several records (the other part of the correspondence, other documents mentioned by the sender and the recipient, oral messages, and so on), which James Keenan would describe as "known unknowns."[40] They constitute textual fragments that we know we have lost.

This raises further questions. How should we consider these oral messages, already qualified as documents by the authors? Do we have to consider them as belonging with other lost written documents, or are they only elevated to the status of "documentary nobility" when they are mentioned in a text? And, if we accept verbal communication as documents, should non-communication be included by this same reasoning, as suggested by the author of *P.Oxy.* XXXIV 2728? This author writes in his letter: "I am surprised that even now when Horigenes comes to me you let me know nothing about anything. I know that I weigh heavily upon you. Let part be set aside [?]. For among philosophers silence is an answer."[41]

Another question that arises is what a letter becomes if the informative purpose, which was constitutive of this kind of document, has been transferred to the messenger. Whenever the letter is devoid of its informative aim, which is occasionally delegated to the bearer, it becomes something valuable, the tangible demonstration of the correspondents' relationship, which attempts to deviate from the classical formal obligation in favor of an intimate conversation. *P.Mert.* I 12, a Roman letter from a doctor to a colleague, seems to suggest this conception: "I may dispense with writing to you with a great show of thanks; for it is to those who are not friends that we must give thanks in words."[42] In the long run, this new conception of the letter leads to the emptiness of the literary letter, which scholars have discussed as the "deconcretization" of the letter: it no longer has concrete contents and therefore becomes a rhetorical object.[43]

---

40 J. Keenan, "'Known Unknowns': Thoughts on (Lost) Papyrus Evidence," unpublished lecture, Princeton University, July 16, 2014.
41 *P.Oxy.* XXXIV 2728, 5–9 (ca. 312–318 CE according to BL VIII, 261): θαυμάζω | πῶς καὶ νῦν, τοῦ Ὡριγένους ἐρχομένου | πρὸς ἐμέ, οὐδέν μοι ἐδή[λ]ωσας [[ου]] περὶ οὐδενός· | ἐπίσταμαι ὅτι πολλὰ β\αρ/οῦμαί σε· ἀποταγῇ μέρος· | σιγὴ γὰρ παρὰ φιλοσόφο[ις] ἀπόκρισις. Trans. by the editor.
42 *P.Mert.* I 12, 6–9 (Oxyrhynchus or Hermopolis; April 26, 59 CE according to BL VIII, 207): Γράφειν δὲ | σοι μεγάλας εὐχαριστίας παρετέρ(ν)· | δεῖ γὰρ τοῖς μὴ φίλοις οὖσι διὰ λόγων | εὐχαριστεῖν (trans. Stowers 1986, 61). For an analysis of the letter, see Boehm 2014, 113–118.
43 See Karlsson 1962, 15–33; Garzya 1983, 141–143; Fournet 2009, 50–52. More generally, see Fournet 2009 for a deep and diachronic analysis of the changes undergone by the letter during the third and the fourth century CE.

Of course, the role of the messenger, verbal bearer of the authentic message, is not the only cause of this phenomenon. Garzya highlighted the importance of rhetoric in late antiquity, along with the "ceremonious politeness" typical of the elites, who wrote according to the conventions of φιλοφρόνησις.[44] In addition, it should be recalled here that I am taking into consideration private letters from cultivated people, the so-called "private literary letters,"[45] messages which had both a functional purpose and an artistic aspect.[46] Administrative letters, as well as private letters from people of lower social backgrounds, responded to other criteria and continue to show more of a stress on informational function.

The sociable, or perhaps we could say "amicable," letter is thus designed as a genuine gift, a personal act that requires one to dedicate time and attention to the recipient.[47] This idea is already apparent in the treatise *De elocutione*, where Demetrius states that a letter differs from a speech as "it is written and is sent in some manner as a present."[48] The circulation of this work among late antique epistolographers probably stimulated the development and the strengthening of this notion.[49] The same idea is, in fact, expressed in BKT IX 94, a manual of epistolography on papyrus from the sixth century CE. In the fragmentary section dedicated to sending letters to friends, titled πρὸς φίλον, the correspondence between friends is represented as an exchange of presents.[50] The need to maintain a confidential epistolary connection as a sign of friendship, at a time where rhetoric influenced every genre and was an important part of communication, contributed to the evolution of the late antique letter as a garnished, sterile document. Gregory of Nyssa tried to resist this conception, as shown in a letter to Eusebius, where he opposed the dry rhetoric that one expected to find in the gift letter to the richness of Christianity.[51]

---

44 Garzya 1983, 122–142.
45 The appellation is made by Garzya 1983, 117–118.
46 On this concept, see Pascale 2007, 9.
47 F. Bernard has recently maintained that the gift letter was not only an ornamental exercise, as suggested by Karlsson 1962, 112–128 and Littlewood 1976, 221, but a symbol of "mutual intellectual admiration" (see in general Bernard 2011, esp. 11).
48 Demetr. *Eloc.* 224.3: ἡ δὲ γράφεται καὶ δῶρον πέμπεται τρόπον τινά.
49 Mullett 1981, 82–83.
50 See Luiselli 1995, 644–645 for the transcription and the translation of the passage.
51 Gr. Nyss. *Ep.* 4.3 (Pasquali 1959: 28): ξένιον δὲ ἡμέτερον τὸ διὰ τοῦ γράμματός σοι προσαγόμενον αὐτὸ τὸ γράμμα ἐστίν, ἐν ᾧ λόγος μέν τις περιηνθισμένος ταῖς καλλιφώνοις τε καὶ εὐσυνθέτοις τῶν λέξεων ἔστιν οὐδείς, ὡς διὰ τοῦτο δῶρον τὴν ἐπιστολὴν τοῖς φιλολόγοις νομίζεσθαι, ἀλλ' ὁ μυστικὸς χρυσὸς ὁ τῇ πίστει τῶν Χριστιανῶν οἷόν τινι ἀποδέσμῳ ἐνειλημμένος γένοιτο ἄν σοι δῶρον, ἐξαπλωθεὶς ὡς οἷόν τε διὰ τῶν γραμμάτων καὶ τὴν κεκρυμμένην λαμπηδόνα

While in literary letters this trend is widespread, documentary letters provide less evidence. The few examples that we have are still very important, because they prove that this procedure was not exclusive to literary circles. I will make use of two texts from the archive of Dioscorus of Aphrodite, the most extensive archive from the late antique period, to demonstrate this point. The first is *P.Cair.Masp.* III 67295, II, 24–35, a letter from a *notarios* to a colleague.[52] The sender quotes Homer and invokes several epistolary *topoi*, showing remorse at his inability to express himself in a dignified way. The whole text concerns acknowledgments for a refined letter received, and prayers to receive more letters. This letter is even more significant because it is part of a selection of four documents assembled and copied by Dioscorus himself for their style and literary interest.[53] The little collection is composed of a petition by the philosopher Horapollo and three letters. Documents conceived for private employment thus become models to imitate and a source of inspiration. This letter, originally private, is preserved like a literary piece.

The second text is almost unique. *P.Aphrod.Lit.* IV 38 (end of 565/early 566–573 CE?) is a letter in iambic trimeters addressed to a certain Theodoros or Dorotheos.[54] Jean-Luc Fournet, who found a parallel in the versified letter addressed to Seleukos and falsely attributed to Gregory of Nazianzus, stressed the exceptional status of this type of letter, raised to the literary genre.[55] The letter,

---

προδείξας ("and the offering we bring to you through this letter is the letter itself. Here is no discourse wreathed with mellifluous and well-constructed phrases, that this letter might be thought a gift in literary circles. Instead, may the mystical gold, which is wrapped up in the faith of Christians as in a kind of envelope, be my present to you — that it is, when it has been unwrapped in these lines as far as it may, and has shown its hidden lustre"; trans. Silvas 2007, 133–134).

52 A new edition and a translation of the text is given in Fournet 2012, 143–144.
53 The anthology is accurately analyzed by Fournet 2009, 61–63.
54 A new English translation of the text and an updated commentary has been published by Alexander Riehle in Kubina and Riehle 2021, 122–123 and 285–287 (number 8 of the Anthology).
55 Fournet 1999, 273–274. The letter is in fact now attributed to Amphilochius of Iconium: see Crimi and Costa 1999, 9, 31. Dioscorus' verse letter is considered exceptional since it was originally conceived as a document, in opposition to the flourishing fictional epistolography in the Hellenistic and Imperial periods (see Rosenmeyer 2001, 169–338). On the difficulty of defining Byzantine epistolary poetry, see Kubina and Riehle 2021, 17–29. Two more examples at the edge between literary and documentary piece can be found in the *Greek Anthology*, *Anth. Graec.* 5.9 (a love letter by Rufinus to Elpis) and 11.44 (an invitation from Philodemus to Lucius Calpurnius Piso Caesoninus). Finally, it is worth mentioning the remarkable verse letter of Gerardos, a prolific copyist from the fifteenth century CE. His autograph letter-poem is the only case of a private letter preserved as an original outside of epistolary correspondence on papyrus.

whose contents are entirely encomiastic, makes use of typical themes, such as the inability of the sender's quill to worthily praise the addressee. It begins with a prayer to the recipient to accept the present letter from his friend (1–5):

> Δέχου, φέριστε, τοῦ φίλου τὰ γράμματα
> ἐμοῦ φιλοῦντος ὡς ἄνυδρος τὴν θέα[ν]
> προϊκάνων ἕνερα θεωρῆσ[α]ι ῥάθους
> τῆς σῆς, ἐράσμιε, γλυκ[υ]τάτης τριβῆς.
> Θεοῦ τὸ δῶρον οὐκ ἀνεκπίπ[τ]ει ποτέ.

Receive, the best of men, a letter from your friend, from me, who love your sight as a thirsty man who would come out of the earth to contemplate your person, who is for me, amiable friend, a sweet subject of attention. Never decline the gift of God.

In the last line of the excerpt, the letter is introduced as a present offered to the recipient.[56] The letter here draws upon literary taste, probably according to a contemporary trend relating to the maturation of the τέχνη ἐπιστολική,[57] but as part of a sophisticated game between scholars: Dioscorus apologizes for not knowing how to honor his friend, revealing instead the exact opposite by the surprising stylistic choice of his letter, written in verse. Everything is performed through rhetoric and literary divertissement, which gives the letter a new purpose. This remarkable literary document proves the fact that the late antique letter — at least the elite one — has become "personal poetry."[58] Given these examples, the borders of the conventional tripartite division of letters (documentary, literary, and fictitious) are immediately less well defined.

4 Conclusions

If we return to the two definitions that I quoted at the beginning of this paper, it is now rather difficult to agree with them. Through a quick review of documentary and literary letters I have stressed the double role of the messenger, bearer of both a verbal and a written communication. While in documentary texts it

---

The text, translation, and commentary are given by Alexander Riehle in Kubina and Riehle 2021, 254–257 and 359–363; see p. 392 for an image of the letter.

56 The same definition of the letter as a "gift of God" is also present in Letter 84 from Hierotheos the Thesmothete, for which I refer to Darrouzès 1972, 216.

57 See Fournet 1999, 273.

58 On the poetical perception of the letter, see Garzya 1983, 147 and Mullett 1981, 82: "Epistolography, which distills emotions in frozen time, has taken the place of lyric poetry."

was common for citizens to look for a trusted person to deliver the message, in literary texts people also looked for someone competent who could adequately represent the sender. So, the letter is not a written speech between two people, as Pseudo-Libanius asserted, but rather, as Jenkins wrote: "The epistolary discourse often consists of three, not two individuals."[59] There is therefore a thread of continuity with the official communication carried out by heralds in classical times, when the oral word was more trustworthy than private messages,[60] and with the significance of the oral declaration on the written record.[61]

I have also asked whether the letter must necessarily be a written text, since the letter-bearer was entrusted with the most important message and he was called a "living letter" among ancient epistolographers. It is even sometimes claimed by Christian authors that a letter is not necessary, because Christians themselves represent the Lord's message. Finally, if the informational purpose of the text is transferred to the messenger, what is left of Pseudo-Libanius' definition? The late antique letter, when it originates from a high social context, becomes a social emblem more than a social object, and, deprived of concrete contents, is adorned with literary flourishes that can lead to the production of literary pieces, as it is the case of the verse letter *P.Aphrod.Lit.* IV 38. What we qualified as documentary becomes then, in specific circumstances, literary, as long as we are willing to label a human being a lifeless object. My statements are clearly provocative. However, I hope I have shown that the evaluation of secondary evidence, which does not always leave a written trace, can help understanding the evolution of "social objects," as interpreted by Ferraris. In other words, as Pieter J.J. Botha stated: "By realizing how impoverished our conventional perception of tradition has become we also become conscious of the plight of our infatuation with things written and learn to value the living and abiding voice of our fellow humans."[62]

---

[59] See Jenkins 2006, 34.
[60] See Sarri 2018, 7–10.
[61] See Bodel in this volume for the documentary development of the oral stage in classical antiquity.
[62] See Botha 2012, 38.

References

Allen, P./Bronwen, N. (2020), *Greek and Latin Letters in Late Antiquity. The Christianisation of a Literary Form*, Cambridge.
Arzt-Grabner, P. (2009), "'I was intending to visit you, but …': Clauses Explaining Delayed Visits and Their Importance in Papyrus Letters and in Paul", in: C.A. Evans/H.D. Zacharias (eds.), *Jewish and Christian Scripture as Artifact and Canon*, London, 220–231.
Bagnall, R.S./Cribiore, R. (2006), *Women's Letters from Ancient Egypt. 300 BC–AD 800*, Ann Arbor.
Bernard, F. (2011), "'Greet me with words': Gifts and Intellectual Friendships in Eleventh-Century Byzantium", in: M. Grünbart (ed.), *Geschenke erhalten die Freundschaft. Gabentausch und Netzwerkpflege im europäischen Mittelalter. Akten des internationalen Kolloquiums Münster, 19–20. November 2009*, Berlin, 1–12.
Bernard, F. (2020), "Epistolary Communication: Rituals and Codes", in: A. Riehle (ed.), *A Companion to Byzantine Epistolography*, Leiden/Boston, 307–332.
Boehm, I. (2014), "Lettres de médecins", in: J. Schneider (ed.), *La lettre gréco-latine. Un genre littéraire?*, Lyon, 101–120.
Botha, P.J.J. (2012), *Orality and Literacy in Early Christianity*, Eugene, OR.
Bülow-Jacobsen, A. (2001), "Drinking and Cheating in the Desert", in: T. Gagos/R.S. Bagnall (eds.), *Essays and Texts in Honor of J. David Thomas*, Oakville, CT, 119–123.
Courtonne, Y. (1973), *Un témoin du IVᵉ siècle oriental. Saint Basile et son temps d'après sa correspondance*, Paris.
Crimi, C./Costa, I. (1999), *Gregorio Nazianzeno. Poesie*, vol. 2, Rome.
Daris, S. (2015), "Corrispondenza privata e curiosità lessicali", in: *ZPE* 193, 219–222.
Darrouzès, J. (1972), *Littérature et histoire des textes byzantins*, London.
Deferrari, R.J. (ed. and trans.) (1930), *Saint Basil: The Letters*, London.
Dickey, E. (ed. and trans.) (2015), *The Colloquia of the Hermeneumata Pseudodositheana*, vol. 2, Cambridge.
Doty, W.G. (1973), *Letters in Primitive Christianity*, Philadelphia.
Elmaghrabi, M.G. (2013), "Two Letters Exchanged between the Roman Forts of Dios and Xeron", in: *BIFAO* 112, 139–146.
Ferraris, M. (2013), "On New Realism", in: *Kairos* 8, 45–65.
Ferraris, M. (2015), "Collective Intentionality or Documentality?", in: *Philosophy and Social Criticism* 41, 423–433.
Fournet, J.-L. (1999), *Hellénisme dans l'Égypte du VIᵉ siècle. La bibliothèque et l'œuvre de Dioscore d'Aphrodité*, Cairo.
Fournet, J.-L. (2009), "Esquisse d'une anatomie de la lettre antique", in: S. Delmaire/ J. Desmulliez/P.-L. Gatier (eds.), *Correspondances. Documents pour l'histoire de l'Antiquité tardive*, Lyon, 23–66.
Fournet, J.-L. (2012), "Homère et les papyrus non littéraires: le poète dans le contexte de ses lecteurs", in: G. Bastianini/A. Casanova (eds.), *I papiri omerici. Atti del convegno internazionale di studi. Firenze, 9–10 giugno 2011*, Florence, 125–158.
Garzya, A. (1983), *Il mandarino e il quotidiano. Saggi sulla letteratura tardoantica e bizantina*, Naples.
Gillett, A. (2012), "Communication in Late Antiquity: Use and Reuse", in: S.F. Johnson (ed.), *The Oxford Handbook of Late Antiquity*, Oxford, 815–846.

Gorce, D. (1925), *Les voyages, l'hospitalité et le port des lettres dans le monde chrétien des IVe et Ve siècles*, Paris.

Harmon, M.S. (2014), "Letter Carriers and Paul's Use of Scripture", in: *Journal for the Study of Paul and his Letters* 4.2, 129–148.

Head, P.M. (2009), "Named Letter-Carriers among the Oxyrhynchus Papyri", in: *Journal for the Study of the New Testament* 31, 279–299.

Jenkins, T. (2006), *Intercepted Letters: Epistolarity and Narrative in Greek and Roman Literature*, Lanham, MD.

Karlsson, G. (1962), *Idéologie et cérémonial dans l'épistolographie byzantine. Textes du Xe siècle analysés et commentés*, Uppsala.

Kubina, K./Riehle, A. (eds.) (2021), *Epistolary Poetry in Byzantium and Beyond. An Anthology with Critical Essays*, New York/London.

Leone, P.A.M. (ed.) (1991), *Maximi monachi Planudis epistulae*, Amsterdam.

Littlewood, A. (1976), "An 'ikon of the soul': The Byzantine Letter", in: *Visible Language* 10, 197–226.

Luiselli, R. (1995), "Un nuovo manuale di epistolografia di epoca bizantina (P.Berol. inv. 21190): presentazione e considerazioni preliminari", in: B. Kramer/W. Luppe/M. Herwig/P. Günter (eds.), *Akten des 21. Internationalen Papyrologenkongresses. Berlin, 13.–19.8.1995*, Stuttgart/Leipzig, 643–651.

Luiselli, R. (2008), "Greek Letters on Papyrus. First to Eighth Centuries: A Survey", in: E. Mira Grob/A. Kaplony (eds.), *Documentary Letters from the Middle East: The Evidence in Greek, Coptic, South Arabian, Pehlevi, and Arabic (1st – 15th c CE)*, Études Asiatiques 62.3, Bern, 677–737.

Malherbe, A. (1988), *Ancient Epistolary Theorists*, Atlanta.

Morelli, F. (2007), "*Grammatêphoroi* e vie della giustizia nell'Egitto tardo antico", in: E. Cantarella (ed.), *Symposion 2005. Vorträge zur griechischen und hellenistischen Rechtsgeschichte (Salerno, 14.–18. September 2005)*, Vienna, 351–372.

Mullett, M. (1981), "The Classical Tradition in the Byzantine Letter", in: M. Mullett/R. Scott (eds.), *Byzantium and the Classical Tradition*, Birmingham, 75–93.

Mullett, M. (1990), "Writing in Early Mediaeval Byzantium", in: R. McKitterick (ed.), *The Uses of Literacy in Early Medieval Europe*, Cambridge, 156–185.

Oates, J.F. et al. (2001), *Checklist of Editions of Greek, Latin, Demotic, and Coptic Papyri, Ostraca and Tablets*, BASP Suppl. 9. 5th edn., Oakville, CT.

Paoli-Lafaye, E. (2002), "Messagers et message: la diffusion des nouvelles de l'Afrique d'Augustin vers les régions au-delà des mers", in: J. Andreau/C. Virlouvet (eds.), *L'information et la mer dans le monde antique*, Rome, 244–259.

Pascale, G. (2007), *Massimo Planude. Epistole a Melchisedek*, Alessandria.

Pasquali, G. (ed.) (1959), *Gregorii Nysseni epistulae*, Leiden.

Perretti, P. (ed.) (2017), *Teodoreto di Cirro. Commento alle lettere di Paolo*, Milan.

Richards, E.R. (2004), *Paul and First-Century Letter Writing: Secretaries, Composition, and Collection*, Downers Grove, IL.

Rosenmeyer, P.A. (2001), *Ancient Epistolary Fictions: The Letter in Greek Literature*, Cambridge.

Sarischouli, P. (1997), "Ἄνθρωπος in Papyri of the Byzantine Period (late 3rd–mid 7th c.)", in: B. Kramer/W. Luppe/M. Herwig/P. Günter (eds.), *Akten des 21. Internationalen Papyrologenkongresses. Berlin, 13.–19.8.1995*, Stuttgart/Leipzig, 889–901.

Sarri, A. (2018), *Material Aspects of Letter Writing in the Graeco-Roman World, 500 BC–AD 300*, Materiale Textkulturen 12, Berlin/Boston.

Schubert, P. (2021), *The Bearers of Business Letters in Roman Egypt*, Papyrologica Bruxellensia 41, Brussels.
Silvas, A.M. (trans.) (2007), *Gregory of Nyssa: The Letters*, Leiden.
Stowers, S.K. (1986), *Letter Writing in Greco-Roman Antiquity*, Philadelphia.
Teske, R. (2001), *The Works of Saint Augustine: A Translation for the 21st Century: Letters 1–99*, New York.
Teske, R. (2004), *The Works of Saint Augustine: A Translation for the 21st Century: Letters 156–210*, New York.
Thraede, K. (1970), *Grundzüge griechisch-römischer Brieftopik*, Munich.
White, J.L. (1986), *Light from Ancient Letters*, Philadelphia.

Epilogue

Mireille Corbier
The Ancient Historian and His Documents: Reader, Interpreter, and/or Author?

Abstract: Confronted with Ferraris's philosophical theory, this chapter reflects on the historian's and epigraphist's relationship to 'documents.' Various examples demonstrate that Buckland's response to Ferraris on the theme of "What is a document?", in particular his tripartite division of documents, can be applied to the study of ancient history. However, far from being mutually exclusive, the three definitions — made as, made into, considered as — most often interfere in our use of documents, and indeed they did interfere at the time these objects were produced. And they also interfere in their 'second' life (afterlife) as searched for and studied objects. It is the scholar who 'makes the document' and not the other way round. For many relics of antiquity, the recognition of their status as documents is a recent fact. The most interesting thing for a historian is to ask a question, preferably a new one, and to try to identify a group of traces that can be used to answer it, in order to create documents that can be used scientifically for this purpose.

In the first place, of course, I speak as an epigraphist (I have been the editor of *L'Année épigraphique* for thirty years) but mainly as a historian. As such, the history to which I lay claim to is a history of antiquity that has been profoundly renewed during recent decades, as a result of the calls from colleagues working on later periods — specifically the Middle Ages and the Early Modern period. This is also a result of the research of pre- and proto-historians who have transformed the methods, questions, and ambitions of archaeology's increased association with anthropology.

In this regard, I have been interested in a long history extending at least to the nineteenth century, or even nearer to us. Thus my sensitivity to all the questions bound up with the theme of our present debate: namely the role of writing and connections to it — especially in reference to orality — in social and institu-

---

I would like to thank the organizers of the meeting that generated this volume for their invitation. It was a great pleasure for me to be back in Stanford University twenty-eight years after my first visit, thanks to the invitation of Michael Jameson (whose memory I salute) and Susan Treggiari. I am also grateful to Kenneth L. Brown for translating the French of the original paper into English.

tional forms and practices of communication and the circulation of information. But I have been just as profoundly struck by the research of archaeologists and anthropologists who have freed us by relativizing the privileged and exclusive connection that has long been considered a principle between history and writing: the idea that, without written documents, no history is possible. On the contrary, in the second half of the twentieth century, history went through a double revolution. On the one hand, there was a spectacular increase in the mass of objects, of traces, of results from chemistry, physics, biology, etc., which could be used as documents — a transformation summarized and anticipated in 1933 by Lucien Febvre in his inaugural lecture at the Collège de France, when he spoke about the sources of history: "The texts, yes, but all the texts ... the texts, yes, but not only the texts."[1] On the other hand, there was a methodological revolution — inspired by archaeology but today largely accepted in the field of social sciences — centered around the transformation of the *object* discovered, without any scientific value of its own, into a document. This object as document was defined by the totality of the details that provide context and enable us to analyze it as such in order to derive all of the information it contains, and also to develop the multiplicity of relations which may be established between each particular object and all the others — and, for texts, the multiplicity of their possible readings.

The discipline of epigraphy has been transformed in recent decades by this double revolution. The first one led specialists to take into consideration the totality of texts and fragments of texts that have reached us: graffiti, stamps on tiles or bricks, etc. They appropriated for themselves, without formulating it as such, the law proposed by Ferraris, viz. object (social object) = written act,[2] but with the terms reversed: every written act is an object — that is to say, a social object, a witness to an intentionality by its author, even if not intended to be read by anyone else, or only by a divinity. This has also led epigraphists to question the manner in which these written acts might have been read, understood, interpreted, and finally internalized and appropriated by their readers according to their mentalities, their cultures, and their representation of the world.

The second revolution led the same epigraphists to take a further important step, making use of the lessons learned by their archaeological and anthropological colleagues. For the former, all objects found at every level of an excavation (grains and pollens, animal bones, the remains of food or latrines, fragments of stone, wooden or metal tools), if correctly analyzed, can provide a very

---

[1] Febvre 1953, 5–6.
[2] Ferraris 2012.

large amount of information. Much of this, but not all, is beyond any specific intention on the part of their creators; but the objects do reveal techniques that were practiced, rules and social representations, environmental constraints, religious beliefs, which anthropologists can help reconstruct, etc. Even if we extend as far as possible the field of "written acts" to include figurative representations — like the paintings of Lascaux (18,000 years old) or the Grotte Chauvet (36,000 years old), or all the examples of "rock art" — that allow us to follow the progressive elaboration of rules and codes for the representation of human bodies (which take us well beyond the invention of writing), we need to perceive that the "law" proposed by Ferraris does not apply to a large proportion of the cited documents. *Not only is every written act an object, but not all the objects are written acts.* Many of them are simple "traces," without a link to a deliberate intention, that the scientific work of the researcher does its best to transform and constitute as "documents." Collecting and analyzing these objects have prodigiously enlarged the mass of documentation available to historians, extending further into the past the "time of history": the so-called Neolithic revolution has replaced the invention of writing as the fundamental beginning of human history. But it has also put into question, for times belonging to traditional periods of history, some of the conclusions based on the study of texts and figurative representations, such as the "familial" pig as the basis of meat supply for the peasants of the Middle Ages.[3]

Once these basic reservations have been established, there is no fundamental difference between ancient societies and our contemporary ones other than the accelerated growth of the mass of information accumulated and susceptible to circulation, the great majority of which will not be "read," "seen," or "heard"; the accelerated refinement of tools used (the combination of computer and mobile phone, according to Ferraris); and the increasingly tight association between image, sound, and writing, as well as the new possibilities opened up by the virtual. We can see from this that the classification into three groups proposed by Buckland may be perfectly applied to the epigraphic documentation that has been kept, discovered, and studied for the Roman world: made as (a document); made into (a document); and considered as (a document).[4] Pierre Schneider's chapter in this volume has also illuminated how Buckland's categories of classification can be profitably applied to documentary conceptions of

---

3 Audoin-Rouzeau 1995.
4 Buckland 2014.

landscapes in the ancient world.⁵ But we should apply Buckland's categories only on the condition of emphasizing immediately that each of these three "classes" is itself divided into different subgroups.

In the first class, "made as," the dominant dimension of the discipline of epigraphy for a long while privileged texts that came from the domain of political authority: texts written on solid objects and displayed in public space so as to be able — and almost indeed to demand — to be read, or at least seen and known by everyone: the document was identified as a monument. However, the discipline needed to make room too for all forms of texts from private origins, beginning with epitaphs inscribed on tombs put up by individuals or families along roads leaving cities so that they might be read by passers-by. Moreover, epigraphists also had to take into consideration, especially in cities, everything written on walls of houses and shops, and on less "noble" and more fragile supports — namely, coatings — and in the interiors of houses themselves, on the walls of some rooms as decorations or added on as graffiti, as frequently by visitors as by the residents of the house.

This led to the questions which I personally posed: "What was written on the walls of Rome?" and those in *L'Écriture dans la maison romaine*.⁶ I am reminded thereby that a good deal of public display of official information took the form of temporary notices, the *tabulae dealbatae* (Figure 4); these could be removed to make place for other more recent communications, whose display might or might not be preceded by a public reading. Moreover, the quality of material in the case of bronze did not protect a document against the temptation to reuse it for other needs, and even stone itself could be hammered in various ways to prolong the life of a document at the cost of a few necessary corrections, as we can see on Roman milestones.

---

5 Schneider in this volume.
6 Corbier 2006; Corbier 2011; Corbier and Guilhembet 2011; and Corbier 2013.

Fig. 4: *Tabulae dealbatae*, the Forum of Pompei, House of Julia Felix. Museo Archeologico Nazionale, Napoli, inv. 9068.

In the second class, "made into (a document)," it is impossible not to give priority to the metallic money that is handled by the discipline of numismatics. Money usually combines two images and one or two inscriptions similar to monumental inscriptions. It is always a strong political symbol, carrying authority, but its main purpose remains economic: its use as a means of payment and reference for commercial exchange, also thereby defining the maintenance of value. Its content lends itself to every possible form of manipulation — in quality and in weight — through forgery and usury (the latter leading one to think that the most used coins are those which circulated the most, and that the best preserved are those which were hoarded). On the other hand, the image of the *princeps* and the accompanying texts make it possible to fix the date and place of minting. Nonetheless, it is difficult to date the beginnings of a coin's afterlife; some of them escaped re-minting, remaining in circulation to be used for everyday purposes (small coins, which are always much too rare in the historical record) or to be put aside for saving and hoarding. In the case of hoards, we have a good index from the composition of those that have been discovered and in which coins of very different dates may be found together.

In contrast to money, we have all of the markings (stamps) placed on manufactured objects such as tiles, bricks, amphoras, and ceramic dishes. It is tempting to associate them with the real or supposed signatures and guarantees of origin represented today by labels on clothing and many of our manufactured objects; all of these markings were equally intentional in antiquity. Moreover, we also distinguish graffiti, the object of systematic study for some years now, in which a sort of zero-grade writing is often considered. It is more personal, spontaneous, and free. We identify in these practices many more cultural than social regularities, such as habits, favored locations, themes, and vocabularies.

For the third class, the quantity and diversity of artifacts today "considered as (documents)," or susceptible to such consideration, have extended almost infinitely. However, only a few decades ago they were not considered thus and their study was carried out by specialized disciplines (bronzes, sculptures, works of art, ceramics — decorated or not and at times inscribed — everyday objects, mosaics, etc.). In parallel, the types of use for research purposes have become differentiated. The traditional form favored comparison of each object with others of the same nature in order to analyze its inclusion in a series. To this was added the study of the association and presence of different objects from the same place and date, thus constituting a cultural setting.

The three definitions — "made as," "made into," "considered as" — far from excluding one another, more often combine in the use that we make of the documents at hand. Nonetheless, we need to remember that these definitions had already come together at the time when these objects were produced and collected. The intentions of their author in producing them offer only one possible lens for the analysis of each object, and these convergences make it possible to define the complexity of a culture. They also converge in the "second" life (the "afterlife") of the items as objects of research and study by the scientific disciplines concerned; they are employed to define precisely the documentary value and status which a researcher may give these items or choose to give them today.

Of these two successive lives, the "written" texts inscribed on a material object that were produced in the ancient Roman world and have come down to us, represent an original and remarkable example. The Roman world, as well as those different political and cultural entities that preceded it around the Mediterranean since the invention of writing, constituted and preserved its own archives, mostly for political purposes: taken in the widest sense, and therefore including diplomacy, administration, finances, and the economy. In the second half of the fourth century BCE the Romans reconstituted the consular lists of the previous periods using familial archives and oral traditions, at least. The different cities that made up the Roman world, from the largest to the smallest, did the same, even if they often did so less systematically. These archives were used on a daily basis by local authorities, but also by the historians of the time: Tacitus and others, like Pliny the Younger, consulted the *acta senatus*. They were used as sources and evidence for rewriting particular moments from the past.

However, these archives as such have disappeared. The documents upon which we work today not only represent a tiny minority of those produced at the time (it is impossible to propose even a rough percentage), but they are not necessarily the most significant. They are the product of selection by other, often much later, authors and actors. Since the Renaissance they have been constituted as such by more than five centuries of the erudition of ambitious scholars. During that time, these texts have been identified and transcribed, and their material support was sometimes, but not always, removed in order to be conserved in private collections, some of which later became public. Some of these have been published, but it was not until the mid-nineteenth century that all of the known texts — whether with or without their material support — were integrated into a corpus. This took place after a rereading of the original or through identification in a manuscript. Such corpora aimed to be exhaustive, assembling information around the text itself that made it possible to orient the study — transcription, location, dating, etc. — while responding to the accepted rules of presentation. A corpus always had to conform to one form or another of selection from those items which, in the opinion of the editors and researchers, deserved the status of a document having the value of scientific use.

The criteria of selection were progressively extended to texts previously neglected by editors of these collections and to new objects brought up to date by archaeologists who put them into documentary format. The collection of fragments of amphoras accumulated in Rome in the Testaccio may be compared from that point of view with the Geniza documents of Cairo (eleventh and twelfth centuries) used by Salomon Goitein.[7] In both cases, it is a matter of deposits of "documents" which could not be destroyed, but for quite different reasons. In the latter case, these were mostly of a religious nature: the fragments of written papers had to be saved as such without recognizing their status as documents, let alone archives. These may be compared, despite their differences, with the curses (*defixiones*) thrown into the Sulis Minerva spring in Bath.[8] In the former case, however, the reason was purely technical: the amphoras reached Rome filled with oil and wine and could not be used again on the spot, nor returned to their senders. The simplest solution was to break them and pile up the pieces, year after year, in a dump in the open air. It was not until recent decades that this dump began to be the object of systematic exploitation for a study of the supplies of Rome during the Imperial period, based on a stratigraphy adapted to the modalities of its composition. This study gave the status of documents to the fragments of amphoras that maintained an element of their initial form (which made it possible to classify them according to the type of original container), and/or included written indications in the forms of stamps and *dipinti* which could provide information about the origin of the transported product, the quantities, and so forth. Both in Bath and Testaccio and even for the fragments of diverse letters and texts from the Geniza, the authority attributed to a document by recent researchers has little, if anything to do with the intent of the document's author. Rather, it belongs to the scientific project defined in our time by researchers who chose to study them. The knowledge, training, and intent of the reader, as DiGiulio's analysis of Aulus Gellius in this volume reveals, all imbue the document with authority.[9] It is the researcher who "makes the document" and not the creator.

A taxonomy may, of course, be useful as an intermediate step for classifying and distinguishing objects according to well-defined criteria. However, it will not suffice — just as the simple opposition between past and present (based on consequences of the increased magnitude and modes of storage and circulation

---

7 Rodriguez Almeida 1984; Blázques Martínez and Remesal Rodríguez 1999–2014; and Goitein 1967–1993.
8 Tomlin 1988.
9 DiGiulio in this volume.

of information brought about by contemporary tools) will not suffice. The aim of the researcher is based on another ground: that of defining the problems that they want to study, the sources that they can identify and use, and the methods that they will apply to reach the anticipated results. For me, the main ambition of today's historical research, whatever its epoch, is to bring back to life the elements of the past that contain a collection of seemingly new information, or that may be envisaged from another point of view within a cultural context that may have served actors of this past as a framework of actions and reactions, as well as ways of thinking, interpreting, and giving meaning.

Contrary to what Ferraris has written, a mountain is not only a non-social object which exists independently of human presence on earth.[10] It is also a social and cultural object whose history (for Europe) began being written between the eighteenth and nineteenth centuries on the theme of "the discovery of the mountain" — or if you prefer, "the discovery of humanity's and society's relation to the mountain." The field of geography, established as a discipline in the nineteenth century, took upon itself all aspects of description: the physical description of formations, relief and types, and the geological history of their formation, as well as the description of human societies living there and using their resources. Special attention was paid to the migrations of people and of flocks — particularly to the transhumanism of the latter, for which we have numerous direct or indirect written documents,[11] as well as the multiple inscribed traces in the soil, like the *calles* left by the flocks from the Imperial epoch. Fourteen or fifteen centuries later, these were followed, with some differences and variations under the name of *tratturi*, by the flocks of the Dogana delle Pecore ("Customs of the Sheep"). More recently in the *longue durée* of the history of the earth, while astrophysicists reflected upon the existence or absence of mountains on the planets that surround us, geophysics provided an account of the formation and evolution of the mountains on earth.

The case of the mountain is only one example among others of a more general process of the socialization of nature, which, during the past two or three centuries, has accompanied and preceded the understanding that the human species has become a "geological force," capable of modifying and even disrupting the "earth system." The frontier between "social" and "non-social" has shifted. Without realizing it, we have entered into the era of the Anthropocene.

Documentality emphasizes written texts issued by an authority as means of proof. But for a historian, as I will show, these are only one category of docu-

---

10 Ferraris 2012, 33.
11 Cf. the debate regarding the *Saepinum* inscription in Corbier 2006, chapter 9.

ments among many others. Antiquity, which is not taken in consideration at all by theoreticians of documentality, also possessed this type of written text. Let me give some examples.

In this regard, the most remarkable dossier for the Roman world is the leather pouch of Babatha found in a cave in Israel.[12] Lost by its owner during Hadrian's Jewish war of 132–133 CE, it contains all the private documents that this Jewish woman, living in the Roman province of Arabia with the status of a *peregrina* (foreigner), chose to take in her flight: various certificates of her somewhat complicated family life (Babatha had been twice married, to a "Jesus" and a "Judah"; she had a son from the first marriage and a step-daughter from the second, and had been twice widowed), property deeds, and contracts for loans, notably a loan on hypothec of 60 *denarii* contracted by her late husband from a Roman centurion. All of these were private documents written in Greek, Aramaic, and Nabataean-Aramaic, authenticated by the signatures of the contracting parties and witnesses. The Roman state was represented therein, notably by means of a copy of a property declaration for date orchards from the census of 127 CE, displayed on a basilica wall at Rabbath, and by requests addressed to the Roman law courts. Written in ink on papyrus, these documents have a quite modern look. In their time, they were *made as* documents.

The very idea of retaining written documents was, of course, their value in later disputes or suits. Many of these papyri were what are called "double documents," the text being written twice on the same papyrus. The upper (in fact, inner) portion of the papyrus was rolled up and fastened with string to protect the text. The copy on the lower (outer) portion would be accessible and its veracity could be checked, if necessary, by comparison with the upper text.[13] These papyri have been transformed in our day into documents of a very different sort. They are used to study multilingualism and language contacts in the Near East and the various uses of Aramaic and Greek; (il)literacy (Babatha did not sign); Jewish family structures, e.g., the possibility of bigamy; the application of Jewish law or Roman law, notably in regard to the guardianship of orphans and women; the relations of inhabitants with the Roman army, with the help of an interpreter; and more.

As my second example, from Italy, the dossier of *tabulae* that the freed slave Lucius Venidius Ennychus stored in the archives of his house at Herculaneum (the Casa del Salone Nero) bears witness to the acquisition of Roman citizenship

---

[12] P. Yadin in Lewis/Yadin/Greenfield 1989, 1–35 and P. Yadin in Yadin *et al.* 2002, 36–64. A part of the document is published in the first volume, the other in the latter.
[13] N. Lewis in Lewis/Yadin/Greenfield 1989, 6–10.

by a family of Latini Iunani thanks to the procedure of *anniculae probatio*.¹⁴ Known from Gaius (1.29), a jurist of the second century CE, and the *Rules of Ulpian*, a compilation of the fourth century CE (*Tituli ex corpore Ulpiani*, 3.3), the procedure set up by the *lex Aelia Sentia* of 4 CE permitted a freedman Latinus Iunianus who was freed by his owner before the legal age of thirty (if married according to the rules of this *lex*) to request Roman citizenship from the urban praetor in Rome, or the governor of the province. This was on the condition of his having procreated within that marriage a child still alive at one year of age (i.e. *anniculus* or *annicula*), who had thus survived the most difficult period of infant mortality.

The dossier of wooden tablets from L. Venidius Ennychus is the only one to reveal the real documents established at each step of a procedure, thereby demonstrating it to be more complex than what may be understood from Gaius' brief note. The final document (dated March 22, 62 CE) that is taken as proof by the interested party, the wooden triptych *TH* 89, does not attest citizenship delivered by the Roman authority but is a private copy of the decision of the magistrate (his *edictum*), the urban praetor in Rome, displayed in front of his tribunal.¹⁵ It is a copy that conforms to the usual formula *descriptum et recognitum*, certified by twelve witnesses whose names are accompanied by their respective seals. The edict was supported by another document that was given directly to the magistrate in Rome by four *decuriones* from Herculaneum. This document was a *decretum* of decurions of Herculaneum which certified, following verification of the rights of L. Venidius Ennychus, of his wife (*uxor*) Livia Acte, and of their *annicula* daughter, whose name is not even mentioned, that they could apply to benefit from the status of Roman citizens by virtue of the *lex Aelia Sentia*. The praetor, who alone was authorized to take the decision, needed proof that the two necessary conditions had been met, namely a living child of a year or more, born from a legitimate marriage (according to the *lex Aelia Sentia*). The *decurionum decretum* served as proof.

The archive of L. Venidius Ennychus also contains a *tabula* that is a vestige of a triptych in which Ennychus declares the birth of a girl on July 24, 60 CE. It has the names of eight *signatores* authenticating it. Another fragment of a *tabula* has the beginning of a *decurionum decretum*, dated July 25, 61 CE, exactly one year after the birth; the date certifies that this text was an exact copy of the decree of *probatio* validating the request.

---

14 Camodeca 2006 (= *AE* 2006: nos. 305–307). See now Camodeca 2017, 57–84.
15 Restored, reread, and completed by Camodeca after the incomplete first edition in *FIRA*², III, 5 *bis*. b.

One century later, Apuleius refers to the same kind of documents, again called *tabulae*, in a literary text: his own advocacy, which he wrote to defend himself against an alleged charge of magical seduction of the rich widow he had married (Apul. *Apol.* 102.8). He argues that the *tabulae dotis, donationis*, and *testamenti* that he can submit should be sufficient proof of his unselfishness.

There are other writings from the same period whose object is to serve as proof of, for instance, Roman citizenship granted to soldiers (who had been freed in this case from service), in a way quite characteristic of their time. These are bronze diptychs called "military diplomas" by modern historians, but not by contemporary soldiers (Figures 5a and 5b). The beneficiaries were mainly soldiers of auxiliary troops. They received them along with their *honesta missio* and kept them in their places of retirement until they died. These artifacts, which were *made as* documents and manufactured in Rome (as is now accepted) in order to prove the Roman citizenship of their owners, are *made into* documents by historians for other purposes. They can be used to compare the two dates: one of the imperial titulature and the other a consular date. These are authentic documents copied from the original imperial constitution reporting a precise year, month, and day and authenticated by witnesses.

These documents also enable scholars to carry out prosopographical studies; to reconstitute *fasti* of provincial governors; to identify the auxiliary troops, *cohortes* and *alae* present in a province at one time or another, according to the period; and, for each of these auxiliary troops, to reconstitute their movements by comparing the various dated diplomas showing the names of the same unit. They can be used to identify the ethnic origin, and thus the geographical origin, of the soldiers recruited by their registered name, which includes this information; to examine their onomastics and that of their children; and to study the various privileges accorded — before and after 140 CE, when Antoninus Pius cancelled the clause granting citizenship to children of beneficiaries (both boys and girls) born during their service. Diplomas also allow the study of the names of the seven witnesses required to attest that the soldier's name can be clearly read on the bronze tablet containing the imperial constitution displayed in Rome in a precise place where everyone (in Rome) can verify it. A system for avoiding fraud was used: the diptych was closed with wire covered by the seven seals of the witnesses. Access to the inner text, in case of doubt about the identity of the mentioned beneficiary, was only possible by breaking the seals. Emperor Nero imposed the same system on wills written on wax tablets.

Fig. 5: Military diplomas outside (5a) and inside (5b). In: Corbier 2006, 133–134, fig. 98 a-b.

In fact, the major interest for those studying these whole or fragmentary documents, which are very numerous (more than 900 spread throughout the entire empire), is to be able to put them into serial studies. Their interpretation is not always obvious: for example, the reasons for Antoninus Pius having decided to no longer legitimize and grant Roman citizenship to children born during military service — illegitimate by definition, because soldiers, whether citizens or not, did not have the right to marry — are still disputed. The authenticity of military diplomas is best proven by discovering them *in situ* during an excavation. Those found with a metal detector and sold on the antiquarian market have lost the essential element of their provenance, but their original status can be confirmed by checking their internal coherence.[16]

It seems unnecessary to multiply examples of artifacts *made as* documents and then *made into* documents by historians. They are numerous. I have considered here three types of written materials all characteristic of Roman times: papyri, wooden tablets, and bronze tablets. For each of them, we can speak of two lives; passing from the first life to the second, the focus can be reversed. For a military diploma, which was a simple extract of a long imperial constitution engraved on a large bronze tablet displayed at Rome, the place of display where everyone could check that the soldier's name was written there and could verify what the witnesses had seen was well known by all at this time. Now, however, the situation is reversed. Like other historians, using the proximity of one to the other, I have attempted to situate the monuments mentioned (from Claudius to Domitian) as places of display (now lost) on the Capitol's area in the first century CE.[17] Similarly, the place of display of the praetor's edict in favor of Lucius Venidius Ennychus (*Romae in foro Augusto sub porticu Iulia*) is the only evidence we have available today to identify the site of the praetor's tribunal in Rome in 62 CE under Nero.

As a Roman historian and an epigraphist like me, John Bodel has discussed two of my examples in his contribution to this volume: the *tabulae Herculanenses* and the military diplomas.[18] But the first example I analyzed, the famous dossier of Babatha, would also illustrate the various modalities for establishing and checking individual identities during the first centuries CE that were the main purpose of his own inquiry. To put it more clearly, I would underline

---

16 As an aside, I might mention that I decided not to publish any scientific edition on the basis of photographs of military diplomas that had been sent to me by antique dealers. They no longer send them to me ...
17 Corbier 2006, chap. 4.
18 Bodel in this volume.

that the cases of Petronia Iusta and Venidius Ennychus are the best documented in the tablets from Herculaneum and, for this very reason, have been well studied by scholars. My choice of Venidius Ennychus was inspired by the new readings of the documents provided by Giuseppe Camodeca, which have enriched our understanding of the whole story. We can enlarge the reflection: even when documents remain the same, the reading of the texts can be improved and their interpretation is a continuous creation of scholarly research.

Some documents may have more than two lives. They beckon the reader to conduct a veritable police investigation and to discover that from time to time the notion of a "document" has changed.[19] A bronze tablet kept in the Capitoline Museum in Rome, on which a long Latin inscription was engraved and bronze appliqués were affixed, gave me the opportunity for such an investigation (Figure 6). In 1664 the *tabula* was an object in a collection, exhibited in Rome in the house of Paolo Maccarani near the Trevi Fountain, and visited by all lovers of antiquities. It was still the property of the same family in the middle of the eighteenth century at the time of Maffei. The collection made up one of the first core sections of the Capitoline Museum; from the second half of the eighteenth century, the *tabula* was registered and described in all the museum's catalogues, and it remains exhibited in a case on the ground floor. The exact place and probable date of the discovery were ignored until 2004, when Cristina Zaccagnino, an Italian archaeologist, published a letter found in the Biblioteca Marucelliana in Florence; it was from Trastevere and dated from the reign of Pope Urban VIII Barberini (1623–1644). On the basis of notes from the nineteenth-century excavations, she situated the room in the firemen's barracks.[20]

The status of the *tabula* has changed with photography: thanks to A. E. Gordon and subsequently to the editors of the 1999 *Supplementa Italica Imagines*, the *tabula* became an image. The editors had no doubt that this image corresponded to the original document which had simply lost a figurine.[21] What they ignored was the fact that the *tabula*, which was considered a work of art, an object for collection, had been drawn soon after its discovery: these little-known drawings preserved in manuscripts showed that one of them, dated c. 1650, provided the exact traits of each of the three figurines (Figure 7), while the two others, dated respectively before 1647 and 1662, had their respective positions on top of the *tabula* — in fact, different according to the two authors.

---

[19] Corbier 2008 (= *AE* 2008, no. 164) and Corbier 2014 (= *AE* 2014, no. 121).
[20] Zaccagnino 2004 (= *AE* 2004, no. 181).
[21] Gordon 1983 and Gregori/Mattei 1999, no. 2226.

Fig. 6: Bronze tablet dedicated by the *Vigiles*. Museo Capitolino, Roma.

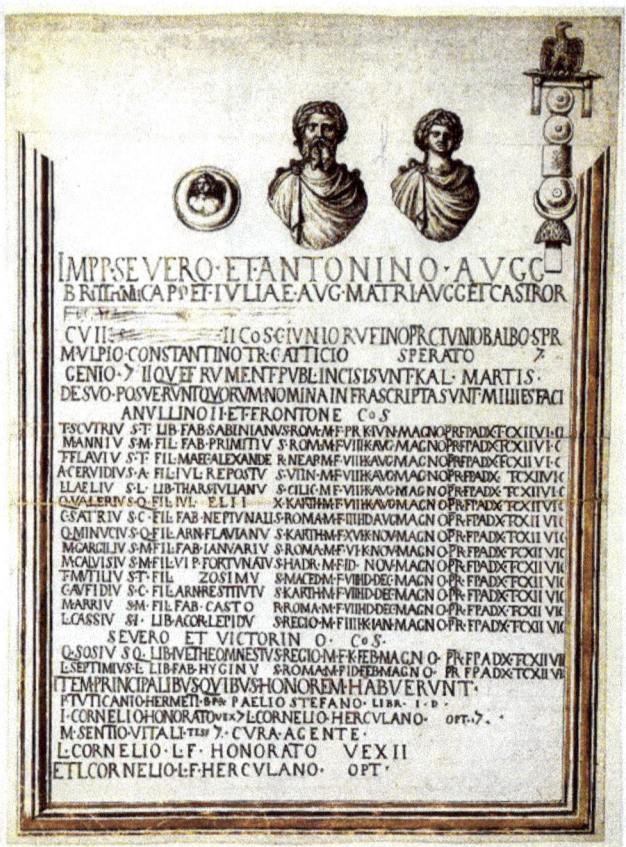

Fig. 7: Cartaceum Museum. British Museum, inv. 2005,0927.52.

In 1876, with the publication of the first volume of the *Corpus Inscriptionum Latinarum* VI, the *tabula* became a "document" according to the term used during the time of Mommsen — that is, a text correctly established on the basis of an "autopsy" by Henzen from twenty years earlier. Thus, the authors of the *Corpus* fixed the interpretation as that of a text (*CIL* VI 220), which can be exploited by its content (a dedication offered by firemen, *vigiles*), and indeed this has been the case until now (Figure 8).

```
220 tabula aenea. In aedibus Pauli Maccarani eq. R. ad radices montis Quirinalis prope aquam Virginem avp. Apud marchionem Maccaranium
FABR. MAFF.  Nunc in museo Capitolino. — Milites quorum est haec tabula vigiles esse nomen Iunii Rufinii praefecti comprobat, quippe qui prae-
fectus vigilum dicatur sub Severo et Antonino in Digest. 1, 15, 4 et a. 205 in titulo quartae cohortis vigilum edito a de Rossio Ann. Inst. 1858
p. 286. Iam vero cum Maccaranii, in quorum aedibus haec tabula fuit, possederint vineam in Aventino sitam, hodie Torloniae principis, trans
viam e regione eius, in qua aedicula centuriae alicuius coh. IV vigilum loco suo antiquo adhuc extat (cf. n. qui praecedit), satis certo deduci potest
tabulam in illa Maccaraniorum vinea repertam esse et ad eandem coh. IV vigilum pertinere. Quam coniecturam iam antequam aedicula illa nota
esset, aliis argumentis ingeniose usus proposuit de Rossi l. l. p. 288 sq.
```

    effigies Severi   *effigies Getae*   *effigies Antonini*

```
            IMPP · SEVERO · ET · ANTONINO · AVGG
         B R i T T A N I C I S · PP·ET·IVLIAE· AVG·MATRI·AVGG·ET·CASTROR·
         E T   F V L V I A E   PLAVTILLAE AVG  C  FVLVIO PLAVTIANO PR PR
            C · V · Π · P SEPTIMIO GETA Π · CoS·C · IVNIO · RVFINO · PR · C · IVNIO · BALBO · S · PR    a.p.C.203
            M · VLPIO · CONSTANTINO · TR · C · ATTICIO · SPERATO · ꝗ
         GENIO · ꝗ · II · QVI · FRVMENT · PVBL · INCISI SVNT · KAL · MARTIS ·
         DE · SVO · POSVERVNT · QVORVM · NOMINA · INFRA SCRIPTA SVNT · MILITES · FACT
                ANVLLINO · Π · ET · FRONTONE · Cos                                        a.p.C 199
         T · SCVTRIV   S · T · LIB · FAB · SABINIANVS · ROM · M · F · PR · K · IVN · MAGNO   PR F P A D X·T·CXLIVKC
         M · ANNIV    S · M · FIL · FAB · PRIMITIV S · ROM · M · F · VIII · K · AVG · MAGNO   PR F P A D X·T·CXL·IVKC
         T · FLAVIV   S · T · FIL · MAEC · ALEXANDER · NEAP · M · F · VIII · K · AVG · MAGNO   PR F P A D X·T·CXL·IVKC
         A · CERVIDIV  S · A · FIL · IVL · REPOSTV S · VTIN · M · F · VIII · K · AVG · MAGNO   PR F P A D X·T·CXLIV KC
         L · LAELIV   S · L · LIB · THARS · IVLIANV S · CILIC · M · F · VIII · K · AVG · MAGNO   PR F P A D X T CXLIVKC
         Q · VALERIV  S · Q · FIL · IVL · FELI    X · KARTH · M · F · VIII · K · AVG · MAGNO   PR·F·P·A·D X · T CXLIVK C
         C · SATRIV   S · C · FIL · FAB · NEPTVNALIS · ROMA · M · F · IIII · ID · AVG · MAGNO   PR F P·A · D X · T · CXLIVK A  etc
         Q · MINVCIV  S · Q · FIL · AKN · FLAVIANV S · KARTH · M · F · XVI · K · NOV · MAGNO   PR F P A D X·T·CXLIVKC
         M · GARGILIV  S · M · FIL · FAB · IANVARIV S · ROMA · M · F · VI · K · NOV · MAGNO   PR F P A D X T CXLIVK
         M · CALVISIV  S · M · FIL · VLP · FORTVNATVS · HADR · M · F ·   ID · NOV · MAGNO   PR F P A D X T CXLIVK
         T · MVTILIV  S · T · FIL ·         ZOSIMV  S · MACED M · F · VIII · ID · DEC · MAGNO   PR F P A D X T CXLIVKC
         C · AVFIDIV  S · C · FIL · ARN · RESTITVTV S · KARTH · M · F · VII · ID · DEC · MAGNO   PR F P A D X · T · CXLIVK
         M · ARRIV   S · M · FIL · FAB · CASTO    R · ROMA · M · F · VIII · ID · DEC · MAGNO   PR F P A D X·T·CXLIVK
   adDYT L · CASSIV  S · L · LIB · AGOR · LEPIDV   S · REGIO · M · F · IIII · K · IAN · MAGNO   PR F P A D X·T CXLIVKC
                   S E V E R O · E T · V I C T O R I N O · C O S                           a.p.C. 200
         Q · SOSIV   S · Q · FIL · IVL · THEOMNESTVS · REGIO · M · F · K · FEB · MAGNO   PR F P A D X T CXLIV K
      SD L · SEPTIMIV S · L · LIB · FAB · HYGINV   S · ROMA · M · F · ID · FEB · MAGNO   PR F P A D X T CXLIV C
         ITEM · PRINCIPALIBVS · QVIBVS · HONOREM · HABVERVNT
         P · TVTICANIO · HERMETI · B PR · P · AELIO STEFANO · LIBR · I · D
         L · CORNELIO · HONORATO · VEX · ꝗ · L · CORNELIO · HERCVLANO · OPT · ꝗ ·
         M · SENTIO · VITALI · TESS · ꝗ · CVRA · AGENTE
         L · CORNELIO · L · F · HONORATO ·           VEXIL · ꝗ
         ET · L · CORNELIO · L · F · HERCVLANO ·    OPT · ꝗ
Descripsi; contulit Bormann. Exhibent Gudius ms. f. 19; Fabretti col. Trai. 37; Maffei M. V. 309 (inde Donati 175, 3); Guasco M. C. 95; Keller-
mann Vig. 12. Vv. 1—9 et 23—31 edidi ipse Or. Henzen 6752.
```

Fig. 8: *CIL*, VI, 220.

In 1876, according to the *Corpus*, the three figurines were considered to be still affixed on the tablet, but there was no drawing and they were simply identified by their names as Septimius Severus, Caracalla, and Geta. As a matter of fact, the Septimius Severus figurine was already in the British Museum, which had purchased it in 1872, and the youthful head had probably been stolen from the Capitoline Museum at the same time. In any case, at some indeterminate date the Capitoline Museum had covered up a part of the emptiness by making a head of Julia Domna. Why a woman? Because the printed catalog had mentioned Septimius Severus, Caracalla, and Julia Domna since that time when the first catalog editor, Guasco, had taken the beardless head on the right for the head of a woman.[22]

---

22 Guasco 1775.

It is now possible by combining all the information to reconstruct the "document," according to the intention of its initiators, and to replace it in its context at the time that it was covered up. It was a small bronze monument consecrated by a group of *vigiles* (the firemen of Rome) in their barracks at Trastevere in homage to the emperor and his family, as well as to the *Genius*, the protector divinity of their *centuria*. The *tabula*, paid for by this group of soldiers and created under the responsibility of two upper-rank comrades, was decorated by three appliqués: the curly-haired spirit, flanked by Septimius Severus and Caracalla. It was displayed near statues of the emperors in a room where *vigiles* kept guard night and day. In this room, excavated in the nineteenth century, there were dozens of graffiti composed by the *vigiles* to relieve their boredom; among them was an exceptional drawing which represented an imagined dedication by a soldier, under the reign of Severus Alexander, who took as a model our *tabula*, or possibly other similar tablets which were displayed in the same room (Figure 9).

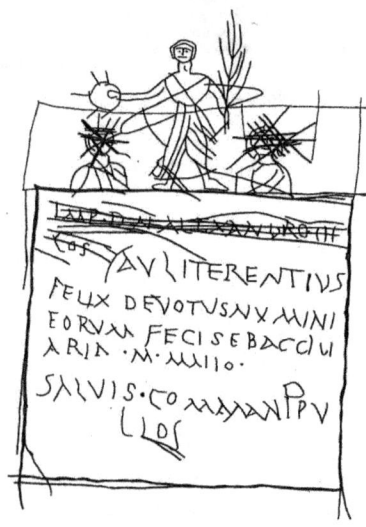

Fig. 9: Graffiti in the barracks of the *Vigiles*. Roma, Trastevere.

Our *tabula* had at least four lives: a decorative monument bearing witness to the loyalty of a group of soldiers who had displayed it in their place of work; an object of collection, admired and copied in the house of a collector; an inscription registered in the *Corpus Inscriptionum Latinarum* which no one had reason to go and see on the spot; and an exhibited museum piece.

What is of most interest for a historian is to pose a preferably new question and to attempt to identify a group of vestiges of all sorts that provide a response. We should not forget that every document that we use today must be situated by us in its history. It is the historian himself or herself, alone or with the help of other social and (more often) natural scientists, who defines the status of a document that we apply to it today. My general considerations on the recent developments of historical research and the specific examples I have given, all of them related to the best-known part of the Roman period (mainly the end of the Republic and the first two centuries of the Empire), illustrate quite well the differences between the approaches of the philosopher and those of the historian. The analysis and the theoretical model elaborated by Ferraris are indeed fascinating. Both propose a very clear interpretation of the increasingly rapid and far-reaching changes in the social world engendered during recent decades by the revolutionary expansion of the techniques and procedures of communication. His ontology of the social world aims to build a theory of the subject, based on what he calls idioms, i.e., all the traces that we can find in social objects of the presence and of the intention of a single person to assert their own individuality: identity, style, and signature. Seen from the *Documentality* point of view, the registration or the writing of any kind of statement on whatever material is the necessary condition today for its socialization. But was this true at all social levels and in all societies of the past?

Most of the classifications and definitions that constitute the core of Ferraris's proposals will, of course, encourage and help the historian of past centuries and millennia to look in a different way at the various direct and indirect traces that they are used to considering as "documents," and to pose a set of new questions to them. The same situation may be observed in the field of economic studies, where the development of a more and more mathematical economy during the last 150 years has strongly and positively influenced the study and understanding by economic historians of the economies of human societies all over the world before the industrial revolution. In both cases, the results of this challenge by the present to the past can be divided into two main categories. On the one hand, we have been through a deep renewal of our disciplines, of their interrogations, conceptualizations, and methods. On the other, we have become more clearly conscious of the structural differences between the different societies we study, and between the methods of analysis they require on our part. The coherence of the analytical framework has made possible a major formalization and has helped us to overcome the traditional limits of mere description based on written texts, which are fewer and fewer as we move farther and farther into the past.

At the same time, through a deeper collaboration with anthropology and archaeology, history has fundamentally changed its definition and conception of "documents," and has gone in the opposite direction from Ferraris's proposal, which was exclusively "authentication-oriented." Every historian today knows that they should not be blinded by the institutional origin of any written document. All the documents they study contain a large range of traces: some are intentional but many others are not, and all have the same importance, the *unintentional* sometimes more, for the scholar. All of them need to be analyzed and studied from different points of view, and in their own different contexts, in order to deliver their full informational potential. The distinction between a "strong" and a "weak" document means very little to a historian and, as Arthur-Montagne's analysis of school texts in this volume demonstrates, may fluctuate depending on the information we choose to prioritize in our analyses.[23] On the contrary, most if not all of these documents do not "say" anything by themselves: they need to be interpreted by scholars, through a long and continuous process that is never quite completed.

A good example would be Jan Van Eyck's *Arnolfini Portrait* (also called *The Arnolfini Wedding*, *The Arnolfini Marriage*, or *The Arnolfini Double Portrait*), quoted by Ferraris himself as the perfect example of a document, with the married couple, the witnesses of their marriage, and the signature of the painter in Latin (*Johannes de Eyck fuit hic 1434*).[24] If we look to the vast literature published by generations of scholars on this painting, we will see that the presentation of Ferraris is only one — and the most traditional, though formulated by Erwin Panofsky — of the many hypotheses that have been proposed to analyze and understand this painting.[25] It remains an enigma, with all the elements capable of being seen and read in very different ways: the identities of both the man and of the woman, the ceremony itself (the lady looks pregnant), the symbolic sense of all the objects and other details in the room, and even the real meaning of Van Eyck's signature.

If we keep in mind that, during recent decades, history has adopted a long perspective, much broader than a few centuries (six for Van Eyck's painting) or even than the five millennia that started with the invention of writing, the same conclusion would be true for all the documents used today by historians. Historians should be open to discussions with philosophers, and, more broadly, with all the scholars who study the present world; they have much to learn from the

---

23 Arthur-Montagne in this volume.
24 Ferraris 2009, 335.
25 Panofsky 1934.

analysis, interpretations, theoretical proposals, and methods of others. But historians cannot limit themselves to mere passive appropriation. They need to elaborate the scientific instruments of their own research, in order to be able to follow their own path.

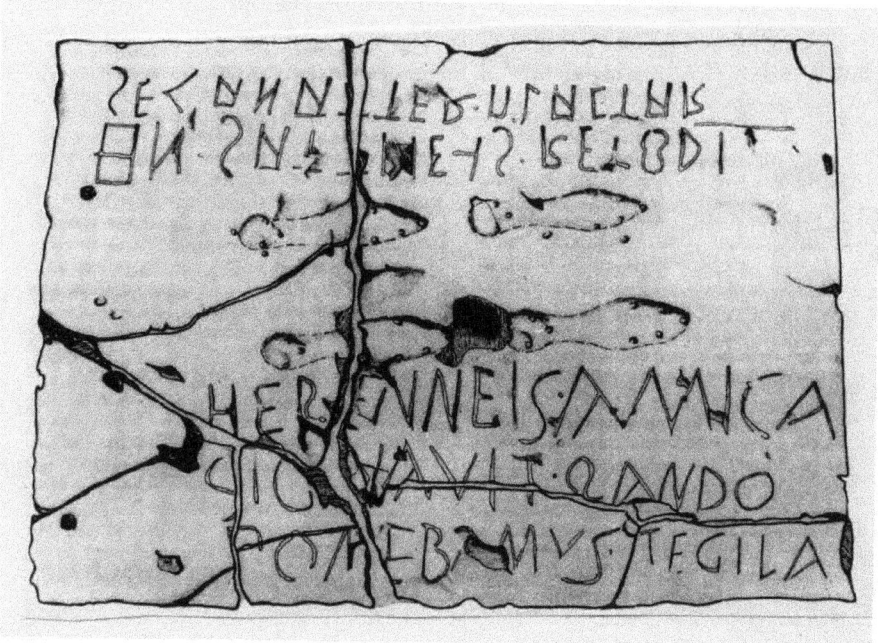

Fig. 10: Graffiti on a tegula. Pietrabbondante.

The remote origins of the assertion of privacy and of individual identities that we can observe in the present time have been taken as evident by archaeologists and prehistorians. But did they mean the same thing for their authors as they mean for us today? Let us take two examples that can be seen as intentional traces left by human beings. The first is the colored hands we find on the walls of so many prehistoric caves, starting from the oldest example, the "grotte Chauvet." These handprints are commonly interpreted as a kind of "signature" of the painter himself, who put his hands in the color he had used for the painting. The second is the graffiti of Pietrabbondante (Samnium, Italy), where two women pressed their feet, shod in clogs, into a (not yet dry: *quando ponebamus tegilam*) tile. Their footprints appear alongside two inscriptions, one written in

Latin and the other in Oscan, that give their names, their social status (both are slaves), and the name of their owner (Figure 10).[26] Is this formal resemblance sufficient to bridge the gap between us today and prehistoric societies ten or twenty millennia before the invention of writing, or a rural society of the Roman period, living 2,100 years ago in a mountainous region of central Italy? If we look at the large range of interpretations that have been proposed for these two sets of images, and if we want to avoid all kinds of anachronism, we must say that it is not. In looking at formal resemblance against cultural differences, culture always makes the difference.

References

Audoin-Rouzeau, F. (1995), "Compter et mesurer les os animaux: pour une histoire de l'élevage et de l'alimentation en Europe de l'Antiquité aux Temps Modernes", in: *Histoire et Mesure* 10, 277–312.

Blázquez Martínez, J.M./Remesal Rodríguez, J. (eds.) (1999–2014), *Estudios sobre el Monte Testaccio (Roma)*, 6 vols., Collecció Instrumenta 6, 10, 14, 24, 35, 47, Barcelona.

Buckland, M.K. (2014), "Documentality beyond Documents", in: *The Monist* 97, 179–186.

Camodeca, G. (2006), "Per una riedizione dell'archivio ercolanese di L. Venidius Ennychus", in: *CErc* 36, 188–211.

Camodeca, G. (2017), Tabulae Herculanenses. *Edizione e commento*, vol. 1, Vetera 20, Rome.

Corbier, M. (2006), *Donner à voir, donner à lire. Mémoire et communication dans la Rome ancienne*, Paris.

Corbier, M. (2008), "Texte et image: du Musée Capitolin au British Museum. Tradition et interprétation", in: *Ktema* 33, 433–443.

Corbier, M. (2011), "Présentation: l'écrit dans l'espace domestique", in: Corbier/Guilhembet 2011, 7–40.

Corbier, M./Guilhembet, J.P. (eds.) (2011), *L'écriture dans la maison romaine*, Paris.

Corbier, M. (2013), "Writing in Roman Public Space", in: G. Sears/P. Keegan/R. Laurence (eds.), *Written Space in the Latin West, 200 BC to AD 300*, London, 13–47.

Corbier, M. (2014), "Lo stesso e l'altro: le vite successive di un artefato iscritto. Le même et l'autre: les vies successives d'une inscription", in: A. Donati (ed.), *L'iscrizione e il suo doppio. Atti del Convegno Borghesi 2013*, Faenza, 51–78.

Corbier, M. (2016a), "Autour des graffitis dans le monde romain: normes, codes, transgressions", in: T. Itgenshorst/P. Le Doze (eds.), *La norme sous la République et le Haut-Empire romains*, Bordeaux, 501–515.

Corbier, M. (2016b), "L'efficacia della scrittura esposta", in: A. Donati (ed.), *L'iscrizione esposta. Atti del Colloquio Borghesi 2015*, Faenza, 9–24.

---

26 Corbier 2016a.

Corbier, M. (2016c), "Interrogations actuelles sur la transhumance", in: *MEFRA*, 128.2, doi.org/10.4000/mefra.3762.
Corbier, M. (2019a), "Nascondere il testo, mascherare il senso", in: A. Sartori (ed.), *L'iscrizione nascosta, Atti del Colloquio Borghesi 2017*, Faenza, 9–23.
Corbier, M. (2019b), "L'historien et le philosophe: document et documentalità", in: G. Baratta/ A. Buonopane/J. Velaza (eds.), *Cultura epigráfica y cultura literaria. Estudios en homenaje a Marc Mayer i Olivé*, Faenza, 125–133.
Febvre, L. (1953), *Combats pour l'histoire*, Paris.
Ferraris, M. (2009), *Documentalità. Perché è necessario lasciar tracce*, Rome.
Ferraris, M. (2012), *Documentality: Why It is Necessary to Leave Traces*, transl. R. Davies, New York.
Goitein, S.D. (1967–1993), *A Mediterranean Society. The Jewish Communities of the Arab World as Portrayed in the Documents of the Cairo Geniza*, 6 vols., Berkeley.
Gordon, A.E. (1983), *Illustrated Introduction to Latin Epigraphy*, Berkeley.
Gregori, G.L./Mattei, M. (eds.) (1999), *Supplementa Italica Imagines. Supplementi fotografici ai volumi italiani del CIL. Roma (CIL, VI)*, vol. 1: *Musei Capitolini*, Rome.
Guasco, F.E. (1775), *Musei Capitolini antiquae inscriptiones*, Rome.
Lewis, N./Yadin, Y./Greenfield, J.C. (eds.) (1989), *The Documents of the Bar-Kokhba Period in the Cave of Letters: Greek Papyri, Aramaic and Nabatean Signatures and Subscriptions*, Jerusalem.
Panofsky, E. (1934), "*Jan van Eyck's* Arnolfini Portrait", in: *Burlington Magazine* 64 (372), 117–119 and 122–127.
Rodriguez Almeida, E. (1984), *Il Monte Testaccio. Ambiente, storia, materiali*, Rome.
Tomlin, R.S.O. (1988), Tabellae Sulis: *Roman Inscribed Tablets of Tin and Lead from the Sacred Spring at Bath*, Oxford.
Yadin, Y./Greenfield, J.C./Yardeni, A./Levine, B.A. (eds.) (2002), *The Documents of the Bar-Kokhba Period in the Cave of Letters: Hebrew, Aramaic, and Nabatean-Aramaic Papyri*, Jerusalem.
Zaccagnino, C. (2004), "*Hercules Invictus*, l'*excubitorium* della *VII cohors vigilum*, il Meleagro Pighini: note sulla topografia di Trastevere", in: *Ostraka* 13, 101–124.

List of Contributors

Yasmine Amory is a postdoctoral research fellow at Ghent University.

Jacqueline Arthur-Montagne is Assistant Professor of Classics at the University of Virginia.

John Bodel is the W. Duncan MacMillan II Professor of Classics and Professor of History at Brown University.

Mireille Corbier is Directeur de recherche émérite at the Centre national de la recherche scientifique (France) and Director of *L'Année épigraphique*.

Scott J. DiGiulio is an Assistant Professor of Classics and a Senior Research Associate of the Cobb Institute of Archaeology at Mississippi State University.

Jean-Luc Fournet is Professor and Chair in Written Culture in Late Antiquity and Byzantine Papyrology at Collège de France (Paris).

Sjoukje M. Kamphorst is a PhD student in Ancient History at the University of Groningen.

Inger N.I. Kuin is Assistant Professor of Classics General Faculty at the University of Virginia.

Karen ní Mheallaigh is Professor of Classics at Johns Hopkins University.

Pierre Schneider is Professor of Ancient History at the University of Artois.

Index Locorum

Agatharchides of Cnidus
Erythr. 41 Müller
  (= Diod. Sic. 3.18.4)   137
Erythr. 79 Müller
  (= Diod. Sic. 3.38.1)   137
Erythr. 110 Müller
  (= Photios *Bibl.* 460b) 136–7

Aeschylus
Cho. 205–210   91–2

Alexander Romance
3.22   21

Apuleius
Apol. 102.8   264
Met. 2.30   20

Arrian
Anab. 1.1.1–3   147–8
Anab. 4.28–30   88
Anab. 6.1.2–6   139–40

Augustine
Ep. 31.2 (= *PL* 33.122)   240
Ep. 186.1.1 (= *PL* 33.815–816)   240

Augustus
Ep. fr. 5 Malcovati   193
Ep. fr. 22 Malcovati   190–91
Fr. 50 Malcovati   191

Aulus Gellius
Praef. 1   182
Praef. 2   73n36, 182
Praef. 20–21   182
1.22.19   187
4.9.6   188
4.18.9–12   200–1
10.1.9   196
10.11.5   191
10.24.lem   192
10.24.2   191–2
11.17.1   204
11.18.4   202–3
12.2   194–5
12.13   188, 202
13.25   198–9
15.7   192
15.7.3   190–1
20.1.5   203
20.5.10   185
20.10.9   203

Basil of Caesarea
Ep. 104   222–3
Ep. 205.5–9   239
Ep. 245.1–8   241n34

Cicero
Arch.
8   47
9   47
Att.
9.5.2   188
Fam.
2.4   186
4.4.4   188
4.13   186
Flac.
23   186
Rab. Post.
10.27   146
Sest.
58   188
II Verr.
3.207   188

Colloquium Celtis
27b   75

Cornelius Nepos
Att. 16.3   186

Cosmas Indicopleustes
Top. Christ. 11.21   139

Demetrius
Eloc. 223	186
Eloc. 223.3–6	235
Eloc. 224.3	243
Eloc. 227	186

Diodorus Siculus
3.37.8–9	141

Diogenes Laertius
6.5	72

Euripides
El. 532–537	92

Evagrius
Eccl. hist. 2.18	216–7

Fronto
104.6–9 VdH (= *Ep. ad Ant.* 3.8.2)	189
104.12–14 VdH (= *Ep. ad Ant.* 3.8.2)	189
182.5–7 VdH (= *Ep. ad amicos* 1.19)	195

Gregory of Nyssa
Ep. 4.3	243–4

Homer
Il. 1.108–154	64–5
Il. 2.527–546	67

Herodotus
2.44.2	98n62
4.82	122n49

Hesiod
Op. 347	62

Horace
Carm. 3.30.1	97

John Malalas
Chronographia 10.12	224–6

Leontius of Neapolis
Life of John the Almsgiver 11	219–20

Livy
Praef. 10	9–10
4.20	10
23.35.5	10

Longus
3.19	21

Lucian of Samosata
Alex.
10–11	116
19–21	117
26	116–7
36	117
55	116

Apol.
3	115

DDS
16	127
28	126–7
60	126

Dear. iud.
7	108

Deor. conc.
14	125
19	125

Dial. mar.
7	108

Dial. meretr.
4.3	119–20
10.3–4	120

Dips.
6	125

Hist. conscr.
62	84, 118–9

Ind.
4–5	76

Sat.
1–9	126
13–18	126

Scyth.
2	125

Symp.
21–33	108
35	108

VH
1.3–4	84

1.7	13, 85–93, 97, 122	**Seneca the Younger**	
		Ep. mor. 27.6–7	76
1.20	85, 93–6, 123	*Ep. mor.* 33.8	73
1.32	123	*Ep. mor.* 114	194
2.3	123	*Ep. mor.* Book 22	194–5
2.11	98		
2.28	85, 97–101, 124–5	**Strabo**	
		1.1.2	150
Maximus Planudes		1.2.3	150
Ep. 85	240	1.2.35	149
		15.1	149–50
Menander Rhetor		15.1.8–9	148
Sentent. 460	61	15.1.9–10	149
Sentent. 705	61	15.1.22 (= Onesicritus, FGrH 134 F22)	140–1
New Testament		15.1.28	149
2 Cor. 3:1–2	239	16.4.15	145
Pausanias		**Suetonius**	
1.13.3	19	*Aug.*	
1.26.4	19	71	193
2.7.2	19	76	193
2.27.2	19	87.1	193
		88	193
Pliny the Elder		*Calig.*	
HN 6.105	137–8	15.4	11
HN 6.139–140	139	30.2	11
HN 37.75	98		
		Synesius	
Plutarch		*Ep.* 85	238
Arist. 7	113		
Mor. 9e	71	**Tacitus**	
		Ann. 3.65.1	12
Pseudo-Libanius		*Ann.* 15.73.1–2	11–12
Epist. Charact. 2	234		
		Theodoret of Cyrus	
Quintilian		*II Ep. Paul. Cor.* 3.2 (= *PG* 82.392C) 239	
1.1.27	59–60		
1.1.28	66	**Thucydides**	
1.4.3	22	5.18	93–5
11.2.29	72	5.23	93–5
11.2.32	66		
		Ulpian	
Seneca the Elder		37.11.1.pr	36–7
Controv. pr. 2–3	73		
		Varro	
		Ling. 6.62	9, 181n5

Xenophon
Cyr. 2.1.27	12
Symp. 3.5	71

ACO
II/1: 66.23–67	214–5

CIL
VI 896	197

IG
XII 2.35	169n46
XII 2.58	165–70, 173–4

IK
Priene 107	160–4, 171–2

Ostraca and Tablets
O.Bodl. II 2170	67
Tabula ceratae graecae Assendelftianae	
1v	62–3

Papyri
BKT IX 94	243
P.Aphrod.Lit. IV 1	227–8
P.Aphrod.Lit. IV 38	244–5
P.Berl.Sarisch. 16	237–8
P.Cair.Zen. III 59308	235
P.Col. III 6	237
P.Iand.Zen. 24	237
P.Köln II 70	64–5
P.Lond.Lit 253	61–2
P.Mert. I 12	242
P.Mich. VIII 492	238
P.Oxy. II 213	64–5
P.Oxy. VII 1070, 45–6	237–8
P.Oxy. XXXIV 2728	242
P.Ryl. III 545	66–7
P.Thomas 8	235
P.Thomas 9	235
SB I 4323	237
SB XVIII 13867	238
SB XX 14606	211–212

TH
20	44
24	43–4

Index Rerum

Acta Conciliorum Œcumenicorum 213–6
Actium 165–8, 168n40, 170
aerarium 17, 200
Aeschylus 13, 63, 91, 92n39,
Aethiopia 135n7, 140, 140n23, 141–2, 145n41
Agatharchides of Cnidus 136–7, 137n9, 141, 143, 146, 149n47,
Alexander the Great 15, 21, 88, 88n28, 88n29, 88n31, 89, 97, 135, 135n7, 136, 139–40, 148, 159–60, 184n10, 185
Alexander Romance 21, 81n8, 88, 88n28–30, 97n60
Alexandria 22, 98–9, 136–7, 141–3, 145, 166n38, 201n45, 214–5, 217, 219
Anaglypha Traiani 17, 17n63,
Anaphora Pilati 21
Anastasius 219, 219n16, 228
Antioch 46, 166, 168, 170, 214
Antisthenes 72
Antoninus Pius 50n38, 187, 264, 267
Apollo 94n49, 116, 168n40
Appius Claudius Pulcher 47
Apuleius 20, 264
Archias 46, 48–9, 51
archives 6, 15, 39n11, 41–2, 82, 92, 137, 142–3, 180, 193, 193n25, 210, 244, 259–60, 262–3
Aristobulus 140, 148
Aristophanes 182
army 15–16, 49–51, 52n41, 210, 262–7, 272
– Macedonian 88n30, 139
Arrian 88, 147–8,
Astypalaia 160, 160n19, 161, 161n23, 162, 171
Athens 15, 18–9, 86–7, 87n25, 94n46–47, 94n49, 96n54, 113, 125, 153, 153n2, 161, 202
Augustine 71n34, 240–1, 241n35
Augustus 10, 17n62, 41, 48–9, 49n33, 52–3, 136, 165, 167–8, 168n41, 168n45, 169–70, 173, 184, 190, 190n21, 191–3, 193n23, 193n27

Aulus Gellius 19, 26, 73, 73n37, 182–204, 260
Austin, J. L. 156
authentication 5, 14, 18, 18n64, 21, 21n75, 38, 38n8, 41n15, 42–6, 48, 50–3, 57–8, 69, 81–2, 83n12, 89, 91, 95, 99–100, 184–5, 199n42, 219, 227, 243, 262–4, 267, 274

Basil of Caesarea 221, 239, 239n26, 241, 241n34
Bathaba 27, 41–2, 262, 267
beryl 97–9, 101, 124
birth certificates 5, 21, 39–43, 45, 48–9, 49n33, 50, 52, 52n41, 53, 263
Bibliotheca Ulpia 83n12, 199–200, 204
Briet, Suzanne 68n25, 144, 144n36, 145, 147
bronze 50n37, 85, 87–9, 91, 96–8, 116, 122, 126, 169n46, 226, 256, 258, 264, 267–9, 272
Brundisium 165–6, 168, 168n41, 170
Buckland, Michael 7n25, 8, 27, 37n7, 38n8, 68n25, 134, 144, 145n42, 255–6

Calatoria Themis 39, 39n11, 40–1, 41n15, 42, 44
Caligula 11
Capitoline 50n37, 165, 169, 268, 271, 267
– Museum 268–71
Caracalla 23, 52, 271–2
Chwe, Michael 25, 157, 157n11
Cicero 17n60, 18n66, 46–7, 47n28, 47n30, 48, 51, 146, 183n5, 184–5, 185n12, 186, 186n14, 186n15, 187, 187n19, 188–91, 194, 196–8,
citizenship 15, 23, 40, 42–3, 46–50, 52–3, 262–4, 267
coinage *see numismatics*
Colloquium Harleianum 237
common knowledge 25, 53, 58, 155, 157, 157n11, 158n17, 159, 163, 164n31, 170–1
Constantine 53
Constitutio Antoniniana 53

copying 8, 23–4, 42, 58–61, 63–8, 70, 72–5, 115, 162n25, 163, 165, 169, 210, 213, 218, 223, 227, 244n55, 262–3
Cornelius Nepos 186, 186n16,
Cosmas, Alexandrian landowner 219–221
Cosmas Indicopleustes 138–9, 139n20
Council of Ephesus 213–5
Cronus 126
Ctesias 89, 89n34, 92, 149
Cyril of Alexandria 214
Cyril of Scythopolis 219, 223n29

debt records 17
Demetrius 186, 235, 243
Derrida, Jacques 4–5, 36n2
dictation 59, 59n6, 61, 62n12, 63–5
diplomacy 25, 259
diplomata 27, 50, 50n37, 51, 52n41, 264, 267
Diocletian 53
Dionysus 13, 85, 88, 88n28, 89, 89n33, 90–1, 97, 122–7, 149, 160–1
Dioscorus of Aphrodite 19, 223, 223n31, 227–8, 244, 244n55, 245
documents
– acts and act-driven 69, 70, 74–5
– ancient accessibility of 9, 17, 17n59, 18, 18n66, 19, 73, 82, 95, 98, 110, 114, 153, 158n17, 170, 182, 192, 193n25, 262, 264
– ancient terminology for 2–3, 8–15, 36n3, 37, 60, 136, 146, 154, 181n1, 182n2, 183, 183n5, 183, 187n17, 201, 203, 236, 236n14, 254, 270
– ancient vs. modern 2–3, 3n8, 8–10, 12–4, 16, 16n57, 22–3, 26–7, 36–9, 41n15, 53–4, 58–9, 67–8, 74, 90–1, 109–12, 114, 134–5, 142–9, 149n49, 183–6, 189–190, 203–4, 210, 234–5, 255 262, 264
– authority of 1, 4, 6, 11–4, 17–24, 26–7, 43–53, 53n48, 68–9, 74, 80–1, 81n8, 82–4, 89, 91, 97, 99, 101, 116–21, 127–9, 144, 148, 157n10, 183–4, 188, 191–95, 197, 199, 199n42, 200–201, 203–4, 256–63
– as carriers of information 3n8, 8, 10–1, 19–20, 27, 48, 84, 124, 133–6, 136n8, 137–8, 138n14, 139–42, 142n29, 143–9, 149n49, 150, 156–8, 158n17, 159, 163, 163n30, 171, 181, 186, 189, 193n25, 219, 226 234–9, 241–3, 246, 254–6, 259–61, 264, 272, 274
– definition of 3, 3n8, 4–9, 12n42, 13–4, 27, 36–7, 42–3, 46, 59, 67–8, 68n25, 70, 75–7, 90–1, 110–2, 133–6, 142, 142n29, 143, 143n33, 144–9, 182, 201–204, 210–13, 218, 233–4, 245–6, 254–62, 273–4
– destruction of 11, 17, 17n62, 47, 50n37, 66, 74, 200, 200n43, 201, 201n45, 202, 260
– and documentality 6–9, 14–5, 19, 22–5, 35, 38–9, 41n15, 53–4, 57, 57n1, 58, 77, 79–81, 84–5, 90–2, 100, 109, 134, 144, 150, 233, 261–2, 273
– and "documentarization" of literary texts 200, 203, 209–11
– and "documentary nobility" 242
– fact-driven 69–70, 75
– and historiography 3–5, 10, 84, 93, 93n43, 95, 95n52, 123–4, 183
– and literature 1, 1n3, 2, 2n4, 13, 17n59, 18–26, 58–61, 70–3, 76, 80, 92, 100–1, 114n26, 128–9, 143, 182–3, 201, 209–11, 213, 218, 227–9
–living things as 140–5, 189n17, 236, 238–41, 246
– and materiality 3, 3n8, 5, 7–8, 10n36, 11, 11n37, 12, 15–6, 17n59, 19, 21–7, 35–6, 36n5, 37, 50n37, 57–61, 66–8, 75, 80–2, 83n11, 85–91, 95–8, 98n62, 99, 101, 111, 111n12, 116–7, 119, 122, 126–7, 133, 135–43, 143n33, 144–9, 153, 153n2, 156, 158, 158n15, 181–83, 200–11, 201n45, 233–4, 236, 254–6, 258–9, 263–4, 267–8, 272–3
– and or as objects 3–8, 12–3, 20–1, 23–5, 27, 35–36, 36n3, 38, 45, 57, 68–9, 81n4, 109–11, 115–7, 121–4, 127–9, 134, 144, 153, 155–6, 159, 170, 187n18, 233–4, 242, 246, 254–61, 273–4

– pseudo- 1, 1n3, 21–2, 81–3, 84n17, 117, 184n10, 185
Domitius Modestus 221

Egypt 15–6, 20, 49, 54n48, 82n11, 88n31, 98, 110n9, 112–4, 115n28, 136–7, 139–40, 140n22, 140n23, 141–2, 142n28, 143–5, 201n45, 212–4, 219, 236n13, 236n14, 260
Electra 13, 91–2, 122n49
electrum 95–6
elegantia 185, 189–91, 201
emperor worship 44, 165, 168–71, 181, 272
epigraphy 2, 7, 10, 21–2, 36–7, 79–80, 84, 95–6, 96n58, 101, 109–11, 115–25, 127–9, 135, 144, 153, 153n2, 154, 154n4, 155–6, 160n19, 164, 170, 253–6, 267
– dedicatory 19, 20n71, 118, 118m39, 121–24, 127, 196, 270–2
– diplomatic/political 6, 15, 25, 48, 93–4, 94n49, 95, 95n51, 96, 114n27, 119, 125, 125n57, 125n58, 153–4, 154n4, 155–64, 164n31, 165–71, 256–9
– and "epigraphic habit" 18, 18n65, 22, 79–80, 84, 110, 110n8, 115, 124–5
– funerary 80, 101, 121, 125, 153n2, 196n34
– honorific 154n4, 155, 160–1, 161n21, 162, 162n25, 163–4
– legal 3, 12, 14, 48, 82, 86–7, 93, 109, 125–6, 203
– in literature 1n3, 2n4, 10, 11n39, 13, 18n66, 19–20, 60, 79–81, 81n8, 82, 82n11, 84, 84n17, 85–8, 88n30, 89–95, 95n51, 96–101, 101n74, 108, 108n4, 110, 110n9, 114n25, 116–8, 118n39, 119–21, 121n46, 122–5, 125n57, 126–9, 183, 196, 196n34, 197–201
– monumental 19–20, 20n69, 20n69, 20n70, 20n71, 82, 82n11, 85–6, 86n22, 87, 89, 89n33, 97–101, 116, 118, 118n39, 119–20, 123, 161, 197, 197n36–7, 198–201, 203, 257–8
– and performativity 156, 156n9, 162
Eris 107, 107n1, 108, 108n4

Euripides 13, 92, 149
Evagrius 216–8

Favorinus 198, 198n38, 198n39, 199
Febvre, Lucien 254
Ferraris, Maurizio; *see also documentality* 5–8, 14, 20, 23–7, 35, 35n1, 36, 36n2, 36n3, 37–9, 39n10, 41n15, 43–4, 53–4, 57, 57n1, 58, 68, 68n25, 70, 81n4, 109, 134, 145n42, 154, 156, 156n9, 158n16, 182–3, 187, 187n18, 201, 203–4, 233–5, 246, 254–5, 261, 273–4
fiction 1, 1n3, 2, 20, 24, 58, 79–81, 81n4, 82–5, 87, 89, 90–1, 93, 95–6, 98–101, 109–11, 119, 121–2, 124–5, 125n56, 126–8, 134, 141, 145n42, 149, 154, 156, 156n9, 158n16, 182–3, 184n10, 187, 187n18, 201, 203–4, 211, 233–5, 244n55, 245–6, 254–5, 261, 273–4
forgery 1–2, 18n64, 21–2, 46–8, 48n31, 48n32, 75, 82–3, 91, 101, 111, 116, 126–9, 199n40, 226–7, 258
Forum Traiani 198–9, 201
Fronto 189–190, 195, 195n32–3

Gabinius, Publius 47
gems 98–9
Geniza deposits 260
geography 87, 134–5, 135n7, 136–42, 142n27, 143–8, 148n46, 149n47, 150
– and autopsy 136, 136n8, 139–40, 143, 145, 148
– and hearsay accounts 136, 136n8, 138, 142–3
– and popular knowledge 141–2
Geta 271
graffiti 16n58, 17n59, 112n13, 119–20, 120n45, 121, 254, 256, 258, 275
Gregory of Nyssa 243

Hadrian 17, 17n62, 41, 51, 193n25, 197, 197n36, 197n37, 262
hagiography 211, 218–221, 229
handwriting 59–60, 64–5, 210
Heraclea 46–7

Heracles 13, 85, 86n22, 87, 87n27, 88, 88n28, 88n29, 89–90, 96n57, 97–8, 122, 122n49, 123–5, 127, 148
Herculaneum 39–41, 41n14, 113n18, 262–3, 268
Herod I 224–5
Herodotus 84n17, 89, 92, 98, 98n62, 126
Hesiod 62–3, 75–6, 98–9, 196n34
Hierapolis 126
Homer 64–7, 71, 75–6, 81, 90, 97–101, 124, 124n55, 149–50, 182, 196n34, 198, 210, 223, 244
honestiores et humiliores 52
Horace 97, 184
Horapollo 210n1, 223, 223n31, 244
horoi 86–7, 87n24–5, 91
hypomnêmata 137, 143, 146, 226

illiteracy 8, 16, 44, 63, 80, 109–14, 114n26, 119–21, 127–9, 202–3
– modern 112, 114
– in papyri 112–3, 113n18
– and women 119–20, 120n43, 121, 129, 262
India 88, 88n28, 127, 135, 135n7, 136–41, 148–9
intentionality 4–7, 13–4, 36–7, 41n15, 45, 67–70, 74–5, 90, 120, 145n42, 148, 154, 183–4, 187, 187n18, 203n51, 213–4, 218, 254–5, 258–9, 272–5
internet, the 8, 14

John the Almsgiver 219–221
John the Baptist 226–7
John Malalas 224–7
Journal of the Trojan War of Dictys of Crete 21, 81–2, 82n11
Juba 138–9, 139n19, 143
judgment of Paris 107, 107n1, 108, 108n4
Julia Domna 271
jurists 23, 36–7, 144, 202n47, 263

Koepsell, David 8

La Pérouse 146–7
law 1, 3n8, 18, 36, 40–9, 57, 87, 125–6, 202–3, 220, 222
– and lawcourts 82, 262
Leontius of Neapolis 219–21
letters 21, 73, 82, 88n28, 108, 116, 120, 140, 233–46, 268
– and carriers as "living letters" 236–8
– and the Christian tradition 21, 209–29, 240, 243–6
– distinction between literary and documentary 184–95, 209–29, 241–6
– informative purpose of 189, 242
– late antique collections of 189, 211, 221–23, 229
– manuals for writing 211, 221, 223, 243
– and messengers in literary letters 238–41
– petitions as 209–29
– and orality 37, 186, 234–42, 246
– and voyeurism 192
lex Aelia Sentia 48, 263
lex Papia Poppaea 49
lex Plautia Papiria 46
lex Junia 40–1, 49
lex Visellia 49
libraries 16n57, 73, 76, 83, 181, 187, 201n45, 204, 210, 223
– of the mind 57–77
linguistic turn 5
literacy 16–7, 44, 71, 74, 107–29
– definition of 111–5
– functional 16n55, 111–2
Livy 10, 146
Longus 21
Lucian of Samosata 13, 79–119, 149n48, 197

manumission 40–1, 44–5, 48–9, 53, 262–4
Marrou, Henri-Irénée 133–4
Massalia 166–8
material turn 5–6
maxims 61, 73
Maximus Planudes 240
Megasthenes 149
Memnon Colossus 20
memory 5–6, 8, 17, 20, 28, 42–3, 47, 57–9, 61–7, 71–73, 76–7, 168, 195, 221–22, 234, 238

Menander 61, 63, 75
metapoetics 92–3, 98–9
miscellanies 181–83, 187n17
mnemonic turn 5
Momus 125
mountains 86–7, 108, 125, 261
Mytilene 165–71, 175–6

Nero 11, 17n62, 45–6, 48, 264, 267,
Niceratus 71
Nile river, sources of 139–40
Nisyros 160–2, 172–4
numismatics 3n8, 17, 46, 257–8

Octavia 165–6
Octavian see Augustus
oracles 116–7, 120, 128
orality 8, 14, 37, 42–8, 53, 55n16, 58, 60–4, 75, 109n6, 112, 114n27, 142–3, 162, 166, 169, 186, 219, 234–42, 246, 253–4, 259
Orestes 13, 91–2, 122n49
ostraca 58, 67, 75, 113
Otlet, Paul 144–7

paideia 58, 67, 71, 75–6
Pantheon (temple) 197
papyri 1–2, 16, 58–9, 72, 74–5, 112–3, 117, 125n57, 209–11, 220n23, 223, 233, 235–8, 243–4, 262, 267
Paul 220, 239–41
Paulinus of Nola 240–1
Pausanias 19–20, 86, 89
Peirce, Charles 91
Pergamon 165–7
peritext 24, 80, 99–101, 121
Persian Gulf 138–9
petitions; see letters
Petronia Iusta 39–45, 48, 268
Petronia Vitalis 40, 44
Petronius Stephanus 40, 44
Pharos 84, 118, 121
Phokaia 160–2, 171–2
Pisonian conspiracy 11–2
Plato 66
Pliny the Elder 96n56, 98, 118n39, 137–9, 143–4, 146

Pliny the Younger 184, 186, 259
Plutarch 71–2, 86, 88n29, 113–4
Posidippus 98–9
praetors 40, 46–7, 143, 203n49, 204, 263
Priene 160–3, 171–2
Probus 53
proskynêmata 20, 88–9
proxeny 154, 164
Pseudo-Libanius 234, 246
Ptolemy I 147–8
Ptolemy II 141–2, 144, 149n47

Quintilian 22, 59–60, 66–7, 72, 190n21, 194

Red Sea 137, 149n47
Rome 16n55, 40–2, 46, 50n37, 83, 164–5, 168–71, 183, 260, 263–4, 267–8, 172

Sabas 219
schools 2, 57–77, 111, 144, 185, 274
Scipio Africanus 200–1, 203
Searle, John 4–6, 58n1
Second Sophistic 58, 60, 71, 182n2
semiotics 7n25, 24, 68n25, 80, 91, 96, 101, 134, 236
Seneca the Elder 73, 185n12
Seneca the Younger 73–4, 76, 184, 185n12, 194–5
Septimius Severus 271–2
Severus Alexander 272
Sidonius Apollinaris 228
signatures 18, 43–5, 69, 75, 95, 99, 112, 143, 258, 262, 273–5
slavery 39–41, 44–5, 48–9, 53, 76, 238, 262–4, 276
Smith, Barry 8n29, 38n8, 58n1–2
Sostratus of Cnidus 118–9, 121–2, 128
speech act theory 36, 155–7
sphragis 99–100
spolia opima 10
Strabo 87n27, 118n39, 135–6, 140–2, 145–50
successor kingdoms (*diadochoi*) 159
Suetonius 11, 190n21, 192–4
Sulpicius Apollinaris 188, 202

Synesius 238
tablets 16, 18, 21, 36–7, 43, 48, 57, 82–3n11, 116–7, 144, 167n39, 267–9, 271–2
– legal 39–42, 50, 263–4
– as metaphor for memory/cognition 58, 67, 72, 144, 239–40
– school 58–62, 66, 75
tabulae dealbatae 256–7
tabulae Herculanenses 39–45, 262–3, 267
Tacitus 11–2, 259
Tarraco 165–8
teachers 59, 62–5, 70–5, 120, 188, 220
Terrone, Enrico 7–8, 38, 43, 51, 54, 57–9, 68–70, 74–5, 81n4, 90, 109n6, 156n9
Testaccio, amphora fragments 260
testationes 43, 47–8, 50–3
testimonia 40, 42–3, 74
Tiberius 12, 21
Theater of Pompey 196–7
Theoderet of Cyrus 239
Theodorus of Petra 219
Thucydides 95, 124n53

traces 13, 28, 35, 59–60, 66, 68–75, 86, 90–1, 109, 122, 144, 161n23, 165, 169, 187, 240, 246, 254–5, 261, 273–5
Tullius Tiro 185n12, 196
Twelve Tables 202n47, 203

Ulpian 36–7

vadimonia 40–2
Van Eyck, Jan 274
Varro 9, 183n5, 184n9, 187, 196
Venidius Ennychus, L. 41–2, 48–9, 262–3, 267–8
vigiles 269–272
Vergil 71, 114, 187, 194
vestal virgins 18, 166

White, Hayden 3–5
wills 1, 18, 21–2, 36–7, 43, 48n31–2, 264
– Antony's will 18
witnesses 14, 41–46, 48, 50–3, 82n11, 143, 262–4, 267, 274

www.ingramcontent.com/pod-product-compliance
Lightning Source LLC
Chambersburg PA
CBHW060351190426
43201CB00044B/1982